Technical
Analysis
Explained

Also by Martin J. Pring

How to Forecast Interest Rates: A Guide to Profits for Consumers, Managers, and Investors (1981)

Technical Analysis Explained

The Successful Investor's Guide to Spotting Investment Trends and Turning Points

Martin J. Pring

President
The International Institute
for Economic Research, Inc.
Washington Depot, Connecticut

Third Edition

McGraw-Hill, Inc.

New York St. Louis San Francisco Auckland Bogotá
Caracas Hamburg Lisbon London Madrid
Mexico Milan Montreal New Delhi Paris
San Juan São Paulo Singapore
Sydney Tokyo Toronto

Library of Congress Cataloging-in-Publication Data

Pring, Martin J.
    Technical analysis explained : the successful investor's guide to
  spotting investment trends and turnings points / by Martin J. Pring.
  — 3rd ed.
        p.   cm.
    Includes bibliographical references and index.
    ISBN 0-07-051042-3 :
    1. Investment analysis.   I. Title.
HG4529.P75   1991
332.63'22—dc20   91-9075
                                                                  CIP

    3 4 5 6 7 8 9 0   DOC/DOC   9 7 6 5 4 3

ISBN 0-07-051042-3

*The sponsoring editor for this book was Betsy N. Brown, the editing supervisor
was Olive H. Collen, and the production supervisor was Suzanne W. Babeuf. It
was set in Baskerville by McGraw-Hill's Professional Book Group composition
unit.*

Printed and bound by R. R. Donnelley & Sons Company.

Contents

Preface

There is no reason why anyone cannot make a substantial amount of money in the financial markets, but there are many reasons why most people will not. As with most endeavors in life, the key to success is knowledge and action. This book has been written in an attempt to cast some light on the internal workings of the markets and to help expand the "knowledge" component, leaving the "action" to the patience, discipline, and objectivity of the individual investor.

The mid- to late 1980s saw the expansion of investment and trading opportunities to a global scale, in terms of both the cash and the futures markets. This third edition of *Technical Analysis Explained* has been expanded to keep abreast of these changes and to include some technical innovations that have evolved since the second edition was published.

The material in this edition has been thoroughly reworked and expanded. Considerable attention is still focused on the U.S. equity market, but coverage of international equity markets and commodity and currency markets has been greatly expanded. Technical analysis was as valid in Wall Street in 1850 as it is in Tokyo in 1990 and will be in Moscow in the year 2000. This is true because price action in financial markets is a reflection of human nature, and human nature remains more or less consistent. Where appropriate, the concepts are illustrated with up-to-date examples.

Three new chapters have been added. Chapter 1, Market Cycle Model, builds the framework for the whole book by explaining the idea

of the three main trends—primary, intermediate, and short-term—and
how they interact.

The important concept of momentum has been significantly expanded and is now covered in two chapters. Momentum indicators such
as the relative strength indicator (RSI), stochastics, and moving average
convergence divergence (MACD) have been included because they have
become popular with futures traders in recent years.

Another new chapter (Chapter 25, Automated Trading Systems) is
presented as a starting point for a more formalized and disciplined approach to technical analysis rather than a shortcut to profits.

The treatments of breadth, moving averages (MAs), sentiment, seasonality, relative strength (RS), and volume have been expanded.

A new appendix (Appendix A, Candle Charts) has been included, in
response to the resurgence of interest in this method of plotting price
data.

Finally, two "new" concepts are presented. These are the *weighted
summed rate of exchange* (know *sure thing*," or KST) and *seasonal momentum*. The word "new" is in quotation marks because these concepts
are not revolutionary but represent old ideas that have been reworked
and presented in a different and more practical format.

In the past two decades the time horizon of virtually all investors has
shrunk considerably. As a result, technical analysis has become very
popular for implementing short-term timing strategies. This use may
lead to great disappointment: In my experience there is a rough corre-
lation between the reliability of the technical indicators and the time
span being monitored. This is the paramount reason for orienting most
of the discussion here toward intermediate- and long-term trends.

To be successful, technical analysis should be regarded as the art of
assessing the technical position of a particular market with the aid of
several scientifically researched indicators. While many of the mechanistic techniques described in this book offer reliable indications of
changing market conditions, all suffer from the common characteristic
that they can and often do fail to operate satisfactorily. This characteristic presents no problem to the consciously disciplined investor, since a
good working knowledge of the principles underlying major movements in financial markets and a balanced view of this overall technical
position offer a superior framework within which to operate.

There is, after all, no substitute for independent thought. The action
of the technical indicators illustrates the underlying characteristics of
any market, and it is up to the analyst to put the pieces of the jigsaw
puzzle together and develop a working hypothesis.

The task is by no means easy, as initial success can lead to overconfidence and arrogance. Charles H. Dow, the father of technical analysis,

once wrote that "pride of opinion caused the downfall of more men on Wall Street than all the other opinions put together." This is true because markets are essentially a reflection of people in action. Normally such activity develops on a reasonably predictable path. Since people can — and do — change their minds, price trends in the market can deviate unexpectedly from their anticipated course. To avoid serious trouble, investors must adjust their attitudes as changes in the technical position emerge.

In addition to pecuniary rewards, a study of the market can also reveal much about human nature, both from observation of other people in action and from the aspect of self-development. As investors react to the constant struggle through which the market will undoubtedly put them, they will also learn a little about their own makeup. Washington Irving might well have been referring to this challenge of the technical market when he wrote: "Little minds are taxed and subdued by misfortune but great minds rise above it."

Martin J. Pring

Acknowledgments

The material for the third edition of this book has been gathered from a substantial number of sources, and I am deeply indebted to the many organizations that have given their permission to reproduce charts and diagrams without which the book would not have been possible. In particular, special thanks go to Ned Davis Research for providing most of the illustrations in the chapter on sentiment. I would also like to thank Steve Nison for his encouragement and help on the appendix covering candlestick charting.

Acknowledgment is also due to Bill Dilani for his useful suggestions and updates on Chapter 3, "Dow Theory." Thanks also to Ian Notley, North America's leading cycles analyst, for his comments on Chapter 16, "Time: Longer-Term Cycles."

Thanks also go to my colleagues at the International Institute, especially to Renee Pike for her constant encouragement and constructive suggestions, and to Sheila Silvernail, who, along with Olive Collen at McGraw-Hill, worked tirelessly to uncover my many errors and omissions.

Above all, this book would not have been possible without the help and encouragement of my wife, Danny. Not only was she able to stay awake while reading the manuscript, but she was also able to translate it into readable English and come up with a great title.

Technical
Analysis
Explained

Introduction

To investors willing to buy and hold common stocks for the long term, the stock market has offered excellent rewards over the years in terms of both dividend growth and capital appreciation. The market is even more challenging, fulfilling, and rewarding to resourceful investors willing to learn the art of cyclical timing through a study of technical analysis.

The advantages of cyclical investing over the "buy-and-hold" approach were particularly marked between 1966 and 1982. The market made no headway at all—as measured by the Dow Jones Industrial Average (DJIA)—in the 16 years between 1966 and 1982. Yet there were some substantial price fluctuations. Although the DJIA failed to record a net advance between 1966 and 1982, the period included five major advances totaling over 1500 Dow points. The potential rewards of cyclical investing were therefore significant.

A long-term investor fortunate enough to sell at the five tops in 1966, 1968, 1973, 1979, and 1981 and to reinvest the money at the troughs of 1966, 1970, 1974, 1980, and 1982 would have seen the total investment (excluding transactions costs and capital gains tax) grow from a theoretical $1000 (that is, $1 for every Dow point) in 1966 to over $10,000 by October 1983. In contrast, an investor following a buy-and-hold approach would have realized a mere $250 gain over the same period. Even during the spectacular rise which began in August 1982, technical analysis would have proved useful, since that period witnessed a considerable variation in performance between different industry groups.

A bull market like the one that occurred in the 1980s is a once-in-a-generation affair. This implies that the 1990s will be a more difficult and challenging period and that market timing will prove to be of crucial importance.

In practice, of course, it is impossible to buy and sell consistently at exact cyclical market turning points, but the enormous potential of this approach still leaves plenty of room for error even when commission costs and taxes are included in the calculation. The rewards for identi-

1

fying major market junctures and taking the appropriate action can be substantial.

Originally, technical analysis was applied only in the equity market, but its popularity has gradually expanded to embrace commodities, debt instruments, currencies, and other international markets. To be successful, the technical approach involves taking a position contrary to the expectations of "the crowd." This requires the patience, objectivity, and discipline to acquire a financial asset at a time of depression and gloom and liquidate it in an environment of euphoria and excessive optimism. The aim of this book is to explain the technical characteristics to be expected at major market turning points and to help to assess them objectively. The book has been designed to give the reader a better understanding of market action and to enable the investor to capitalize on major swings and minimize potential mistakes.

Technical Analysis Defined

The technical approach to investment is essentially a reflection of the idea that prices move in trends which are determined by the changing attitudes of investors toward a variety of economic, monetary, political, and psychological forces. The art of technical analysis—for it is an art—is to *identify trend changes at an early stage and to maintain an investment posture until the weight of the evidence indicates that the trend has reversed.*

Human nature remains more or less constant and tends to react to similar situations in consistent ways. By studying the nature of previous market turning points, it is possible to develop some characteristics that can help to identify major market tops and bottoms. Technical analysis therefore is based on the assumption that people will continue to make the same mistakes they have made in the past. Human relationships are extremely complex and never repeat in identical combinations. The markets, which are a reflection of people in action, never duplicate their performance exactly, but the recurrence of similar characteristics is sufficient to enable technicians to identify major juncture points. Since no single indicator has signaled or indeed could signal every cyclical market juncture, technical analysts have developed an arsenal of tools to help isolate these points.

Three Branches of Technical Analysis

Technical analysis can be broken down into three essential areas: sentiment, flow-of-funds, and market structure indicators. Data and indicators for all three areas are available for the U.S. stock market. For other financial markets the statistics are more or less confined to the market structure indicators. The major exceptions are futures markets based in the United States, for which short-term sentiment data can now be obtained. The following comments on sentiment and flow-of-funds indicators relate to the U.S. stock market.

Sentiment Indicators

Sentiment or *expectational indicators* monitor the actions of different market participants, e.g., the so-called odd lotters, mutual funds, and floor specialists. Just as the pendulum of a clock continually moves from one extreme to another, so the sentiment indexes (which monitor the emotions of investors) move from one extreme at a bear market bottom to another at a bull market top. The assumption on which these indicators is based is that different groups of investors are consistent in their actions at major market turning points. For example, insiders (i.e., key employees or major stockholders of a company) and New York Stock Exchange (NYSE) members as a group have a tendency to be correct at market turning points; in aggregate, their transactions are on the buy side toward market bottoms and on the sell side toward tops.

Conversely, advisory services as a group are often wrong at market turning points, since they consistently become bullish at market tops and bearish at market troughs. Indexes derived from such data show that certain readings have historically corresponded to market tops, while others have been associated with market bottoms. Since the consensus or majority opinion is normally wrong at market turning points, these indicators of market psychology are a useful basis from which to form a contrary opinion.

Flow-of-Funds Indicators

The area of technical analysis that involves what are loosely termed *flow-of-funds indicators* analyzes the financial position of various investor groups in an attempt to measure their potential capacity for buying or selling stocks. Since there has to be a purchase for each sale, the "ex post," or actual dollar balance between supply and demand for stock, must always be equal. The price at which a stock transaction takes place has to be the same for the buyer and the seller, so naturally the amount of money flowing out of the market must equal that put in. The flow-of-funds approach is therefore concerned with the before-the-fact balance between supply and demand, known as the *ex ante relationship*. If at a given price there is a preponderance of buyers over sellers on an ex ante basis, it follows that the actual (ex post) price will have to rise to bring buyers and sellers into balance.

Flow-of-funds analysis is concerned, for example, with trends in mutual fund cash positions and other major institutions such as pension funds, insurance companies, foreign investors, bank trust accounts, and customers' free balances, which are normally a source of cash on the buy side; and new equity offerings, secondary offerings, and margin debt on the supply side.

This money flow analysis also suffers from disadvantages. While the data measure the availability of money for the stock market, e.g., mutual fund cash position or pension fund cash flow, they give no indication of the inclination of market participants to use this money for the purchase of stocks, or of their elasticity or willingness to sell at a given price on the sell side. The data for the major institutions and foreign investors are not sufficiently detailed to be of much use, and in addition they are reported well after the fact. In spite of these drawbacks, flow-of-funds statistics may be used as background material.

A superior approach to flow-of-funds analysis is derived from an examination of liquidity trends in the banking system, which measures financial pressure not only on the stock market but in the economy as well.

Market Structure Indicators

This area of technical analysis is the main concern of this book, embracing *market structure* or the *character of the market indicators*. These indicators monitor the trend of various price indexes, market breadth, cycles, volume, etc., in order to evaluate the health of bull and bear markets.

Most of the time, price and internal measures, such as market breadth, momentum, and volume, rise and fall together, but toward the end of market movements the paths of many of these indicators diverge from the price. Such divergences offer signs of technical deterioration during advances, and technical strength following declines. Through judicious observation of these signs of latent strength and weakness, technically oriented investors are alerted to the possibility of a reversal in the trend of the market itself.

Since the technical approach is based on the theory that the price is a reflection of mass psychology ("the crowd") in action, it attempts to forecast future price movements on the assumption that crowd psychology moves between panic, fear, and pessimism on one hand and confidence, excessive optimism, and greed on the other. As discussed here, the art of technical analysis is concerned with identifying these changes at an early phase, since these swings in emotion take time to accomplish. Studying these market trends enables technically oriented investors to buy or sell with a degree of confidence, on the principle that once a trend is set in motion it will perpetuate itself.

Price movements may be classed as primary, intermediate, and short-term. Major movements (sometimes called *primary* or *cyclical*) typically work themselves out in a period of 1 to 3 years and are a reflection of investors' attitudes toward the business cycle. *Intermediate movements* usually develop over a period of 3 weeks to as many months, sometimes longer. While not of prime importance, they are nevertheless useful to identify. It is clearly important to distinguish between an intermediate reaction in a bull market and the first downleg of a bear market, for example. *Short-term movements,* which last less than 3 or 4 weeks, tend to be random in nature.

Discounting Mechanism of the Market

All price movements have one thing in common: they are a reflection of the trend in the hopes, fears, knowledge, optimism, and greed of the investing public. The sum total of these emotions is expressed in the price level, which is, as Garfield Drew[1] noted, "never what they [stocks] are worth but what people think they are worth."

This process of market evaluation was well expressed by an editorial in *The Wall Street Journal*[2]:

> The stock market consists of everyone who is "in the market" buying or selling shares at a given moment, plus everyone who is not "in the market" but might be if conditions were right. In this sense, the stock market is potentially everyone with any personal savings.
>
> It is this broad base of participation and potential participation that gives the market its strength as an economic indicator and as an allocator of scarce capital. Movements in and out of a stock, or in and out of the market, are made on the margin as each investor digests new information. This allows the market to incorporate all available information in a way that no one person could hope to. Since its judgments are the consensus of nearly everyone, it tends to outperform any single person or group....[The market] measures

[1]Garfield Drew, *New Methods for Profit in the Stock Market,* Metcalfe Press, Boston, 1968, p. 18.
[2]*The Wall Street Journal,* Oct. 20, 1977. Reprinted by permission of *The Wall Street Journal.* Copyright Dow Jones and Co. Inc. 1977. All rights reserved.

the after-tax profits of all the companies whose shares are listed in the market, and it measures these cumulative profits so far into the future one might as well say the horizon is infinite. This cumulative mass of after-tax profits is then, as the economists will say, "discounted back to present value" by the market. A man does the same thing when he pays more for one razor blade than another, figuring he'll get more or easier shaves in the future with the higher-priced one, and figuring its present value on that basis.

This future flow of earnings will ultimately be affected by business conditions everywhere on earth. Little bits of information are constantly flowing into the market from around the world as well as throughout the United States, and the market is much more efficient in reflecting these bits of news than are government statisticians. The market relates this information to how much American business can earn in the future. Roughly speaking, the general level of the market is the present value of the capital stock of the U.S.

This implies that investors are looking ahead and taking action so that they can liquidate at a higher price when the anticipated news or development actually takes place. If expectations concerning the development are better or worse than originally thought, then through the market mechanism investors sell either sooner or later, depending on the particular circumstances. Thus the familiar maxim "sell on good news" applies on when the "good" news is right on or below the market's (i.e., the investors') expectations. If the news is good but not as favorable as expected, a quick reassessment will take place, and the market (other things being equal) will fall. If the news is better than anticipated, the possibilities are obviously more favorable. The reverse will, of course, be true in a declining market. This process explains the paradox of equity markets peaking out when economic conditions are strong, and forming a bottom when the outlook is most gloomy.

The reaction of any market to news events can be most instructive, for if the market, as reflected by price, ignores supposedly bullish news and sells off, it is certain that the event was well discounted, i.e., already built into the price mechanism, and the reaction should therefore be viewed bearishly. If a market reacts more favorably to bad news than might be expected, this in turn should be interpreted as a positive sign. There is a good deal of wisdom in the saying "A bear argument known is a bear argument understood."

The Financial Markets and the Business Cycle

The major movements in bond, stock, and commodity prices are caused by long-term trends in the emotions of the investing public. These emotions reflect the anticipated level and growth rate of future economic activity, and the attitude of investors toward that activity.

For example, there is a definite link between primary movements in the stock market and cyclical movements in the economy, because trends in corporate profitability are an integral part of the business cycle. If the stock market were influenced by basic economic forces only, the task of determining the changes in primary movements of the market would be relatively simple. In practice it is not, and this is due to several factors.

First, changes in the direction of the economy can take some time to materialize. As the cycle unfolds, other psychological considerations — for example, political developments or purely internal factors such as a speculative buying wave or selling pressure from margin calls — can affect the equity market and result in misleading rallies and reactions of 5 to 10 percent or more.

Second, changes in the market usually precede changes in the economy by 6 to 9 months, but the lead time can sometimes be far shorter or longer. In 1921 and 1929, the economy turned before the market did.

Third, even when an economic recovery is in the middle of its cycle, doubts about its durability often arise. When these doubts coincide with political or other adverse developments, sharp and confusing countercyclical price movements usually develop.

Fourth, profits may increase, but investors' attitudes toward those profits may change. For example, in the spring of 1946 the DJIA stood at 22 times the price/earnings ratio. By 1948, the comparable ratio was 9.5 when measured against 1947 earnings. In this period profits had almost doubled and price/earnings ratios had fallen, but stock prices were lower.

Changes in bond and commodity prices are linked much more directly to economic activity than are stock market prices, but even here psychological influences on price are very important. Currencies do not fit well into business cycle analysis. Though data reported several months after the fact are very good at explaining currency movements, technical analysis has been most useful for timely forecasts and the identification of emerging trends.

Technical Analysis—Trend Determination

Since technical analysis involves a study of the action of markets, it is not concerned with the difficult and subjective tasks of forecasting trends in the economy, or assessing the attitudes of investors toward those changes. Technical analysis tries to identify turning points in the *market's* assessment of these factors.

The approach taken here differs from that found in standard presentations of technical analysis. The various techniques used to determine trends and identify their reversals will be examined in Part 1, Trend-Determining Techniques, which deals with moving averages (MAs), rates of change (ROCs), trendlines, price patterns, etc. These principles apply to *all* markets, stocks, and time frames. Part 2, Market Structure, is principally concerned with analysis of the U.S. equity market, although examples using other equity markets are included to demonstrate that the principles are universally applicable. All that is required is the appropriate data. This section offers a more detailed explanation of the various indicators and indexes. It also shows how they can be combined to build a framework for determining the quality of the internal structure of the market. A study of market character is a cornerstone of technical analysis, since reversals of price trends in the major averages are almost always preceded by latent strength or weakness in the market structure. Just as a careful driver does not judge the performance of a car from the speedometer alone, so technical analysis looks further than the price trends of the popular averages. Trends of investor confidences are responsible for price movements, and this emotional aspect is examined from four viewpoints, or dimensions, namely, price, time, volume, and breadth.

Changes in prices reflect changes in investor attitude, and *price*, the first dimension, indicates the level of that change.

Time, the second dimension, measures the recurrence and length of cycles in investor psychology. Changes in confidence go through distinct cycles, some long and some short, as investors swing from excesses of optimism toward deep pessimism. The degree of price movement in the market is usually a function of the time element. The longer it takes for investors to move from a bullish to a bearish element, the greater the ensuing price change is likely to be. The examples in the two chapters on time relate mainly to the U.S. stock market, but are equally valid for commodities, bonds, currencies, or stocks.

Volume, the third dimension, reflects the intensity of changes in investor attitudes. For example, the level of enthusiasm implied by a price rise on low volume is not nearly as strong as that implied by a similar price advance accompanied by very high volume.

The fourth dimension, *breadth*, measures the extent of the emotion. This is important, for as long as stocks are advancing on a broad front, the trend in favorable emotion is dispersed among most stocks and industries, which indicates a healthy and broad economic recovery and a widely favorable attitude toward stocks in particular. On the other hand, when interest has narrowed to a few blue-chip stocks, the quality of the trend has deteriorated, and a continuation of the bull market is highly suspect.

Technical analysis measures these psychological dimensions in a number of ways. Most indicators monitor two or more aspects simultaneously; for instance, a simple price chart measures both price (on the vertical axis) and time (on the horizontal axis). Similarly, an advance/decline line measures breadth and time.

Part 3, Interest Rates and the Stock Market, examines some of the technical indicators that have been useful in identifying reversals in debt prices and interest rates. The relationship between changes in interest rates and the stock market is also discussed.

Part 4, Other Aspects of Market Behavior, deals with the importance of speculation and with other aspects of market sentiment. Finally, Part 5, Specific Financial Markets, considers the application of technical analysis to other financial markets including gold, currencies, and commodities.

Candle charts and the Elliott wave principle are covered in the appendixes. The glossary explains some terms used but not defined in the text.

Conclusion

Financial markets move in trends caused by the changing attitudes and expectations of investors with regard to the business cycle. Since investors continue to repeat the same type of behavior from cycle to cycle, an understanding of the historical relationships between certain price averages and market indicators can be used to identify turning points. No single indicator can ever be expected to signal all trend reversals, and so it is essential to use a number of them together to build up a consensus.

This approach is by no means infallible, but a careful, patient, and objective use of the principles of technical analysis can put the odds of success very much in favor of the investor or trader who incorporates these principles into an overall investment strategy.

PART 1

Trend-Determining Techniques

1
Market Cycle Model

In the Introduction *technical analysis* was defined as the art of identifying a *trend reversal* at an early stage and riding that trend until the weight of the evidence proves that it has been reversed. In order to identify a reversal, we must first know what a trend is. This chapter, therefore, explains and categorizes the various trends, and concludes with a discussion of one of the basic trend-determining techniques, *peak-and-trough progression*.

Peak-and-trough progression is one of the simplest, and perhaps the most effective, trend-identification techniques used in technical analysis. It forms a building block for many of the other techniques discussed later.

Three Important Trends

A trend is a time measurement of the direction in price levels covering different time spans. There are many trends, but the three that are most widely followed are primary, intermediate, and short-term.

Primary Trend

The primary trend generally lasts between 1 and 2 years and is a reflection of investors' attitudes toward unfolding fundamentals in the business cycle. The business cycle extends statistically from trough to trough for approximately 3.6 years, so it follows that rising and falling primary

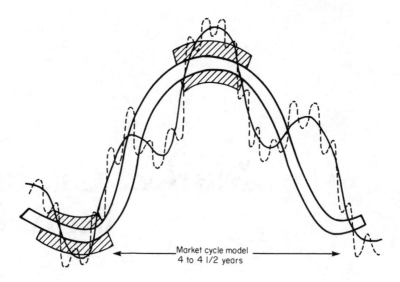

Market cycle model
4 to 4 1/2 years

Figure 1.1. Market cycle model.

trends (bull and bear markets) last for 1 to 2 years. Since building up takes longer than tearing down, bull markets generally last longer than bear markets.

The primary trend cycle is operative for bonds, equities, and commodities. Primary trends also apply to currencies, but since currencies reflect investors' attitudes toward the interrelationship of two different economies, analysis of currency relationships does not fit neatly into the business cycle approach discussed in Chapter 2.

The primary trend is illustrated in Figure 1.1 by the double line. In an idealized situation the primary uptrend (bull market) is the same size as the primary downtrend (bear market), but in reality of course their magnitudes are different. Because it is very important to position investments in the direction of the main trend, a significant part of this book is concerned with identifying reversals in the primary trend.

Intermediate Trend

Anyone who has looked at a price chart will notice that prices do not move in a straight line. A primary upswing is interrupted by several reactions along the way. These countercyclical trends within the confines of a primary bull market are known as *intermediate price movements.* They last anywhere from 3 weeks to as long as 6 months or more.

Intermediate-term trends of the stock market are examined in greater detail in Chapter 4 and are shown as a thin solid line in Figure 1.1.

It is important to have an idea of the direction and maturity of the primary trend, but an analysis of intermediate trends is also helpful for improving success rates in trading, as well as for determining when the primary movement may have run its course.

Short-Term Trends

Short-term trends, which last from 1 to 3 or 4 weeks, interrupt the course of the intermediate cycle, just as the intermediate-term trend interrupts primary price movements. Short-term trends are shown in the market cycle model (Figure 1.1) as a dashed line. They are usually influenced by random news events and are far more difficult to identify than their intermediate or primary counterparts. Generally speaking, *the longer the time span of the trend, the easier it is to identify.*

Market Cycle Model

It is apparent by now that the price level of any market is influenced simultaneously by several different trends, and it is important to understand which type is being monitored. For example, if a reversal in a short-term trend has just taken place, a much smaller price movement may be expected than if the primary trend had reversed.

Long-term investors are principally concerned with the direction of the primary trend, and thus it is important for them to have some perspective on the maturity of the prevailing bull or bear market. However, *long-term investors must also be aware of intermediate- and, to a lesser extent, short-term trends.* This is because an important step in the analysis is an examination and understanding of the relationship between short- and intermediate-term trends, and how they affect the primary trend.

Very short term traders in the futures markets are principally concerned with smaller movements in price, but they *also need to know the direction of the intermediate and primary trends.* This is because surprises occur on the upside in a bull market, and on the downside in a bear market. In other words, rising short-term trends within the confines of a bull market are likely to be much greater in magnitude than short-term downtrends, and vice versa. A trading loss usually happens because the trader is positioned in a countercyclical position against the main trend. In effect, *all market participants need to have some kind of working knowledge of all three trends,* although the emphasis will depend on whether their orientation comes from an investment or a short-term trading perspective.

Intraday Trends

In recent years, computers and real-time trading have enabled traders to identify hourly and even tick-by-tick movements. The principles of technical analysis apply equally to these very short term movements, and are just as valid. There are two main differences. First, reversals in the hourly charts have only a very short term implication and are not significant for longer-term price reversals. Second, extremely short term price markets are much more influenced by psychology and instant reaction to news events than are longer-term ones. Decisions therefore have a tendency to be emotional, knee-jerk reactions. Intraday price action is also more susceptible to manipulation. As a consequence, price data used in very short term charts are much more erratic and less reliable than those that appear in the longer-term charts.

Secular Trend

The primary trend consists of several intermediate cycles, but the secular, or very long term, trend is constructed from a number of primary trends. This "super cycle," or long wave, extends over a substantially greater period, usually lasting well over 10 years, and often as long as 25 years. It is discussed more fully in Chapter 16. A diagram of the interrelationship between a secular and a primary trend is shown in Figure 1.2. It is certainly very helpful to understand the direction of the secular trend. Just as the primary trend influences the magnitude of the intermediate-term rally relative to the countercyclical reaction, so the secular trend influences the magnitude and duration of a primary-trend rally or reaction. For example, in a rising secular trend, primary bull markets will be of greater magnitude than primary bear markets. In a secular downtrend, bear markets will be more powerful, and will take longer to unfold, than bull markets.

Peak-and-Trough Progression

Technical analysis, as pointed out before, is the *art* of identifying a (price) trend reversal based on the weight of the evidence. As in a court

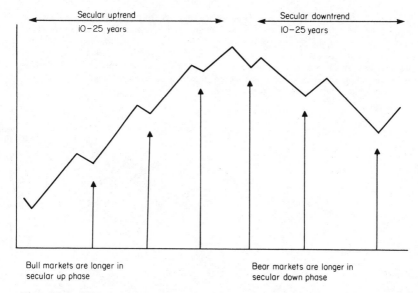

Figure 1.2. Relationship between the secular and the primary trend.

of law, a trend is presumed innocent until proved guilty! The "evidence" is the objective element in technical analysis. It consists of a series of indicators or techniques that work well most of the time in the trend-identification process. The "art" consists of combining these indicators into an overall picture and recognizing when that picture resembles a market peak or trough.

Widespread use of computers has led to development of some very sophisticated trend-identification techniques in market analysis. Some of these indicators work reasonably well, but most do not. The continual search for the "holy grail," or perfect indicator, will undoubtedly continue, but it is unlikely that such a technique will ever be developed. Even if it were, news of its discovery would soon be disseminated and the indicator would gradually be discounted.

In the quest for sophisticated mathematical techniques, some of the simplest and most basic techniques of technical analysis are often overlooked.

Peak-and-Trough Progression

One simple, basic technique that has been underused is peak-and-trough progression (see Chart 1.1), which relates to Charles Dow's original observation that a rising market moves in a series of waves, each

Chart 1.1. Moody's AAA corporate bond yields between 1944 and 1990. The solid line above the yield corresponds to the primary bull and bear markets. The series of rising cyclical peaks and troughs extended from the end of World War II until the early 1980s. This was a very long period, even by secular trend standards. In 1985 the series of rising peaks and troughs was violated, confirming that the secular uptrend was completed in 1981. This peak-and-trough signal indicated a change in trend, but gave no indication of the magnitude or duration of the new secular downtrend.

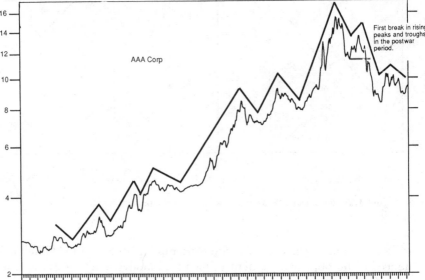

rally and reaction being higher than its predecessor. When the series of rising peaks and troughs is interrupted, a trend reversal is signaled. To explain this approach, Dow used an analogy with the ripple effect of waves on a seashore. He pointed out that just as it was possible for someone on the beach to identify the turning of the tide by a reversal of receding wave action at low tide, so the same objective can be achieved in the market by observing the price action.

In Figure 1.3 the price has been advancing in a series of waves, with each peak and trough reaching higher than its predecessor. Then, for the first time, a rally fails to move to a new high and the subsequent reaction pushes it *below the previous trough*. This occurs at point *X*, and gives a signal that the trend has reversed. Figure 1.4 shows a similar situation, but this time the trend reversal is from a downtrend to an uptrend.

This idea of the interruption of a series of peaks and troughs is the basic building block for both Dow theory (Chapter 3) and price pattern analysis (Chapter 5).

The significance of a peak-and-trough reversal is determined by the duration and magnitude of the rallies and reactions in question. For exam-

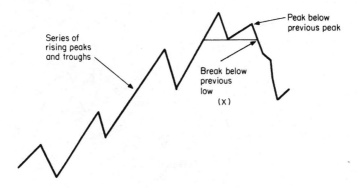

Figure 1.3. Reversal of rising peaks and troughs.

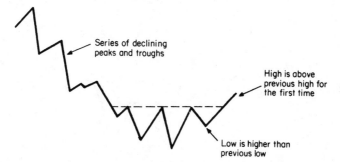

Figure 1.4. Reversal of falling peaks and troughs.

ple, if it takes 2 to 3 weeks to complete each wave in a series of rallies and reactions, the trend reversal will be an intermediate one, since intermediate price movements consist of a series of short-term (2- to 3-week) fluctuations. Similarly, the interruption of a series of falling intermediate peaks and troughs by a rising one signals a reversal from a primary bear to a primary bull market.

A Peak-and-Trough Dilemma

Occasionally peak-and-trough progression becomes more complicated than the examples shown in Figures 1.3 and 1.4. In Figure 1.5, example *a*, the market has been advancing in a series of rising peaks and troughs, but following the highest peak the price declines at point *X* to a level which is below the previous low. At this juncture the series of rising troughs has been broken but *not* the series of rising peaks. In other words, *at point* X *only half a signal has been generated.*

The complete signal of a reversal of both rising peaks and troughs

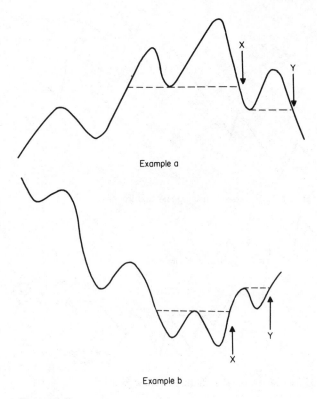

Example a

Example b

Figure 1.5.

arises at point Y, when the price slips below the level previously reached at point X.

At point X there is quite a dilemma because the trend should still be classified as positive, and yet the very fact that the series of rising troughs has been interrupted indicates underlying technical weakness. On the one hand, we are presented with half a bearish signal, while on the other hand, waiting for point Y would mean giving up a substantial amount of the profits earned during the bull market.

The dilemma is probably best dealt with by referring back to the second half of the definition of technical analysis given at the beginning of this chapter: "and riding that trend until the *weight of the evidence* proves that it has been reversed."

In this case, if the "weight of the evidence" from other technical indicators, such as moving averages (MAs), volume, momentum, and breadth (discussed in later chapters), overwhelmingly indicates a trend reversal, it is probably safe to anticipate a change in trend, even though peak-and-trough progression has not *confirmed* the situation. It is still a wise policy, though, to view this signal with some degree of skepticism until the reversal is confirmed by an interruption in *both* series of rising peaks as well as troughs.

Figure 1.5, example *b*, shows this type of situation for a reversal from a bear to bull trend. The same principles of interpretation apply at point *X* as in Figure 1.5, example *a*.

Occasionally the determination of what constitutes a rally or reaction becomes a subjective process. One way around this problem is to choose an objective measure such as categorizing rallies greater than, say, 5 percent. This can be a tedious process, but some software programs such as MetaStock enable the user to establish such benchmarks almost instantly in graphic format (see Resources section).

Summary

1. A number of different trends simultaneously influence the price level of any market.

2. The three most important trends are primary, intermediate, and short-term.

3. The principles of technical analysis apply to intraday trends, but since they are more random in nature, the analysis is generally less reliable than for longer-term trends.

4. Very long term, or secular, trends influence the magnitude of primary bull and bear trends.

5. Peak-and-trough progression is the most basic trend-identification technique and is a basic building block of technical analysis.

2
Financial Markets and the Business Cycle

Introduction

The basic concern of this book is the technical approach, but it is also important to understand that primary trends of stocks, bonds, and commodities are determined by the *attitude* of investors toward unfolding events in the business cycle. Each market has a tendency to peak and trough at different points during the business cycle in a consistent, chronological manner. An understanding of the interrelationship of debt, equity, and commodity markets provides a useful framework for identifying major reversals in each market. The following discussion will use the U.S. dollar price of gold bullion as a proxy for the commodity markets. From time to time, the price performance of gold bullion has differed from general commodity price trends, but nevertheless it has proved a useful measure of inflationary expectations. In the 1980s the gold price led major turning points in commodities by several months, but this is not a sufficient period to conclude that this discounting mechanism is permanent.

The Discounting Mechanism of Financial Markets

The trend of all financial markets is essentially determined by investors' expectations of movements in the economy, the effect those changes are likely to have on the price of the asset in which a specific financial market deals, and the psychological attitude of investors to these fundamental factors. Market participants typically anticipate future economic and financial developments and take action by buying or selling the appropriate assets, with the result that a market normally reaches a major turning point well ahead of the actual development.

An expanding level of economic activity is usually favorable for stock prices, a weak economy is bullish for bond prices, and an inflationary economy is favorable for gold and gold-related assets. These three markets often move in different directions at the same time because they are trying to discount different things.

An economy is rarely stable; generally, it is either expanding or contracting. As a result, financial markets are also in a continual state of flux. A hypothetical economy, as shown in Figure 2.1, revolves around a point of balance known as *equilibrium*. Roughly speaking, equilibrium can be thought of as a period of zero growth in which the economy is neither expanding nor contracting. In practice, this state of affairs is rarely if ever attained, since an economy as a whole possesses tremendous momentum in either the expansionary or the contractionary phase, so that the turnaround rarely occurs at an equilibrium level. In any event, the "economy" consists of a host of individual sectors, many of which are operating in different directions at the same time. Thus, at the beginning of the business cycle, leading economic indicators such as housing starts might be rising, while lagging indicators such as capital spending or employment levels could be falling. Investors in financial markets are not concerned with periods of extended stability or equilibrium, for such periods do not produce volatile price swings and opportunities to make quick profits.

Since the financial markets lead the economy, it follows that the greatest profits can be made just before the point of maximum economic distortion, or disequilibrium. Once investors realize that an econ-

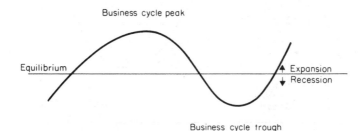

Figure 2.1. A hypothetical business cycle. (*Source: Martin J. Pring, International Investing Made Easy, McGraw-Hill, New York, 1981, p. 16.*)

omy is changing direction and returning toward the equilibrium level, they discount this development by buying or selling the appropriate asset. Obviously, the more dislocated and volatile an economy becomes, the greater is the potential, not only for a return toward the equilibrium level, but for a strong swing well beyond it to the other extreme. Under such conditions, the possibilities for making money in financial markets are greater because they too will normally become subject to wider price fluctuations.

Market Movements and the Business Cycle

The major movements of interest rates, equities, and gold prices are related to movements in the level of business activity. Figure 2.2 represents a business cycle which typically has a life of between 3 and 5 years between troughs. The horizontal line reflects a level of zero growth, above which are periods of expansion and below which are periods of contraction. After the peak is experienced, the economy continues to grow, but at a declining rate, until the line crosses below the equilibrium level and contraction in economic activity takes place. The arrows in Figure 2.2 show the idealized peaks and troughs of the financial markets as they relate to the business cycle.

Periods of expansion generally last longer than periods of contraction, because it takes longer to build something up than to tear it down.

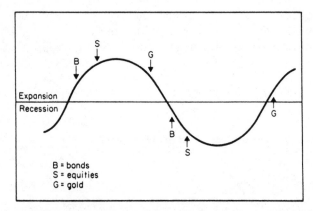

Figure 2.2. A hypothetical business cycle showing peaks and troughs. (*Source: Martin J. Pring, International Investing Made Easy, McGraw-Hill, New York, 1981, p. 20.*)

For this reason, bull markets for equities and gold generally last longer than bear markets. Conversely, bond, bear markets generally last longer than bull markets.

Figure 2.3 shows how the three markets of interest rates, gold, and equities also relate to the typical business cycle. In the example, interest rates have been plotted inversely to correspond with bond prices. A bull market for bonds is marked by a rising line, and a bear market by a descending one. Referring back to Figure 2.2, we can see that the bond market is the first financial market to begin a bull phase. This usually occurs after the growth rate in the economy has slowed down considerably from its peak rate and quite often is delayed until the initial stages of the recession. Generally speaking, the sharper the economic contraction, the greater the potential for a rise in bond prices will be (i.e., a fall in interest rates). Alternatively, the stronger the period of expansion, the smaller the amount of economic and financial slack, and the greater the potential for a decline in bond prices (and a rise in interest rates).

Following the bear market low in bond prices, economic activity begins to contract more sharply. At this point, participants in the equity market are able to "look through" the valley in corporate profits, which are now declining sharply because of the recession, and to begin accumulating stocks. After the recovery has been under way for some time, investors start to feel uncomfortable about the outlook for inflation; therefore a bottom occurs in the gold asset markets if it has not done so already. At this point all three financial markets are in a rising trend.

Gradually the economic and financial slack which developed as a result of the recession is substantially absorbed, putting upward pressure

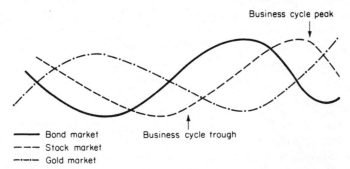

Figure 2.3. The interaction of financial markets during a typical business cycle. (*Source: Martin J. Pring, International Investing Made Easy, McGraw-Hill, New York, 1981, p. 22.*)

on the price of credit, i.e., interest rates. Since rising interest rates mean falling bond prices, the bond market peaks out and begins its bear phase. Because some excess plant and labor capacity still exists, rising business activity results in improved productivity and a continued positive outlook. Because the stock market discounts trends in corporate profits, it remains in an uptrend until investors sense that the economy is becoming overheated and the potential for an improvement in profits is very low. At this point there is less reason to hold equities, and they in turn enter into a bear phase.

The price of gold is determined basically by the interaction of two types of market participants. The first group deals in gold as an industrial commodity affected by fundamental demand/supply relationships; the second invests in gold as a hedge against inflation. Essentially, the level of business activity has a more or less identical effect on both types of market participants, since both the trend of industrial demand and the growth rate of price inflation normally rise during a business cycle expansion and fall during a contraction. The price of gold and gold-related assets therefore discounts trends in business activity but lags behind equity prices. This happens because both forms of market demand for gold — i.e., commodity and investment demand — are oriented to lagging indicators of an economic cycle. Since gold is considered to be a good store of value, for example, its investment demand depends substantially on the rate of price inflation. Because the peak rate of price inflation is typically experienced around the beginning of the recessionary stage of the business cycle, theoretically the cyclical high in the price of gold should be achieved several months ahead of the point at which the rate of price inflation turns down.

Once this juncture has been reached, all three financial markets begin to fall. They will continue to fall until the debt markets bottom out. This final stage, which develops around the same time as the beginning of the recession, is usually associated with a free-fall in prices in at least one of the financial markets. If a panic is to develop, this is one of the most likely points for it to take place.

Longer Cycles

Some expansions encompass much longer periods, and they usually include at least one slowdown in the growth rate followed by a second round of economic expansion. This has the effect of splitting the overall expansion into two or three parts, each of which results in a complete cycle in the financial markets. An example of this phenomenon is illustrated in Figure 2.4.

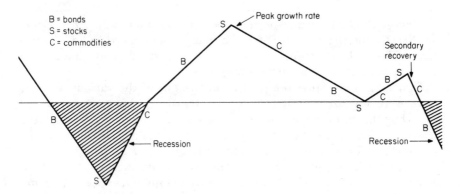

Figure 2.4. The growth track of the economy in a double cycle.

Market Experience, 1964–1990

Figure 2.5 shows how peaks and troughs developed for the various markets between 1964 and 1982. The horizontal line corresponds to periods when the economy moved from a stage of expansion to a stage of contraction in a manner similar to that shown in Figure 2.1. The jagged lines represent a rough approximation of the peaks and troughs of economic growth throughout the period. *B*, *S*, and *G* relate to the prices of short-term (i.e., money-market) debt instruments: the New York Stock

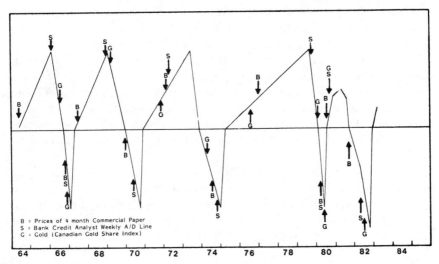

Figure 2.5. Peaks and troughs in U.S. financial markets, 1964–1982. (*Source: Pring Market Review.*)

Exchange (NYSE) advance/decline line[1] as published in the *Pring Market Review* and the Toronto Stock Exchange Gold Share Index, respectively. The Gold Share Index has been used instead of the actual gold price because it has a longer trading history.

Figure 2.5 shows that the peaks and troughs of the various markets have, in reality, turned out very much as they might have been expected to. While the chronological sequence has been more or less perfect, the leads and lags in each cycle have varied considerably, because special circumstances can affect a particular market and cause it to reverse at an earlier or later point than a study of the business cycle might suggest. For example, in the 1970–1974 cycle, most commodities peaked during the spring of 1974, but the U.S. dollar price of gold bullion made its cyclical high later in the year because the legalization of gold purchases for American residents in December 1974 had the effect of delaying the bearish phase of the cycle. The Gold Share Index, however, peaked in March 1974.

In 1980, on the other hand, the Toronto Stock Exchange Gold Share Index peaked almost simultaneously with the stock market. In forecasting, this sequential approach is most useful as a framework or road map. For example, if the technical position of the debt markets suggests that they have made a peak while the gold and stock markets are still acting well, the framework suggests that the next major top is going to be that of equities, and so forth. Similarly, if it is evident that the gold price has peaked, the technical position of the debt markets should be assessed in anticipation of a bear market low, etc.

Chart 2.1 brings the same approach up to date by illustrating the actual price action in the three markets. The arrows join the *peaks associated with business cycle peaks*, and Chart 2.2 highlights the troughs over the same period. The chronological *sequence* in each of these cycles was more or less normal, but the leads and lags were very different. For example, the high in money-market prices was reached in early 1977, but the stock market was still making a new high more than 3 years after that point. This is in sharp contrast to the January 1983 money-market peak, which was followed only 5 months later by a top in the stock market.

The recovery that began in 1982 consisted of three minicycles. The first (as measured by money-market prices) troughed out at the end of 1981, the second in mid- to late 1984, and the third in the spring of 1989. (Note their approximate 4-year separation.) It is important to understand that the financial market lows that occurred after 1982 were

---

[1]This indicator is discussed at length in Chapter 17.

Chart 2.1. Three financial markets (peaks).

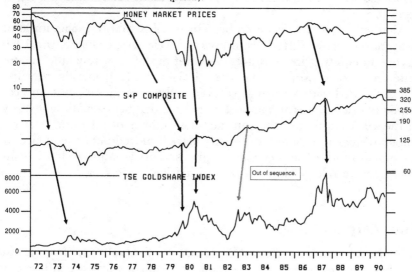

Chart 2.2. Three financial markets (troughs).

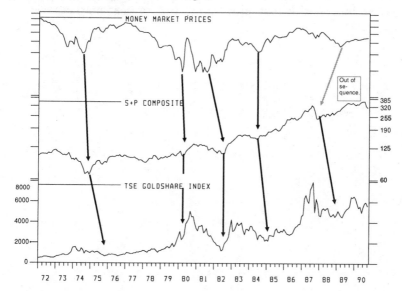

associated with slowdowns in the economy rather than with full-fledged recessions.

Another important factor to bear in mind is that the magnitude of each market move differs from cycle to cycle. For example, the 1980 decline in equity prices was not only brief but of relatively little magnitude, in sharp contrast to the 1983–1984 setback. Ironically, the first was associated with an actual recession, the second with just an economic slowdown. It is also important to note that because of the severity of the 1987 crash, and the considerable number of takeovers that resulted in stock retirement, the equity market moved out of sequence. It bottomed *ahead* of money-market prices. This is unusual, but it confirms that no relationship in financial markets is perfect.

Summary

1. A typical business cycle embraces three individual cycles for interest rates, equities, and gold and commodities, all of which are influenced by the same economic and financial forces but each of which responds differently.

2. The leads and lags vary from cycle to cycle and have little forecasting value.

3. The chronological sequence of peaks and troughs in the various financial markets can be used as a framework for identifying the position of a specific market within its bull or bear market cycle.

3

Dow Theory

The Dow theory is the oldest and by far the most publicized method of identifying major trends in the stock market. An extensive account will not be necessary here, as there are many excellent books on the subject. A brief explanation, however, is in order, because the basic principles of the Dow theory are used in other branches of technical analysis.

The goal of the theory is to determine changes in the primary or major movement of the market. Once a trend has been established, it is assumed to exist until a reversal is proved. Dow theory is concerned with the *direction* of a trend and has no forecasting value as to the ultimate duration or size of the trend.

Starting in 1897, an investor who purchased the stocks in the Dow Jones Industrial Average (DJIA) following each Dow theory buy signal, liquidated the position on sell signals, and reinvested the money on the next buy signal, would have seen the original investment of $44 in 1897 grow to about $51,268 by January 1990.[1] If instead the investor had held onto the original $44 investment throughout that period, the investment would also have grown, but only to about $2500. In reality, the substantial profit earned by following the Dow theory would have been trimmed by transaction costs and capital gains taxes. Even if a wide margin for error is allowed, the investment performance using this approach would still have been far superior to the results of a buy-and-hold strategy.

It should be recognized that the theory does not always keep pace with events; it occasionally leaves the investor in doubt, and it is by no

---

[1]This assumes that the averages were available in 1897. Actually, Dow theory was first published in 1900.

means infallible, since small losses are sometimes incurred. These points emphasize that, while mechanical devices can be useful for forecasting the stock market, there is no substitute for obtaining additional supportive analysis on which to base sound, balanced judgment.

Dow theory evolved from the work of Charles H. Dow, which was published in a series of *Wall Street Journal* editorials between 1900 and 1902. Dow used the behavior of the stock market as a barometer of business conditions rather than as a basis for forecasting stock prices themselves. His successor, William Peter Hamilton, developed Dow's principles and organized them into something approaching the theory as we know it today. These principles were outlined rather loosely in Hamilton's book *The Stock Market Barometer,* published in 1922. It was not until Robert Rhea published *Dow Theory* in 1932 that a more complete and formalized account of the principles finally became available.

The theory assumes that the majority of stocks follow the underlying trend of the market most of the time. In order to measure "the market," Dow constructed two indexes, which are now called the *Dow Jones Industrial Average,* which was originally a combination of 12 (but now includes 30) blue-chip stocks, and the *Dow Jones Rail Average,* comprising 12 railroad stocks. Since the Rail Average was intended as a proxy for transportation stocks, the evolution of aviation and other forms of

Chart 3.1. DJIA, 1952–1968, showing Dow theory buy and sell signals.

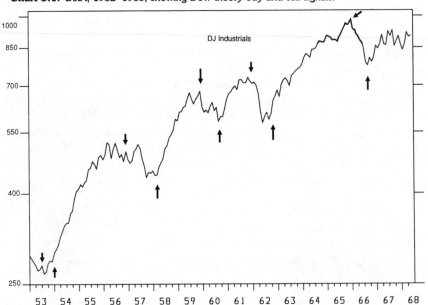

Chart 3.2. DJIA, 1968–1990, showing Dow theory buy and sell signals.

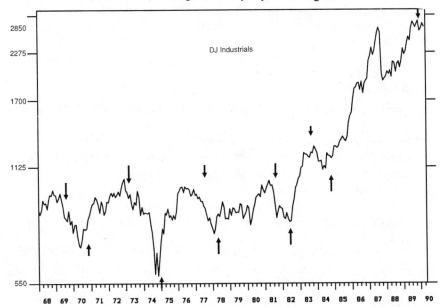

transportation has necessitated modifying the old Rail Average in order to incorporate additions to this industry. Consequently, the name of this index has been changed to *Transportation Average.*

Interpreting the Theory

In order to interpret the theory correctly, it is necessary to have a record of the daily closing[2] prices of the two averages and the total of daily transactions on the New York Stock Exchange (NYSE). The six basic tenets of the theory are as follows:

1. The Averages Discount Everything

Changes in the daily closing prices reflect the aggregate judgment and emotions of all stock market participants, both current and potential. It is therefore assumed that this process discounts everything known and

[2]It is important to use closing prices, since intraday fluctuations are more subject to manipulation.

predictable that can affect the demand/supply relationship of stocks. Although acts of God are obviously unpredictable, their occurrence is quickly appraised and their implications are discounted.

2. The Market Has Three Movements

There are simultaneously three movements in the stock market.

Primary Movement.   The most important is the *primary* or *major trend*, more generally known as a bull (rising) or bear (falling) market. Such movements last from less than 1 year to several years.

A *primary bear market* is a long decline interrupted by important rallies. It begins as the hopes on which the stocks were first purchased are abandoned. The second phase evolves as the levels of business activity and profits decline. The bear market reaches a climax when stocks are liquidated regardless of their underlying value (because of the depressed state of the news or because of forced liquidation caused, for example, by margin calls). This represents the third stage of the bear market.

A *primary bull market* is a broad upward movement, normally averaging at least 18 months, which is interrupted by secondary reactions. The bull market begins when the averages have discounted the worst possible news, and confidence about the future begins to revive. The second stage of the bull market is the response of equities to known improvements in business conditions, while the third and final phase evolves from overconfidence and speculation when stocks are advanced on projections that usually prove to be unfounded.

Secondary Reactions.   A *secondary* or *intermediate reaction* is defined as "an important decline in a bull market or advance in a bear market, usually lasting from 3 weeks to as many months, during which interval the movement generally retraces from 33 to 66 percent of the primary price change since the termination of the last preceding secondary reaction."[3] This relationship is shown in Figure 3.1.

Occasionally a secondary reaction can retrace the whole of the previous primary movement, but normally the move falls in the one-half to two-thirds area, often at the 50 percent mark. As discussed in greater detail below, the correct differentiation between the first leg of a new primary trend and a secondary movement within the existing trend provides Dow theorists with their most difficult problem.

[3]Robert Rhea, *Dow Theory*, Barron's, New York, 1932.

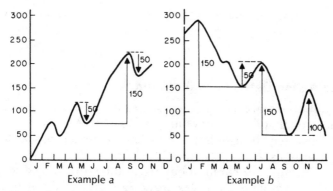

Figure 3.1. Secondary retracements.

Minor Movements. The *minor movement* lasts from a matter of hours up to as long as 3 weeks. It is important only in that it forms part of the primary or secondary moves; it has no forecasting value for longer-term investors. This is especially important since short-term movements can be manipulated to some extent, unlike the secondary or primary trends.

3. Lines Indicate Movement

Rhea defined a line as "a price movement two to three weeks or longer, during which period the price variation of both averages moves within a range of approximately 5 percent (of their mean average). Such a movement indicates either accumulation [*stock moving into strong and knowledgeable hands and therefore bullish*] or distribution [*stock moving into weak hands and therefore bearish*]."[4] (Words in italics added.)

An advance above the limits of the "line" indicates accumulation and predicts higher prices, and vice versa. When a line occurs in the middle of a primary advance, it is really forming a horizontal secondary movement and should be treated as such.

4. Price/Volume Relationships Provide Background

The normal relationship is for volume to expand on rallies and contract on declines. If volume becomes dull on a price advance and expands on a decline, a warning is given that the prevailing trend may soon be reversed. This principle should be used as background information only,

[4]Ibid.

since the conclusive evidence of trend reversals can be given only by the price of the respective averages.

5. Price Action Determines the Trend

Bullish indications are given when successive rallies penetrate peaks while the trough of an intervening decline is above the preceding trough. Conversely, bearish indications come from a series of declining peaks and troughs.

Figure 3.2 shows a theoretical bull trend interrupted by a secondary reaction. In example *a* the index makes a series of three peaks and troughs, each higher than its respective predecessor. The index rallies following the third decline but is unable to surpass its third peak. The next decline takes the average below its low point, confirming a bear market as it does so at point X. In example *b*, following the third peak in the bull market, a bear market is indicated as the average falls below the previous secondary trough. In this instance the preceding second-

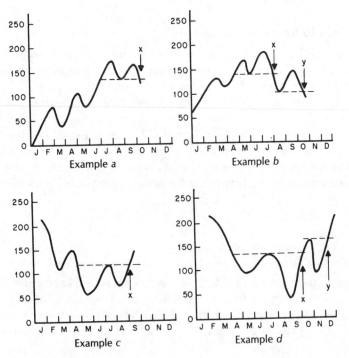

Figure 3.2. Primary reversals.

ary was part of a bull market, not the first trough in a bear market, as shown in example *a*. Many Dow theorists do not consider penetration at point *X* in example *b* to be a sufficient indication of a bear market. They prefer to take a more conservative position by waiting for a rally and subsequent penetration of that previous trough marked as point *Y* in example *b*.

In such cases, it is wise to approach the interpretation with additional caution. If a bearish indication is given from the volume patterns and a clearly identifiable speculative stage for the bull market has already materialized, it is probably safe to assume that the bearish indication is valid. In the absence of such characteristics, it is wiser to give the bull market the benefit of the doubt and adopt a more conservative position. Remember, technical analysis is the art of identifying trend reversals based on *the weight of the evidence*. Dow theory is one piece of evidence, so if four or five other indicators are pointing to a trend reversal, it is usually a good idea to treat the "half" signal at point *X* as an indication that the trend has reversed. Examples *c* and *d* represent similar instances at the bottom of a bear market.

The examples in Figure 3.3 show how the primary reversal would appear if the average had formed a line at its peak or trough. The importance of being able to distinguish between a valid secondary movement and the first leg of a new primary trend is now evident. This is perhaps the most difficult part of the theory to interpret, and unquestionably the most critical.

It is essential to establish that the secondary reaction has retraced at least one-third of the ground of the preceding primary movement, as measured from the termination of the preceding secondary. The secondary should also extend for at least 3 to 4 weeks.

Vital clues can also be obtained from volume characteristics and from

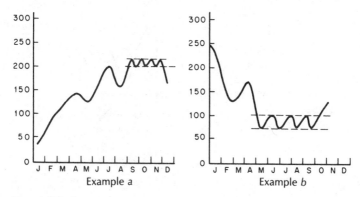

Figure 3.3. Lines.

an assessment of the maturity of the prevailing primary trend. The odds of a major reversal are much greater if the market has undergone its third phase, characterized by speculation and false hopes during a primary upswing, or a bout of persistent liquidation and widespread pessimism during a major decline. A change in the primary trend can occur without a clearly identifiable third phase, but generally such reversals prove to be relatively short-lived. On the other hand, the largest primary swings usually develop when the characteristics of a third phase are especially marked during the preceding primary movement. Hence, the excessive bouts of speculation in 1919, 1929, and 1968 were followed by particularly sharp setbacks. Intermediate-term movements are discussed more extensively in Chapter 4.

6. The Averages Must Confirm

One of the most important principles of Dow theory is that the movement of the Industrial Average and the Transportation Average should always be considered together; i.e., the two averages must confirm each other.

The need for confirming action by both averages would seem fundamentally logical, for if the market is truly a barometer of future business conditions, investors should be bidding up the prices both of companies that produce goods and of companies that transport them in an expanding economy. It is not possible to have a healthy economy in which goods are being manufactured but not sold (i.e., shipped to market). This principle of confirmation is shown in Figure 3.4.

In example *a*, the Industrial Average is the first to signal a bear trend (point *A*), but the actual bear market is not indicated until the Transportation Average confirms at point *B*. Example *b* shows the beginning of a new bull market. Following a sharp decline, the industrials make a

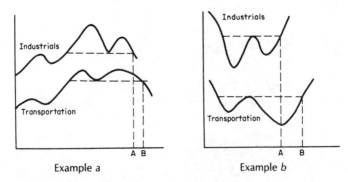

Example *a*   Example *b*

Figure 3.4. Industrial and transportation confirmations.

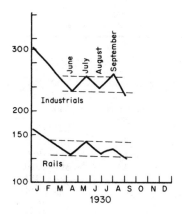

Figure 3.5. 1930 example.

new low. A rally then develops, but the next reaction holds above the previous low. When prices push above the preceding rally, a bull signal is given by the industrials at point *A*. In the meantime the Transportation Average makes a series of two succeeding lows. The question that arises is, Which average is correctly representing the prevailing trend? Since *it is always assumed that a trend is in existence until a reversal is proved*, the conclusion should be drawn at this point that the Transportation Average is indicating the correct outcome.

It is only when this average exceeds the peak of the preceding secondary at point *B* that a new bull market is confirmed by both averages, resulting in a Dow theory buy signal.

The movement of one average unsupported by the other can often lead to a false and misleading conclusion, which is well illustrated in Figure 3.5 by the following example, from 1930.

The 1929–1932 bear market began in September 1929 and was confirmed by both averages in late October. In June 1930 both averages made a new low and then rallied and reacted in August. Following this correction, the industrials surpassed their previous peak. Many observers believed that this signaled the end of a particularly sharp bear market and that it was only a matter of time before the rails would follow suit. As it turned out, the action of the industrials was totally misleading; the bear market still had another 2 years to run.

Additional Considerations

Dow theory does not specify a time period beyond which a confirmation of one average by the other becomes invalid. Generally, the closer the

Table 3.1.

Buy signals			Sell signals		
Date of signal	Price of Dow	Percentage gain from sell signal when short	Date of signal	Price of Dow	Percentage gain from buy signal
Jul. 1897	44		Dec. 1899	63	43
Oct. 1900	59	6	Jun. 1903	59	0
Jul. 1904	51	14	Apr. 1906	92	80
Apr. 1908	70	24	May 1910	85	21
Oct. 1910	82	4	Jan. 1913	85	3
Apr. 1915	65	24	Aug. 1917	86	32
May 1918	82	5	Feb. 1920	99	22
Feb. 1922	84	16	Jun. 1923	91	8
Dec. 1923	94	(loss) 3	Oct. 1929	306	226
May 1933	84	73	Sep. 1937	164	95
Jun. 1938	127	23	Mar. 1939	136	7
Jul. 1939	143	5	May 1940	138	(loss) 7
Feb. 1943	126	8	Aug. 1946	191	52
Apr. 1948	184	4	Nov. 1948	173	(loss) 6
Oct. 1950	229	(loss) 32	Apr. 1953	280	22
Jan. 1954	288	(loss) 3	Oct. 1956	468	63
Apr. 1958	450	4	Mar. 1960	612	36
Nov. 1960	602	2	Apr. 1962	683	13
Nov. 1962	625	8	May 1966	900	43
Jan. 1967	823	9	Jun. 1969	900	9
Dec. 1970	823	9	Apr. 1973	921	12
Jan. 1975	680	26	Oct. 1977	801	18
Apr. 1978	780	3	Jul. 1981	960	23
Aug. 1982	840	13	Feb. 1984	1186	41
Jan. 1985	1261	(loss) 6	Jan. 1990	2546	102
Average of all cycles, 10%			Average of all cycles, 38%		

*When considering the results, note that these signals are the result of interpretation, in some cases with the benefit of hindsight. Some Dow theorists would disagree with my interpretation, but none would dispute the fact that, in general, the theory works.

confirmation, the stronger the following move is likely to be. For example, confirmation of the 1929–1932 bear market was given by the Rail Average just one day after the Industrial Average. The sharp 1962 break was confirmed on the same day.

One of the major criticisms of Dow theory is that many of its signals have proved to be late, often 20 to 25 percent after a peak or trough in the averages has occurred. One rule of thumb that has enabled Dow theorists to anticipate probable reversals at an earlier date is to observe the dividend yield on the industrials. When the yield on the Industrial Average has fallen to 3 percent or below, it has historically been a reliable indicator at market tops. Similarly, a yield of 6 percent has been a reliable indicator at market bottoms.

Dow theorists would not necessarily use these levels as actual buying or selling points, but would probably consider altering the percentage of their equity exposure if a significant nonconfirmation developed between the Industrial Average and the Transportation Average when the yield on the Dow reached these extremes. This strategy would help to improve the investment return of the Dow theory but would not always result in a superior performance. At the 1976 peak, for example, the yield on the Dow never reached the magic 3 percent level, and prices fell 20 percent before a mechanical signal was confirmed by both averages.

Over the years many criticisms have been leveled at the theory on the basis that from time to time (as in periods of war) the rails have been overregulated, or that the new Transportation Average no longer reflects investors' expectations about the future movement of goods. The theory has stood the test of time, however, as Table 3.1 indicates. Indeed, criticism is perfectly healthy, for if the theory gained widespread acceptance and its signals were purely mechanistic instead of requiring experienced judgment, they would be instantly discounted, which would render Dow theory useless for profitable investment.

Summary

Dow theory is concerned with determining the direction of the primary trend of the market, not the ultimate duration or size of the trend. Once confirmed by both averages, the new trend is assumed to be in existence until an offsetting confirmation by both averages takes place.

Major bull and bear markets each have three distinct phases. Both the identification of these phases and the appearance of any divergence in the normal volume/price relationship offer useful indications that a reversal in the major trend is about to take place. Such supplementary evidence is particularly useful when the action of the price averages themselves is inconclusive.

4

Typical Parameters for Intermediate-Term Trends

Some Basic Observations

The two previous chapters discussed the main or primary trend, i.e., the price movement that corresponds to changes in economic activity over the course of a typical 3- to 4-year business cycle. Though it is clearly important to have an idea of the direction and maturity of the primary trend, it is also helpful to have some understanding of the typical character and duration of the intermediate trend for the purpose of improving success rates in trading, and also to help assess when the primary movement may have run its course.

Successful analysis of intermediate trends for any market or stock offers the following advantages:

1. Changes in intermediate trends aid in identification of turning points in the primary trend.

2. Intermediate-term trading involves fewer transactions than trading of minor price movements and therefore results in lower commission costs.

3. Intermediate-trend reversal points occur several times a year and can, if properly interpreted, allow a relatively high and quick return on capital.

Intermediate Cycles Defined

A primary trend typically consists of five intermediate trends, three of which form part of the prevailing trend while the remaining two run counter to that trend. In a bull market the intermediate countertrends are represented by price declines; in a bear market they form rallies that separate the three intermediate downwaves as shown in Figure 4.1.

It is apparent from the discussion above that there are essentially two types of intermediate price movements. The first, which goes in the direction of the primary trend, may be called a *primary intermediate price movement*. The second is an important price movement that lasts from 3 weeks to 3 months (occasionally longer) and normally retraces between one-third and two-thirds of the preceding primary intermediate movement. This price movement, which runs counter to the main trend, is called a *secondary movement* or *reaction*. Since a primary intermediate price movement operates in the same direction as the primary or main market trend, it almost always lasts longer than its secondary counterpart. Its price magnitude is normally much greater as well.

These countertrends or reactions against the main trend are notoriously difficult to forecast in terms of character, magnitude, and duration. Therefore they should generally be avoided from a trading point

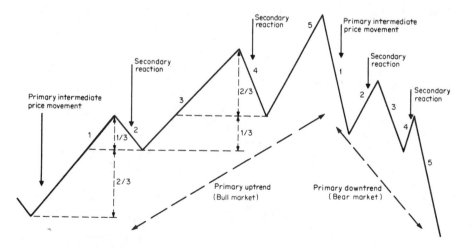

Figure 4.1.

of view, as they will almost invariably be subject to confusing whipsaws. By their very nature they tend to fool the majority and are usually extremely treacherous. It is possible to design successful mechanized systems based on intermediate price movements, but poor or losing signals usually come from secondary market movements that occur against the main trend. Intermediate-term trends that move in the same direction as the primary trend generally are easier to profit from. Traders who do not have the patience to invest for the longer term will find that successful analysis of intermediate movements offers superior results, especially as the day-to-day or minor swings are to a large degree random in nature and therefore even more difficult to capitalize on. This tendency has been most pronounced in recent years when increasingly sharp price movements have resulted from emotional knee-jerk reactions to the release of unexpected economic data.

A secondary reaction does not have to be a decline in a bull market or a bear market rally. It can also take the form of a sideways movement or consolidation, under the same idea as Charles Dow's line formation (see the discussion in Chapter 3).

Intermediate movements can go either with or against the main trend, which means that there is an intermediate cycle, just as there is a primary one. An intermediate cycle consists of a primary intermediate price movement and a secondary reaction. It extends from the low of one intermediate trend to the low of the other, as shown in Figure 4.2.

In a bull market the up phase of the cycle should be longer in time and greater in magnitude. The low on the secondary reaction should be higher than its predecessor. In a bear market the reverse conditions hold true; i.e., declines are longer and greater while rallies are short

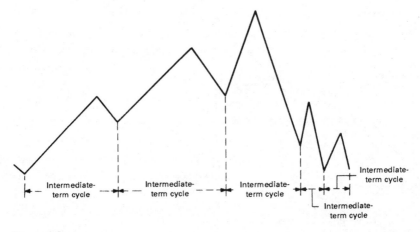

Figure 4.2.

and sharp, but of less magnitude. Accordingly, technicians are alerted first to the possibility of a reversal in the primary trend when a third intermediate cycle is nearing completion. It is also important to note whether the overall technical structure looks weak (strong in a bear market) as the previous intermediate low (high) is approached and, finally, to note whether that level is decisively broken on the downside (upside).

This does not mean that primary movements can never encompass more or fewer than three primary intermediate price movements, for often they do. Expect three as a normal event, but do not be caught off guard if there are fewer or more.

Causes of Secondary Reactions

Since the primary trend of stock prices is determined by the *attitudes* of investors to the future flow of profits, which are in turn determined to a large degree by the course of the business cycle, it would seem illogical at first to expect longer-term movements to be interrupted by what often prove to be very uncomfortable reactions (or in the case of a bear market, very deceptive rallies).

History shows that secondary reactions occur because of technical distortions which arise in the market as a result of overoptimism (or overpessimism), and also because new factors emerge which suggest that business conditions are not going to be as extreme as was originally anticipated, or even that they are going to materialize in the opposite direction. For example, after the first intermediate-term rally in a bull market for equities, a reaction may develop because investors who had discounted a strong recovery now see some chinks appearing that might even forecast an actual decline in business conditions. Such fears eventually prove ungrounded but are sufficient to cause a countercyclical intermediate reaction. Another possibility might be fear of rising interest rates which could choke off the recovery. Since prices had discounted a strong recovery, this change in perception causes investors to pull back and prices to fall accordingly. At the same time, many investors get carried away during the rally phase and leverage themselves up. As prices begin to fall, this causes their equity to shrink and forces them to liquidate, which adds further fuel to the price decline.

A bear market rally for stocks generally takes place because of an improved outlook for business conditions over what was anticipated. A bear market rally for bonds develops under the opposite set of conditions. Corrections in commodity and currency markets all have their roots in a changed, but incorrect, perception of the underlying (primary) economic trend. The catalyst to the rally is the rush by traders and investors to cover their short positions (for a definition and explanation of short selling, see the Glossary). It should be added that the *apparent* motivating force for the correction need not necessarily be directly linked to the outlook for business or interest rates. It could be linked to the anticipated resolution or worsening of a political or military problem, for example. Essentially the change in anticipated conditions combined with the unwinding of the technical distortions of the previous primary intermediate trend and its associated sharp price movement are sufficient to confuse the majority. Only when business conditions are correctly expected to change from recovery to recession (or vice versa) is the primary trend of equities likely to reverse.

In his excellent book *Profits in the Stock Market,* H. M. Gartley[1] pointed out that in the 40 years ending in 1935 two-thirds of all bull market corrections in the U.S. stock market developed in two waves of liquidation separated by a minor rally that retraced between one-third and two-thirds of the first decline. Observation of such corrections since 1935 also bears out the finding that most intermediate corrections consist of two, rather than one or three, phases of liquidation. Unfortunately, intermediate corrections within a bear market cannot be so easily categorized since some are one-move affairs or consist of a rally out of a small base, while still others unfold as a very volatile sideways movement. Even though Gartley's observations were concerned with the equities, this form of correction applies to all financial markets.

Relationship between Primary Intermediate Moves and Subsequent Reactions

In *Profits in the Stock Market* Gartley published a series of diagrams using the classification of intermediate trends established by Robert Rhea. Gartley's conclusion was that the smaller in magnitude the primary intermediate-term movement was, the larger the retracement tended to be, and vice versa. He noted that this was just as valid for bull market reactions as for bear market rallies. Observations of the period since 1933 for virtually all markets appear to support this hypothesis. For example, the rally off the 1962 stock market low was only 18 percent compared to the mean average of 30 percent between 1933 and 1982. This represented part of a double bottom formation and there-

[1]Lambert Gann Publishing, Pomeroy, Wash., 1981.

fore the first primary intermediate rally. This relatively small advance was followed by a somewhat larger 71 percent retracement. However, the ensuing rally from late 1962 until mid-1963 was 32 percent and was followed by a small 25 percent retracement of the gain. Interested readers may wish to be satisfied that what goes up does not necessarily come down, and vice versa.

The 1976–1980 gold bull market was very powerful, but the intermediate corrections were quite brief. On the other hand, the rallies between 1982 and 1990 were far less strong but were followed by corrections of much greater magnitude proportionally.

Using Intermediate Cycles to Identify Primary Reversals

Number of Intermediate Cycles

A primary movement may normally be expected to encompass 2½ intermediate cycles (see Figure 4.3). Unfortunately, not all primary movements correspond to the norm; an occasional primary movement may

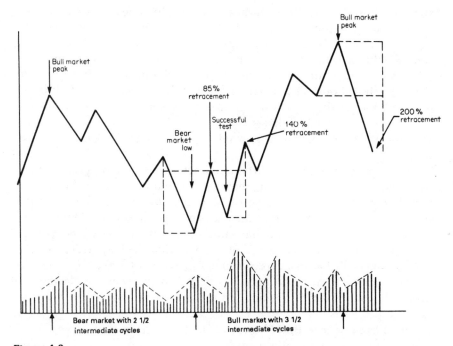

Figure 4.3.

consist of 1, 2, 3, or even 4 intermediate cycles. Furthermore, these intermediate cycles may be of very unequal length or magnitude, making their classification and identification possible only after the event. Even so, intermediate-cycle analysis can still be used as a basis for identifying the maturity of the primary trend in most cases.

Whenever prices are well advanced in a primary intermediate trend following the complication of two intermediate cycles, technicians should be alerted to the fact that a reversal of the primary trend itself may be about to take place. Again, if only one intermediate cycle has been completed, the chances of prices reaching higher levels (lower levels in a bear market) are quite high.

Characteristics of Final Intermediate Cycle in a Primary Trend

In addition to actually counting the number of intermediate cycles, it is also possible to compare the characteristics of a particular cycle with those of a typical pivotal or reversal cycle of a primary trend. These characteristics are discussed below.

Reversal from Bull to Bear Market.   Since volume leads price, the failure of volume to increase above the levels of the previous intermediate-cycle up phase is a bearish sign. Alternatively, if, over a period of 3 to 4 weeks, volume expands on the intermediate rally close to the previous peak in volume but fails to move prices significantly, it represents churning and should also be treated bearishly. Coincidence of either of these characteristics with a downward crossover of a 40-week moving average (see Chapter 8) or a divergence in an intermediate-term momentum index (see Chapter 9) would be an additional reason for caution.

There are essentially two broad characteristics that suggest that the downward phase of an intermediate cycle could be the first downleg of a bear market. The first is a substantial increase in volume during the price decline. The second is a cancellation or retracement of 80 percent or more of the up phase of that same intermediate cycle. The greater the retracement, the greater the probability that the basic trend has reversed, especially because a retracement in excess of 100 percent means that any series of rising troughs has been broken, thereby placing the probabilities in favor of a change in the primary trend.

Reversal from Bear to Bull Market.   The first intermediate up phase of a bull market is usually accompanied by a substantial expansion in volume that is significantly greater than those of previous intermediate up phases. In other words, the first upleg in a bull market attracts noticeably more volume than any of the intermediate rallies in the previous bear market. Another sign of a basic reversal occurs when prices retrace at least 80 percent of the previous decline. Again, the greater the proportion of retracement, the greater the odds of a reversal in the basic trend. If the retracement is greater than 100 percent, the odds clearly indicate that a reversal in the downward trend has taken place, because the series of declining troughs will have broken down.

Since volume normally expands substantially as the intermediate down phase during a bear market reaches a low, a shrinkage in volume during an intermediate decline could well be a warning that the bear market has run its course. This is especially true if the price does not reach a new low during this intermediate decline, since the series of declining intermediate cyclical lows, which is a characteristic of a bear market, may no longer be intact. An example of this is shown in Chart 5.6*a*, where the overall peak in volume was seen in the June 1962 decline rather than the August–October sell-off. Chart 5.6*b* showed no perceptible slackening of volume at the lows, but the volume expansion during the January rally, combined with the bettering of the October–November high, i.e., a 100 percent retracement, offered a valuable clue that the bear market was over. The final decline in October represented the down phase of the third intermediate cycle in the bear market, which should have warned of its probable maturity.

Intermediate Trends in the U.S. Stock Market, 1897–1982

Amplitude and Duration of Primary Intermediate Upmoves

Between 1897 and 1933, Robert Rhea, the author of *Dow Theory*, classified 53 intermediate-trend advances within a primary bull market, which ranged in magnitude from 7 to 117 percent, as shown in Table 4.1.

I have classified 35 intermediate-term moves between 1933 and 1982, and the median averaged 22 percent from low to high. The results are shown in Table 4.2.

The median average primary intermediate advance since 1897 appears to be around 20 to 22 percent. The median primary intermediate upmove in the 1933–1982 period does not differ from that of the ear-

Table 4.1. Primary Intermediate Upmoves, 1897–1933 (Percentage)

Proportion of intermediate moves	Price magnitude
25	7–14
50	15–28
25	28–117
100	
Median 20	

Table 4.2. Primary Intermediate Upmoves, 1933–1982

	Swings from low to high, percent	Duration, weeks
Mean average	30	22
Median	22	24
Range	10–105	3–137

lier period classified by Rhea. However, the median duration appears to have increased considerably, from 13 weeks in the 1897–1933 period to 24 weeks in the 1933–1982 period.

Amplitude and Duration of Primary Intermediate Downmoves

Using Rhea's classification, 39 cases of a primary intermediate decline developed between 1900 and 1932, as summarized in Table 4.3.

My research shows that between 1932 and 1982 there were 35 primary intermediate declines, with a median of 16 percent (the decline was measured as a percentage from the high). The results are summarized in Table 4.4.

Table 4.3. Primary Intermediate Downmoves, 1900–1932 (Percentage)

Proportion of intermediate moves	Price magnitude
25	3–12
50	13–27
25	28–54
Median 18	

Table 4.4. Primary Intermediate Downmoves, 1932–1982

	Swings from high	Duration (weeks)
Mean average	18	17
Median	16	14
Range	7–40	3–43

The results in the 1932–1982 period did not differ appreciably from those in the 1897–1933 period. Rhea's median average swing was 18 percent, as compared to the more recent 16 percent, whereas the median duration in the earlier period was 13 weeks, as compared to 14 weeks in the 1932–1982 period.

Amplitude, Duration, and Retracement of Bull Market Intermediate Corrections

Bull Market Secondary Reactions.   Between 1898 and 1933, Rhea classified 43 cases of bull market secondaries. In terms of retracement of the previous primary intermediate upmove, they ranged from 12.4 to 180 percent, with a median of 56 percent. This compared with a range in the 1933–1982 period from 25 to 148 percent, with a median of 51 percent. The duration of the median in the earlier period was 5 weeks, as compared to 8 weeks between 1933 and 1982. The median percentage loss from the previous primary intermediate peak was 12 percent (the mean average was 13 percent) between 1933 and 1982.

Bear Market Rallies

Rhea estimated that the median bear market rally retraced 52 percent of the previous decline, which is comparable to my own median estimate of 61 percent in the 1932–1982 period. The two ranges were 30 and 116 percent and 26 and 99 percent, respectively. Median durations were 6 weeks in 1898–1933 and 7 weeks in 1932–1982. Rallies off the low averaged 12 and 10 percent for mean and median, respectively, for the 1933–1982 period.

Summary

1. The typical primary trend can be divided into 2½ primary intermediate cycles, each consisting of an upmove and a downmove. In a bull

market each successive upwave should reach a new cyclical high, and in a bear market each successive downwave of the intermediate cycle should reach a new low. Breaking the pattern of rising lows and falling peaks is an important but *not* unequivocal warning of a reversal in the primary trend. For more conclusive proof, technicians should derive a similar conclusion from a *consensus* of indicators.

2. A secondary movement or reaction is that part of an intermediate cycle which runs counter to the main trend—a downward reaction in a bull market or a rally in a bear market. Secondary intermediate movements typically last from 3 weeks to 3 months and retrace between one-third and two-thirds of the previous primary intermediate price movement. Secondary price movements may also take the form of a line or horizontal trading pattern.

3. The character of intermediate cycles can be used to help identify primary trend reversals.

5
Price Patterns

The techniques discussed in this chapter and in Chapters 6 to 12 are concerned with analysis of any price trend that has been determined by interaction of buyers and sellers in a free market.

The concept of price patterns is demonstrated in Figures 5.1 and 5.2. Figure 5.1 represents a typical stock market cycle in which there are three trends—up, sideways, and down. The sideways trend is essentially a horizontal or transitional one which separates the two major market movements. Sometimes a highly emotional market can change without warning, as in Figure 5.2, but this rarely happens. Consider a fast-moving train, which takes a long time to slow down and then go into reverse; the same is normally true of financial markets.

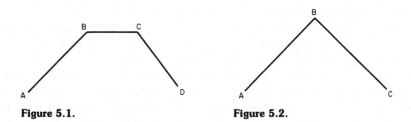

Figure 5.1.   **Figure 5.2.**

To the market technician, the transitional phase has great significance because it marks the turning point between a rising and a falling market. If prices have been advancing, the enthusiasm of the buyers has outweighed the pessimism of sellers up to this point, and prices have risen accordingly. During the transition phase, the balance becomes more or less even until finally, for one reason or another, it is tipped in a new direction as the relative weight of selling pushes the trend (of prices) down. At the termination of a bear market the reverse process occurs.

These transition phases are almost invariably signaled by clearly definable price patterns or formations whose successful completion alerts the technician to the fact that a reversal in trend has taken place.

This phenomenon is illustrated in Figure 5.3, which shows the price action at the end of a long rising trend. As soon as the index rises above line *BB*, it is in the transitional area, although this is apparent only some time after the picture has developed.

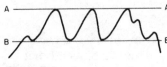

Figure 5.3.

Once into the area, the index rises to line *AA*, which is technically termed a *resistance area*. The word "resistance" is used because at this point the index shows opposition to a further price rise. When the demand/supply relationship comes into balance at *AA*, the market quickly turns in favor of the sellers because prices react. This temporary reversal may occur because buyers refuse to pay up for stock, or because the higher price attracts more sellers, or for a combination of these two reasons. The important fact is that the relationship between the two groups is temporarily reversed at this point.

Following the unsuccessful assault on *AA*, prices turn down until line *BB*, known as a *support level*, is reached. Just as the price level at *AA* reversed the balance in favor of the sellers, so the support level *BB* alters the balance again. This time the trend moves in an upward direction, for at *BB* prices become relatively attractive for buyers who missed the boat on the way up, while sellers who feel that the price will again reach *AA* hold off. For a while there is a standoff between buyers and sellers within the confines of the area bounded by lines *AA* and *BB*. Finally the price falls below *BB*, and a major new (downward) trend is signaled.

To help explain this concept, the contest between buyers and sellers is like a battle fought by two armies engaged in trench warfare. In Figure 5.4, example *a*, armies A and B are facing off. Line *AA* represents army A's defense, and *BB* is army B's line of defense. The arrows indicate the forays between the two lines, as both armies fight their way to the op-

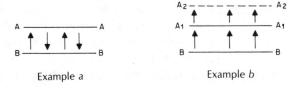

Example a   Example b

Figure 5.4.

posing trench but are unable to penetrate the line of defense. In the second example, army B finally pushes through A's trench. Army A is then forced to retreat and make a stand at the second line of defense (line AA_2). In the stock market, line AA represents selling resistance which, once overcome, signifies a change in the balance between buyers and sellers in favor of the buyers, so that prices will advance quickly until new resistance is met. The second line of defense, line AA_2, represents resistance to a further advance.

On the other hand, army B might quite easily break through AA_2, but the further it advances without time to consolidate its gains, the more likely it is to become overextended and the greater is the probability of its suffering a serious setback. At some point, therefore, it makes more sense for this successful force to wait and consolidate its gains.

If stock market prices extend too far without time to digest their gains, they too are more likely to face a sharp and seemingly unexpected reversal.

The transitional or horizontal phase separating rising and falling price trends is a pattern known as a *rectangle*. This formation corresponds to the "line" formation developed from Dow theory. The rectangle in Figure 5.3, marking the turning point between the bull and bear phases, is termed a *reversal* pattern. Reversal patterns at market tops are known as *distribution* areas or patterns, and those at market bottoms are called *accumulation* patterns (see Figure 5.5, example a). If the rectangle were completed with a victory for the buyers as the price pushed through line AA (see Figure 5.5, example b), no reversal of the rising trend would occur. The "breakout" above AA would therefore have reaffirmed the underlying trend. In this case the corrective phase

Example a   Example b

Figure 5.5.

associated with the formation of the rectangle would temporarily interrupt the bull market and become a consolidation pattern. Such formations are also referred to as *consolidation* or *continuation* patterns.

During the period of formation, there is no way of knowing in advance which way the price will ultimately break; therefore it should always be assumed that the *prevailing trend is in existence until it is proved to have been reversed.*

Size and Depth

The significance of a price formation or pattern is a direct function of its size and depth. In other words, the longer a pattern takes to complete and the greater the price fluctuations within the pattern, the more substantial the following move is likely to be. It is just as important to build a strong base from which prices can rise as it is to build a large, strong, deep foundation upon which to construct a skyscraper. In the case of financial market prices, the foundation is an accumulation pattern that represents an area of indecisive combat between buyers and sellers. The term "accumulation" is used because market bottoms always occur when the news is bad. Such an environment stimulates sales by uninformed investors who were not expecting developments to improve. During an accumulation phase more sophisticated investors and professionals would be positioning or accumulating the asset concerned in anticipation of improved conditions 6 to 9 months ahead. During this period the asset is moving from weak, uninformed traders or investors into strong and knowledgeable hands. At market tops the process is reversed, as those who were accumulating at or near the bottom sell to less sophisticated market participants, who become more and more attracted to the market as prices rise, business conditions improve, and forecasts for the economy are revised upward. Thus, *the longer the period of accumulation, the greater the amount of stock that moves from weak into strong hands, and the larger is the base from which prices can rise.* The reverse is true at market tops, where a substantial amount of distribution inevitably results in a protracted period of price erosion or base building.

The longer the formation of a rectangle pattern takes (see Figure 5.6)

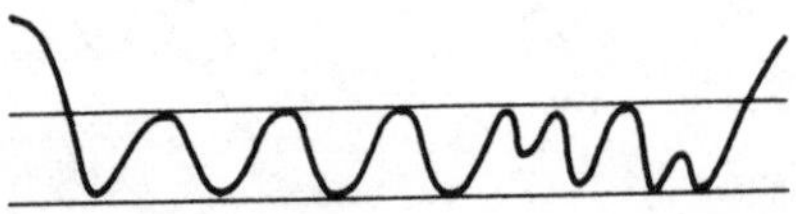

Figure 5.6.

and the more often it fails to break through its outer boundaries, the greater is the significance of the ultimate penetration.

The time taken to complete a formation is important because of the amount of an asset changing hands, and also because a movement in price beyond the boundaries of a pattern means that the balance between buyers and sellers has altered. When the price action has been in a stalemate for a long time and investors have become used to buying at one price and selling at the other, a move beyond either limit represents a fundamental change which has great psychological significance.

Measuring Implications

Most of the results obtained with technical analysis procedures do not indicate the eventual duration of a trend. Price patterns are the exception, since their construction offers some limited forecasting possibilities.

There are two alternative methods of charting, and the choice of scale determines the significance of the measuring implications. The two types of graph used in technical analysis are (1) arithmetic and (2) ratio or logarithmic.

Arithmetic Scale

Arithmetic charts consist of an arithmetic scale on the vertical or y axis, with time shown on the horizontal or x axis, as illustrated in Figure 5.7. All units of measure are plotted using the same vertical distance, so that the difference in space between 2 and 4 is the same as that between 20 and 22. This scale is not particularly satisfactory for long-term price movements, since a rise from 2 to 4 represents a doubling of the price, whereas a rise from 20 to 22 represents only a 10 percent increase. On an arithmetic scale both moves are represented by the same vertical dis-

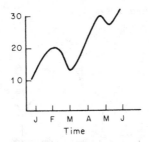

Figure 5.7.

tance. In the U.S. stock market a relatively large move of 30 points is not un-common. A 10-point move in 1932, though, when the average was as low as 5 to 40, represented a 20 to 25 percent change. For this reason, long-term movements are commonly plotted on a ratio or logarithmic scale. The choice of scale does not materially affect daily charts, in which price movements are relatively small in a proportionate sense. For periods over 1 year, in which fluctuations are much larger, I always prefer to use a ratio scale.

Ratio Scale

Prices plotted on a ratio scale show identical distances for identical percentage moves. In Figure 5.8 the vertical distance between 1 and 2 (a 2:1 ratio) is ½ inch. Similarly, the 2:1 distance between 4 and 2 is also represented on the chart as ½ inch. A specific vertical distance on the chart indicates the same percentage change in the price being measured, whatever the level. For example, if the scale in Figure 5.8 was extended, ½ inch would always represent a doubling, from 1 to 2, 16 to 32, 50 to 100, and so on, just as ¼ inch would indicate a rise of 50 percent, and 1 inch would show a quadrupling of prices. Graph paper using ratio or logarithmic scale is easily obtained from any large office supplier. Almost all computer software gives the user the option of choosing between arithmetic and logarithmic scales.

It is important to remember that market prices are a function of psychological attitudes toward fundamental events. Since these attitudes have a tendency to move proportionately, it makes sense to plot them on a scale that reflects proportionate moves equally.

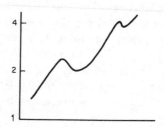

Figure 5.8.

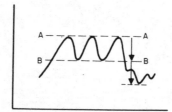

Figure 5.9.

An alternative method of portraying a ratio scale chart is to use arith
metic paper but plot the logarithm of an index instead of the actual index number itself. Hence, the Dow Jones Industrial Average (DJIA) at
1004 would be plotted at 3.001, which is the base 10 logarithm for 1000,
and 758 would be plotted at 2.880, etc.

Figure 5.9 shows a rectangle which has formed and completed a (distribution) top. The measuring implication of this formation is the vertical distance
between its outer boundaries, i.e., the distance between lines *AA* and *BB* projected downward from line *BB*. If *AA* represents 100 and *BB* 50, then the
downside objective will be 50 percent, using a ratio scale. When projected

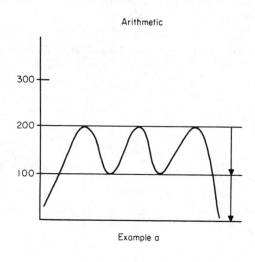

Example a

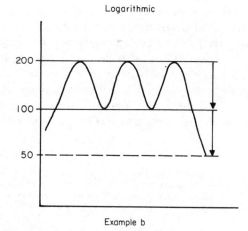

Example b

Figure 5.10.

downward from line *BB,* 50 percent gives a measuring implication of 25. While this measuring formula offers a rough guide, it is usually a *minimum* expectation, and prices often go much further than their implied objective. In a very high proportion of cases the objective level derived from the measuring formula becomes an area of support or resistance when the price trend is temporarily halted.

The importance of using logarithmic scales whenever possible is shown in Figure 5.10, examples *a* and *b.* In example *a* the price has traced out and broken down from a rectangle. Projecting the vertical distance between 20 and 100 downward gives an objective of 0, clearly a very unlikely possibility. On the other hand, example *b* in Figure 5.10 uses the same projection based on a logarithmic scale. In this case a more realistic objective of 50 is obtained.

If a rectangle appears as a bottom reversal pattern or as a consolidation pattern, the measuring rules remain consistent with the example given for the distribution formation. This is shown in the series in Figure 5.11.

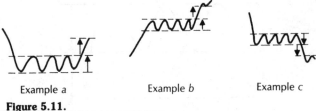

Example *a*   Example *b*   Example *c*

Figure 5.11.

If the minimal objective proves to be the ultimate extension of the new trend, a substantial amount of accumulation or distribution, whichever is appropriate, will have to occur before prices can move in their original direction. Thus, if a 2-year rectangle is completed and the downward price objective is reached, even though further price erosion does not take place, it is still usually necessary for a base (accumulation) to be formed of approximately the same size as the previous distribution (in this case 2 years) before a valid uptrend can take place.[1]

[1]Note: It is very important to remember that price objectives represent the *ultimate* target and are not normally achieved in *one* move. Usually, a series of rallies and reactions in an upside breakout is required, or reaction or retracements in a downside breakout, before the objective is reached.

Confirmation of a Valid Breakout

Price

So far it has been assumed that any move (however small) out of the price pattern constitutes a valid signal of a trend reversal (or resumption, if the pattern is one of consolidation). Quite often misleading moves known as whipsaws occur, so it is helpful to establish certain criteria to minimize the possibility of misinterpretation. Conventional wisdom holds that you should wait for a 3 percent penetration of the boundaries before concluding that the breakout is valid. This filters out a substantial number of misleading moves, even though the resulting signals are less timely.

The problem with this type of fixed approach is that many short-term price movements barely exceed 3 percent in total. Moreover, if you wait for a 3 percent move to buy, and an additional 3 percent decline for a breakdown to sell, it will be extremely difficult to turn a profit. I have no basic objection to the 3 percent rate for longer-term price movements in which the fluctuations are much greater. There is no substitute for judgment based on experience, however, in trying to decide whether a breakout will be valid or not. This judgment would take into consideration such factors as the type of trend being monitored, volume, and momentum characteristics.

Volume

Volume usually goes with the trend; i.e., volume advances with a rising trend of prices and falls with a declining one. This is a normal relationship, and anything which diverges from this characteristic should be considered a warning sign that the prevailing price trend may be in the process of reversing. Figure 5.12 shows a typical volume/price relationship.

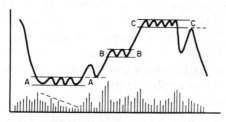

Figure 5.12.

Volume, the number of units of an asset (e.g., shares, contracts) that change hands during a specific period, is shown by the vertical lines at the bottom of Figure 5.12. Volume expands marginally as the price approaches its low, but as the accumulation pattern is formed, activity recedes noticeably. Volume is always measured on a relative basis, so that heavy volume is "heavy" only in relation to a recent period. As the pattern nears completion, disinterest prevails and volume almost dries up. As if by magic, activity picks up noticeably when the index moves above its level of resistance (bounded by the upper line in the rectangle). It is sometimes possible to draw a trendline joining the lower volume peaks, as shown in Figure 5.12. It is this upward surge in trading activity that confirms the validity of the breakout. A similar move on low volume would be suspect and would result in a failure of volume to move with the trend.

Following the sharp price rise from the rectangle, enthusiasm dies down as prices correct in a sideways movement and volume contracts. This is a perfectly normal relationship, since volume is correcting (declining) with price. Eventually volume and price expand together, and the primary upward trend is once again confirmed. Finally the buyers become exhausted, and the index forms yet another rectangle — characterized as before by falling volume, but this time destined to become a reversal pattern.

It is worth noting that while the volume from the breakout in rectangle *B* is high, it is relatively lower than that which accompanied the move from rectangle *A*. In relation to the overall cycle this is a bearish factor, since volume usually leads price. In this case volume makes its peak just before entering rectangle *B*, while the peak in prices is not reached until rectangle *C*.

Volume contracts throughout the formation of rectangle *C* and expands as prices break out on the downside. This expanded level of activity associated with the violation of support at the lower boundary of the rectangle emphasizes the bearish nature of the breakout, although expanding volume is not a prerequisite for a valid signal with downside breakouts, as it is for an upside move. Following the downside breakout, more often than not prices will reverse and put on a small recovery or retracement rally. This advance is invariably accompanied by declining volume, which itself reinforces the bearish indications. It is halted at the lower end of the rectangle, which now becomes an area of resistance.

Chart 5.1 shows an example for the Dow Jones Rail Average at the 1946 bull market high.

Some of the more common reversal formations are head and shoulders, double tops and bottoms, broadening formations and triangles.

Chart 5.1. Dow Jones Rail Average, 1946. This chart shows a classic rectangle formation as traced out by the Rail Average at the peak of the 1942–1946 bull market. Note the declining trend of volume, as indicated by the dashed line, during the formation of the rectangle. Worth special mention is the saucerlike formation of the volume during the late July–early August rally. The expansion of activity accompanying the downside breakdown in late August completed the bearish implication of the successful completion of this pattern.

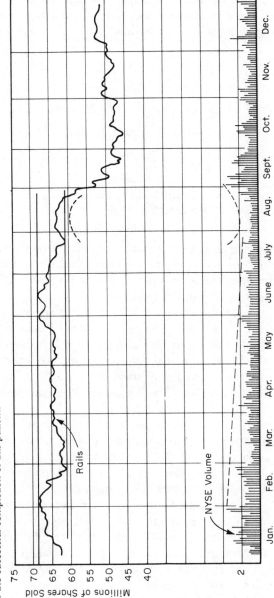

63

Head and Shoulders

The head and shoulders (H&S) is probably the most reliable of all chart patterns. H&S formations occur at both market tops and market bottoms. Figure 5.13 shows a typical distribution pattern. (See also Chart 5.2.)

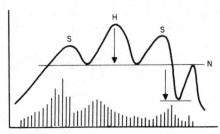

Figure 5.13.

The pattern consists of a final rally (the head) separating two smaller, though not necessarily identical, rallies (the shoulders). The first shoulder is the penultimate advance in the bull market, and the second is in effect the first bear market rally.

Volume characteristics are of critical importance in assessing the validity of these patterns. Activity is normally heaviest during the formation of the left shoulder and also tends to be quite heavy as prices approach the peak. The real tip-off that an H&S pattern is developing comes with the formation of the right shoulder, which is invariably accompanied by distinctly lower volume. The line joining the bottoms of the two shoulders is called the *neckline*.

The measuring formula for this price formation is the distance between the head and the neckline projected downward from the neckline, as shown in Figure 5.13. It follows that the deeper the pattern, the greater its bearish significance once it has been completed. It is essential to wait for a decisive break below the neckline.

H&S patterns can be formed in 3 to 4 weeks or can take several years to develop. The process can take as little as a few hours on real-time, tick-by-tick charts! Generally speaking, the longer the period, the greater the amount of distribution that has taken place, and therefore the longer the ensuing bear trend is likely to be. The larger H&S formations are often very complex and comprise several smaller ones, as shown in Figure 5.14.

The H&S patterns illustrated in Figures 5.13 and 5.14 have a horizontal neckline, but there are many other varieties (as Figure 5.15 shows),

Chart 5.2. *The New York Times* average, 1928. This chart of *The New York Times* average of 50 railroad and industrial stocks shows the formation of an upward-sloping H&S during March, April, and May 1928. The minimum downside objective of about 182 was achieved fairly quickly, but a 3-month period of base building commensurate with the H&S pattern was still necessary before the effect of the distribution was canceled out and prices were able to resume their primary advance. Note the heavy volume on the left shoulder and head and the relatively low volume on the right shoulder. Also, activity declined substantially during the formation of the triangle but began to expand during the breakout in September.

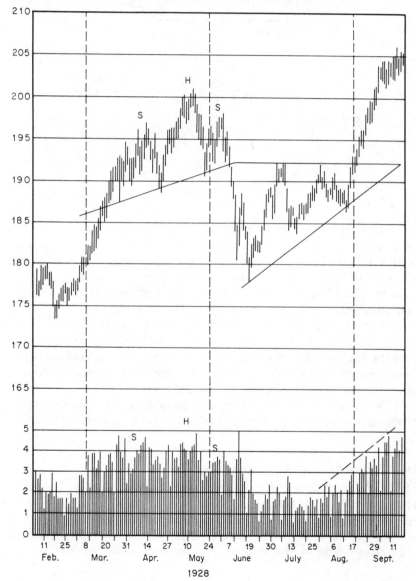

1928

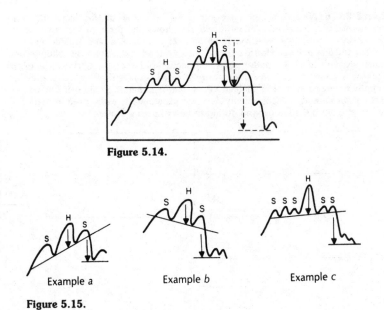

Figure 5.14.

Example *a*   Example *b*   Example *c*

Figure 5.15.

all of which possess the same bearish implications as the horizontal variety once they have been completed. Chart 5.3 shows a classic H&S pattern that formed at the end of 1929. Figure 5.16 shows an H&S pattern at a market bottom; this is usually called an *inverse H&S*.

Normally, volume is relatively high at the bottom of the left shoulder and during the formation of the head. The major factor to watch for is activity on the right shoulder, which should contract during the decline to the trough and expand substantially on the breakout (see Chart 5.4). Like the H&S distribution patterns, the inverse (accumulation) H&S can have a number of variations in trendline slope, number of shoulders, etc. Some of these are shown in Figure 5.17.

H&S patterns are extremely reliable formations, and their successful completion usually gives an excellent indication of a trend reversal.

H&S Formations as Continuation Patterns

H&S and reverse H&S formations occasionally show up on the charts as continuation patterns. Measuring implications and volume characteristics are the same as for the reversal type. The only difference is that these patterns develop *during* a trend rather than at the *end*.

Chart 5.3. *The New York Times* average, 1928–1930. During January and May of 1929 it appeared as if *The New York Times* average, shown here, was forming a broadening top. Three ascending peaks, *O, Q,* and *S,* were separated by two declining troughs, *P* and *R,* but since the third bottom (*T*) remained above *R,* no negative signal was given. The break above the line joining *O, Q,* and *S* indicated that the "top" would not be completed. A sharp upward move followed as prices ran up to the ultimate peak of the 1921–1929 bull market. Even though this formation was never completed, the very fact that prices moved in such a volatile manner was a strong warning of the underlying weakness. A small right-angled broadening formation seemed to develop in July and August, but this would eventually prove to be the left shoulder of a 2½-month H&S pattern, the completion of which terminated the long bull market.

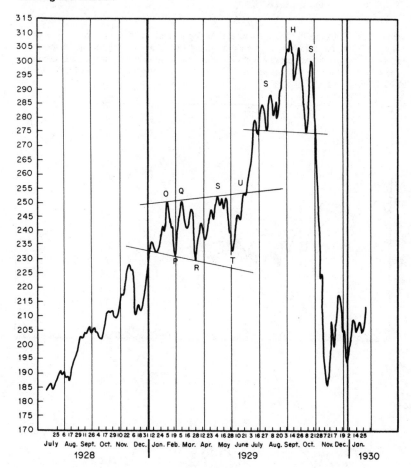

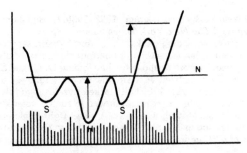

Figure 5.16.

Chart 5.4. DJIA, 1898. This downward-sloping inverse H&S pattern developed in the spring of 1898. Note that the April rally developed on very low volume. The subsequent reaction successfully tested the March low, and the ensuing breakout rally was accompanied by a bullish expansion of volume. By August the DJIA had reached 60.97, and by April 1899 it rose to 77.28.

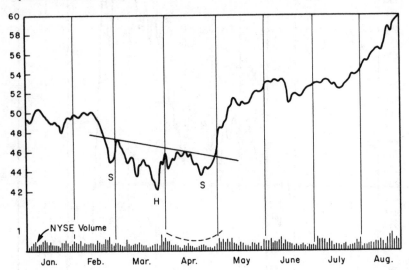

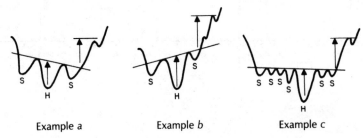

Example *a*   Example *b*   Example *c*

Figure 5.17.

H&S Failures

Sometimes the price action exhibits all the characteristics of an H&S distribution pattern but either refuses to penetrate the neckline or penetrates it temporarily and then starts to rally. This represents an H&S failure and is *usually* followed by an explosive rally. It is probably due to misplaced pessimism. Once the real fundamentals are perceived, not only do new buyers rush in, but traders holding short positions are forced to cover. Since fear is a stronger motivator than greed, these bears bid up the price very aggressively.

Chart 5.6b, which shows the daily close for the DJIA in 1975, illustrates this phenomenon very clearly, as the "failure" of a H&S pattern results in a fairly worthwhile rally. Nevertheless, an H&S that does not "work" indicates that while there is still some life left in the situation, the end may not be far off. In the example cited above, the rally ended rather abruptly in July.

Unfortunately, the pattern itself gives no indication that it is going to fail. Sometimes such evidence can be gleaned from other technical factors. Failures used to be fairly rare but now seem to be more common, which indicates the necessity of waiting for a decisive breakout on the downside. If any action is contemplated, it should be taken when the price breaks above the right shoulder on heavy volume. *Usually* such signals offer substantial profits in a very short period of time and are well worth acting on. Inverse H&S patterns can also fail. Again, the failure is usually followed by an extremely sharp sell-off, as participants who bought in anticipation of an *upward* breakout are flushed out when the new bearish fundamentals become more widely known.

Double Tops and Bottoms

A double top consists of two peaks separated by a reaction or valley in prices. The main characteristic of a double top is that the second top is formed with distinctly less volume than the first (see Chart 5.5).

Minimum downside measuring implications, as shown in Figure 5.18, are similar to H&S patterns. A double bottom is shown in Figure 5.19.

The pattern is typically accompanied by high volume on the first bottom, very light volume on the second, and very heavy volume on the breakout. Usually the second bottom is formed above the first, but these formations are equally valid whether or not the second reaction reaches (or even slightly exceeds) the level of its predecessor.

"Double" patterns may extend to form triple tops or bottoms, or

Chart 5.5. DJIA, 1936–1937. Following a substantial advance from 1932, the first post-Depression bull market ended in 1937. This chart shows a classic double top. Note that the volume during the July–August rally was substantially below that of the January–March peak.

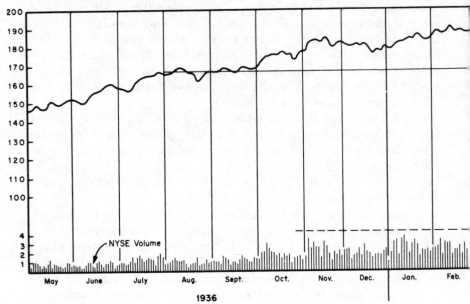

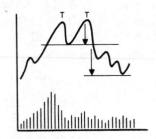

Figure 5.18.

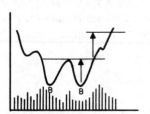

Figure 5.19.

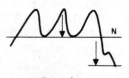

Example *a*

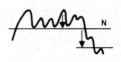

Example *b*

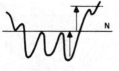

Example *c*

Figure 5.20.

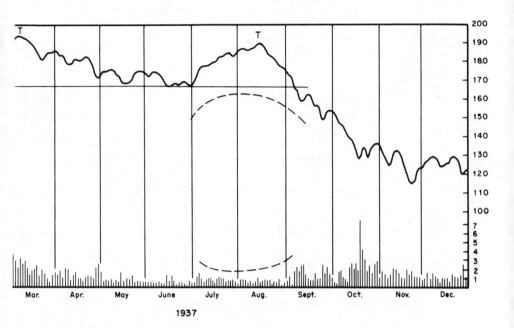

1937

sometimes even quadruple or other complex formations. Some variations are shown in Figure 5.20.

The measuring implications of all these patterns are derived by measuring the distance between the peak (trough) and lower (upper) end of
the pattern and projecting this distance from the neckline. Chart 5.6a
and b shows two classic double bottoms in the DJIA in 1962 and 1974.

Broadening Formations

Broadening formations occur when a series of three or more price fluctuations widen out in size so that peaks and troughs can be connected
with two diverging trendlines. The easiest types of broadening formations to detect are those with a "flattened" bottom or top, as shown in
examples a and b, Figure 5.21.

The pattern in example a is sometimes referred to as a *right-angled
broadening formation.* Since the whole concept of widening price swings
suggests highly emotional activity, volume patterns are difficult to char-
acterize, though at market tops, volume is usually heavy during the rally
phases. The patterns, at both bottoms and tops, are similar to the H&S

Chart 5.6. DJIA, 1962. This chart depicts two classic double bottoms in the DJIA, which formed during 1962 (*a*, at top) and 1974 (*b*, at bottom). Note that the second of each pair was accompanied by lower volume than the first. While volume expanded during the 1962 breakout, the increase in activity was not particularly spectacular. The rise in activity during January 1975 left little doubt that a new bull market had begun.

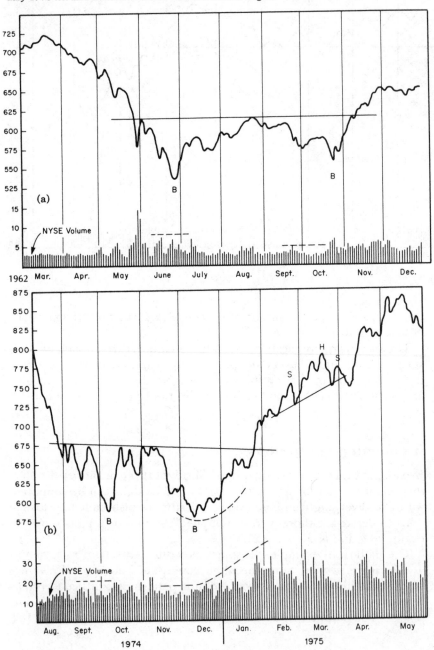

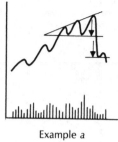

Example a

Example b

Figure 5.21.

variety except that the "head" in the broadening formation is always the last to be formed. A bear signal comes with a decisive downside breakout. Volume can be heavy or light, but additional bearish emphasis arises if activity expands at this point.

Since a broadening formation with a flattened top is an accumulation pattern, volume expansion on the breakout is an important requirement, as shown in example b, Figure 5.21. Examples of broadening formations are shown in Charts 5.7 to 5.9.

These two types of broadening formation can also develop as consolidation patterns, as shown in Figure 5.22.

Broadening formations occasionally fail to work. Possibilities are shown in Figure 5.23. Unfortunately, there does not appear to be a reliable point beyond which it is safe to say that the pattern has failed to operate. The best defense in such cases is to extend the diverging trendlines, i.e., the dashed lines in Figure 5.23, and await a decisive penetration by the price as confirmation.

When completed, right-angled broadening formations of both the reversal and the continuation type result in a particularly dynamic move. It is almost as if they are aborted H&S formations in which the move is so powerful that there is not time to complete the right shoulder.

The final type of broadening formation, known as an *orthodox broadening top,* is shown in Figure 5.24. This pattern comprises three rallies, with each succeeding peak higher than its predecessor, and each peak separated by two bottoms, with the second bottom lower than the first. Orthodox broadening formations are associated with market peaks rather than market troughs.

These patterns are extremely difficult to detect until some time after the final top has been formed, since there is no clearly definable level of support the violation of which could serve as a benchmark. The violent and emotional nature of both price and volume swings further compounds the confusion and increases the complexity of defining these sit-

Chart 5.7. DJIA, 1919–1920. This daily chart of the DJIA during 1919 shows a classic right-angled broadening formation. This period marked the peak of a huge run-up in commodity prices and preceded the 1920–1921 Depression. The extreme volatility of financial markets at this time is clearly reflected not only in the action of the Dow but also in the volume of stocks traded.

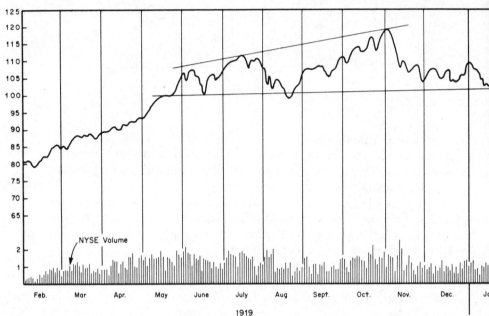

1919

uations. Obviously, a breakout is difficult to pinpoint under such conditions, but if the formation is reasonably symmetrical, a decisive move below the descending trendline joining the two bottoms – or even a decisive move below the second bottom – usually serves as a timely warning that an even greater decline is in store.

Measuring implications are similarly difficult to determine, but normally the volatile character of a broadening top formation implies the completion of a substantial amount of distribution. Consequently, price declines of considerable proportion usually follow the successful completion of such patterns.

Triangles

Triangles, the most common of all the price patterns discussed in this chapter, are unfortunately the least reliable. Triangles may be consoli-

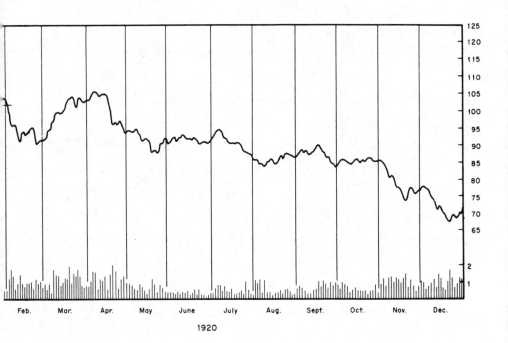

dation or reversal formations, and they fall into two categories, symmetrical and right-angled.

Symmetrical Triangles

A symmetrical triangle is composed of a series of two or more rallies and reactions in which each succeeding peak is lower than its predecessor, and the bottom from each succeeding reaction is higher than its predecessor (see Figure 5.25). A triangle is therefore the opposite of a broadening formation, since the trendlines joining peaks and troughs *converge*, unlike the (orthodox) broadening formation, in which they *diverge*.

These patterns are also known as *coils*, for the fluctuation in price and volume diminishes as the pattern is completed. Finally, both price and (usually) volume react sharply, as if a coil spring had been wound tighter and tighter and then snapped free as prices broke out of the tri-

Chart 5.8. T-bills (90 days).

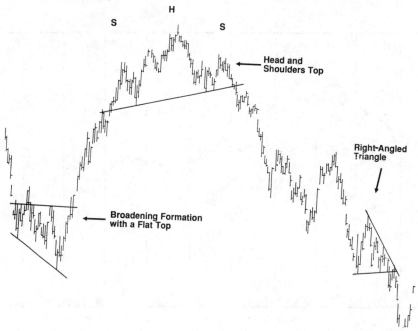

angle. Generally speaking, triangles seem to work best when the breakout occurs somewhere between one-half and three-fourths of the distance between the widest peak and rally and the apex (as in Figure 5.26).

The volume rules used for other patterns are also appropriate for triangles.

Right-Angled Triangles

Right-angled triangles are really a special form of the symmetrical type, in that one of the two boundaries is formed at an angle of 90 degrees, i.e., horizontal to the vertical axis. (These triangle variations are illustrated in Chart 5.9 and Figure 5.27.) The symmetrical triangle does not give an indication of the direction in which it is ultimately likely to break, but the right-angled triangle does, with its implied level of support or resistance and contracting price fluctuations. One difficulty in interpreting these formations is that many rectangles begin as right-angled triangles. Consequently, a great deal of caution should be used when evaluating these elusive patterns. An example is shown in Figure 5.28, where a potential

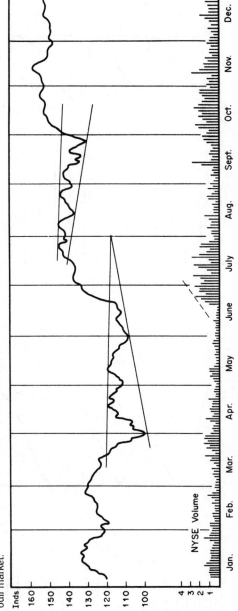

Chart 5.9. DJIA, 1938. This excellent example of a right-angled triangle occurred at the bottom of the 1937–1938 bear market. Note the substantial increase in volume that accompanied the upside breakout. Following the breakout, the average traced out a right-angled broadening formation with a flat top. Usually breakouts from these consolidation patterns are followed by a dramatic rise. In this case, however, the 158 level in November was destined to become the high for the 1938–1939 bull market.

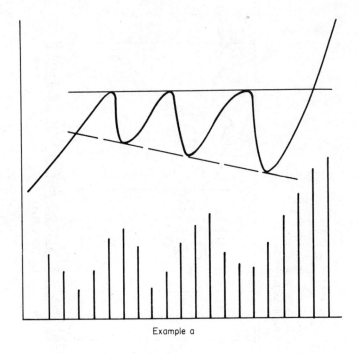

Example a

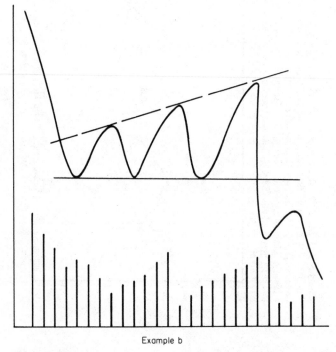

Example b

Figure 5.22.

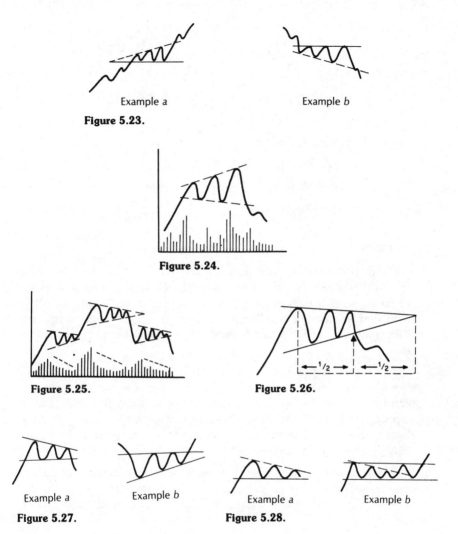

Example a   Example b

Figure 5.23.

Figure 5.24.

Figure 5.25.   **Figure 5.26.**

Example a   Example b   Example a   Example b

Figure 5.27.   **Figure 5.28.**

downward-sloping right-angled triangle in example *a* develops into a rectangle in example *b*.

Measuring objectives for triangles are obtained by drawing a line parallel to the base of the triangle through the peak of the first rally. This line (*BB* in Figure 5.29) represents the price objective which prices may be expected to reach or exceed.

The reverse procedure at market tops is shown in Figure 5.29, examples *c* and *d*. The same technique is used to project prices when triangles are of the consolidation variety.

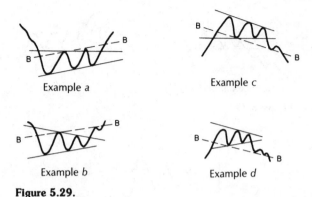

Example a

Example c

Example b

Example d

Figure 5.29.

Summary

1. Prices in financial markets move in trends. A reversal is characterized by a temporary period in which the enthusiasm of buyers and
   sellers is roughly in balance. This transitional process can usually be
   identified by clearly definable price patterns which, when completed,
   offer good and reliable indications that a reversal in trend has taken
   place.

2. Until a pattern has been formed and completed, the assumption
   should be that the prevailing trend is still operative, i.e., that the pattern is one of consolidation or continuation. This principle is more
   important when the trend has been in existence for only a relatively
   short period, because the more mature it is, the greater the probability of an important reversal.

3. Price patterns can be formed over any time period. The longer the
   time required to form a pattern and the greater the price fluctuations within it, the more substantial the ensuing price movement is
   likely to be.

4. Measuring formulas can be derived for most types of patterns, but
   these are generally minimum objectives. Prices usually extend much
   further.

5. Price objectives are not normally achieved in one move but are often
   reached after a series of rallies and reactions has materialized.

6

Flags, Pennants, Wedges, and Gaps

Most of the price patterns described in Chapter 5 can be observed in both reversal and continuation formations. The majority of the formations discussed in this chapter materialize during the course of a price trend and are therefore of the continuation variety.

Flags

A *flag*, as the name implies, looks like a flag on the chart. It represents a quiet pause accompanied by a trend of declining volume which interrupts a sharp, almost vertical rise or decline. As the flag is completed, prices break out in the same direction that they were moving in prior to its formation. Flags for both an up and a down market are shown in Figure 6.1. Essentially they take the form of a parallelogram in which the rally peaks and reaction lows can be connected by two parallel lines. The lines move in a countercyclical direction. In the case of a rising market the flag is usually formed with a slight downtrend, but in a falling market it has a slight upward bias. Flags may also be horizontal.

In a rising market this type of pattern usually separates two halves of an almost vertical rise. Volume is normally extremely heavy just before the point at which the flag formation begins. As it develops, volume gradually dries to almost nothing, only to explode as the price works its way out of the completed formation. Flags can form in a period as short as 5 days or as long as 3 to 5 weeks. Essentially they represent a period of controlled profit taking in a rising market.

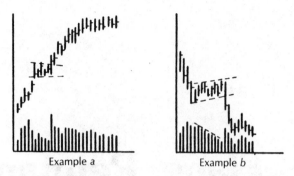

Example a   Example b

Figure 6.1. [*Source: Martin J. Pring (ed.), The McGraw-Hill Handbook of Commodities and Futures, McGraw-Hill, New York, 1985, p. 42-2.*]

The formation of the flag in a downtrend is accompanied by declining volume as well. This type of flag represents a formation with an upward bias in price, so the volume implication is bearish in nature, i.e., rising price with declining volume. When the price breaks down from the flag, the sharp slide continues. Volume tends to pick up as the price moves down below the flag, but it need not be explosive, as in the case of an upside breakout, to be valid.

It is most important to make sure that the price and volume characteristics agree. For example, the price may consolidate following a sharp rise, in what *appears* to be a flag formation, but volume may fail to contract appreciably. In such cases great care should be taken before coming to a bullish conclusion since the price may well react on the downside. A flag that takes more than 4 weeks to develop should also be treated with caution, because these formations are by definition temporary interruptions of a sharp uptrend. A period in excess of 4 weeks represents an unduly long time for profit taking and is therefore suspect.

Flag formations are usually reliable patterns from a forecasting point of view, for not only is the direction of ultimate breakout indicated but the ensuing move is also usually well worthwhile from a trading point of view. Flags seem to form at the halfway point of a move. Once the breakout has taken place, a useful method for setting a price objective is to estimate the size of the price move in the period immediately before the flag formation began and then to project this move in the direction of the breakout. Since flags take a relatively short period to develop, they do not show up on weekly or monthly charts.

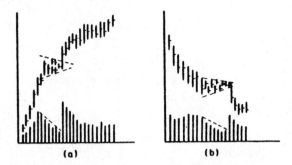

Figure 6.2. [*Source: Martin J. Pring (ed.), The McGraw-Hill Handbook of Commodities and Futures, McGraw-Hill, New York, 1985, p. 42-3.*]

Pennants

A pennant develops under exactly the same circumstances as a flag, and has similar characteristics. The difference is that this type of consolidation formation is constructed from two converging trendlines, as shown in Figure 6.2. In a sense the flag corresponds to a rectangle, and the pennant to a triangle, because a pennant is in effect a very small triangle. If anything, volume tends to contract even more during the formation of a pennant than during that of a flag. In every other way, however, pennants are identical to flags in terms of measuring implication, time taken to develop, volume characteristics, etc.

Wedges

A wedge is very similar to a triangle in that two converging lines can be constructed from a series of peaks and troughs, as shown in Figure 6.3, but whereas a triangle consists of one rising and one falling line, or one horizontal line, the converging lines in a wedge both move in the *same* direction. A falling wedge represents a temporary interruption of a rising trend, and a rising wedge is a temporary interruption of a falling trend. It is normal for volume to contract during the formation of both types of wedge. Since wedges can take anywhere from 2 to 8 weeks to complete, they sometimes occur on weekly charts but are too brief to appear on monthly charts.

Rising wedges are fairly common as bear market rallies. Following their completion, prices usually break very sharply, especially if volume picks up noticeably on the downside.

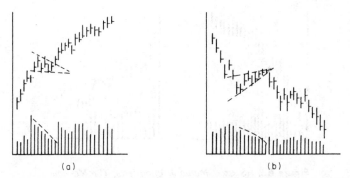

(a)   (b)

Figure 6.3. [*Source: Martin J. Pring (ed.), The McGraw-Hill Handbook of Commodities and Futures, McGraw-Hill, New York, 1985, p. 42-4.*]

Saucers and Rounding Tops

Examples *a* and *b* in Figure 6.4 show the formation of a saucer and a rounding top. A saucer pattern occurs at a market bottom, while a rounding top develops at a market peak. A saucer is constructed by drawing a circular line under the lows, which roughly approximates an elongated or saucer-shaped letter U. As the price drifts toward the low point of the saucer and investors lose interest, downward momentum dissipates. This lack of interest is also characterized by the volume level, which almost dries up at the time the price is reaching its low point. Gradually both price and volume pick up, until eventually each explodes into an almost exponential pattern.

   The price action of the rounded top is almost exactly opposite to that of the saucer pattern, but the volume characteristics are almost the same. As a result, if volume is plotted below the price, it is almost possible to draw a complete circle, as shown in example *b* of Figure 6.4. The tip-off to the bearish implication of the rounded top is the fact that vol-

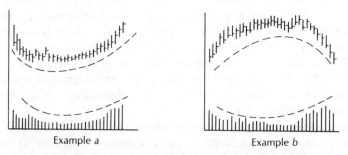

Example *a*   Example *b*

Figure 6.4. [*Source: Martin J. Pring (ed.), The McGraw-Hill Handbook of Commodities and Futures, McGraw-Hill, New York, 1985, p. 42-3.*]

ume shrinks as prices reach their highest levels and then expands as they fall. Both these characteristics are bearish and are discussed in greater detail in Chapter 18.

Rounding tops and bottoms are fine examples of a gradual change-over in the demand/supply balance that slowly picks up momentum in the direction opposite to that of the previous trend. Quite clearly, it is difficult to obtain breakout points for these patterns since they develop slowly and do not offer any clear support or resistance levels on which to establish a potential benchmark. Even so, it is worth trying to identify them since they are usually followed by substantial moves.

Rounding and saucer formations can also be observed as consolidation as well as reversal phenomena and can take as little as 3 weeks to as much as several years to complete.

Key Reversal Days

A key reversal day occurs after a long move, lasting many days or even weeks, has taken place. The key reversal day is the pivotal point that marks the peak of a rally or the bottom of a decline.

The term *key reversal* refers to the fact that at the beginning of the day in question the price continues to move sharply in the direction of the previous trend. Since this usually occurs following a long exponential-type move, it appears as if the price will never reverse its trend. However, by the end of the day the price has key-reversed, so that it closes in the direction opposite to that indicated at the opening. In an up market the price closes down on the day; in a down market the price closes up on the day. Key reversal days are associated with an explosion of volume well above levels of the recent past and represent an exhaustion of buying power at peaks and selling power or liquidation at troughs (see Figure 6.5, examples *a* and *b*).

Since a key reversal is in a sense a 1-day price pattern, it implies a short-term trend reversal. However, because such reversals develop after a long and sustained move, they are often followed by important changes in trend.

The price range on key reversal days often dwarfs anything that has gone before. It is not uncommon for the price to move as much in the first 2 to 4 hours as it would in 2 to 5 normal trading days. For the day to qualify as a key reversal day, the price must make a significant new high or new low. Thus, price action which occurs within a price pattern does not qualify as a key reversal, even though it possesses the appropriate volume characteristics. While such a "pattern-contained" reversal does have some short-term significance, it cannot be treated with any-

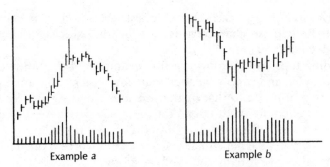

Example a   Example b

Figure 6.5. [*Source: Martin J. Pring (ed.), The McGraw-Hill Handbook of Commodities and Futures, McGraw-Hill, New York, 1985, p. 42-5.*]

where near the reverence accorded a key reversal that takes place after an extended move. Occasionally this type of activity occurs in weekly charts. In this case the pivotal point is represented as a weekly key reversal in which the high (or low) was set early in the week, but the Friday close is lower (or higher) than it was the previous week. Provided that the volume pattern is also consistent with key reversal characteristics, the weekly reversal is of greater significance than a daily one, other things being equal.

Gaps

A gap occurs when the lowest price of a specific trading period is above the highest level of the previous trading period (Figure 6.6, example *a*) or when the highest price for a specific trading period is below the low-

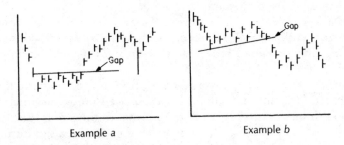

Example a   Example b

Figure 6.6. [*Source: Martin J. Pring (ed.), The McGraw-Hill Handbook of Commodities and Futures, McGraw-Hill, New York, 1985, p. 42-5.*]

est price of the previous trading period (example *b*). On a daily bar chart the trading period is regarded as a day, whereas on a weekly chart, it is a week, etc.

By definition, gaps can occur only on bar charts on which intraday, weekly, or monthly prices are plotted. A gap is represented by an empty vertical space between one trading period and another. Daily gaps are far more common than weekly ones because a gap on a weekly chart can fall only between Friday's price range and Monday's price range; i.e., it has a 1 in 5 chance relative to a daily chart. Monthly gaps are even more rare since such "holes" on the chart can develop only between monthly price ranges. A gap is closed or "filled" when the price comes back and retraces the whole range of the gap. This process sometimes takes a few days, and at other times it takes a few weeks or months. More rarely, the process is never completed. There is an old principle that the market abhors a vacuum and that all gaps are eventually filled. It is certainly true that almost all gaps are eventually filled, but this is not *always* the case. Because it can take months or even years to fill a gap, trading strategies should not be implemented solely on the assumption that the gap will be filled in the immediate future. In almost all cases, some kind of attempt is made to fill the gap, but quite often a partial filling on a subsequent test is sufficient before the price again reverts to the direction of the prevailing trend. Gaps should be treated with respect, but their importance should not be overemphasized. Those that occur during the formation of a price pattern, known as *common gaps,* or *area gaps,* are usually closed fairly quickly and do not have much technical significance. Another type of gap which has little significance is the one that results from a stock going ex dividend.

There are three other types of gaps that are worthy of consideration: breakaway, runaway, and exhaustion gaps.

Breakaway Gaps

A breakaway gap is created when a price breaks out of a price pattern (as in Figure 6.6, examples *a* and *b*). Generally speaking, the presence of the gap emphasizes the bullishness or bearishness of the breakout, depending on which direction it takes. Even so, it is still important for an upside breakout to be accompanied by a relatively high level of volume. It should not be concluded that every gap breakout will be valid, because the "sure thing" does not exist in technical analysis. However, a gap associated with a breakout is more likely to be valid than one that does not. Gap breakouts which occur on the downside are not required to be accompanied by heavy volume.

Continuation or Runaway Gaps

Runaway gaps occur during a straight-line advance or decline when price quotations are moving rapidly and emotions are running high. Either they are closed very quickly, e.g., within a day or so, or they tend to remain open for much longer periods and are not generally closed until the market makes a major or intermediate swing in the opposite direction to the price movement that was responsible for the gap. This type of gap often occurs halfway between a previous breakout and the ultimate duration of the move. For this reason continuation gaps are sometimes called *measuring gaps* (see Figure 6.7, examples *a* and *b*).

Exhaustion Gaps

A price move sometimes contains more than one runaway gap. This indicates that a very powerful trend is in force, but the presence of a second or third gap should also alert the technician to the fact that the move is likely to run out of steam soon. Hence there is a possibility that a second or third runaway gap will be the final one. An exhaustion gap is therefore associated with the terminal phase of a rapid advance or decline and is the last in a series of runaway gaps (see Figure 6.7, example *b*).

One clue that an exhaustion gap may be forming is a level of volume that is unusually heavy in relation to the price change of that day. In such a case, volume usually works up to a crescendo well above previous levels. Sometimes the price will close near the vacuum (or gap) and well away from its extreme reading. If the next day's trading creates an "island" on which the gap day is completely isolated by a vacuum from the previous day's trading, this is usually an excellent sign that the gap day was in fact *the* turning point. This indicates only temporary exhaustion

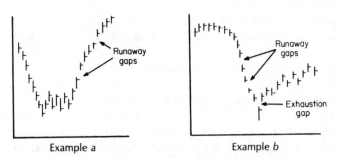

Figure 6.7. [*Source: Martin J. Pring (ed.), The McGraw-Hill Handbook of Commodities and Futures, McGraw-Hill, New York, 1985, p. 42-6.*]

but should be a red flag that signals to highly leveraged traders that they should liquidate or cover their positions.

If the gap is the first one during a move, it is likely to be a runaway rather than a breakaway type, especially if the price objective called for by a price pattern has not yet been achieved. An exhaustion gap should not be regarded as a sign of a major reversal but merely as a signal that, at the very least, some form of consolidation should be expected.

Island Reversals

An island reversal is a compact trading range created at the end of a sustained move and isolated from previous price behavior by an exhaustion gap and a breakaway gap. A typical island reversal is shown in Figure 6.8 and Chart 6.1.

The island itself is not usually a pattern denoting a major reversal. However, islands often appear at the end of an intermediate or even a major move and form part of an overall price pattern such as the top (or bottom) of a head-and-shoulders (H&S) pattern (or an inverse H&S pattern). Islands occasionally occur as 1-day phenomena, as shown in Chart 6.2.

Summary

1. Flags, pennants, and wedges are short-term price patterns that usually develop halfway along a sharp price movement. Their development is normally complete within 3 weeks, and they represent periods of quiet price movement and contracting volume. They are almost always continuation patterns.

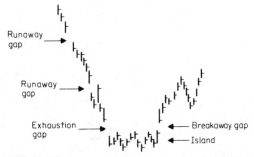

Figure 6.8.

Chart 6.1. Deutsch mark and island reversals.

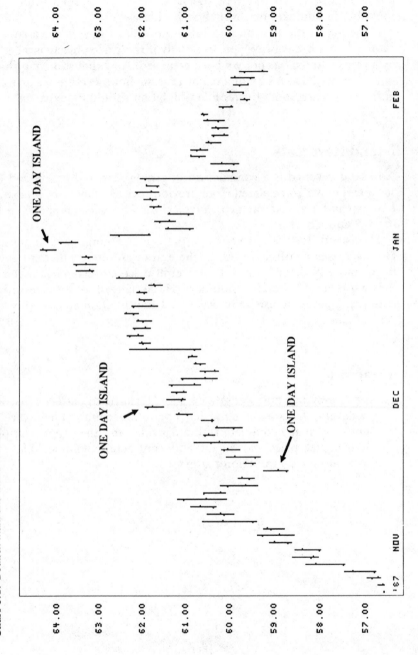

Chart 6.2. AMR and an island reversal.

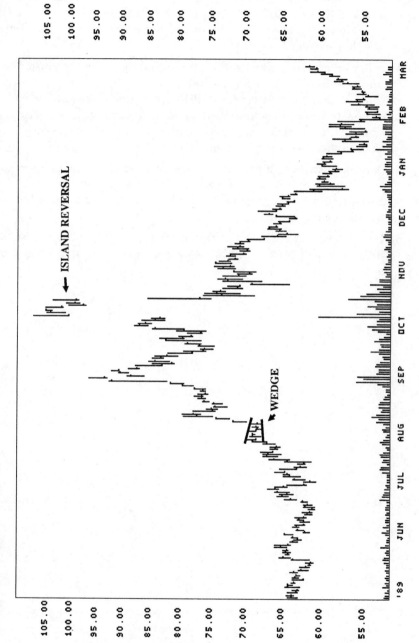

2. Saucer formations and rounding tops are usually reversal formations and are typically followed by substantial price movements. In both formations, volume contracts toward the center and is at its highest at either extremity.

3. A key reversal day signals that a price movement has exhausted itself for at least a temporary period and has three characteristics. It should occur after prices have made a sustained move to a new high or low. It must be accompanied by heavy volume, and the price must close in the direction opposite to the previous move; e.g., it must close higher following a downmove.

4. A gap is essentially a vacuum or hole in a bar chart. Ex dividend and area gaps have little significance. Breakaway gaps develop at the beginning of a move, runaway gaps in the middle of a move, and exhaustion gaps at the end.

5. Island reversals are small price patterns or congestion areas isolated from the main price trend by two gaps. They often signal the termination of an intermediate move.

7

Trendlines

A review of any chart will quickly reveal that prices usually move in trends. Quite often a series of ascending bottoms in a rising market can be joined together by a straight line, and so can the tops of a descending series of rally peaks. These lines, known as *trendlines,* are a simple but invaluable addition to the technical arsenal (see Figure 7.1).

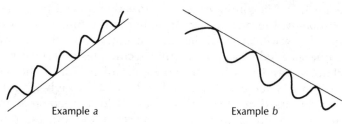

Example *a*   Example *b*

Figure 7.1.

Trendline Breaks Can Signal
Reversals or Consolidation

Some trends can be sideways, so it follows that trendlines can also be drawn horizontally. The neckline of a head-and-shoulders (H&S) pattern or the upper or lower boundary of a rectangle is really a trendline. The penetration of these lines warns of a change in trend, as does the penetration of rising or falling trendlines. In effect these lines represent points of support (rising trendline).and resistance (declining trendline).

The completion of a rectangle pattern can signify either (1) a reversal in the previous trend, in which case it becomes known as a *reversal pattern,* or (2) a resumption of the previous trend, when it is defined as a *consolidation* or *continuation pattern.* Similarly, the penetration of a

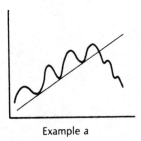

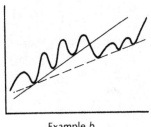

Example a   Example b

Figure 7.2.

trendline will result in either a reversal of that trend or its continuation. Figure 7.2 illustrates this point from the aspect of a rising price trend. In example *a* the trendline joining the series of troughs is eventually penetrated on the downside. The fourth peak represented the highest point in the bull market, so the downward violation of the trendline signals that a bear market is under way.

The upward price trend and trendline penetration in example *b* are identical to those in example *a*, but the action following this warning signal is entirely different because the trendline violation merely signals that the advance will continue, but at a greatly reduced pace.

Unfortunately, there is no way of telling at the time of the violation which possibility will prove to be the outcome. Nevertheless, valuable clues can be gleaned by applying other techniques described in subsequent chapters, and by evaluating the state of health of the market's overall technical structure (examined in Parts 2 through 4). Using the techniques discussed in Chapter 5 can also help. For example, in a rising market a trendline penetration may occur at the time of, or just before, the successful completion of a reversal pattern. Some possibilities are shown in Figure 7.3. In example *a* the rising trendline joins a series of bottoms, but the last two troughs represent reactions from a right shoulder and head which are part of an ascending H&S pattern. Examples *b* and *c* represent a similar situation for a rectangle and a broadening top.

Figure 7.4 illustrates the same phenomenon from the aspect of a bear market reversal. If the violation occurs simultaneously with, or just after, the completion of a reversal pattern, the two breaks have the effect of reinforcing each other; but sometimes, as in Figure 7.5, the trendline violation occurs *before* the completion of the pattern. In such cases, the break should be regarded as a sign of an interruption of the prevailing movement rather than as a sign of reversal, because a trend is assumed

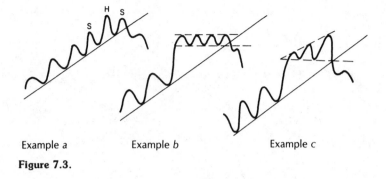

Example a					Example b					Example c

Figure 7.3.

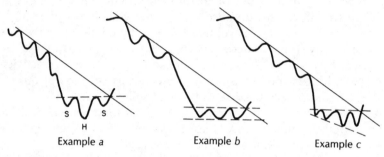

Example a					Example b					Example c

Figure 7.4.

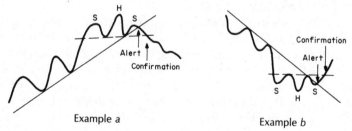

Example a								Example b

Figure 7.5.

to continue until the weight of the evidence indicates a reversal. During an advance, a setback below the previous trough should develop. This would confirm an actual reversal.

The opposite will occur in the case of a declining market (see Figure 7.5, example *b*). Further clues to the significance of a specific trendline violation can be gleaned from volume characteristics, as described in Chapters 2 and 18. For example, if a series of ascending peaks and troughs is accompanied by progressively lower volume, it is a sign that

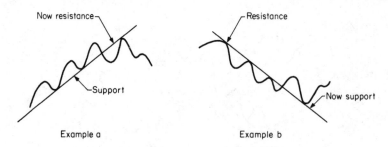

Figure 7.6.

the advance is running out of steam (since volume is no longer going with the trend). In this instance a trendline violation is likely to be of greater significance than if volume had continued to expand with each successive rally. It is not necessary for a downside penetration to be accompanied by high volume, but a violation that occurs as activity expands emphasizes the bearish undertone because of the obvious switch in the demand/supply balance in favor of sellers.

Because a return move often happens following a breakout from a price pattern, a similar move, known as a *throwback,* sometimes develops following a trendline penetration. Example *a* in Figure 7.6 shows a trendline reversing its previous role as support while the "throwback" move turns it into an area of resistance. Example *b* shows the same situation for a declining market.

The importance of plotting charts on logarithmic as opposed to arithmetic paper was discussed in Chapter 5. The choice of scale is even more critical for a timely and accurate use of trendline analysis, because at the end of a major movement prices tend to accelerate in the direction of the prevailing trend; i.e., they rise faster at the end of a rising trend (Figure 7.7) and decline more sharply at the termination of a bear market. In a bull market, prices rise slowly after an initial burst, and then

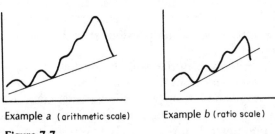

Example *a* (arithmetic scale)   Example *b* (ratio scale)

Figure 7.7.

Chart 7.1. Standard & Poor's (S&P) Composite, 1982–1989 (plotted arithmetically). (*Source: Pring Market Review.*)

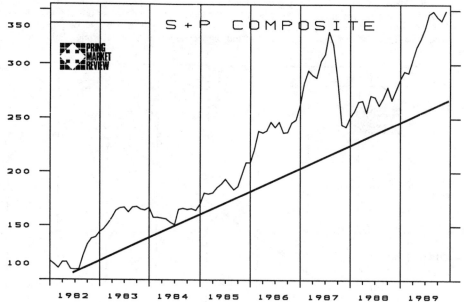

advance at a steeper and steeper angle as they approach the ultimate peak, looking rather like the left-hand cross section of a mountain.

Chart 7.1 shows that this exponential movement takes the price well away from the trendline if the index concerned is being plotted on an arithmetic scale. Consequently, the price has to fall that much further before a penetration of the trendline can take place. As a result, *up trendlines are violated more quickly on a logarithmic than an arithmetic scale.* Conversely, *down trendlines are violated sooner on an arithmetic scale.*

The four examples in Charts 7.1 to 7.4 show that penetration of a logarithmically drawn trendline is normally far more accurate in reflecting trend reversals than is penetration of an arithmetically drawn trendline.

Significance of Trendlines

It has been established that a break in trend caused by penetration of a trendline results in either an actual trend reversal or a slowing in the pace of the trend. Although it may not always be possible to assess

Chart 7.2. S&P Composite, 1982–1989 (plotted logarithmically). Charts 7.1 and 7.2 show the S&P Composite plotted on an arithmetic and logarithmic scale respectively. Since the bull market trendline was not violated during the 1987 crash on the arithmetic scale, no indication of a loss in momentum was given. On the other hand, the logarithmic trendline was broken; not only did it serve to warn of a major loss of upside momentum, but the extended line also proved to be insurmountable resistance at the end of the retracement rally. (*Source: Pring Market Review.*)

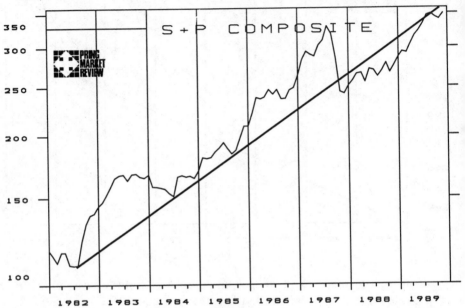

which of these alternatives will develop, it is still important to understand the significance of a trendline penetration; the guidelines described below should help in evaluation.

Length of the Line

The size or length of a trend is an important factor, as with price patterns. If a series of ascending bottoms occurs over a 3- to 4-week span, the resulting trendline is only of minor importance. If the trend extends over a period of 1 to 3 years, however, its violation marks a significant juncture point.

Chart 7.3. S&P Composite, 1972–1976 (plotted arithmetically). (*Source: Pring Market Review.*)

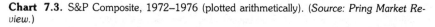
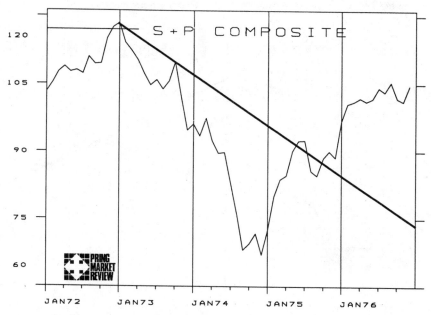

Number of Times the Trendline Has Been Touched or Approached

A trendline derives its authority from the number of times it has been touched or approached; i.e., the larger the number, the greater the significance. This is true because a trendline represents an area of support or resistance. Each successive "test" of the line contributes to the importance of this support or resistance, and thus the authority of the line is a true reflection of the underlying trend.

Angle of Ascent or Descent

A very sharp trend (as in Figure 7.8) is difficult to maintain and is liable to be broken rather easily, even by a short sideways movement.

All trends are eventually violated, but the steeper ones are likely to be ruptured more quickly. The violation of a particularly steep trend is not as significant as that of a more gradual one. Penetration of a steep line

Chart 7.4. S&P Composite, 1972–1976 (plotted logarithmically). In charts 7.3 and 7.4 note that the premature trendline violation on the arithmetic scale resulted in a whipsaw. This was not true of the violation in Chart 7.4, which proved to be a much more reliable signal of a major trend reversal. (*Source: Pring Market Review.*)

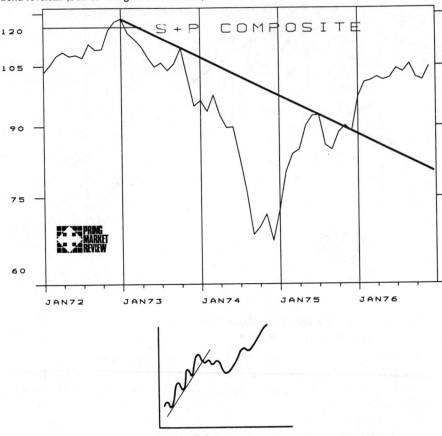

Figure 7.8.

usually results in a short corrective movement, following which the trend resumes but at a greatly reduced and more sustainable pace. Usually the penetration of a steep trendline represents a continuation rather than a reversal break.

Trendline Construction—A Matter of Judgment

The construction of trendlines is often dependent upon judgment that has been acquired through trial and error. For example, in Figure 7.9 two bottoms are formed at marginally different levels, so that the re-

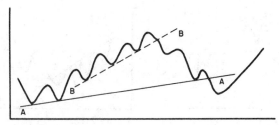

Figure 7.9.

sulting trendline *AA* becomes relatively flat; consequently, its penetration is of no use in signaling a breakdown or reversal of the major trend. Although trendline *BB* is shorter than *AA* in this case, it more closely resembles the trend, and its violation is that much more significant, for by the time prices violate *AA*, the bear market is almost over.

Measuring Implication

Trendlines have measuring implications when they are broken, just as price patterns do. The vertical distance between the peak in the price and the trendline is measured during a rising trend (A_1 in Figure 7.10).

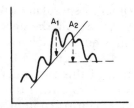

Figure 7.10.

This distance is then projected down from the point at which the violation occurs (A_2).

The term *price objective* is perhaps misleading. Objectives are usually reached when a trendline violation turns out to be a reversal, but because they are more often exceeded (as with price patterns), the objective becomes more of a minimum expectation. When prices move significantly through the objective, as in Figure 7.11, this area often becomes one of resistance to the next major rally, or support for a subsequent reaction. Figure 7.12 shows the same possibilities for an upside breakout.

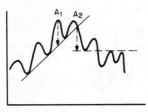

Figure 7.11

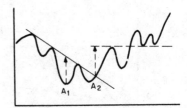

Figure 7.12.

Time and again, these price objective areas prove to be important support or resistance points. Unfortunately there is no way to determine where the actual juncture point will be for any rally or reaction. This emphasizes a point made earlier that there is no known way of consistently determining the duration of a price movement. It is only possible to speculate on the *probability* that a specific area will prove to be an important turning point.

Corrective Fan Principle

At the beginning of a new primary bull market, the initial intermediate rally is often explosive, and so the rate of ascent is unsustainably steep. This happens because the advance is often a technical reaction to the previous overextended decline, as speculators who were caught short rush to cover their positions. As a result, the steep trendline constructed from the first minor reaction is quickly violated.

This is represented as line *AA* in Figure 7.13. A new trendline is then constructed, using the bottom of this first intermediate decline (*AB*). The new line rises at a less rapid rate than the initial one. Finally the process is repeated, resulting in construction of a third line, *AC*. These lines are known as *fan lines*. There is an established principle that

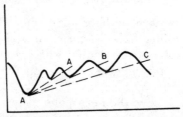

Figure 7.13.

once the third trendline has been violated, the end of the bull market is confirmed. In some respects these three rally points and trendlines can be compared to the three stages of a bull or bear market, as outlined in Chapter 3. The fan principle is just as valid for downtrends, and can also be used for determining intermediate as well as cyclical movements.

Trend Channels

So far, only the possibilities of drawing trendlines joining bottoms in rising markets and tops in declining ones have been examined. It is also useful to draw lines that are parallel to those "basic" trendlines, as shown in Figure 7.14. In a rising market the parallel line, known as a *return trendline*, joins the tops of rallies (*AA* in example *a*), and during declines the return line joins the series of bottoms (*BB* in example *b*). The area between these trend extremities is known as a *trend channel*.

The return line is useful from two points of view. First, it represents an area of support or resistance, depending on the direction of the trend. Second, and perhaps more important, penetration of the return trendline represents a signal that either the trend will accelerate or a reversal of at least a temporary proportion in the basic trend is about to take place.

In Figure 7.15, example *a*, the violation of the return line signifies that the price advance has begun to accelerate. Example *b* shows the same idea for a downside breakout. In effect, the channel in example *a* represents a rising rectangle and the trendline violation represents a breakout.

On the other hand, if the angle of the trend channel is much steeper, as in Figure 7.16, example *a*, the violation of the return line represents

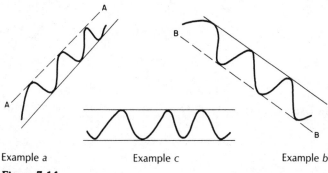

Example *a*   Example *c*   Example *b*

Figure 7.14.

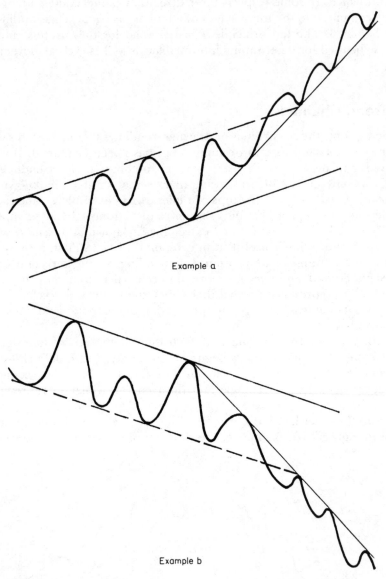

Example a

Example b

Figure 7.15. (a) Successful trend channel breakout. (b) Trend channel breakdown.

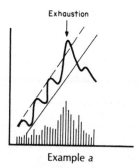

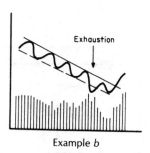

Figure 7.16.

an exhaustion move. The failure of the price to hold above (below) the return line then signals an important reversal in trend. This is often the case if the action is accompanied by high volume.

Consider a situation in which a man is sawing a thick piece of wood. At first his sawing strokes are slow but deliberate; gradually he realizes that his task is going to take some time, becomes frustrated, and slowly increases the speed of his strokes. Finally he bursts into a frantic effort and is forced to give up his task for at least a temporary period because of complete exhaustion. Example *b* in Figure 7.16 shows an exhaustion move in a declining market. In this case the expanding volume at the low represents a selling climax. As a general rule, the steeper the channel, the more likely it is that the breakout will turn out to be an exhaustion move (see Chart 7.5).

Summary

1. Trendlines are perhaps the easiest technical tool to understand, but considerable experimentation and practice are required before the art of interpreting them can be successfully mastered.

2. Trendline violations signal either a temporary interruption or a reversal in the prevailing trend. It is necessary to refer to other pieces of technical evidence to determine which is being signaled (see Chart 7.6).

3. The significance of trendlines is a function of their length, the number of times they have been touched or approached, and the steepness of the angle of ascent or descent.

4. A good trendline reflects the underlying trend and represents an important support and resistance zone.

Chart 7.5. S&P Composite, 1966–1988. This chart shows that a resistance trendline joining the 1974 low and 1978 and 1981 highs was temporarily violated. This proved to be an exhaustion move since the S&P Composite was unable to hold above the line. This failure was followed by the 1987 crash. Not all exhaustion moves result in such dynamic consequences, but they certainly warn of potential trouble and should never be ignored.

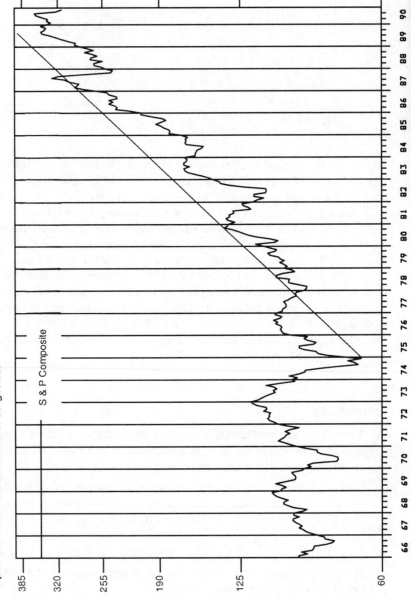

S & P Composite

Chart 7.6. Value Line Composite Index, 1989–1990. This represents a classic example of a major trendline violation occurring in combination with a price pattern completion. In this case the formation was a broadening one with a slightly rising up trendline. Some form of poetic license is often required in interpreting charts since this particular one could not strictly be interpreted as a broadening formation with a flat bottom, but the effects were certainly the same. (*Source: Pring Market Review.*)

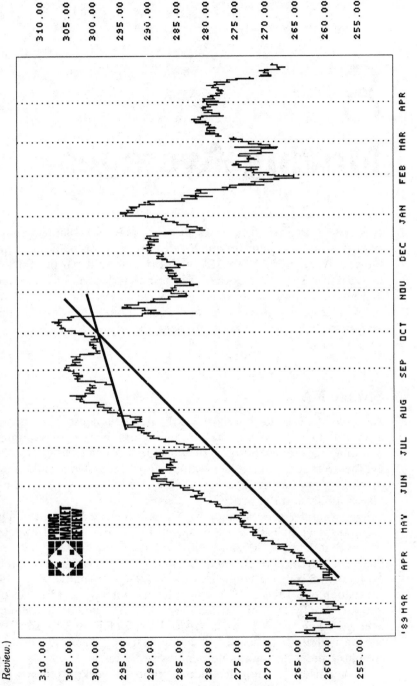

8
Moving Averages

It is evident that trends in stock prices can be very volatile, almost haphazard at times. One technique for dealing with this phenomenon is the moving average (MA). An MA attempts to tone down the fluctuations of stock prices into a smoothed trend, so that distortions are reduced to a minimum. Three basic types of MAs are used in the technical analysis of stock trends: simple, weighted, and exponential. The construction and use of these averages are different; therefore each type will be dealt with in turn.

Simple MA

A simple MA is by far the most widely used. It is constructed by totaling a set of data and dividing the sum by the number of observations. The resulting number is known as the *average* or *mean average*. In order to get the average to "move," a new item of data is added and the first item on the list subtracted. The new total is then divided by the number of observations, and the process is repeated.

For example, the calculation of a 10-week MA would follow the method shown in Table 8.1. On March 12 the total of the 10 weeks ending on that date was 966, and 966 divided by 10 results in an average of 96.6. On March 19 the number 90 is added, and the observation of 101 on January 8 is deleted. The new total of 955 is then divided by 10. The calculation of a 13-week MA would require totaling of 13 weeks of data and dividing by 13. This calculation is then repeated in order to get the average to "move." A 13-week MA is shown in Figure 8.1, example *a*, by the dashed line. Generally speaking, a rising MA indicates market strength, and a declining one denotes weakness.

A comparison of the price index with its 13-week MA shows that the

Table 8.1.

Date	Index	10-week total	MA
Jan. 8	101		
15	100		
22	103		
29	99		
Feb. 5	96		
12	99		
19	95		
26	91		
Mar. 5	93		
12	89	966	96.6
19	90	955	95.5
26	95	950	95.0
Apr. 2	103	950	95.0

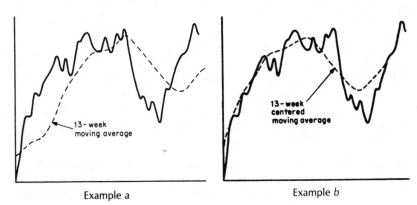

Example *a*   Example *b*

Figure 8.1.

average changes direction well after the peak or trough in the price and is therefore "late" in changing direction. This is because the MA is plotted on the thirteenth week, whereas the average price of 13 weeks of observations actually occurs halfway through the 13-week time span, i.e., in the seventh week. If it is to reflect the underlying trend correctly, the latest MA should be centered, i.e., plotted, on the seventh week, as shown in Figure 8.1, example *b*.

If the centering technique had been used in the example, it would have been necessary to wait 6 weeks before ascertaining whether the average had changed direction.

A time delay, though it is an irritant, is not particularly critical when analyzing other time series such as economic data. However, given the relatively rapid movement of prices in the financial markets and consequent loss of profit potential, a delay of this nature is totally unacceptable. Technicians have found that, for the purpose of identifying trend reversals, the best results are achieved by plotting the MA on the final week.

Changes in the price trend are identified not by a reversal in direction of the MA, but by the price itself crossing its MA. A change from a rising to a declining market is signaled when the price moves below its MA. A bullish signal is triggered when the price rallies above the average. Since the use of MAs gives clear-cut buy and sell signals, it helps to eliminate some of the subjectivity associated with the construction and interpretation of trendlines.

More often than not, it pays to take action based on MA crossovers, since this technique is one of the most reliable tools in the technical arsenal. The degree of accuracy depends substantially on the choice of MA, as discussed below. First we need to examine some of the characteristics of MAs in greater detail.

1. An MA is a smoothed version of a trend, and the average itself is an area of support and resistance. In a rising market, price reactions are often reversed as they find support in the area of the MA. Similarly, a rally in a declining market often meets resistance at an MA and turns down. The more times an MA has been touched, i.e., acts as a support or resistance area, the greater the significance when it is violated.

2. A carefully chosen MA should reflect the underlying trend; its violation therefore warns that a change in trend may already have taken place. If the MA is flat or has already changed direction, its violation is fairly conclusive proof that the previous trend has reversed.

3. If the violation occurs while the MA is still proceeding in the direction of the prevailing trend, this development should be treated as a preliminary warning that a trend reversal has taken place. Confirmation should await a flattening or a change in direction in the MA itself or should be sought from alternative technical sources.

4. Generally speaking, the longer the time span covered by an MA, the greater is the significance of a crossover signal. For instance, the violation of an 18-month MA is substantially more important than a crossover of a 30-day MA.

5. Reversals in the *direction* of an MA are usually more reliable than an MA crossover. In instances in which a change in direction occurs

close to a market turning point, a very powerful and reliable signal is given. However, in most instances an average reverses well after a new trend has begun and so is only useful as a confirmation.

In short, think of an average as a type of "moving trendline" which, like a trendline, obtains its significance from its length (time span), the number of times it has been touched or approached, and its angle of ascent or descent.

What Is a Valid Crossover?

A *crossover* is any penetration of an MA. However, close observation of any chart featuring an MA will usually reveal a number of whipsaw, or false, signals. How can we tell which ones are going to be valid? Unfortunately there is no way of knowing for certain. Indeed, many whipsaws cannot be avoided and should be regarded as a fact of life. However, it is possible to avoid some of these close calls by using filtering techniques. The type of filter to be used depends on the time span in question and is very much a matter of individual experimentation. For example, we may decide to take action on MA crossovers for which a 3 percent penetration takes place, and to ignore all others. Violations of a 40-week MA might result in an average price move of 15 to 20 percent. In this instance a 3 percent penetration would be a reasonable filter. On the other hand, since 3 percent would probably encompass the whole move signaled by a 10-day MA crossover, this kind of filter would be of no use whatsoever.

Some analysts, recognizing that one-period whipsaws are quite common, require an MA crossover to hold for at least that period. In the case of daily data, this approach would mean waiting for the second or third day before concluding that the average had been violated. A more sensible method is to use a combination of the period *and* percentage penetration for deciding whether a crossover is valid.

A useful tip is to wait for an MA crossover to take place at the same time a trendline is violated or a price pattern completed. Such signals strongly reinforce the trendline or price pattern signal and therefore need less in the form of a filter requirement.

MAs are usually constructed from closing data. Closing prices are more reliable than others because they reflect positions that investors are willing to carry overnight or, in the case of weekly charts, over the weekend. Intraday trading can be subject to manipulation or distorted by an unwarranted emotional attitude to news events. For this reason it is best to wait for the closing price to penetrate the average before con-

Chart 8.1. The Canadian dollar and two MAs. (*Source: Pring Market Review.*)

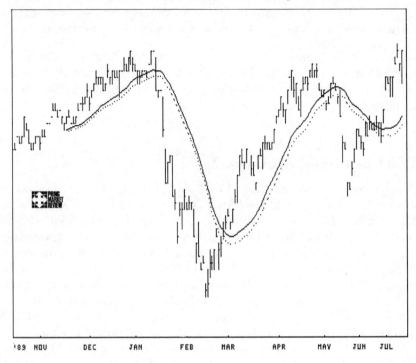

cluding that a crossover has taken place. If intraperiod activity is used for MA violations, it is usually best to calculate an MA based on daily lows or highs. In Chart 8.1 the dotted line shows a 25-day MA calculated from intraday lows. The solid line represents the same average based on closing-only data. If intraday crossovers of the former had been used as stop-loss signals on the downside, considerably fewer whipsaws would have been generated than if the MA had been based on closing data.

Choice of Time Span

MAs can be constructed for any time period, whether a few days, several weeks, many months, or even years. Choice of length is very important. For example, if it is assumed that a complete bull and bear cycle lasts for 4 years, an MA constructed over a time span longer than 48 months will not reflect the cycle at all. This is because it smoothes out all the fluctuations that take place during the period and will appear more or less as a straight line crossing through the middle of the data. On the other hand, a 5-day MA will catch every minor move in the stock cycle and will be useless for the purpose of identifying the actual top and bottom of the overall cycle. Even if the 48-month average were shortened to 24 months and the 5-day average expanded to 4 weeks, for example (see Figure 8.2), using the crossover signals would still cause the 24-month average to give an agonizingly slow confirmation of a change in trend. The 4-week average would be so sensitive that it would continually give misleading or whipsaw signals. Only an MA that can catch the movement of the actual cycle will provide the optimum tradeoff be-

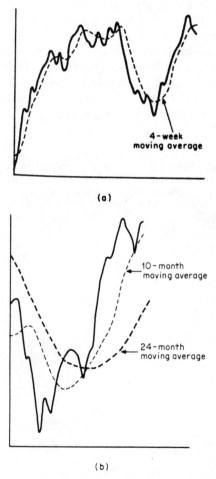

Figure 8.2. (a) MA not centered. (b) MA centered.

tween lateness and oversensitivity, such as the 10-month MA in Figure 8.2*b*.

The choice of MA depends on the type of market trend that is to be identified, i.e., short, intermediate, or primary. Because different markets have different characteristics and the same markets go through different cyclic phenomena, there is no such thing as a "perfect" MA. In recent years extensive computer research has been done on the optimum MA time span. *The conclusion from all sources is that there is no one perfect time span.*

What may work extremely well in one market over one specific period of time is unlikely to be duplicated in the future. When we talk about choice of time span, we are really trying to identify an MA that will work most of the time with a specific time frame, i.e., short, intermediate, or long. Generally speaking, long-term time spans are less influenced by manipulation and knee-jerk random reactions to unexpected news than are short-term ones. This is why long-time spans usually give the best test results; both daily and weekly averages work best at, or above, a 40-period span (Chart 8.2). Research also shows that

Chart 8.2. Standard & Poor's (S&P) Composite, yen, and gold, and 40-week MAs. This chart shows a 40-week MA at work in three different markets. Crossovers of each index are subject to whipsaws from time to time, but on balance this average is still fairly reliable. Note that the 40-week average is continually being used as a support or resistance level.

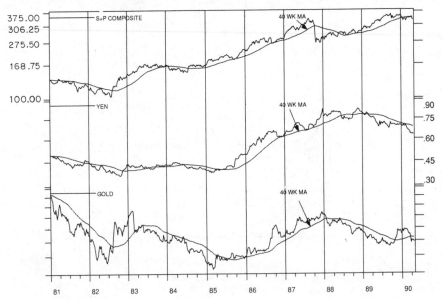

Table 8.2. Time Frame

Short-term	Intermediate-term	Long-term
10-day	30-day	200-day/40-week/9-month*
15-day	10-week (50-day)	45-week†
20-day	13-week (65-day)	
25-day	20-week	12-month‡
30-day	26-week	18-month
	200-day	24-month

*Recommended by William Gordon, *The Stock Market Indicators,* Investors Press, Palisades Park, N.J., 1968.
†Reported by Robert W. Colby and Thomas A. Meyers in *The Encyclopedia of Technical Market Indicators,* Dow Jones–Irwin, Homewood, Ill., 1988, to be the best average for the U.S. stock market using weekly data.
‡Ibid.; reported to be the best average for the U.S. stock market using monthly data.

simple averages generally outperform weighted and exponential ones.[1] Recognizing these limitations, the time spans in Table 8.2 are suggested.

The important thing to remember is that an MA is *one* technical tool in the technical arsenal, which is used with other techniques as part of the *art* of identifying trend reversals.

Advanced MAs

A technique that has a lot of potential, but is not widely used, is to advance an MA. In the case of a 25-day MA, for example, the actual plot would not be made on the twenty-fifth day but advanced to the twenty-eighth or thirtieth, and so forth. The advantage of this approach is that it delays the crossover and filters out occasional whipsaws or false signals. In *Profits in the Stock Market,* H. M. Gartley[2] calculated that during the period 1919–1933, which covered almost all kinds of market situations, use of a simple 25-day MA crossover netted 446 Dow points (slightly better than 433 points for the 30-day MA and far better than 316 and 216 for 40- and 15-day MAs, respectively). However, when the 25-day average was plotted on the twenty-eighth day, crossovers resulted in an increase of 231 points to 677. The 30-day MA, when advanced 3 days, also produced superior results, with an addi-

[1]Weighted MAs and exponential moving averages (EMAs) are explained later, in this chapter.
[2]Lambert Gann Publishing, Pomeroy, Wash., 1981.

tional gain of 204 points for a total of 637. Chart 8.3 represents three MAs as calculated by Gartley. Although these MAs are plotted normally, the whipsaw signals would be avoided by moving the MA forward 3 days, as shown on the chart.

Although the 25-day MA advanced 3 days may not ultimately prove to be the best combination, the technique of advancing an MA is clearly one that could be usefully incorporated into the technical approach. It is always difficult to know how much to advance an MA. Experimentation is the answer. One possibility is to advance the average by the square root of the time span; e.g., a 36-week MA would be advanced by 6 days (the square root of 36 = 6).[3]

Convergence of Averages

A sharp price move is often preceded by a gradually narrowing trading range. In effect, decreasing price fluctuations reflect a very fine balance between buyers and sellers. When the balance is tipped one way or the other, the price is then free to embark upon a major move.

This kind of situation can often be identified by plotting several MAs and observing when they are all at approximately the same point. Chart 8.4, for example, shows the daily price between 1989 and 1990. Note how the three MAs almost completely converge just before the price embarks on a sharp decline. The convergence of the averages warns that a major move is likely, but the actual signal comes from the violation of the trendline.

Multiple MAs

Some techniques of trend determination involve more than one MA at a time. Signals are given by a shorter-term MA crossing above or below a longer one. This procedure has the advantage of smoothing the data twice, which reduces the possibility of a whipsaw, yet it warns of trend changes fairly quickly after they have taken place (see Chart 8.5). Two averages which have been found reliable in determining primary market moves are the 10- and 30-week MAs, when used together. For the purpose of simplifying the calculation, the weekly closing price is used, rather than a 5-day average.

Signals are given when the 10-week average moves below the 30-week

---

[3]Arthur Skarlew, *Techniques of a Professional Commodity Chart Analyst,* Commodity Research Bureau, New York, 1980.

Chart 8.3. The Dow Jones Industrial Average (DJIA) and three MAs. (*Source: H. M. Gartley, Profits and the Stock Market, Lambert Gann Publishing, Pomeroy, Wash., 1981.*)

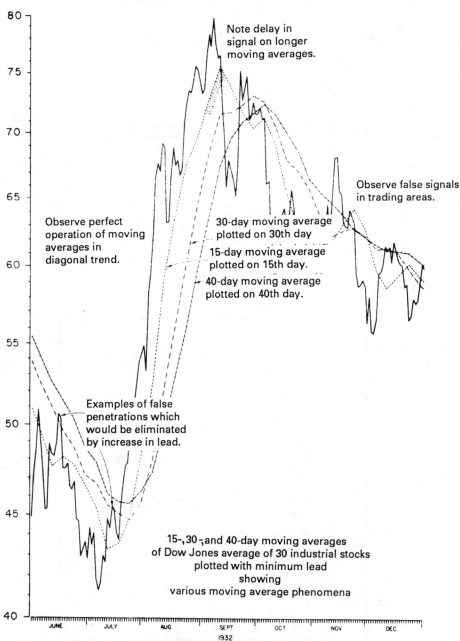

Chart 8.4. Palladium and three MAs.

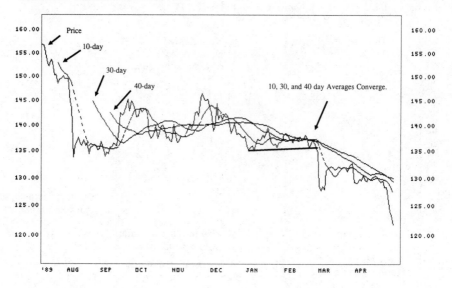

Chart 8.5. The DJIA versus 30-week and 10-week MAs.

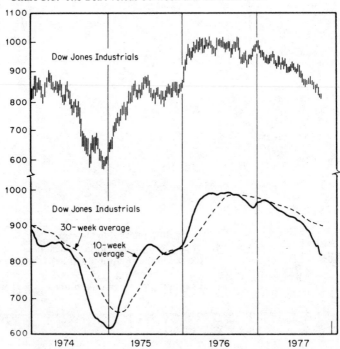

average and when the 30-week average itself is declining. This development warns that the major trend is down. It is not assumed to have reversed until both averages are rising simultaneously, with the 10-week higher than the 30-week MA. A valid signal is not given if the 10-week average rises above the 30-week average while the longer average is still declining (and vice versa for bull markets). By definition, these warning signals always occur after the ultimate peak or trough of stock prices, and serve as a *confirmation* of a change in trend rather than as actual juncture points in themselves.

MAs should *always* be used in conjunction with other indicators. This is because prices occasionally fluctuate in a broad sideways pattern for an extended period of time, resulting in a series of misleading signals. Chart 8.6, showing the 1946–1949 bear market in U.S. equities, shows an example of a period in which many misleading crossovers were experienced. Usually such frustrating trading-range action is followed by an extremely strong trend in which the losses incurred from the trendless period of whipsaw signals are more than made up for.

Weighted MAs

An MA can correctly represent a trend from a statistical point of view only if it is centered, but centering an average delays the signal, for the reasons discussed earlier. One technique that attempts to overcome this problem is to weight the data in favor of the most recent observations.

Chart 8.6. DJIA, 1946–1951.

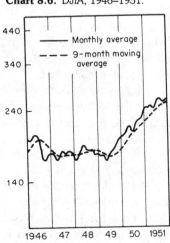

An MA constructed in this manner is able to "turn" or reverse direction much more quickly than a simple MA, which is calculated by treating all the data equally.

There are countless ways in which data can be weighted, but the most widely used method is a technique whereby the first period of data is multiplied by 1, the second by 2, the third by 3, and so on until the latest one. The calculations for each period are then totaled. The divisor for a simple MA is the number of periods, but for this form of weighted average, the divisor is the sum of the weights; i.e., $1 + 2 + 3 + 4 + 5 + 6 = 21$. For a 10-week weighted MA, the sum of the weights would be $1 + 2 + 3 + 4 + 5 + 6 + 7 + 8 + 9 + 10 = 55$. Table 8.3 illustrates how the calculations are made.

Another method is to calculate a simple MA, but, in doing so, to use the most recent observation twice, which doubles its weight. The calculation of a 6-week weighted MA using this approach and the data from Table 8.3 would be as shown in Table 8.4.

The interpretation of a weighted average is different from that of a simple average, because the weighted average is more sensitive. A warning of a trend reversal is given by a change in direction of the average rather than by a crossover.

Exponential Moving Averages

Weighted MAs are helpful for the purpose of identifying trend reversals. However, the time-consuming calculations required to construct and maintain such averages greatly detract from their usefulness (unless, of course, a computer is within easy reach). An exponential moving average (EMA) is a shortcut to obtaining a form of weighted MA. In order to construct a 20-week EMA, it is necessary to calculate a simple 20-week MA first, i.e., the total of 20 weeks of observations divided by 20. In Table 8.5 this has been done for the 20 weeks ending January 1, and the result appears as 99.00 in column 6.

The 20-week average becomes the starting point for the EMA. It is transferred to column 2 for the following week. Next, the entry for the twenty-first week (January 8 in the example above) is compared with the EMA, and the difference is added or subtracted and posted in column 3; i.e., $100 - 99 = 1.00$. This difference is then multiplied by the exponent, which for a 20-week EMA is 0.1. This exponentially treated difference, 1.00×0.1, is then added to the previous week's EMA, and the calculation is repeated each succeeding week. In the example, the exponentially treated difference for January 8 is 0.1, which is added to the previous week's average, 99.00, to obtain an EMA for January 8 of

Table 8.3.

Date	Index (1)	6 × col. 1 (2)	5 × col. 1 1 week ago (3)	4 × col. 1 2 weeks ago (4)	3 × col. 1 3 weeks ago (5)	2 × col. 1 4 weeks ago (6)	1 × col. 1 5 weeks ago (7)	Total cols. 2–7	Col. 8 ÷ 21 (9)
Jan. 8	101								
15	100								
22	103								
29	99								
Feb. 5	96								
12	99	594	480	396	309	200	101	2080	99.1
19	95	570	495	384	297	206	100	2052	97.7
26	91	546	475	396	288	198	103	2006	95.5
Mar. 5	93	558	455	380	297	192	99	1981	94.3
12	89	534	465	364	285	198	96	1924	92.5

Table 8.4.

Week	Index
1	101
2	100
3	103
4	99
5	96
6	96
Total	595

$$\frac{\text{Total}}{\text{Weeks}} = \frac{595}{6} = 99.2$$

Table 8.5.

Date	Price (1)	EMA for previous week (2)	Difference (col. 1 − col. 2) (3)	Exponent (4)	Col. 3 × col. 4 ± /− (5)	Col. 2 + col. 5 EMA (6)
Jan. 1	...	...	...	...	...	99.00
8	100.00	99.00	1.00	0.1	+0.10	99.10
15	103.00	99.10	3.90	0.1	+0.39	99.49
22	102.00	99.49	2.51	0.1	+0.25	99.74
29	99.00	99.64	(0.64)	0.1	−0.06	99.68

99.10. This figure in column 6 is then plotted. Figure 8.3 shows an example of a 13-week EMA.

If the difference between the new weekly observation and the previous week's EMA is negative, as in the reading 99.00 versus 99.64 for January 29, the exponentially treated difference is subtracted from the previous week's EMA.

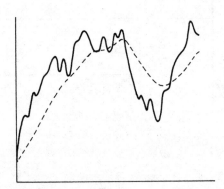

Figure 8.3.

Table 8.6.

Number of weeks	Exponent
5	0.4
10	0.2
15	0.13
20	0.1
40	0.05
80	0.25

The exponent used varies with the time span of the MA. The correct exponents for various time spans are as shown in Table 8.6, where the time periods have been described as weekly. In effect, however, the exponent 0.1 can be used for any measure of 20−days, weeks, months, years, or an even longer period.

Exponents for time periods other than those shown in the table can easily be calculated by dividing 2 by the time span. For example, a 5-week average will need to be twice as sensitive as a 10-week average; thus 2 divided by 5 gives an exponent of 0.4. On the other hand, since a 20-week average should be half as sensitive as for a 10-week period (0.2), its exponent is halved to 0.1.

If an EMA proves to be too sensitive for the trend being monitored, one solution is to extend its time period. Another is to smooth the EMA by another EMA. This method uses an EMA, as calculated above, and repeats the process using a further exponent. There is no reason why a third or fourth smoothing could not be tried, but the resulting EMA, while smoother, would be far less sensitive. Remember, all forms of MAs represent a compromise between timeliness and sensitivity.

By definition, EMA crossovers and reversals occur simultaneously. Buy and sell signals are, therefore, triggered in the same way as simple MA crossovers.

In their book *The Encyclopedia of Technical Market Indicators*,[4] Colby and Meyers tested all the time spans between 1- and 75-week EMAs for the U.S. stock market between 1968 and 1987. They discovered that the 42-week EMA gave the best performance, offering an equity gain of 97+ points, but lagged behind the 45-week simple MA, which experienced a gain of 111+ points.

Envelopes

It has already been established that MAs can act as important juncture points in their role as support and resistance areas. In this re-

[4]Robert W. Colby and Thomas A. Meyers, *The Encyclopedia of Technical Market Indicators*, Dow Jones–Irwin, Homewood, Ill., 1988.

spect, the longer the time span, the greater the significance of MAs. This support and resistance principle can be taken one step further by constructing symmetrical lines parallel to an MA, called *envelopes* (see Figure 8.4). This technique is based on the principle that stock prices fluctuate around a given trend in cyclical movements of reasonably similar proportion. In other words, just as the MA serves as an important juncture point, so do certain lines drawn parallel to that MA. Looked at in this way, the MA is really the center of the trend, and the envelope consists of the points of maximum and minimum divergence from it.

There is no hard-and-fast rule about the exact position at which the envelope should be drawn, since that can be discovered only on a trial-and-error basis with regard to the volatility of the price being monitored and the time span of the MA. This process can be expanded, as in Figure 8.5, to include four or more envelopes (i.e., two above and two below the MA), each drawn at an identical proportional distance from its predecessor. In this example the envelopes have been plotted at 10 percent intervals. If the MA is at 100, for example, the envelopes should be plotted at 90, 110, etc.

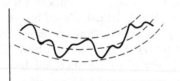

Figure 8.4.

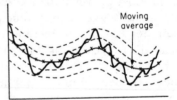

Figure 8.5.

Chart 8.7 shows that the envelope technique can be very useful from two aspects: (1) developing a "feel" for the overall trend and (2) discerning when a rally or reaction is overextended. The disadvantage is that there is no certainty that the envelope will prove to be the eventual turning point. This method, like all techniques that attempt to forecast the duration of a move, should be used on the basis that if the index reaches a particular envelope, there is a good probability that it will reverse course at that juncture. The actual trading, or investment decision, should be determined by an assessment of a number of characteristics, of which envelope analysis is one ingredient.

Chart 8.7. DJIA, 1972–1974.

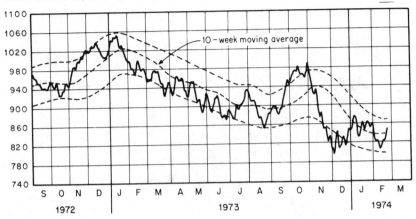

Bollinger Bands

A useful addition to envelope analysis is a new approach devised by John Bollinger.[5] Rather than being plotted as fixed percentages above and below an MA, Bollinger bands are plotted as standard deviations above and below an average based on closing prices.

The bands have the following characteristics:

A continuation of the trend is implied when prices move outside the band, provided the band is not rising or falling too steeply.

A move that starts at one band usually carries over to the other one.

The bands tighten as volatility shrinks. This is usually followed by a sharp price move.

Rallies and reactions that temporarily take prices outside the bands usually represent exhaustion and are associated with trend reversals.

The calculation and plotting of either regular envelopes or Bollinger bands are time-consuming. Two computer programs that plot these indicators automatically are MetaStock and Computrac (see the Resources section at the end of the book). Chart 8.8 shows the British pound together with 2.0 percent Bollinger bands.

[5]John Bollinger, Bollinger Capital Management, P.O. Box 3358, Manhattan Beach, Calif., 90266.

Chart 8.8. The British pound using 2.0 percent Bollinger bands.

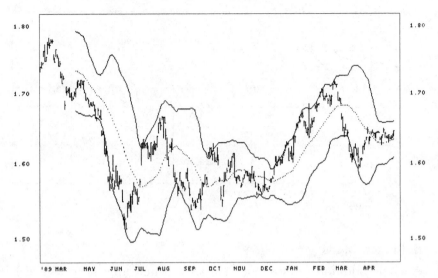

Summary

1. One of the basic assumptions of technical analysis is that stocks move in trends. Since major trends comprise many minor fluctuations in prices, an MA is constructed to help smooth out the data so that the underlying trend will be more clearly visible.

2. Ideally, a simple MA should be plotted at the halfway point of the time period being monitored (a process known as *centering*), but since this would involve a time lag during which stock prices could change rapidly and lose much of the potential profit of a move, it is plotted at the end of the period in question.

3. This drawback has been largely overcome by the use of MA cross-overs, which provide warnings of a reversal in trend, and by the use of weighted or EMAs, which are especially more sensitive to changes in the prevailing trend since they weight data in favor of the most recent periods.

4. There is no such thing as a perfect average. The choice of time span always represents a trade-off between timeliness — catching the trend at an early stage — and sensitivity — catching the trend turn too early and causing an undue amount of whipsaws. For short-term trends, 25- and 40-day spans are suggested, but for longer-term time spans 40- and 45-week averages are recommended. A helpful time span using monthly data is 12 months.

9

Momentum I

The methods of trend determination considered so far have been concerned with analysis of the movement of the price itself through trendlines, price patterns, and moving-average (MA) analysis. These techniques are extremely useful, but they identify a change in trend *after it has taken place*. The use of *momentum* indicators can warn of latent strength or weakness in the indicator or price being monitored, often well ahead of the final turning point.

This chapter will examine the general principles of momentum interpretation that apply in some degree or other to *all* momentum indicators. Rate of change will be used as a case study. The next chapter will discuss other specific momentum indicators.

Introduction

The concept of upside momentum is illustrated in the following example. When a ball is thrown into the air, it begins its trajectory at a very fast pace; i.e., it possesses strong momentum. The speed at which the ball rises gradually diminishes, until it finally comes to a temporary standstill. The force of gravity then causes it to reverse course. This slowing-down process, known as a *loss of upward momentum,* is a phenomenon that is also experienced in financial markets. The flight of a ball can be equated to a market price. The price's rate of advance begins to slow down noticeably before the ultimate peak in prices is reached.

On the other hand, if a ball is thrown inside a room and hits the ceiling while its momentum is still rising, the ball and the momentum will reverse at the same time. Unfortunately, momentum indicators in the marketplace are not dissimilar. This is because there are occasions on which momentum and price peak simultaneously, either because a ceiling of selling resistance is met or because buying power is temporarily exhausted. Under such conditions the *level* of momentum is often as helpful as its *direction* in assessing the quality of a price trend.

The idea of downward momentum may be better understood by comparing it to a car that is pushed over the top of a hill. The car begins to roll downhill and, as the gradient of the hill steepens, to accelerate; at the bottom, it reaches maximum velocity. Although its speed then begins to decrease, the car continues to travel, but finally it comes to a halt. Market prices act in a similar fashion: the rate of decline (or loss of momentum) often slows ahead of the final low. This is not always the case, however, since momentum and price sometimes (as at peaks) turn together, as prices meet a major level of support. Nevertheless, momentum leads price often enough to warn of a potential trend reversal in the indicator or market average that is being monitored.

Momentum is a generic term. Just as "fruit" describes apples, oranges, grapes, etc., so "momentum" embraces many different indicators. Examples include rate of change (ROC), the relative strength indicator (RSI), moving-average convergence divergence (MACD), breadth oscillators, and diffusion indexes.

There are essentially two broad ways of looking at momentum. The first uses price data for an individual series, such as a currency, commodity, stock, or market average, and manipulates it in a statistical form that is plotted as an oscillator. We will call this *price momentum.* The second is also plotted as an oscillator but is based on statistical manipulation of a number of market components, such as the percentage of New York Stock Exchange (NYSE) stocks above a 30-week MA. This measure is referred to as *breadth momentum* and is discussed in Chapter 19. *Price momentum can be constructed for any price series, but breadth momentum can be calculated only for a series that can be broken down into various components.*

The principles or characteristics of momentum interpretation are the same for all indicators, but some are specially constructed to bring out a particular characteristic. This chapter outlines the eight basic principles. We will be using ROC as an example, but you should remember that it is only *one* type of price momentum indicator. Chapters 10 and 19 will discuss other individual indicators for price and breadth momentum respectively. Breadth indicators for the international markets, gold, commodities, and currencies will be discussed in the appropriate chapters in Part 5.

It should be noted that the type of trend reversal signaled by a momentum indicator depends upon the time span over which it has been calculated. It is accepted practice to use daily data for identifying short-term trends, weekly data for intermediate trends, and monthly data for primary trends.

It is very important to note that the use of momentum indicators assumes that markets or stocks are experiencing a normal cyclic rhythm which is expressed in price action by rallies and reactions. However, in some instances countercyclical reactions are almost nonexistent. Price movement is then reflected as a linear uptrend or downtrend. This is an unusual phenomenon and when it develops, momentum indicators fail to work. This is why *it is of paramount importance to use momentum analysis in conjunction with some kind of trend-reversal signal in the price series itself.*

Rate of Change (ROC)

The simplest way of measuring momentum is to calculate the rate at which a market average changes price over a given period of time. If it is desired, for example, to construct an indicator measuring a 10-week rate of change, the current price is divided by the price 10 weeks ago. If the latest price is 100 and the price 10 weeks ago was 105, the ROC or momentum indicator will read 95.2, that is, 100 divided by 105. The subsequent reading in the indicator will be calculated by dividing next week's price by the price 9 weeks ago (see Table 9.1). The result is a series that oscillates around a central reference point. This horizontal equilibrium line represents the level at which the price is unchanged from its reading 10 weeks ago (Figure 9.1). If a ROC calculation were made for a price that remained unchanged, its momentum index would be represented by a straight line.

When an ROC indicator is above the reference line, the market price that it is measuring is higher than its level 10 weeks ago. If the ROC indicator is also rising, the difference between the current reading of the price and its level 10 weeks ago is growing. If an ROC indicator is above the central line but is declining, the price is still above its level 10 weeks ago, but the difference between the two readings is shrinking. When the ROC indicator is below its central line and falling, the price is below its level 10 weeks ago, and the difference between the two is growing. If the indicator is below its central line but rising, the price is still lower than its level 10 weeks ago, but its rate of decline is slowing.

In short, *a rising ROC indicator implies expanding velocity, and a falling one implies a loss of momentum.* Rising momentum should be interpreted as a bullish factor, and declining momentum as a bearish one.

There are two methods of scaling an ROC chart. Since the choice does

Table 9.1.

Date	DJIA (1)	DIJA 10 weeks ago (2)	10 week rate of change (col. 1 ÷ col. 2) (3)
Jan. 1	985		
8	980		
15	972		
22	975		
29	965		
Feb. 5	967		
12	972		
19	965		
26	974		
Mar. 5	980		
12	965	985	98.0
19	960	980	98.0
26	950	972	97.7
Apr. 2	960	975	98.5
9	965	965	100.0
16	970	967	100.3
23	974	972	100.2
30	980	965	101.6
May 7	985	974	101.1

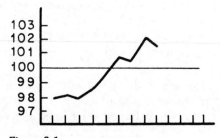

Figure 9.1.

not affect the trend or level of the index, the method used is not important, but a brief explanation is in order because the two alternatives can be confusing. The first method is the one described above and shown in Figure 9.1, where 100 becomes the central reference point. In the example, 100 (this week's observation) divided by 99 (the observation 10 weeks ago) is plotted as 101, 100 divided by 98 as 102, 100 divided by 102 as 98, and so on.

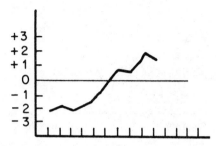

Figure 9.2.

The alternative is to take the difference between the indicator and the 100 level and plot the result as a positive or negative number, using a reference line of 0. In this case, 101 is plotted as +1, 102 as +2, 98 as -2, and so on (see Figure 9.2).

Selection of Time Span

Choice of the correct time span is important. For longer-term trends, a 12-month or 52-week momentum is generally the most reliable, although a 24- or 18-month period can also prove useful. For intermediate trends, a 9-month, 26-week (6-month), or 13-week (3-month) momentum works well. Price movements of even shorter duration are often reflected by a 10-, 20-, 25-, or 30-day span.

It is important to remember that *the analysis of any technical situation will be enhanced by the calculation of a momentum indicator for several different time spans.* In this way trendlines, price patterns, or divergences which may not be apparent in one period are more apparent in another. The discovery of signs of a trend reversal in several indicators constructed from different time spans adds further fuel to the weight of the evidence.

Principles and Applications of Momentum Indicators

The following description of the principles and use of momentum indicators applies to all forms of oscillators, whether constructed from an individual price series or from an index that measures internal market momentum, such as those described in Chapter 19.

Momentum is usually plotted below the price series that it is measuring, as in Figure 9.3.

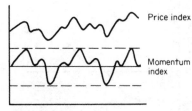

Figure 9.3.

1. Overbought and Oversold Levels

Perhaps the most widely used method of momentum interpretation is the evaluation of overbought and oversold levels. This concept can be compared to a person taking an unruly dog for a walk on a leash. The leash is continually being pulled from one side of the person to the other as the dog struggles to get free. Despite all its activity, however, the dog can move no farther away than the length of the leash.

The same principle holds true for momentum indicators in the marketplace, except that the market's "leash" should be thought of as made of rubber, so that it is possible for particularly strong or weak price trends to extend beyond the normal limits known as *overbought* and *oversold* levels. These areas are drawn on a chart at some distance above and below the equilibrium level, as in Figure 9.3. The actual boundaries will depend on the volatility of the price being monitored and the time period over which the momentum indicator has been constructed. For example, an ROC indicator has a tendency to move to wider extremes over a longer period than over a shorter one. It is highly unlikely that a price will move 10 percent over a 10-day period; yet over the course of a primary bull market, extending over a 12-month period, a 25 percent increase would not be uncommon. Some indicators, such as RSI and stochastics, have been specially constructed to move within definite predetermined boundaries.

In view of the variability of indicators such as ROC, there is no hard-and-fast rule about where the overbought and oversold lines should be drawn. This can be determined only by studying the history and characteristics of the market or stock being monitored. The lines should be drawn such that they will act as pivotal points which, when touched or slightly exceeded, are followed by a reversal in the oscillator. When a particularly sharp price movement takes place, these boundaries will become totally ineffective. Unfortunately, this is a fact of life, but by and large it is usually possible to construct overbought and oversold benchmarks that are price-sensitive.

The maturity of the trend, whether primary or intermediate, will have an effect on the limits that an oscillator might reach. For example, when a bull market has just begun, there is a far greater tendency for an oscillator to move quickly into overbought territory and to remain at very high readings for a considerable period of time. In such cases the overbought readings tend to give premature warnings of declines. During the early phases of the bull cycle, when the market possesses strong momentum, reactions to the oversold level are much more responsive to price reversals and such readings therefore offer more reliable signals. *It is only when a bull trend is maturing, or during bear phases, that overbought levels can be relied upon to signal that a rally is shortly to be aborted.* The very fact that an indicator is unable to remain at, or even to achieve, an overbought reading for long is itself a signal that the advance is losing momentum. The opposite is true for a bear trend.

A further indication of the maturity of a trend is given when the momentum index moves strongly in one direction but the accompanying move in the price index is a much smaller one. Such a development suggests that the price index is tired of moving in the direction of the prevailing trend, for despite a strong push of energy from the momentum index, prices are unable to respond. This unusual, but powerful, phenomenon is illustrated for both tops and bottoms in Figure 9.4, examples *a* and *b*.

Notwithstanding the above, an overbought reading is generally a point at which one should think about selling or certainly taking profits, while an oversold reading indicates a good place to buy. Again, the market "leash" is made of rubber and can remain in overbought or oversold territory for long periods. Consequently, it is essential to get confirmation from a reversal in the trend of the price itself before taking any drastic action.

In most cases, excellent buy and sell alerts are generated when the momentum indicator exceeds its extended overbought or oversold boundary and then recrosses back through the boundary on its way to zero. Figure 9.5 demonstrates this possibility. This approach filters out

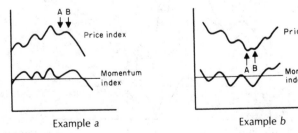

Example *a*   Example *b*

Figure 9.4.

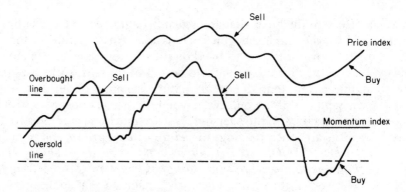

Figure 9.5. Overbought oversold crossovers.

a lot of premature buy and sell signals generated as the indicator just reaches its overextended boundary, but one should still wait for a trend reversal in the price itself before taking action.

2. Divergences

The ball example used at the beginning of the chapter showed that maximum velocity was obtained fairly close to the point at which the ball leaves the hand. Similarly, prices in financial markets usually reach their maximum level of momentum ahead of the final peak in prices. In Figure 9.6 this is shown at point A. If the price makes a new high which is confirmed by the momentum index, no indication of technical weakness arises. On the other hand, if momentum fails to confirm (point B), a *negative* divergence is set up between the two series, and a warning of a weakening technical structure is given. Such discrepancies normally in-

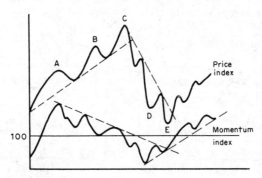

Figure 9.6.

dicate that the price will undergo a corrective process. This process can take the form of either a sideways or a horizontal trading range, or (more likely) a downward one. However, the price will sometimes continue upward to a third top and be accompanied by even greater weakness in the momentum index (point *C*). Occasionally, the third peak in the momentum index may be higher than the second but lower than the first. Either circumstance requires some degree of caution, since this characteristic is a distinct warning of a sharp reversal in price or a long corrective period.

It is extremely important to note that a negative divergence only warns of a weakening market condition and does not represent an actual signal to sell.

Whenever any divergence between momentum and price occurs, it is essential to wait for a confirmation from the price itself that its trend has also been reversed. This confirmation can be achieved by (1) the violation of a simple trendline, as shown in Figure 9.6 and Chart 9.1, (2) the crossover of an MA, or (3) the completion of a price pattern. This form of insurance is well worth taking, since it is not unknown for an index to continually lose and regain momentum without suffering a break in trend during a long cyclical advance. Examples of this phenomenon occurred during the 1962–1966 bull market in U.S. stocks, and in Japanese stocks between 1982 and 1987.

Chart 9.1. The Hang Seng Index (weekly) and an advance warning of a top. The price action of the Hang Seng Index experienced no sign of distribution prior to the 1987 crash. However, the 39-week ROC indicator had been showing signs of weakness for several months. (*Source: Pring Market Review.*)

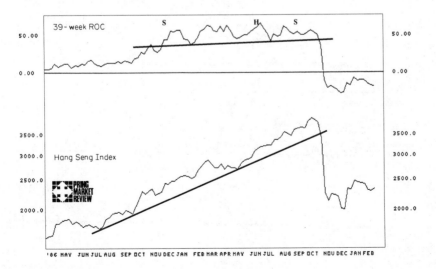

As a general rule, the greater the number of negative divergences, the weaker the underlying structure. At point *C* in Figure 9.6 the price moves to a significant new high, but the momentum index is barely able to remain above the 100 reference line. Such a situation demands the utmost caution *when accompanied by a trend break,* for it is usually a sign of extreme technical weakness and is often followed by a very sharp decline. The opposite type of situation in a bear market should be viewed as a very positive characteristic, especially if the upward trend break in price is accompanied by high volume. The more explosive the volume, the more reliable the signal is likely to be.

A good example of price and momentum interaction can be seen in Chart 9.2, which shows the Nikkei Dow violating an important 3½-year secondary trendline after the 13-week ROC indicator had negatively diverged several times with the index. As a result, the final rally was accompanied by very little in the way of upside momentum. It would have been a mistake to sell on any of the prior divergences, but a very timely sell signal was generated by waiting for a confirmation in the form of a trend break in the index itself.

Chart 9.2. The Nikkei Dow and a 13-week ROC indicator. This chart shows how the Nikkei worked its way higher between 1987 and 1990, but the momentum indicator was tracing out a series of four declining peaks. Those were confirmed when the 1986–1990 trendline was violated.

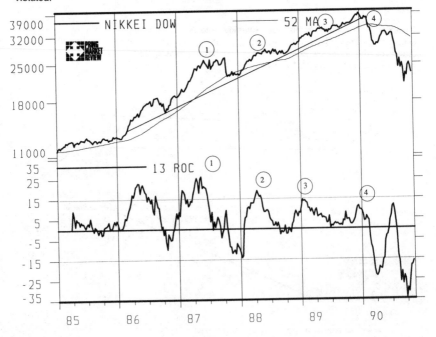

In a sense it is possible to equate momentum divergences and price trend breaks with dark clouds and rain. If you look up at the sky and observe dark clouds, common sense tells you that it will probably rain, but you don't know for sure until you can hold out your hand and actually feel rain falling. In other words, the clouds (like the divergences) warn of the deteriorating weather (technical condition), but the change in weather is signaled only by the first raindrop (reversal in the price). It is possible to take the analogy a step further by concluding that the darker the clouds (the greater the number of divergences), the heavier the rainstorm (the sharper the price decline) will be.

3. Complex Divergences

It is widely recognized that price movements are simultaneously influenced by several cyclic phenomena. Because a single momentum indicator can monitor only one of these cycles, it is always a good idea to compare several different momentum indicators based on differing time spans.

One approach is to plot two momentum indicators of differing time spans on the same chart, as shown in Figure 9.7. Since this method tries to monitor two separate cycles, it's as well to choose two widely different time spans. For example, not much could be gained from the comparison of a 12- and a 13-week ROC since they would move very closely

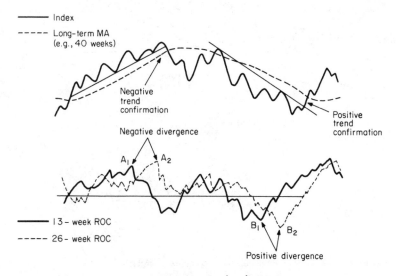

Figure 9.7. Momentum interpretation—complex divergences.

together. On the other hand, a combination of 13- and 26-week spans would clearly reflect different cycles. An approximation of this idea is shown in Figure 9.7.

Most of the time the two indicators are moving in gear, so this study does not give us much information. On the other hand, when the longer-term indicator reaches a new peak and the shorter one is at or close to the horizontal line, they are clearly in disagreement or out of gear (point A_2, Figure 9.7). This normally, but not necessarily, indicates that a reversal in trend will take place, and it's usually an important one. Even so, it is very important to make sure that any such divergence is confirmed by a reversal in the price trend itself. In Figure 9.7 a trend break does occur, but in Figure 9.8 no reversal took place and the price continued on upward.

Complex divergences also occur in a positive combination as indicated at point B_1 in Figure 9.7, but again, it is mandatory to wait for that trend-reversal signal in the price itself.

An example using the West German deutsch mark with a 13- and a 26-week ROC is shown in Chart 30.6. Typically, both ROC indexes move in the same direction. A warning sign of an important change in trend is given when the two series diverge noticeably, as in late 1980,

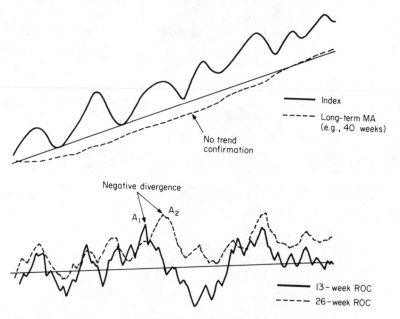

Figure 9.8. Momentum interpretation—complex divergences (*continued*).

early 1982, and mid-1983. Each occurrence was followed by an important sell-off.

4. Trendline Violations

Occasionally the momentum index peaks simultaneously with price (as shown in Figure 9.9). Under these circumstances, no advance warning of an imminent price decline is given. Nevertheless, a clue to potential weakness is given when a trendline joining a series of troughs in the momentum indicator is violated.

The construction and significance of the break should be based on the principles outlined in Chapter 7. This type of momentum weakness must be regarded as an alert, and action should be taken only when confirmed by a break in the price trend itself (indicated by line *AA* in Figure 9.9). In effect the momentum trend break is reinforcing the price trend break, and it offers an additional piece of evidence that the trend has reversed.

5. Momentum Price Patterns

Momentum indexes are also capable of tracing out price patterns. Because of the shorter lead times normally associated with reversals of falling momentum, a breakout from an accumulation pattern, when accompanied by a reversal in the downward trend of the index itself, is usually a highly reliable indication that a worthwhile move has just begun. An example is shown in Figure 9.10 and Chart 9.3.

It is important to use a little common sense in interpreting momentum price patterns. Figure 9.11, for example, shows a breakout from a

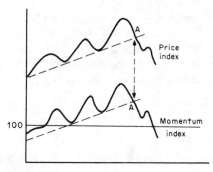

Figure 9.9.

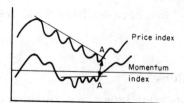

Figure 9.10.

Chart 9.3. Carnival Cruise Lines and a 20-day ROC indicator. This chart of Carnival Cruise Lines shows the completion of an H&S top in the 20-week momentum indicator, and a trendline and price pattern break in the price itself in September 1989. In March 1990 a reverse H&S and a price trendline break occurred simultaneously. The continuation of the price trendline involved use of a little poetic license. While the October 1989 rally broke through the line, it nevertheless represented the underlying (down) trend since it was touched or approached on numerous occasions. (*Source: Pring Market Review.*)

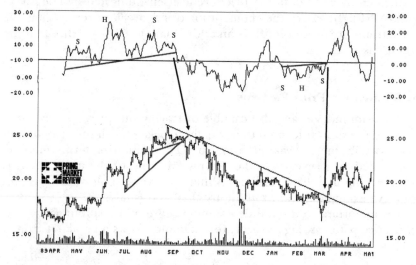

reverse head-and-shoulders (H&S) pattern that takes place as a result of an overbought condition. This is not to say that such signals will never be valid, but it stands to reason that a breakout from an extreme level is very unlikely to result in a sustainable price move. Remember, technical analysis deals with probabilities, and the odds of a favorable outcome in this case are low.

6. Equilibrium Crossovers

Some technicians have devised indicators that offer buy and sell signals when the momentum indicator crosses above and below its equilibrium

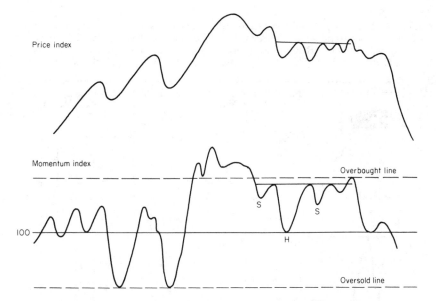

Figure 9.11. Pattern completion continued, pattern failure from overbought level.

or zero line. Many markets do not lend themselves to this approach, so its implementation depends very much on a trial-and-error basis through experimentation. In any event it is always a good idea to use this method in conjunction with a reversal in the price itself. Chart 9.4 shows how zero crossovers used in conjunction with 12-month MA crossovers consistently gave buy signals for the Economist All Items Commodity Index.

7. Momentum and Moving Averages

By now it is apparent that all the trend-determining techniques used for price are also applicable to momentum. Interpretation of momentum indexes, as described above, depends to a considerable extent on judgment. One method of reducing this subjectivity is to smooth the ROC index by using an MA. Warnings of a probable trend reversal in the price being monitored are offered by MA crossovers, as in Figure 9.12.

One of the problems associated with this approach is that the momentum indicator is often much more jagged than the price index that it is trying to measure, causing generation of an unacceptable number of whipsaw signals. It is possible to filter out some of these whipsaws by using a combination of two MAs, as shown in Figure 9.13. Buy and sell

Chart 9.4. The Economist All Items Commodity Index and a 12-month ROC indicator. Very good buy signals have been generated for the Economist All Items (dollar) Commodity Index when its 12-month ROC indicator crossed above zero. Also worthy of note is the 2½-year H&S top in this oscillator that was associated with a 7-year high in the price index

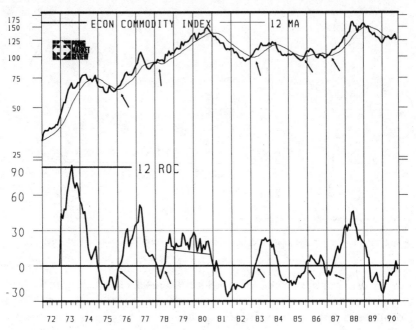

alerts are given when the shorter-term MA crosses above or below its longer-term counterpart.

This interpretation of momentum is explained in greater detail in the next chapter, since momentum forms the basis of the trend deviation and MACD indicators.

8. Smoothed Momentum Indicators

Another way of incorporating MAs into momentum studies is to smooth the momentum indicator by a long-term MA. The meaning of "long-term" in this case will depend on the type of trend being monitored. For example, a 20- to 30-day time span would be suitable for a short-term price movement, but a 6-, 9-, or even 12-month smoothing is more appropriate for a primary trend. Warnings of a probable trend reversal in the price would be offered by a reversal in the smoothed momentum index itself, shown in Figure 9.14, example *a*, or by a penetration of the

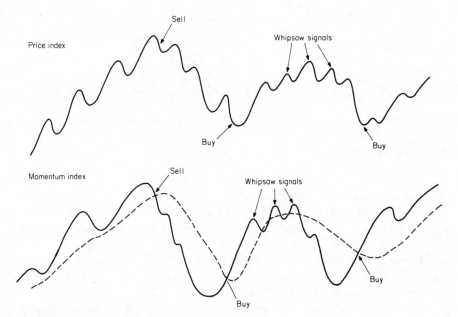

Figure 9.12. MA crossovers.

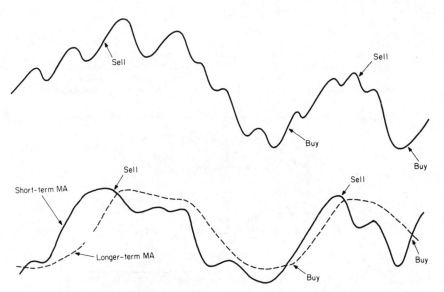

Figure 9.13. MA crossovers smoothed.

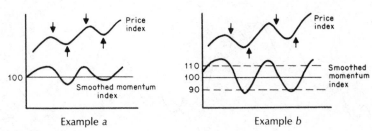

Example *a*   Example *b*

Figure 9.14.

MA through a designated overbought or oversold level, as in example *b*. The level of the dashed overbought and oversold barrier would be determined on a trial-and-error basis, with reference to a historical study of the relationship between the price and the momentum curve.

If the momentum curve is found to be unduly volatile, it is always possible to smooth out fluctuations by calculating an even longer-term MA, or by smoothing the MA itself with an additional calculation.

Another possibility is to construct a momentum index by combining the MAs of three or four ROCs and weighting them according to their time span. This possibility is discussed at length in Chapter 10.

Chart 9.5 shows the effectiveness of combining two smoothed ROC indicators. In this case the smoothing is a 10-month weighted average of 11- and 14-month rates of change of Dow Jones Industrial Average

Chart 9.5. Long-term price momentum indicator, 1960–1975. This momentum indicator has a long history of successful buy signals and is plotted up to December 1975 on this chart. It turned up in the following month and successfully confirmed the 1974–1976 bull market. (*Source: Derived from data developed by E. S. C. Coppock, Trendex Research, San Antonio, Tex.*)

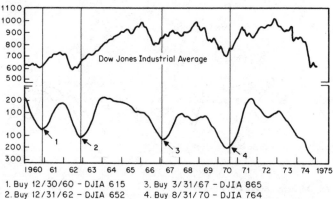

1. Buy 12/30/60 – DJIA 615   3. Buy 3/31/67 – DJIA 865
2. Buy 12/31/62 – DJIA 652   4. Buy 8/31/70 – DJIA 764

(DJIA) monthly closing prices. Since this indicator has been found useful for market bottoms rather than tops, the momentum curve is significant only when it falls below the 0 reference line and then rises.

A further variation on construction of a smoothed momentum index is to take the ROC of an MA of a price index itself. This method reverses the process described above, for instead of constructing an ROC and then smoothing the resulting momentum index, the price index itself is first smoothed with an MA, and an ROC is taken of that smoothing.

Summary

1. Momentum measures the rate at which prices rise or fall. It gives useful indications of latent strength or weakness in a price trend. This is because prices usually rise at their fastest pace well ahead of their peak, and normally decline at their greatest speed before their ultimate low.

2. Since markets generally spend more time in a rising than a falling phase, the lead characteristic of momentum indicators is normally greater during rallies than during reactions.

3. Markets are usually more sensitive to (i.e., more likely to reverse from) an oversold condition in an uptrend, and to an overbought reading in a downtrend.

4. Under certain circumstances the *level* of momentum can also be used to predict a reversal in the price trend itself.

5. An extremely overbought condition at the beginning of a bull market is a sign of strength and is the exception to the rule that overbought conditions represent a weak technical condition.

6. Momentum signals should *always* be used in conjunction with a trend-reversal signal by the actual price.

10
Momentum II

We will examine a number of specific momentum indicators in this chapter. It is recommended that you study them all and then choose two or three in which you have confidence and with which you intuitively feel comfortable. Following too many indicators will be likely to lead to confusion.

The RSI

The relative strength indicator (RSI) was developed by Wells Wilder.[1] It's a momentum indicator, or oscillator, that measures the relative internal strength of a stock or market against *itself*, instead of comparing one asset with another, or a stock with a market. The formula for the RSI is as follows:

$$RSI = 100 - \left[\frac{100}{1 + RS} \right]$$

where RS = the average of x days' up closes divided by the average of x days' down closes. The formula aims to overcome two problems involved in construction of a momentum indicator: (1) erratic movements and (2) the need for a constant trading band for comparison purposes. Erratic movements are caused by sharp alterations in the values, which are dropped off in the calculation. For example, in a 20-day rate-of-change (ROC) indicator, a sharp decline or advance 20 days in the past can cause sudden shifts in the momentum line even if the current price is little changed. The RSI attempts to smooth out such distortions.

The RSI formula not only provides this smoothing characteristic but

---

[1] *New Concepts in Technical Trading Systems,* Trend Research, Greensboro, N.C., 1978.

also results in an indicator that fluctuates in a constant range between 0 and 100. Overbought and oversold lines are traditionally drawn at the 70 and 30 levels. The RSI can be plotted for any time span. Wilder recommended a 14-day period, but some people argue that a 22-day span is more accurate. A 9-day span works well for *very* short term movements. Remember, the shorter the time period, the greater the swings up and down. Shorter-term time spans help to point out overbought and oversold conditions, but since they are not very useful for the purpose of constructing trendlines or price patterns, there is a bit of a trade-off.

In an article entitled "How RSI Behaves,"[2] Peter W. Aan argued that the average value of an RSI top and bottom occurred close to the 72 and 32 levels, respectively. This research would indicate that the 70 and 30 levels recommended by Wilder should be moved further apart to better reflect the average overbought and oversold value.

The volatility of the RSI is considerably reduced when longer periods are taken into consideration, and thus the frequency at which the market moves to the extreme overbought and oversold bands can be manipulated by changing the time span.

The RSI can also be constructed from weekly and monthly data. For longer-term charts, covering perhaps 2 years of weekly data, a time span of about 8 weeks offers enough information to identify intermediate-term turning points. A 26-week RSI results in a momentum series that oscillates in a narrower range, but nevertheless usually lends itself to trendline construction. Very long term charts, going back 10 to 20 years, seem to respond well to a 12-month time span. Crossovers of the 30 percent oversold and 70 percent overbought barriers give a very good idea of major long-term buying and selling points. When the RSI pushes through these extremes and then crosses back toward the 50 level, it often warns of a reversal in the primary trend.

To isolate major buy candidates, it's important to remember that the best opportunities lie where long-term momentum, such as a 12-month RSI, is oversold. If you can also identify an intermediate- and a short-term oversold condition, all three trends—primary, intermediate-term, and short-term—are then in a classic conjunction to give a high-probability buy signal.

RSI Interpretation

Some of the principal methods used to interpret the RSI are reviewed in the following sections.

[2]*Futures*, January 1985.

Extreme Readings and Failure Swings. Any time an RSI moves above the 70 level, or below the 30, it indicates an overbought or oversold condition. The significance depends upon the time frame under consideration. For example, an overbought reading in a 9-day RSI (as shown in Chart 10.1) is nowhere near as significant as an RSI constructed with a 12-month time span (Chart 10.2). An overbought or oversold reading merely indicates that, in terms of probabilities, a counterreaction is overdone or overdue. It presents an *opportunity* to consider liquidation or acquisition, but not an *actual* buy or sell signal. This can come *only* when the price series itself gives a trend-reversal signal.

More often than not, the RSI traces out a divergence, as indicated in Figure 10.1. In this case the second crossover of the extreme level at points *A* and *B* *usually* offers good buy and sell alerts. These divergences are often called *failure swings*.

Trendline Violations and Pattern Completions. The RSI can also be used in conjunction with trendline violations. Generally speaking, the longer the time span for any particular period (i.e., daily, weekly, or monthly), the better the opportunity for trendline construction. Important buy and sell signals are generated when trendlines for both price

Chart 10.1. New York Light Crude and a 9-day RSI. A very short term RSI is constantly moving from overbought to oversold. It also reaches greater extremes than an RSI with a larger span.

Chart 10.2. Gold and a 12-month RSI.

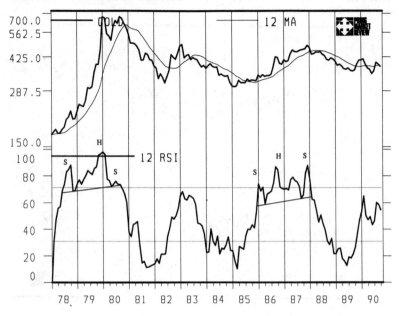

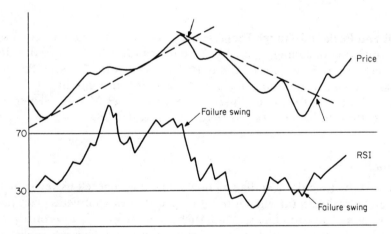

Figure 10.1.

and the RSI are violated within a relatively short period (see Chart 10.3).

An example of the RSI's ability to form price patterns is shown in Chart 10.2, where two sell alerts in 1980 and 1988 were soon confirmed by negative 12-month moving-average (MA) crossovers in the gold price.

Chart 10.3. The deutsch mark and a 52-week RSI. The weekly deutsch mark-dollar relationship is shown, using a 52-week RSI.

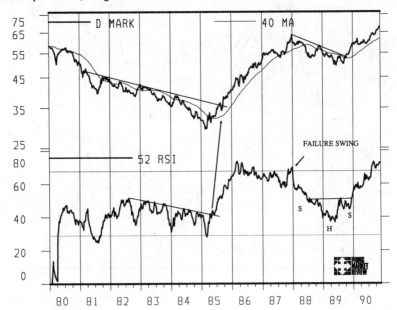

RSI and Peak-and-Trough Progression. The RSI often traces out a series of rising or falling peaks and troughs which, when reversed, offer important buy or sell alerts. Chart 10.4 shows that the 52-week RSI for gold reversed a declining series of peaks and troughs in 1985, just around the time the price crossed above its 40-week MA. A sell alert by the RSI on the same lines was *confirmed* in early 1988.

Conclusion

Most of the time the RSI, like all oscillators, does not tell us very much. It can be really useful when it triggers divergences, completes price patterns, or violates trendlines. When such an occurrence is *also* confirmed by a trend-reversal signal in the price itself, it is usually a wise policy to pay attention, because the RSI has a good record of reliability.

Trend Deviation

A trend-deviation indicator is obtained by dividing a market price or stock price by an MA. Since the average represents the trend being

Chart 10.4. Gold and the 52-week RSI.

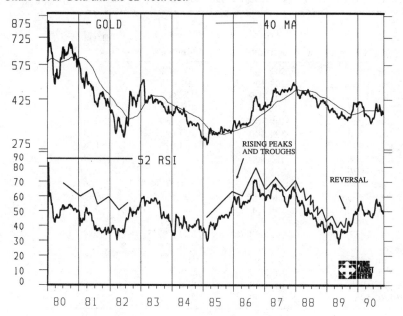

monitored, the momentum indicator shows how fast the price is advancing or declining in relation to that trend. An oscillator based on a trend-deviation calculation is in fact a horizontal representation of the envelope analysis discussed in Chapter 8. Examples *a* and *b* in Figure 10.2 show these two approaches for the same indicator. The upper and lower envelopes are both drawn at a level that is 10 percent from the actual MA, which means that when the price touches the 100 line, it is really at the same level as the MA. When the momentum index is at 110, the price index is 10 percent above its MA, and so on.

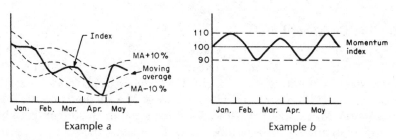

Figure 10.2.

Table 10.1. Gold Price and 30-Day Deviation Calculation

Date	(1) P.M. fix	(2) 30-day MA	(3) Deviation (1) ÷ (2)
12 Dec. 1986	391.500	395.627	0.990
15 Dec. 1986	394.300	395.403	0.997
16 Dec. 1986	393.100	394.967	0.995
17 Dec. 1986	392.000	394.433	0.994
18 Dec. 1986	390.750	393.950	0.992
19 Dec. 1986	394.800	393.493	1.003
22 Dec. 1986	393.025	393.025	1.000
23 Dec. 1986	389.200	392.307	0.992
24 Dec. 1986	391.000	391.807	0.998
26 Dec. 1986	391.000	391.273	0.999
29 Dec. 1986	390.100	390.693	0.998
30 Dec. 1986	388.750	390.430	0.997
31 Dec. 1986	401.900	390.357	1.030
02 Jan. 1987	403.500	390.773	1.033
05 Jan. 1987	398.950	390.958	1.020
06 Jan. 1987	401.700	391.370	1.026
07 Jan. 1987	400.400	391.777	1.022
08 Jan. 1987	402.650	392.515	1.026
09 Jan. 1987	402.000	393.123	1.023

This indicator provides essentially the same information as the envelope analysis, but it also shows subtle changes of underlying technical strength and weakness.

The calculation for a 30-day trend deviation for the gold price using a simple MA is illustrated in Table 10.1.

The interpretation of a trend-deviation indicator is based on the same principles described in Chapter 9. This method can be used to identify divergences and overbought and oversold zones, but it appears to come into its own when used in conjunction with trendline construction and MA crossovers.

Trendline Construction

Chart 10.5 shows the Dow Jones Basic Materials Index between 1982 and 1990. This series is constructed from various basic industry stocks such as steels, chemicals, and papers. Underneath is a trend-deviation indicator, which is constructed from a 3-week MA of the close divided by a 40-week MA, lagged by 10 weeks. I have found this formula to be very useful in analysis of a number of different markets.

Most of the time the indicator does not give actionable information,

Chart 10.5. The Dow Jones Basic Materials Index and a trend-deviation indicator.

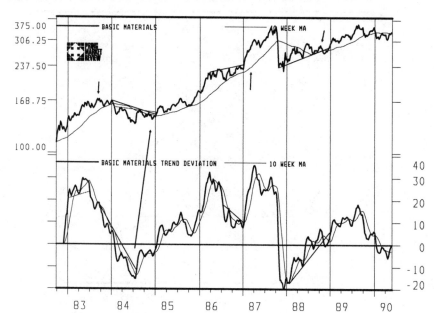

but occasionally a trendline that has been touched at least twice may be constructed. Violation of such a line almost invariably indicates a significant reversal in trend of the price being monitored. Even so, it is very important to make sure that the signal is confirmed by some kind of trend reversal in the price itself.

In the example in Chart 10.5, the trendline violation of the deviation indicator that occurred in mid-1984 was later confirmed by the completion of a small reverse head-and-shoulders (H&S) pattern and by a positive MA crossover in the Basic Materials Index itself. Two joint upside breakouts occurred in January 1987.

The failure of a joint trend break in late 1988 illustrates the point that this approach is by no means infallible, even though the odds will generally work in your favor.

Trend Deviation and MAs

The example in Chart 10.5 incorporates a slight smoothing of the raw data, but even that results in a fairly volatile and random affair. An alternative approach would be to smooth out this volatility with the aid of two MAs, as shown in Chart 10.6. The actual trend-deviation series is

Chart 10.6. The Dow Jones Basic Materials Index and a smoothed trend-deviation indicator.

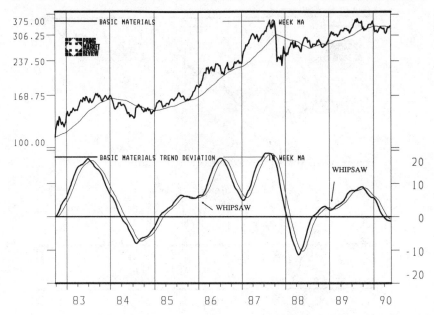

calculated by taking a 26-week MA of the closing price divided by a 40-week MA. The second series is simply a 10-week MA of the first. Buy and sell alerts are then triggered as the smoothed trend-deviation indicator crosses above or below its 10-week MA. This approach worked quite well over most of the period covered by the chart, but there were two whipsaw signals in 1985 and late 1988. In both instances the deviation indicator slipped below its MA and then quickly crossed back above it.

A useful method that greatly reduces such whipsaw activity but still offers timely signals is to lag the 40-week MA by 10 weeks when the trend-deviation calculation is being made. This means that each weekly close is divided by the 40-week MA as it appeared 10 weeks before. This new calculation has been plotted in Chart 10.7. In this example both whipsaws have been filtered out since the trend-deviation indicator fails to cross decisively below its MA.

MACD

The moving-average convergence divergence (MACD) trading method is an oscillator constructed from the division of one MA by another.

Chart 10.7. The Dow Jones Basic Materials Index and a smoothed trend-deviation indicator.

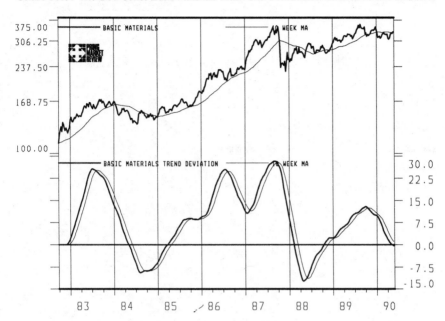

The two MAs are usually calculated on an exponential basis in which more recent periods are more heavily weighted than in the case of a simple MA.

Chart 10.8*a* shows the gold price at the end of 1989 and the beginning of 1990. The solid line represents the price, and the dashed line represents a short-term exponential moving average (EMA). The dotted line is a longer-term average. In the bottom half of Chart 10.8*b* the closing price has been eliminated, leaving the two EMAs.

The MACD shown at the top of Chart 10.8*b* expresses the relationship of these two EMAs in an oscillator format by dividing the shorter MA by the longer one. The horizontal equilibrium line represents the points at which the two EMAs are at identical levels. When the indicator moves through this line, it means that the short-term MA is crossing the longer one. Plots below the horizontal line indicate when the shorter MA is below the longer one and vice versa. For example, since the short MA crosses the longer-term MA at points *A* and *B*, this is where the MACD oscillator moves below and above the horizontal, or equilibrium, level.

The oscillator gets its name from the fact that the shorter MA is continually converging toward and diverging from the longer-term one.

Chart 10.8. (a) Comex gold. (b) Comex gold and a 9- to 15-day MACD.

(a)

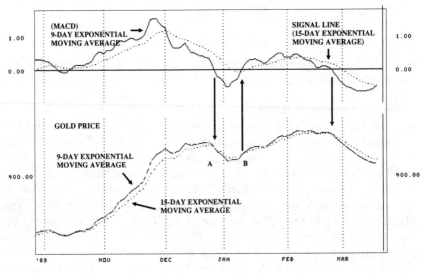

(b)

Chart 10.9. Homestake Mining and an MACD in histogram format. This chart shows a classic upward-sloping H&S pattern. Note that the MACD histogram gradually became weaker as the pattern progressed. This was only a short-term sell signal, but the price eventually fell below the signal level. (*Source: Telescan.*)

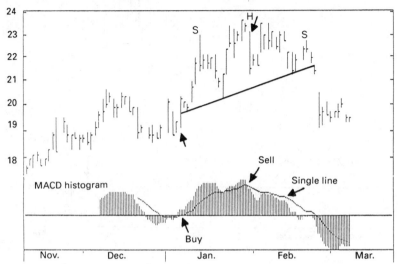

Some technicians use these equilibrium crosses as buy and sell signals, but the MACD system can be expanded to include an additional EMA, known as the *signal line*. This third average is obtained from an MA of the oscillator itself and is also shown in Chart 10.8*b*. Buy and sell alerts are triggered when the oscillator crosses above or below the signal line. The oscillator is sometimes plotted as a histogram and the MA as a solid line, as in Chart 10.9. These examples are shown in Charts 10.10 and 10.11.

MACDs can be used in an infinite number of different time periods. Gerald Appel, of Signalert,[3] who has done a considerable amount of research on the subject, recommends that buy signals on a daily chart be constructed from a combination of 8, 17, and 9 exponential MAs, but he feels that sell signals are more reliable when triggered on the basis of a 12, 25, and 9 combination.

Stochastics

The stochastic indicator has gained a great deal of popularity among futures traders, with the result that the standard formula uses very

[3]150 Great Neck Road, Great Neck, NY 11021.

Chart 10.10. Homestake Mining and an MACD in histogram format. This chart plots a histogram of the difference between the signal line and the histogram in Chart 10.9. Zero crossovers occur when the histogram in Chart 10.9 crosses above or below the signal line. Note that the momentum indicator in this chart gets progressively weaker to the extent that it is well into negative territory when the right shoulder is being formed. (*Source: Telescan.*)

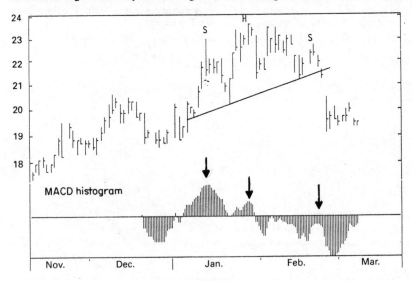

Chart 10.11. Echo Bay Mines showing a price pattern formed by an MACD. This chart of Echo Bay Mines shows an MACD histogram together with a signal line. Crossovers of the signal line were not very useful (as is often the case). However, there were two important trendline breaks that did give good signals. An upside trendline violation occurred in mid-1986. More important, the histogram traced out an H&S top between 1986 and 1987. This should have caused the cautious investor to bail out just as the histogram was completing its top in late 1987. However, an actual bearish signal did not materialize until mid-1968, when a significant price trendline was violated. (*Source: Telescan.*)

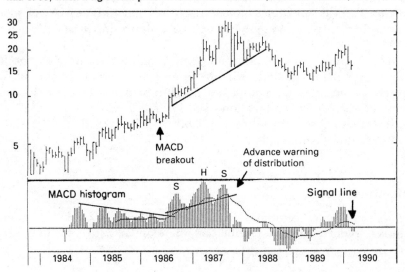

short term time spans. The theory behind the indicator, which was invented by George Lane,[4] is that prices tend to close near the upper end of a trading range during an uptrend. As the trend matures, the tendency for prices to close away from the higher end of the trading range becomes pronounced. In a downward-moving market the reverse conditions hold true.

The stochastic indicator therefore attempts to measure the points in a rising trend at which the closing prices tend to cluster around the lows for the period in question, and vice versa, since these are the conditions which signal trend reversals. It is plotted as two lines, the %K line and the %D line. The %D line is the one that provides the major signals and is therefore more important.

The formula for calculation of %K is

$$\%K = 100[(C - L5\text{close})/(H5 - L5)]$$

where C is the most recent close, $L5$ is the lowest low for the last five trading periods, and $H5$ is the highest high for the same five trading periods. Remember that the calculation of stochastics differs from that of most other momentum indicators in that it requires high, low, and closing data for the period in question.

The stochastic formula is similar to the RSI in that the plots can never exceed 0 or 100, but in this case it measures the closing price in relation to the total price range for a selected number of periods. A very high reading, in excess of 80, would put the closing price for the period near the top of the range, while a low reading, under 20, would put it near the bottom of the range.

The second line, %D, is a smoothed version of the %K line. The normal value is three periods. The %D formula is as follows:

$$\%D = 100 \times (H3/L3)$$

where $H3$ is the 3-period sum of $(C - L5)$ and $L3$ is the 3-period sum of $(H5 - L5)$.

The momentum indicator that results from these calculations is two lines that fluctuate between 0 and 100. The %K line is usually plotted as a solid line, while the slower %D line is usually plotted as a dashed line.

The popularity of the stochastic indicator can no doubt be explained by the smooth manner in which it moves from an overbought to an oversold condition, lulling a trader into a feeling that price trends are much more orderly than would appear from an observation of an RSI or an ROC indicator.

[4]Investment Educators Incorporated, Des Plaines, IL 60018.

Longer-term time frames, used on monthly and weekly charts, appear to work much better than the shorter-term stochastics used on daily futures charts. Colby and Meyers, in *The Encyclopedia of Technical Market Indicators,*[5] noted that the stochastic indicator tested very poorly relative to MA crossovers and other momentum indicators.

Overbought and oversold bands for stochastics are usually plotted in the 75 to 85 percent area on the upside and in the 15 to 25 percent area on the downside, depending on the time span in question. An overbought indication is given when the %D line crosses the extreme band, but an actual sell alert is not indicated until the %K line crosses below it. When the two lines cross, they behave very similarly to a dual MA system. If you wait for the penetration, you can avoid getting trapped into shorting a strongly bullish move or buying an extremely negative one.

General Interpretation

Crossovers.   Normally the faster %K line changes direction sooner than the %D line. This means that the crossover will occur before the %D line has reversed direction, as in Figure 10.3, example *a*. When the %D line reverses direction first, a slow, stable change of direction is indicated, and %D is regarded as a more reliable signal. (See Figure 10.3, example *b*.)

Divergence Failure.   An important indication of a possible change in trend arises when the %K line crosses the %D line, moves back to test its extreme level, and fails to cross the %D line, as in Figure 10.4.

Reverse Divergence.   Occasionally the %D line will make a lower low, which is associated with a higher low in the price (Figure 10.5). This is a bearish omen, and conventional wisdom suggests looking for a selling opportunity on the next rally. This condition is sometimes referred to as a *bear setup*.

Extremes.   Occasionally the %K value reaches the extreme of 100 or 0. This indicates that a very powerful move is under way, since the price is consistently closing near its high or low. If a successful test of this extreme occurs following a pullback, it is usually an excellent entry point.

[5]Robert W. Colby and Thomas A. Meyers, *The Encyclopedia of Technical Market Indicators,* Dow Jones–Irwin, Homewood, Ill., 1988.

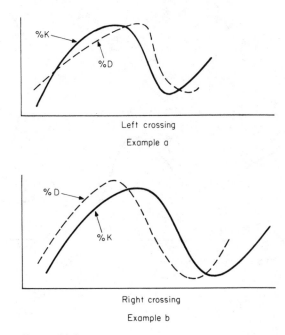

Left crossing

Example a

Right crossing

Example b

Figure 10.3.

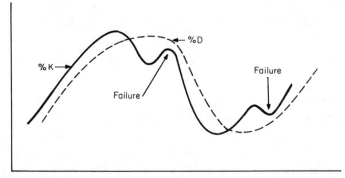

Figure 10.4. Failure.

Hinge.   When either the %K line or the %D line experiences a slow-down in velocity, indicated by a flattening line, the indication is usually that a reversal will take place in the next period (Figure 10.6).

Divergences.   The stochastic indicator often sets up positive and negative divergences in a similar manner to other oscillators. Some possi-

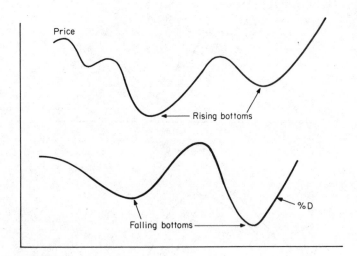

Figure 10.5. Reverse divergence.

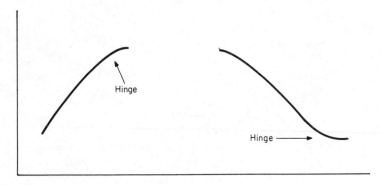

Figure 10.6.

bilities are indicated in Figure 10.7. Buy and sell alerts are triggered when the %K line crosses %D after a divergence has taken place.

Slowed Stochastic.   It is also possible to extend the calculation in order to invoke a slowed version of stochastics. In this instance the %K line is replaced with the %D line, and another MA is calculated for the %D. Many technicians argue that this modified stochastic version gives more accurate signals. Charts 10.12 and 10.13 show a shorter- and a longer-term stochastic indicator respectively.

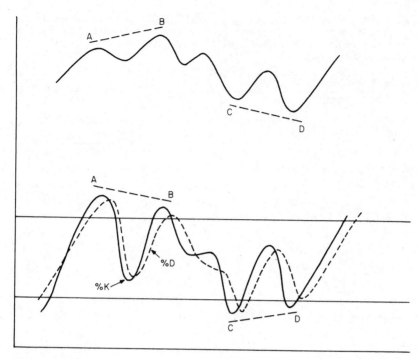

Figure 10.7.

Chart 10.12. Schlumberger and a 5%K, 5%D stochastics indicator.

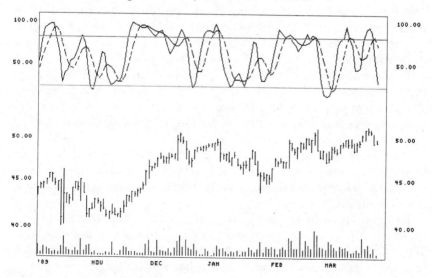

Chart 10.13. London 3-Month Copper and an 18%K, 10%D stochastics indicator. Longer-term stochastics indicators have a tendency to give better buy and sell signals as the crossovers from extreme levels take place. In this respect, a timely sell alert was given at the end of 1988 and a buy signal in mid-1989.

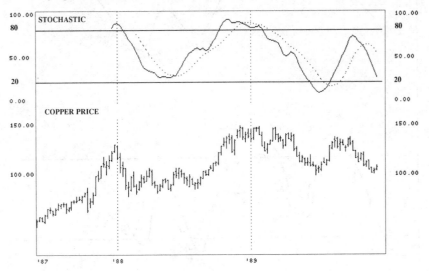

Summed ROC: "Know Sure Thing" (KST)

Chapter 9 explained that ROC measures the speed of an advance or decline over a specific time span and is calculated by dividing the price in the current period by the price N periods ago. The longer the time span under consideration, the greater the significance of the trend being measured. Movements in a 10-day ROC are far less meaningful than those calculated over a 12- or 24-month time span.

The use of an ROC indicator helps to explain some of the cyclical movements in markets, often giving advance warning of a reversal in the prevailing trend. This method comes into its own during wide-trading-range markets, but gives misleading signals when a sustained or linear trend is under way.

Another problem is that a specific time frame used in an ROC calculation reflects only one cycle. If that particular cycle is not operating, is dominated by another one, or is dominated by a combination of cycles, it will be of little value.

This point is illustrated in Chart 10.14, which shows three ROC indicators of different time spans—6 months, 12 months, and 24 months. The solid vertical lines show that at major market turning points all three series also reverse direction. In other words, the first intermediate bull market rally is associated with a bottoming in a number of dif-

Chart 10.14. S&P Composite and three ROC indicators.

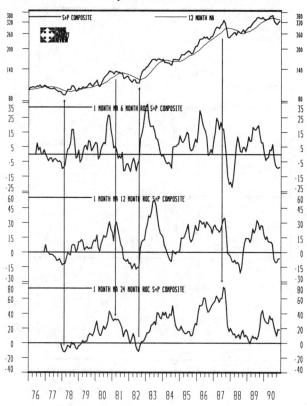

ferent indicators. In a similar vein, the dashed vertical lines show how bear markets start with all three momentum series in a declining mode. It's important to note that at no time during the 1982–1987 advance were *all three* series falling simultaneously. This did not occur until October 1987.

Chart 10.15 shows these same indicators, but this time they have been smoothed so that the direction of their cyclical swings can be identified more easily. The 6-month series is the first to turn, followed by the 12- and 24-month indicators. The 6-month ROC is much more sensitive to price swings and therefore is more timely on most occasions. At other times, it turns long before the data series itself reverses, giving an unduly premature signal. Cycles in the 6-month indicator are not always reflected in 12- or 24-month momentum series, because the price movements are not always of sufficient magnitude to be picked up by the longer-term time spans.

Chart 10.15. S&P Composite and three smoothed ROC indicators.

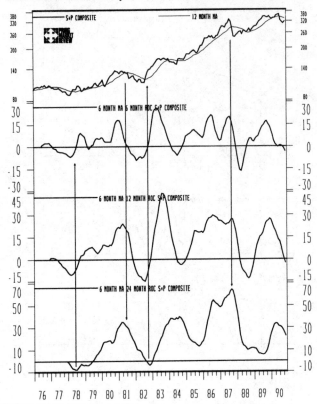

The 6-month series explains virtually every intermediate-term move in the market, but the longer-term 24-month indicator better reflects the major market movements. For example, the mid-1971 bull market correction barely affected the 24-month smoothing but resulted in a major swing for the 6-month indicator.

Several characteristics can be observed from these relationships.

1. The smoothed 24-month ROC sets the scene, or background, for the major move.

2. The strongest price trends usually occur when all three curves move simultaneously in the same direction, e.g., in 1973–1974, early 1975, late 1982, and late 1987.

3. If the 24-month ROC peaks out when the 6- or the 12-month series,

or both, are rising, the implied decline is normally mild because the cycles are conflicting. This has the effect of cushioning a decline or, in the 1984–1985 instance, permitting a gentle advance.

4. If the 24-month indicator is in a rising mode when the 6- and 9-month indicators peak out, the implied decline is either mild or short-lived.

This graphic arrangement can be very instructive, but it does not provide an easily identifiable and objective timing mechanism. One solution is to combine four smoothed ROCs into one indicator, weighting each one in rough proportion to its time span.

Chart 10.16 shows a summed ROC for the U.S. stock market, using this concept. The momentum series has been constructed from smoothed 9-, 12-, 18-, and 24-month ROCs. In this calculation the first three periods are smoothed with a 6-month MA, whereas the 24-month time span is smoothed with a 9-month MA. The resulting series are then weighted in proportion to their respective time spans. This means that the 24-month ROC has a far bigger weighting (4) than its 9-month

Chart 10.16. S&P Composite and a long-term KST indicator. This chart features the S&P Composite and a weighted summed rate of change. Reversals in this indicator are associated with the major primary trend reversals in the S&P, but it's "know sure thing" (KST). The best signals seem to come when the KST crosses above and below its 9-month MA.

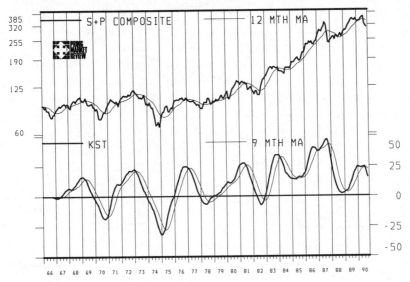

counterpart (1). The indicator signals most of the major movements in the stock market on a *relatively* timely basis and yet does not suffer very much from whipsaw activity.

Periods of accumulation and distribution occur between the time when the summed ROC and its MA change direction. There are really three levels of signaling. The first occurs when the indicator itself changes direction, the second when it crosses its MA, and the third when the MA also reverses direction. *In most cases the MA crossover offers the best combination of timely signals with a minimum of whipsaws.*

For the most part the indicator has been very reliable, but like any other technical approach, it is by no means a perfect technique. For instance, the same calculation is shown in Chart 10.17, but this time for the Nikkei Dow. During periods of a secular or linear uptrend (as occurred for Japanese equities in the 1970s and 1980s), this type of approach is counterproductive since many false bear signals are triggered. However, the vast majority of markets are sensitive to the business cycle, and so the summed ROC concept works extremely well. It is for this reason that I call this indicator the *"know sure thing"* (KST). Most of the time the indicator is reliable, but you "know" that it's not a "sure thing."

Chart 10.17. The Nikkei Dow and a long-term KST indicator. The KST is a smoothed, weighted summed rate of change.

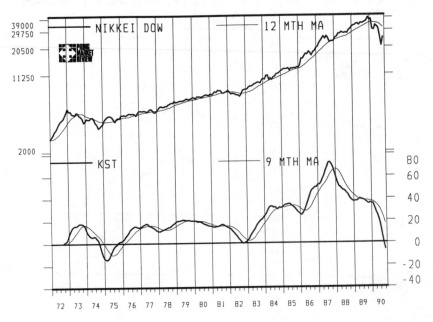

Short- and Intermediate-Term Indicators

Chart 10.18 shows that the same concept can be applied to daily charts for short-term swings. In a similar vein, Chart 10.19 offers a weekly summation suitable for intermediate-term trend decisions. Generally speaking, the monthly KST is far more reliable than its daily and weekly counterparts. The degree of success for any of these time frames will depend on the character of the market being monitored and the nature of the trend. For example, the monthly KST gave premature sell signals during the great linear Japanese bull market of the 1980s. The indicator also failed during the 1980s in the volatile Singapore stock market. By its very construction the formula assumes that markets are influenced by the usual 4-year business cycle. Whenever the time frame is unduly shortened or lengthened the monthly KST suffers in its performance.

The formulas presented in Table 10.2 are by no means the last word and are suggested merely as good starting points for further analysis. Readers may experiment with different formulas for the short- and intermediate-term time frames and obtain superior results.

Chart 10.18. Japanese yen (daily) and a short-term KST indicator. The KST is a smoothed, weighted summed rate of change.

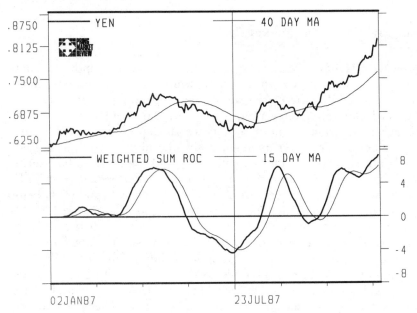

Chart 10.19. The Shearson Lehman Bond Index and an intermediate-term KST indicator. The KST is a smoothed, weighted summed rate of change.

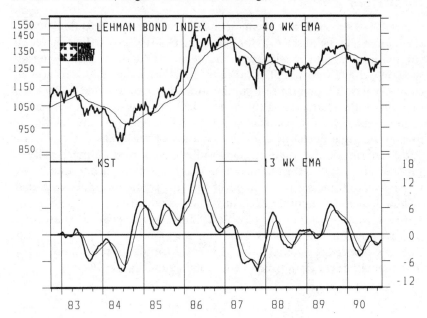

Using the KST in the Market Cycle Model

Three Main Trends. The goal of the KST is to obtain an indicator that captures the major moves while keeping whipsaws to a minimum. Chapter 1 explained that there are several trends operating in the market at any particular time. They range from intraday, hourly trends right through to very long term or secular trends that evolve over a 20- or 30-year period. For investment purposes, the most widely recognized trends are short-term, intermediate-term, and long-term. Short-term trends are usually monitored with daily prices, intermediate-term with weekly prices, and long-term with monthly prices. A hypothetical bell-shaped curve incorporating all three trends is shown in Figure 1.1.

From an investment point of view, it is important to understand the direction of the main, or primary, trend. This makes it possible to gain some perspective on the current position of the overall cycle. The construction of a long-term KST indicator is a useful starting point from which to identify major market cycle junctures. Charts 10.18 and 10.19 show that it is also possible to construct KST indicators that give a rough approximation of short- and intermediate-term trends.

Table 10.2. Suggested KST Formulas*

	ROC	MA	Weight	ROC	MA	Weight	ROC	MA	Weight	ROC	MA	Weight
Short-term†	10	10	1	15	10	2	20	10	3	30	15	4
Short-term‡	3	3¶	1	4	4¶	2	6	6¶	3	10	8¶	4
Intermediate-term‡	10	10	1	13	13	2	15	15	3	20	20	4
Intermediate-term‡	10	10¶	1	13	13¶	2	15	15¶	3	20	20¶	4
Long-term§	9	6	1	12	6	2	18	6	3	24	9	4
Long-term‡	40	26¶	1	52	26¶	2	78	26¶	3	104	39¶	4

*It is possible to program all KST formulas into MetaStock and the Computrac Snap Module (see Resources, at the end of the book).
†Based on daily data.
‡Based on weekly data.
§Based on monthly data.
¶EMA.

Reversals in trend are signaled between the points where the KST and its MA reverse directions. The best signals are given when the KST crosses above or below its MA. The KST gives a very good indication of the prevailing stage of the specific trend that it measures, but like any indicator it is far from perfect, especially in highly volatile markets or markets that do not undergo cyclic correction.

The best investments are made when the primary trend is in a rising mode and the intermediate- and short-term market movements are bottoming out. During a primary bear market, the best selling opportunities occur when intermediate- and short-term trends are peaking out.

In a sense, any investments made during the early and middle stages of a bull market are bailed out by the fact that the primary trend is rising, whereas investors have to be much more agile during a bear market in order to capitalize on the rising intermediate-term swings. Chart 10.16 shows that the long-term KST calculated from monthly data corresponds quite closely to the primary-trend swing indicated in the idealized cycle in Figure 1.1. The weekly and daily charts do not have quite such a close fit but do correspond reasonably well to intermediate- and short-term price movements.

Combining the Three Trends

Ideally, it would be very helpful to track the KST for monthly, weekly, and daily data on the same chart, but plotting constraints do not easily permit this. It is possible though, to simulate these three trends by using different time spans based on weekly data, shown for the Standard & Poor's (S&P) Composite in Chart 10.20. This arrangement facilitates identification of both the direction and the maturity of the primary trend (shown at the bottom), as well as the interrelationship between the short and the intermediate trends.

The best buying opportunities seem to occur either when the long-term index is in the terminal phase of a decline or when it is in an uptrend but has not yet reached an overextended position. These indicators differ from the previous charts in that they are smoothed by EMAs rather than by simple MAs. This results in a number of misleading changes in the *direction* of the indicators but not in signals generated by MA crossovers.

Only an actual crossover should be interpreted as a buy or sell alert for momentum series based on exponential smoothing, not on a reversal in direction.

Bullish intermediate signals that met the two criteria—i.e., correct position on the long-term indicator and EMA crossover on the inter-

Chart 10.20. The S&P Composite and three KST indicators. The KST is a smoothed, weighted summed rate of change. The three series in the chart represent a proxy for short, intermediate, and primary trends. Important buy signals occur when all three series are above their EMAs and vice versa.

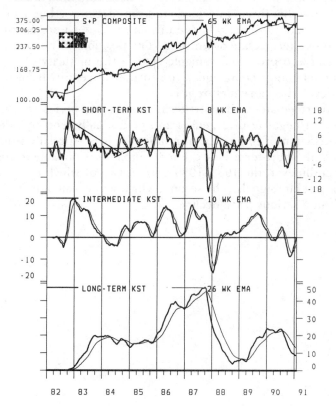

mediate-term indicator—occurred in mid-1984, late 1985, December 1986, and mid-1990. The first three resulted in powerful rallies. The last one, in 1990, did not, but in retrospect the long-term indicator made its peak in early 1990.

On the other hand, as might be expected, bear intermediate-term sell signals are less powerful when they occur against a backdrop of a rising primary-trend KST. Such signals occurred in 1985, early 1986 and 1987, and mid-1989.

This arrangement is helpful from the point of view of trying to assess the maturity of a primary bull or bear market. In the classic conceptual sense, a primary bull market consists of three intermediate uptrends; in certain cases, there is also a fourth. During the 1984–1987 period, there were in fact four intermediate-term buy signals.

During a bear market the same conditions should hold in reverse (i.e., there should be three intermediate-term declines), but during the 1983–1984 and 1987 periods, the primary declines were accompanied by only one intermediate downtrend. The position of the long-term indicator can also provide a valuable clue to the maturity of a primary trend. Other things being equal, the further a trend is from the equilibrium level, the more mature it is.

The intermediate- and short-term momentum series can also flag positive and negative divergences and occasionally lend themselves to the construction of important trendlines. This is especially true of the more volatile short-term index. For example, it is possible to construct three trendlines in the 1983–1989 period, two of which corresponded to important buy signals. The second, which was violated in 1985, failed to result in a serious price decline.

11
Point and Figure Charting

Point and Figure Charts versus Bar Charts

Point and figure charts differ from bar charts in two important ways. First, bar charts are plotted at specific time intervals regardless of whether there is any change in price. A new plot on a point and figure chart, on the other hand, is made only when the price changes by a given amount. Point and figure charts are concerned only with measuring price, whereas bar charts measure both price (on the vertical axis) and time (on the horizontal axis).

The second major difference is that bar charts record every change in price for the period they are measuring, but point and figure charts ignore all price movements that are smaller than a specified amount. For example, if a box is set at price movements of 5 points for the Dow Jones Industrial Average (DJIA), only price changes in excess of 5 points will be recorded, and smaller fluctuations will not appear.

Construction of Point and Figure Charts

Point and figure charts are constructed using combinations of X's and 0's, known as "boxes." The X shows that prices are moving up, the 0 that they are moving down. Once the amount of historical data to be plotted has been established, there are two important decisions to be made before a chart can be constructed.

First, the size of each box must be determined. For individual stocks it is common practice to use a 1-point unit or box for issues trading above $20 and a ½-point unit for lower-priced stocks. However, for very long term charts or for averages consisting of much higher numbers, it is more convenient to use 5-, 10-, or even 20-point boxes. As the box size is decreased, the detail of price movement graphically displayed is increased, and vice versa. In following the price action of a stock or market over many years, it is more convenient to use a relatively large box since small boxes will make the chart unduly large and unmanageable. Often it is a good idea to maintain two or three different versions, just as daily, weekly, and monthly bar charts may be plotted.

The second decision is whether to use a regular point and figure formula or to use a reversal chart (which should not be confused with a "reversal pattern"). The straight point and figure chart is plotted just as the data are recorded. If the price moves from 64 to 65, five X's will be plotted on a 0.20¢-point chart as in Fig. 11.1*b*. If the price reverses from 67 to 66, five 0's will be posted. Reversal charts, on the other hand, follow a predetermined rule: *A new series of X's or 0's cannot begin un-*

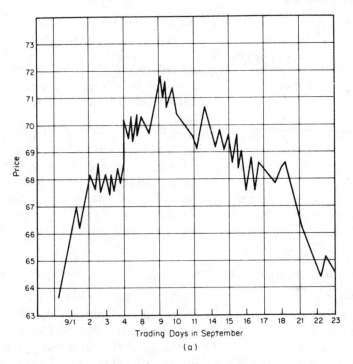

Figure 11.1. [*Source: Martin J. Pring (ed.), The McGraw-Hill Handbook of Commodities and Futures, McGraw-Hill, New York, 1985, p. 50-5.*]

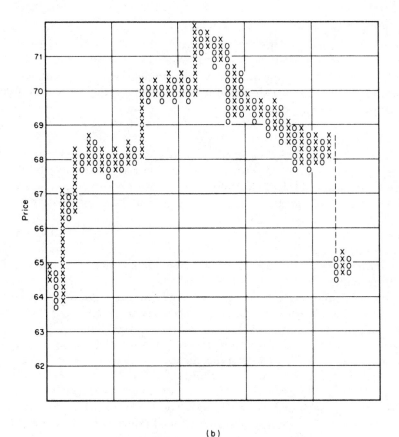

(b)

Figure 11.1. (*Continued*) [*Source: Martin J. Pring (ed.), The McGraw-Hill Handbook of Commodities and Futures, McGraw-Hill, New York, 1985, p. 50-5.*]

til prices have moved by a specified amount in the opposite direction to the prevailing trend. The use of the reversal technique therefore helps to reduce misleading or whipsaw signals, and to greatly compress the size of the chart so that more data can be plotted.

The construction of ½-point charts, 5- or 10-point charts, or charts by any other measure is identical to the above method except that a new box can be posted only when the price has moved by the degree specified, that is, by ½ point, 5 points, 10 points, respectively. Since only price is recorded, it could take several days or even weeks before a new box is plotted. Hence a common practice is to record dates either at the foot of the chart or in the boxes at the appropriate points. A combination of both date locations is used for longer-term charts. For example, the year is recorded at the bottom of the chart against the column for which the first posting of that year was made, and the beginning of each month is recorded in a box using the number of the month — 1 for January, 2 for February, etc.

The decision about unit size (and thus the degree of price change required to trigger a new column of 0's or X's) is essentially based on personal judgment. It is determined by the price range and degree of volatility of the indicator, stock, or market under consideration. Reducing the size of the units (figures) increases the detail of the price movement portrayed. Making the unit larger expands the base of data which can be included but limits the number of fluctuations which can be illustrated. (See Chart 11.1.) Following a market with bar or line charts on a daily, weekly, or monthly basis corresponds to keeping several point and figure charts using various unit sizes.

Point and figure charts are plotted on arithmetically ruled cross-section paper, with 8, 10, or 12 squares to the inch. Occasionally point and figure charts are constructed on semilogarithmic or ratio scale charting paper.

Data published in the financial press covering the high, low, and close for specific stocks are not suitable for accurate point and figure charts. For example, if a $15 stock has an intraday price range of $1½, it is impossible to know for point and figure purposes the actual course of the stock from 14½ to 16. It could have risen from 14½ to 16 in one move, which for a ½-point chart would have been represented by three rising X's. Alternatively it might have moved from 14½ to 15½, back to 14½, and then to 16, which would have resulted in two X's, two 0's, and then a column of three X's. The character of the rally has a very important bearing on the appearance of a point and figure chart.

When dealing with data published in this form, it is better to use larger units so that intraday fluctuations do not distort the chart unduly. If more detail is required, the data should be purchased from a source which publishes intraday price movements.

Accepted rules for plotting point and figure data where the actual prices on the tape are now known are as follows:

1. If the opening price is closer to the high than the low, assume that the course of prices is open, high, low, close.

2. If the opening price is closer to the low, assume open, low, high, close.

3. If the opening price is also the high, assume open, high, low, close.

4. If the opening price is also the low, assume open, low, high, close.

Chart 11.1. Gold price $5 and $2 reversals. These two charts show the gold price plotted on $5 and $2 reversals. The trendlines are self-explanatory. Note that the $5 chart captures 10 years of trading history very concisely. On the other hand, the 2-point reversal chart, which covers March–November 1982, offers far better detail. (*Source: Chart Analysis Ltd., London, England.*)

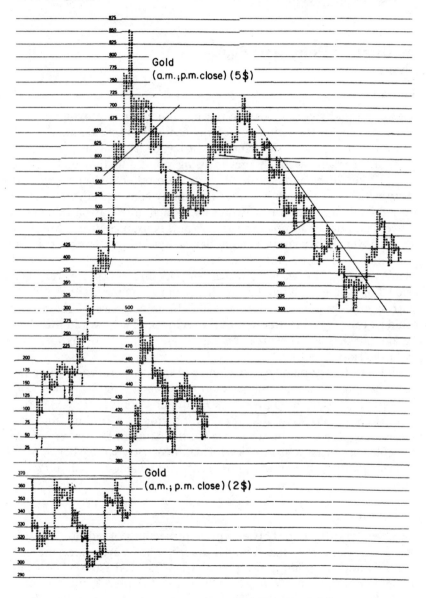

5. If the opening price is the low and the closing price the high, assume open, low, close, high.

6. If the opening price is the high for the day and the close is the lowest price, assume open, high, close, low.

Interpreting Point and Figure Charts

General

Since point and figure charts do not include volume, moving averages (MAs), or time, price action is the only element to be examined.

In this respect the basic principles of bar chart analysis are applied. There are certain disadvantages to using point and figure charts; for example, key reversal days, islands, gaps, and other such formations do not show up. On the other hand, if properly constructed, these charts represent all important price swings even on an intraday basis. They effectively emphasize important support and resistance areas; for example, on a weekly bar chart a single bar representing a weekly price action can take up only one line. However, if there was considerable volatility during the week in which support and resistance were each tested 3 or 4 times, this would most likely show up on a point and figure chart as a congestion area. As a result the importance of these levels would be drawn to the attention of the technician, who would then be in a good position to interpret the significance of any breakout which might develop.

Point and figure patterns are similar in nature to those of price patterns and may be of the continuation or reversal type. The most common ones are shown in Figure 11.2. Head-and-shoulders (H&S) and inverse H&S patterns, double tops and bottoms, rounding tops and bottoms, etc., can easily be recognized as the point and figure equivalent of regular bar or close-only price formations, discussed earlier. Most of the price patterns shown in Figure 11.2 are explained in Chapter 5.

The Count

The essential difference between price projections based on point and figure charts and those based on bar or close-only charts is that the measuring formula of point and figure charts is derived from a horizontal rather than a vertical count. As discussed in Chapter 5, the minimum downside projection from an H&S top is derived by projecting downward the vertical distance from the top of the head to the neckline. In

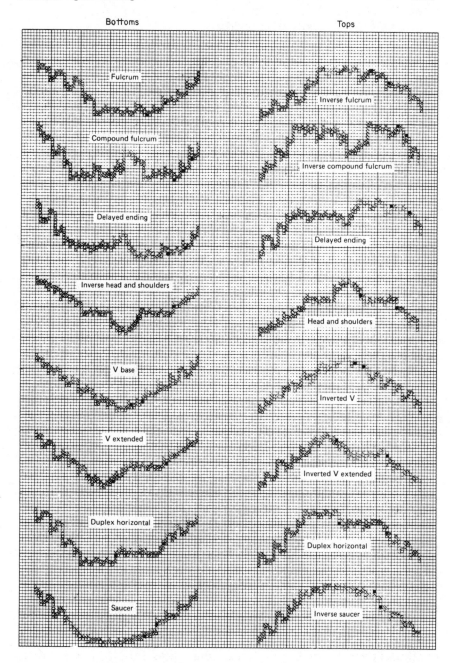

Figure 11.2. *(Source: Study Helps in Point and Figure Technique.)*

point and figure charting the *width* of the pattern is used as the projecting mechanism from the breakout. No one, to my knowledge, has so far satisfactorily explained why this principle appears to work. It seems to be based on the idea that lateral and vertical movements are proportional to each other on a point and figure chart. In other words, the more times a stock or market has undergone price swings within two given levels (as dictated by the price pattern), the greater the *ultimate* move is likely to be once the breakout has taken place. On a point and figure chart the dimensions of the consolidation or reversal pattern can be easily discerned by adding up the number of boxes and projecting the number downward or upward depending on which way prices break out.

The essential problem with the count method is that formations with irregular outlines can generate confusion about where the count should begin. The best approach is to select an important horizontal line in the formation, measure across it, and add (or subtract) the number of boxes in the line to (or from) the level of the line.

Price projections for point and figure formations are by no means 100 percent accurate in all situations. In general, upside projections are likely to be exceeded in bull markets, and downside projections surpassed in bear markets. Projections which are made counter to the prevailing trend have a *tendency* not to be achieved—for example, a downside projection in a bull market.

Trendlines on Point and Figure Charts

It is possible to construct trendlines on point and figure charts by joining a series of declining peaks. Up trendlines are drawn by connecting a series of rising lows, and horizontal trendlines are created by joining identical support or resistance levels. The same principles of interpretation discussed in Chapter 7 apply to trendlines drawn on point and figure charts. The trendline takes its significance from a combination of length, angle of descent or ascent, and the number of times it has been touched. Misleading or whipsaw signals occur occasionally, but if a carefully chosen reversal amount is used as a filter in the construction of the chart, such whipsaws can be kept to a minimum. Another possibility is to draw a parallel line one box above (or below) the actual trendline and use this as the signal to buy (or sell). Although some timeliness is clearly lost with this type of approach, it does offer some protection from misleading price moves.

Summary

1. Point and figure charts measure only one dimension: price.

2. They are constructed from columns of X's and 0's, known as figures, which represent a specified predetermined price movement.

3. Point and figure charts emphasize the number of price swings which take place within a given congestion area.

4. Point and figure charts are interpreted similarly to bar charts, the main exception being the measuring formula which is achieved by the principle of the count.

12

Miscellaneous Techniques for Determining Trends

Two techniques discussed in this chapter, *support and resistance* and *proportion,* are concerned with estimating the potential extent or duration of a trend. This contrasts with most of the indicators previously examined, which attempt to confirm a change in trend after it has already occurred. These techniques should be used only as an indication of the *probable* extent of the move, however, not as the basis of an actual forecast, as there is no known method of predicting the exact magnitude or duration of a price trend.

The third technique to be covered in this chapter is *relative strength* (RS). This method compares the price action of two financial assets to determine which is performing better. It is most widely used by comparing an item with an index — usually "the market," as measured by a stock market average. The performance of General Motors (GM), for example, might be compared to the Dow Jones Industrial Average (DJIA). In Japan, Nippon Telephone and Telegraph might be compared to the Nikkei Dow and so forth.

Declining RS after a long up move is regarded as a sign of weakness, while improving RS after a substantial decline is interpreted as a sign of strength. RS can also be used for comparing the performance of two different assets such as bonds and stocks, or even members of the same asset class such as gold and silver.

Support and Resistance

Support has been defined as "buying, actual or potential, sufficient in volume to halt a downtrend in prices for an appreciable period," and *resistance* as "selling, actual or potential, sufficient in volume to satisfy all bids and hence stop prices from going higher for a time."[1]

A support zone represents a *concentration of demand,* and a resistance zone a *concentration of supply.* The word "concentration" is emphasized because supply and demand are always in balance, but it is their RS or concentration which determines trends.

The reasons for the occurrence of areas of support and resistance and some methods of detecting them in advance are illustrated by the example shown in Figure 12.1. At the beginning of Figure 12.1, the price is in a downtrend. The bear market is interrupted by a consolidation pattern (rectangle), from which prices ultimately break down. The price reaches its low and then after a brief period of consolidation mounts a rally. This advance is halted at the dashed line, which is at the same level as the lower end of the rectangle. People who bought during the period when the rectangle was being formed have all lost money up to this point, and many of them are keen to liquidate their positions and "break even." Consequently there is a concentration of supply at this level, transforming what was formerly a level of support to one of resistance. Such levels are often formed at round numbers such as 10, 50, or 100, since they represent easy psychological points upon which investors often base their decisions.

Prices then fall off slightly and mount another assault on the resistance level, but still more of the asset is put up for sale. Finally prices

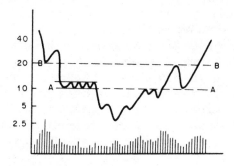

Figure 12.1.

[1]Robert D. Edwards and John Magee, *Technical Analysis of Stock Trends,* John Magee, Springfield, Mass., 1957, p. 211.

and volume pick up, and the resistance is overcome as the available supply at this price is absorbed.

The first rule in assessing the importance of a support or resistance zone relates to the amount of an asset which changed hands in that area. The greater the activity, the more significant the zone.

The next level of resistance in Figure 12.1 is around the level of the "panic" bottom (line *BB*) of the previous bear market. The price is forced back at this point, since the combination of an overextended rally and a substantial level of resistance is overpowering.

The attempt to climb through the resistance level here can be compared to the efforts of a person who, having just finished a 10-mile run, tries unsuccessfully to open a heavy concrete trapdoor. Opening the trapdoor would prove difficult at the best of times, but after such violent physical exercise the person is forced to rest before making another attempt. The same principle can be applied to the market, in that a long, steep climb in price is similar to the 10-mile run, and the resistance level resembles the trapdoor. Consequently, *a second rule for assessing the significance of a support or resistance zone is to assess the speed and extent of the previous move.*

The more overextended the previous price swing, the less resistance or support is required to halt it.

Figure 12.1 shows that the price, having unsuccessfully mounted an assault on the resistance level at *BB*, falls back to the first level at *AA*. It then returns to its previous role of support. This reversal in role is due to the experiences of the investors concerned. In the first place, some who bought at the bear market low may have decided to take profits at *AA*, i.e., $10, and may have been so frustrated by subsequently watching the asset rise to $20 that they decided to repurchase if it ever returned to $10. Similarly, an investor who bought at $10 previously and sold at $20 may wish to repeat this shrewd maneuver.

The third rule for establishing the potency of a support or resistance zone is to examine the amount of time that has elapsed between the formation of the original congestion and the nature of general market developments in the meantime. A supply which is 6 months old has greater potency than one established 10 or 20 years previously. Even so, it is almost uncanny how support and resistance levels repeat their effectiveness time and time again even when separated by many years.

Proportion

The law of motion states that for every action there is a reaction. Prices established in financial markets as reflected in various trends are really the measurement of crowd psychology in motion, and are also subject to this law. The measuring implications of price patterns, trendlines, moving averages (MAs), and envelopes, which were discussed in Chapter 8, are examples of this concept of proportion in practice.

Support and resistance levels can help to give an idea of just where a trend in prices may be temporarily halted or reversed. The principles of proportion can also help, but these principles go much further.

For example, when an index is exploring new, all-time high ground, there is no indication of where a resistance level may occur, because no transactions have taken place. In such cases the concept of proportion offers a clue to potential juncture points.

Perhaps the best-known principle of proportion is the *50 percent rule*. For instance, many bear markets, as measured by the DJIA, have cut prices by half. For instance, the 1901–1903, 1907, 1919–1921, and 1937–1938 bear markets recorded declines of 46, 49, 47, and 50 percent, respectively. The first leg of the 1929–1932 bear market ended in October 1929 at 195, just over half the September high. Sometimes the halfway mark in an advance represents the point of balance, often giving a clue to the ultimate extent of the move in question or, alternatively, indicating an important juncture point for the return move. Thus, between 1970 and 1973 the market advanced from 628 to 1067. The halfway point in that rise was 848, or approximately the same level at which the first stage of the 1973–1974 bear market ended.

By the same token, rising markets often find resistance after doubling from a low; the first rally from 40 to 81 in the 1932–1937 bull market was a double.

In effect, the 50 percent mark falls halfway between the one-third to two-thirds retracement described in Chapter 3 in the discussion of Dow theory. These one-third and two-thirds proportions can be widely observed in the stock market, and also serve as support or resistance zones.

Ratio scale charts are helpful in determining such points, since moves of identical proportion can easily be projected up and down.

The principle of proportion can also be applied to individual stocks. The example in Chart 12.1 shows GM's habit of rising in proportions of about 50 percent. In downmoves this results in a 33 percent decline from high to low. The 55 and 35 percent proportions and multiples thereof tend to act as pivotal points for support and resistance areas. Thus the 1974 low of about 32, when multiplied by 150 percent, results in an objective of just over 65. The 65 area proved to be one of strong support in 1976 and 1977, and it was one of resistance in 1978 and 1979.

Chart 12.1. GM 50 percent swings. (*Source: Securities Research, Boston, Mass.*)

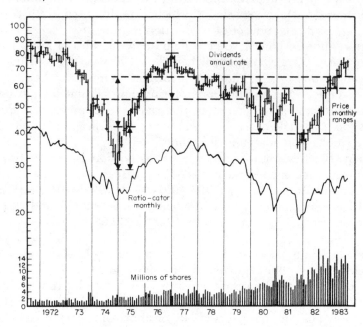

It is not possible to project which proportion will result from a specific move. However, these swings occur with sufficient consistency to offer possible reversal points at both peaks and troughs. If general market conditions and additional technical analysis of the price are consistent, there is a good chance that the projections based on this approach may prove accurate.

Remember that technical analysis deals with probabilities, which means that forecasts using only this method should not be undertaken. If you are making a projection based on the rules of proportion, it is always a good idea to see whether the projection corresponds to a previous support or resistance point. If so, the odds will be much higher that this zone will represent a reversal point or at least a temporary barrier. When a market is reaching new all-time high ground, another possibility is to try to extend up trendlines. The point at which the line intersects with the projection using the rules of proportion may well represent the time and place of an important reversal. Experimentation will show that each market, stock, or commodity has a character of its own, some lending themselves more readily to this approach, others not at all.

Speed Resistance Lines

This concept incorporates the one-third and two-thirds proportions but, instead of incorporating them as a base for a probable price objective, uses them in conjunction with the speed of an advance or a decline.

During a downward reaction, a price may be expected to find support when it reaches a line which is advancing at either ⅔ or ⅓ of the rate of advance from the previous trough to the previous peak. This is illustrated in Figure 12.2. In examples *a* and *b*, *A* marks the peak and *B* the trough. The advance from *A* to *B* is 100 points and takes 100 days, so the speed of the advance is 1 point per day. A ⅓-speed resistance line will advance at ⅓ of that rate (that is, ⅓ point per day), and a ⅔ line will move at ⅔ point per day.

A rally or decline is measured from the extreme intraday high or low and not the closing price. In order to construct a ⅓-speed resistance line from example *a*, it is necessary to add 33 points (i.e., ⅓ of the 100-point advance) to the price at *A* and plot this point directly under *B*. In

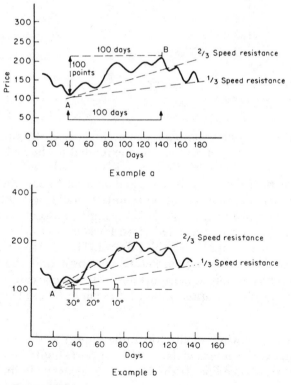

Figure 12.2.

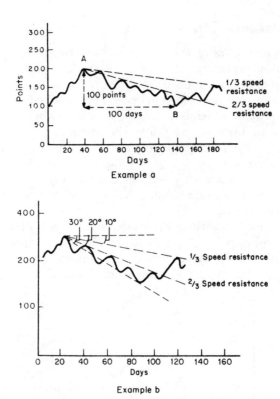

Figure 12.3.

this case A is 100 points, and so a plot is made at 133 under B. This point is then joined to A and the line extended to the right-hand portion of the graph. Similarly, the ⅔ line joins A and the 166 level on the same date as B. If the chart were plotted on a ratio scale, the task would be much easier. All that would be required would be a line joining A and B (this is shown in example b). The angle of ascent, in this case 30 degrees, would then be recorded. Two lines at ⅓ (10 degrees) and ⅔ (20 degrees) of this angle are then drawn. Figure 12.3 illustrates the same process for a declining market. Once constructed, the speed resistance lines act as important support and resistance areas.

More specifically, the application of these lines is based on the following rules:

1. A reaction following a rally will find support at the ⅔-speed resistance line. If this line is violated, the support should be found at the ⅓-speed resistance line. If the index falls below its ⅓ line, the prob-

abilities indicate that the rising move has been completed and that the index will decline to a new low, possibly below that upon which the speed resistance lines were based.

2. If the index holds at the ⅓ line, a resistance to further price advance may be expected at the ⅔ line. If the index moves above the ⅔ line, a new high is likely to be recorded.

3. If the index violates its ⅓ line and then rallies again, it will find resistance to that rally at the ⅓ line.

4. Rules 1 through 3 apply in reverse for a declining market.

Chart 12.2 shows the application of these rules in the marketplace.

Relative Strength (RS)

Introduction

RS is a very important technical concept which measures the relationship between two financial series. There are several ways in which it can be used. The first, and most common, is to compare an individual item in a market to a base. We might compare a stock to a market average — for example, IBM to the Standard & Poor (S&P) Composite. *RS is therefore a very powerful concept for individual stock selection.*

The second approach uses RS to compare one asset to another, in order to decide which one to buy. In this case we might compare gold to bonds to see whether the gold price is in a rising trend *relative* to bonds or vice versa. Another possibility might arise when a review of the technical position indicates that *both* the U.S. and the German stock markets are in a bullish trend. Analyzing the trend of RS between the two would show which market was likely to outperform the other.

A currency as traded in the marketplace is really an RS relationship. In this sense there is no such thing as the "U.S. dollar," only the dollar-pound or dollar-yen cross rate, etc. Each currency is really a relationship between itself and other currencies.

An RS line is obtained by dividing the price of one item by another. Usually the numerator is a stock and the denominator a measurement of "the market," for example, the DJIA or the S&P 500. The concept can also be expanded to the commodity area by comparing the price of an individual commodity, such as sugar, to a commodity index, such as the Commodity Research Board (CRB) Composite, etc. Another possibility might involve the comparison of an individual country's stock or bond index to a global indicator, such as the Morgan Stanley World

Chart 12.2. The DJIA and speed resistance lines.

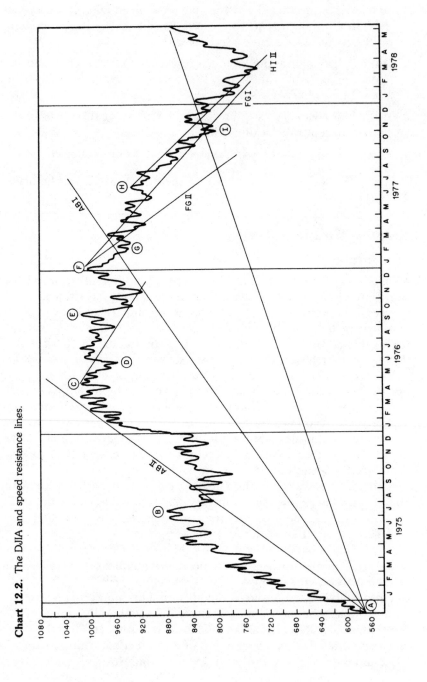

Stock Index or the Salomon World Bond Index. As long as the appropriate currency adjustments are made, the principles are the same.

RS is then plotted as a continuous line underneath the item being measured. A rising line denotes that the item is performing better than the market, and a declining line indicates that it is being outperformed by the market.

RS moves in trends and lends itself to trend-reversal techniques such as price patterns, trendlines, and MAs, described earlier.

As a result, interpretation of trends in RS is subject to exactly that of the price itself. It is important to note that an RS indicator is just what its name implies—relative. A rising line does not mean that an item, such as a stock, is advancing in price, but merely that it is outperforming the market or whatever it is being compared to. For example, the market, as measured by the Dow, may have fallen by 20 percent and the stock by 10 percent. Both have lost value, but the RS line would be rising because the stock retreated less than the market.

When a stock and its RS are both rising and it appears that the RS trend is about to reverse, a warning is given of a possible change in the trend of the price itself. This is because RS typically peaks *ahead* of price. On the other hand, a firming of the RS line during a declining trend indicates a position of growing technical strength. Since the lead time given by such signals varies, it is very important to await a confirmation by a similar trend reversal in the price itself. On the other hand, if the RS is being used to monitor a position of a particular stock, a reversal in RS might justify its sale in favor of one with a rising RS trend.

When both the price and the RS are rising, they are said to be "in gear." Important trends usually begin with both series in gear, but eventually the RS line fails to confirm new highs being set by the price itself (Figure 12.4, example *a*). This type of situation indicates that the stock has begun a period of underperformance against the market. The investor may choose to switch from current holdings to a stock with a

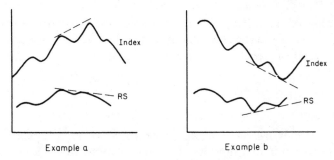

Example a   Example b

Figure 12.4.

more positive *relative* technical picture. However, weakness in RS is not an *absolute* sell signal, i.e., one indicating that the price will go down; it is merely a *relative* signal, i.e., one implying a switch from an issue that has started to go out of favor to one that is coming into favor.

Quite often, though, a divergence or series of divergences between the price and RS represent an early warning sign of trouble, which is later confirmed by a trend-reversal signal in the price itself.

The opposite set of circumstances holds true in a declining market, in which an improvement in RS ahead of price is regarded as a positive sign (Figure 12.4, example *b*). Quite often bear market lows in the equity market are preceded by an improvement of interest-sensitive stocks such as utilities, since they are early leaders as a new bull market gets under way. This idea is discussed at greater length in Chapter 15, in the discussion of group rotation in the stock market.

RS Interpretation and Trendline Violations

Generally speaking, RS indicators are much more volatile than the price itself. For this reason, the best trend-reversal signals appear to come from price pattern completions or more normally from trendline violations.

Figure 12.5 shows that a useful way to identify "buy" candidates is to wait for a trendline violation in both price *and* RS. These joint violations don't occur that often, but when they do, they usually signal an important reversal. The figure also shows a similar joint penetration, on the downside. In effect these joint violations have the effect of reinforcing each other, which makes for a much stronger signal.

Price Patterns

Figure 12.6 shows a price-reversal possibility incorporating a price formation. When a purchase is contemplated, it is very important to wait for some kind of trend reversal in the price itself.

MA Crossovers

Because RS lines are very volatile for almost all relationships, MA crossovers often result in whipsaws. Bearing in mind that MA crossovers always represent a compromise between timeliness and sensitivity,

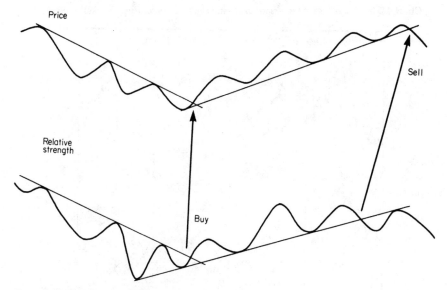

Figure 12.5. RS and trendline violation.

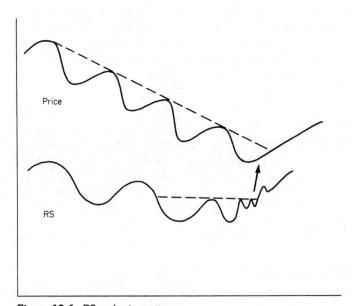

Figure 12.6. RS and price pattern.

Chart 12.3. Texas Instruments and an RS indicator. (*Source: Pring Market Review.*)

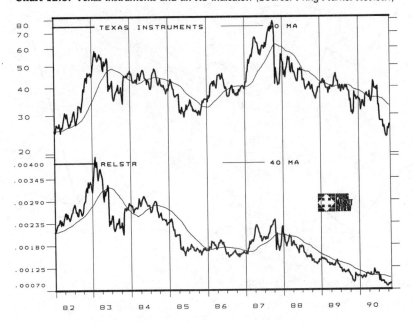

the best way round this dilemma is to smooth the RS line and use the smoothing as a basis for MA crossovers. In the example in Chart 12.3, the solid RS line is actually a 4-week MA of the weekly RS line. Buy and sell signals (for relative strength) occur as the 4-week MA moves above and below its 40-week counterpart. This is a more satisfactory, but far from perfect, solution.

RS Momentum

Trends in RS can also be analyzed from a momentum viewpoint. In effect, any of the individual momentum indicators discussed in Chapters 9 and 10 can be used. Chart 12.4 shows the RS of Texas Instruments against the S&P 500 between 1982 and 1987. A major buying opportunity occurred in 1986, when the RS and its momentum violated important trendlines.

Combining Price and RS

A useful way of analyzing the technical structure of an individual stock is to combine price, price momentum, RS, and relative momentum on one chart, as shown on Chart 12.5.

Chart 12.4. The RS of Texas Instruments and a momentum indicator of RS. (*Source: Pring Market Review.*)

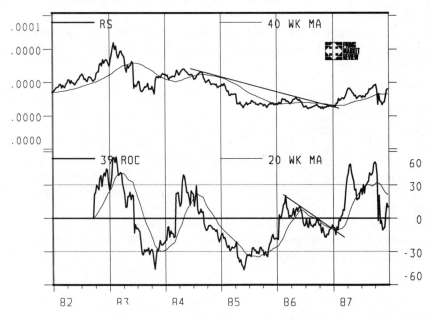

Chart 12.5. The S&P Financial Index and three indicators. (*Source: Pring Market Review.*)

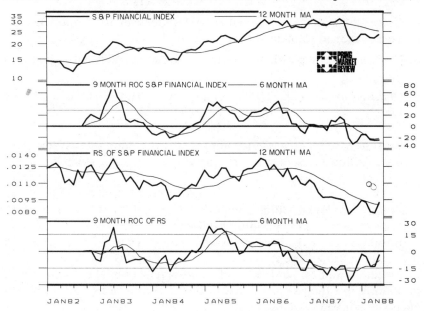

In this way it is possible to see very quickly whether the price is reversing on an absolute basis, and also whether the stock is likely to outperform the market or not.

Readers who wish to pursue this subject more fully should refer to Chapter 15 (Group Rotation) and Chapter 28 (Technical Analysis of Individual Stocks).

Spreads

RS is widely used in the futures markets under the heading "spread trading," in which market participants try to take advantage of market distortions. These discrepancies arise because of unusual fundamental developments, which temporarily affect normal relationships. Spreads are often calculated by subtracting the numerator from the denominator rather than dividing. I prefer the division method because it presents the idea of proportionality. However, if a spread is calculated over a relatively short period, i.e., less than 6 months, it is not important whether subtraction or division is used.

Spread relationships arise because of six principal factors:

1. *Product relationships:* e.g., soybeans versus soybean oil or meal, crude oil versus gasoline or heating oil

2. *Usage:* e.g., hogs, cattle, or broilers to corn

3. *Substitutes:* e.g., wheat versus corn, cattle versus hogs

4. *Geographic factors:* e.g., copper in London versus copper in New York, sugar in Canada versus sugar in New York

5. *Carrying costs:* e.g., when a specific delivery month is out of line with the rest

6. *Quality spreads:* e.g., T-bills versus Eurodollars, S&P versus Value Line

Some of these relative relationships, such as London versus New York copper, really represent arbitrage activity and are not suitable for the individual investor or trader.

On the other hand, the so-called TED Spread, which measures the relationship between ("high"-quality) T-bills and ("low"-quality) Eurodollars is a very popular trading vehicle.

In some cases, spreads move to what was previously an extreme and then proceed to even greater distortion. For this reason it is always important to wait for some kind of trend-reversal signal before taking a position. While the risk associated with such transactions is by no means eliminated, it will certainly be reduced.

Other relationships between various asset categories, etc., are further analyzed in subsequent chapters. These relationships may be used for different purposes, but all are subject to trends, reversals of which can be identified by the techniques already described.

Summary

1. Support and resistance represent a concentration of demand and supply sufficient to halt a price move at least temporarily.

2. The significance of a support or resistance zone depends upon the amount of an asset that previously changed hands in that area, the speed and extent of the previous price move, and the period of time that has elapsed since the zone was last encountered.

3. Price often moves in proportion, and the most common proportions are ½, ⅓, and ⅔.

4. RS usually compares an item with a basket such as a stock with a market average. However, it can also compare different assets or assets within a class, or it can be used as a spread relationship.

5. Trends in RS are analyzed using standard technical tools such as MAs, momentum, and price patterns, but trendline analysis is normally the most reliable.

13
Putting the Techniques Together:

An Analysis of the Dow Jones Utility Average, 1962–1969

The Dow Jones Utility Average was first constructed in 1929. It did not record its secular bottom in 1932, as was the case with most of the other indexes, but its low was delayed until April 1942. From that level (10.42) the index rose irregularly for 23 years until April 1965, at which point it reached an all-time high of 164.39; it then proceeded to lose nearly 100 points in the next 9 years (see Chart 13.1). An examination of the period between 1962 and 1969 is valuable since it covers the culmination of the secular advance and its associated distribution as well as several intervening cycles.

In May 1962 the average was at 99.8, which represented the closing low of a 7-month bear market. At this particular juncture there was nothing to suggest that a reversal in trend had taken place. The first significant signs appeared several months after the bottom. At this point the downtrend in the index (trendline *AA* in Chart 13.2) had been reversed, and the index had crossed above its 40-week moving average (MA). These two signals confirmed the reversal in the downtrend of the weighted momentum index that had taken place earlier (line *AM/AM*).

Chart 13.1. The Dow Jones Utility Average, 1929–1977. (Source: Pring Market Review.)

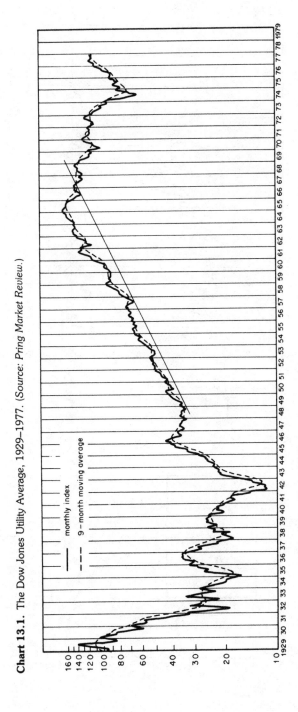

Chart 13.2. The Dow Jones Utility Weekly Average, 1959–1978, and a 40-week MA (with weighted momentum index). (*Source: Pring Market Review.*)

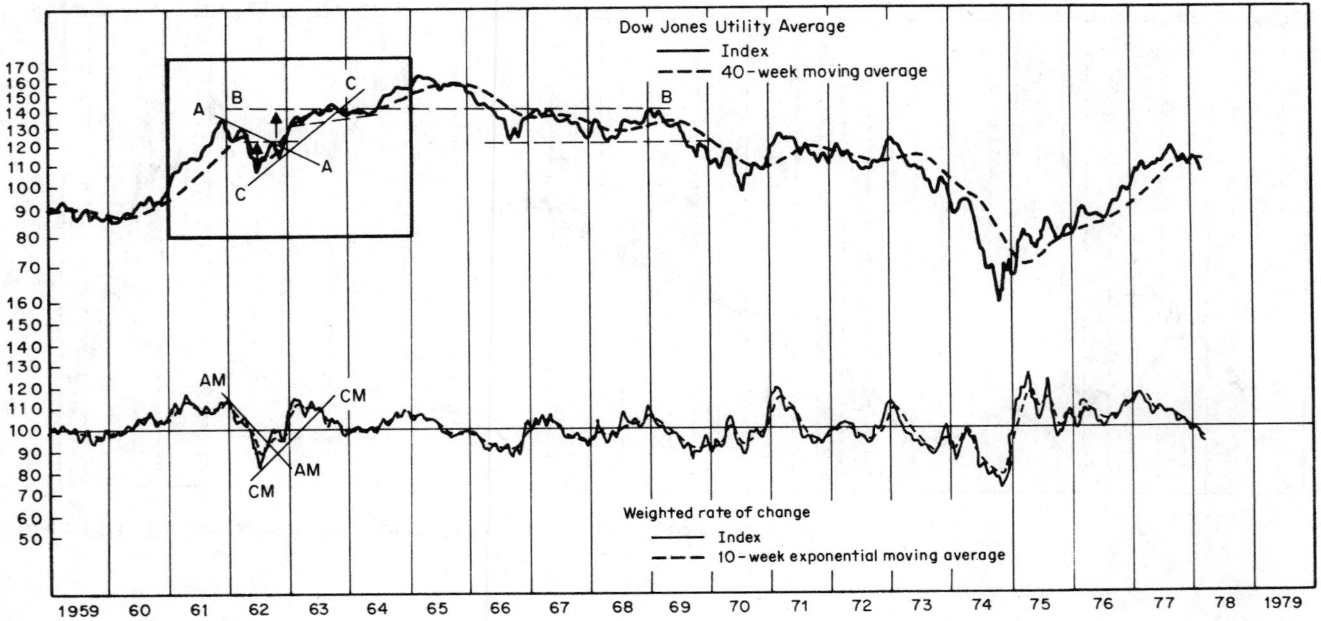

This rate-of-change (ROC) index was constructed by combining 6-, 13-, and 26-week ROC indexes and weighting them according to their respective time periods. These positive signs were also accompanied by the completion of a double bottom by the Utility Average. Since the second decline occurred on lower volume than the first, the breakout to a new recovery high in December indicated that higher prices could be expected.

The average continued to rally until it reached the upside price objective indicated by the double bottom. This level, represented by line *BB* on the chart, proved to be a major resistance level in the 1963–1964 period and later in 1967 and 1969 as well. During the 12 months following the breakout, the initial bull market trendline *CC* remained intact, and the average also remained above its 40-week MA. In late 1963, both the trendline *CC* and the MA were violated. This development, combined with the two declining peaks and the break in trend of the momentum index (line *CM/CM*), suggested that further upside potential in the average would be difficult to achieve. Indeed, the index did not decisively break above the September 1963 high for almost a year.

This break in trend was followed by a long sideways movement. The most significant development during this period was the formation of a head and shoulders (H&S) top between 1963 and 1964. This is shown in more detail in the boxed area of Chart 13.2. The pattern was almost completed, but instead of breaking below the neckline, the index broke above its 40-week MA and began a sharp advance. This type of move is typical of a potential distribution pattern that is never completed. While the ensuing move is usually long and explosively sharp, the formation of the distribution pattern indicates some form of underlying weakness even though it fails. As it happened, the late 1964 advance was to prove to be the last before the significant 1965 peak.

It should be noted that while the late 1963 break in trend indicated that some form of consolidation was likely, at no time did the 14-month exponential moving average (EMA) shown on Chart 13.3 threaten to reverse direction in a way that would have thrown doubt on the entire primary movement. Further reference to Chart 13.3 shows that the early 1964 decline offered a useful benchmark for the construction of a significant bull market trendline (line *AA,* Chart 13.3) by joining this point with the 1962 bottom. It was an important one, since it lasted a long time (2 years) and rose at a fairly shallow angle. Although this particular bull market had another 2 years to run, the average time span for a primary advance is about 2 years. Thus a trendline of this type that remains intact for 2 years represents a relatively long period. Its violation would therefore give a strong signal that the overall trend from 1962 had been reversed. In actual fact, the downward penetration of this line

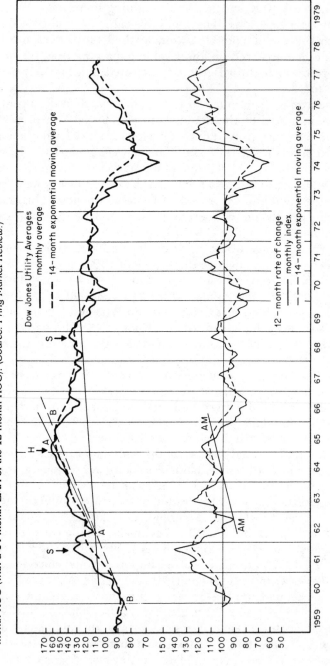

Chart 13.3. The Dow Jones Utility Monthly Average, 1959–1977 (with a 14-month EMA), and a 12-month ROC (with a 14-month EMA of the 12-month ROC). (*Source: Pring Market Review.*)

occurred in early 1965 just after the peak. Further signs of weakness at this point can be seen from the rather dramatic deterioration in RS (see Chart 13.4) that had begun in 1963.

The 12-month momentum index (see Chart 13.3) had also recorded a negative divergence, since it did not confirm the 1965 top in the Utility Average itself.

By late 1965 the technical position had deteriorated even more dramatically. First, from a cyclical point of view the 14-month EMA shown in Chart 13.3 had turned down, and the Utility Average index had also crossed below this important MA. The weakening position of the momentum index was also apparent, as the index itself had broken its uptrend established by the 1962 and early 1964 bottoms (line *AM/AM*). Moreover, the 14-month EMA of this ROC index had also turned down.

From a longer-term point of view, the most significant development was that the 12-month momentum index had made a series of three declining peaks in 1961, 1963, and 1965. This showed that throughout this period the Utility Average was gradually losing its vitality. As long as the trend in the average itself continued to be positive, there was no danger of falling prices, but by late 1965 the important trendline (*BB*, Chart 13.3) joining the 1960 and 1962 bottoms was decisively penetrated on the downside. While no distribution patterns were evident at this point, the break in this important trendline accompanied by a long-term deterioration in the momentum index and RS indicated that the progress of the Utility Average was going to be constrained for a considerable period.

The cyclical decline that began in mid-1965 bottomed out in late 1966. The ensuing bull market was a rather weak one and essentially proved to be a 3-year period of consolidation. In effect the Utility Average, as illustrated by Chart 13.2, was forming a rectangle. By the time the 1969–1970 bear market was under way, it became apparent that the Utility Average had been forming an 8½-year H&S distribution pattern between 1961 and 1969 (Chart 13.3). The completion of this pattern was confirmed when the average broke below its 1968 low in the fall of 1969.

It is worth noting that throughout the 1966–1969 period when the rectangle was being formed, the long-term trend of the Utility Average's relative strength, shown in Chart 13.4, was in a sharp downtrend. The break in the secular uptrend of the average (shown on Chart 13.1), which occurred in 1967, gave an additional bearish warning that the ensuing period would be one of substantial constraint for the Utility Average. This indeed proved to be the case, as the average proceeded to lose over 50 percent of its value in the ensuing 5 years.

Chart 13.4. The Dow Jones Utility Average and RS, 1959–1977. (*Source: Pring Market Review.*)

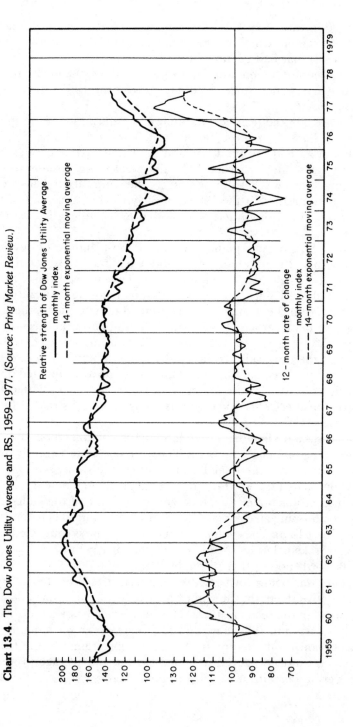

Relative strength of Dow Jones Utility Average
  —— monthly index
  ––– 14-month exponential moving average

12-month rate of change
  —— monthly index
  ––– 14-month exponential moving average

PART 2
Market Structure

14

Price: The Major Averages

Price is the most logical starting point for any attempt to analyze the strength of the overall market structure.

There is no ideal index that represents the movement of "the market." Although the majority of stocks move together in the same direction most of the time, there is rarely a period when specific stocks or several groups of stocks are not moving contrary to the general direction of the trend. There are basically two methods for measuring the general level of stock prices. The first, known as an *unweighted index*, takes a mean average of the prices of a wide base of stocks; the second also takes an average of the prices of a number of stocks, but in this case the prices are weighted by the outstanding capitalization (i.e., the number and market value of shares) of each company. The first method monitors the movement of the vast majority of listed stocks, but since the second gives a greater weight to larger companies, movements in a market average constructed in this way more fairly represent changes in the value of the nation's portfolios. For this reason, weighted averages are usually used as the best proxy for "the market." These averages can be compiled from stocks representing public participation, market leadership, and industry importance.

Several price indexes have been developed which measure various segments of the market. Their interrelationship offers useful clues about the market's overall technical condition. Chapter 3 discussed in detail the relationship between the Dow Jones Industrial Average

(DJIA) and the Dow Jones Transportation Average, but there are many other useful indexes—such as the Utility Average, unweighted indexes, and a few bellwether stocks. These indexes are examined in this chapter in the context of their contribution to the U.S. market's overall technical structure.

Composite Market Indexes

The DJIA is the most widely followed stock market index in the world. It is constructed by totaling the prices of 30 stocks and dividing the total by a divisor. The divisor, which is published regularly in *The Wall Street Journal* and *Barron's,* is changed from time to time because of stock splits, stock dividends, and changes in the composition of the average. Strictly speaking, it is not a "composite" index, since it does not include such industries as banks, transportation, and utilities. Yet the capitalization of the DJIA stocks is equivalent to approximately 25 to 30 percent of the outstanding capitalization on the New York Stock Exchange (NYSE), and it has normally proved to be a reliable indicator of general market movements. The original reason for including a relatively small number of stocks in an average was convenience. Years ago the averages had to be laboriously calculated by hand. With the advent of the computer, the inclusion of a much more comprehensive sample became much easier.

One of the drawbacks of the method used in the construction of the DJIA is that if a stock increases in price and is not split, its influence on the average will become substantially greater, especially if many of the other Dow stocks are growing and splitting at the same time. In spite of this and other drawbacks, the Dow has over the years acted fairly consistently with many of the more widely capitalized market averages.

The Standard and Poor's (S&P) Composite, which comprises 500 stocks representing well over 90 percent of the NYSE market value, is another widely followed bellwether average. It is calculated by multiplying the price of each share by the number of shares outstanding, totaling the value of each company, and reducing the answer to an index number.

Most of the time the DJIA and S&P 500 move in the same direction, but there are times when a new high or low is achieved in one index but not the other. Generally speaking, the greater the divergence, the greater the next move in the opposite direction is likely to be. Chart 14.1*a* shows that in late 1968 the S&P 500 reached a new all-time high, unlike the DJIA, which was not able to surpass its 1966 peak. This development helped to signal a bear market that wiped nearly 40 percent

Chart 14.1a. Key market averages, 1965–1978. (*Source: Securities Research Co., a Division of United Business Service Co.*)

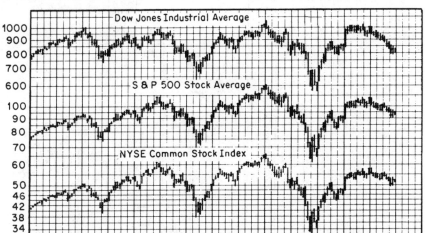

off the value of both averages. On the other hand, the 1973–1974 bear market was completed with a double bottom. In the case of the DJIA the second bottom in December 1974 was lower than the October one, yet the S&P 500 failed to confirm the new low in the DJIA. In the space of the next 2 years the DJIA rose by some 80 percent. This is also shown in Chart 14.1a.

The NYSE compiles an all-encompassing index called the NYSE Composite. In a sense it represents the ideal average, since its value is based on the capitalization of all shares on the exchange. Its movements are very similar to those of the DJIA and the S&P 500. Nevertheless, divergences between the trends of these three averages offer additional confirmation of changes in the overall technical structure.

The most widely followed comprehensive indicator of all is the Wilshire 5000 Equity Index, which represents the value-weighted total, in billions of dollars, of all actively traded common stocks in the United States. Conceptually this is the indicator that should be used for monitoring trends of the overall market, but because of the lethargy of the investment community and the obvious vested interest of the sponsors of the other popular averages, it has not received the widespread recognition which it justly deserves. The Wilshire 5000 is shown in Chart 14.1b.

Chart 16.5 shows a complete history of the U.S. stock market from 1790 to 1976. In reality this is not a consistent 200-year record since new stocks have been substituted from time to time because of mergers

Chart 14.1b. The Wilshire 5000 Index versus the DJIA. (*Source: Pring Market Review.*)

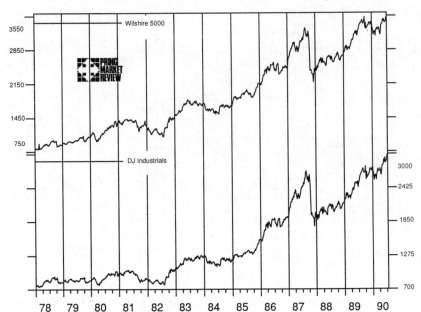

or takeovers. The market in the nineteenth century is represented by several series spliced together to maintain some form of continuity. Thus the interpretation of the actual level of the index in these earlier years should be treated with some caution. However, the timing and size of the various cyclical swings are more reliable.

Because the average has been plotted on a ratio scale, price movements of identical vertical distance are also of the same proportion. The wild gyrations of the market in recent years may appear substantial to those who have been investing during this period, but the chart shows that these movements are relatively mild by historical standards.

Many of the techniques described in Part 1 are useful for identifying trends in the U.S. market. The charts in Chapter 4 offered several illustrations of the use of price pattern analysis with the DJIA. Charts 14.2 and 14.3 illustrate the monthly swings in the S&P Composite from 1929 to 1977. They show that most bull market reversals have been signaled by violation of a simple trendline joining the bear market low in the trough of the first major bull market reaction. This technique signaled termination of nine bull markets at relatively early stages. The 1942–1946 primary uptrend was initially broken in 1943, since it was too steep to be maintained. The violation of the 1962–1966 line was late, but it foreshadowed an extended period of consolidation which

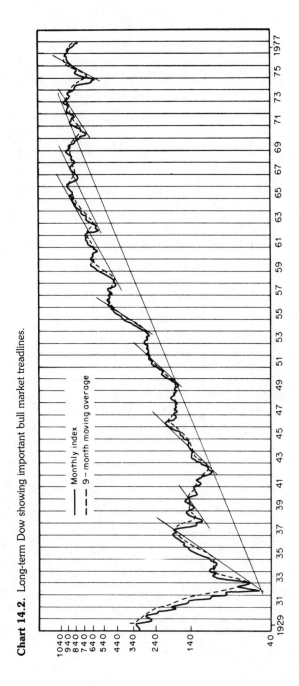

Chart 14.2. Long-term Dow showing important bull market treadlines.

Chart 14.3. Long-term Dow showing important bear market treadlines.

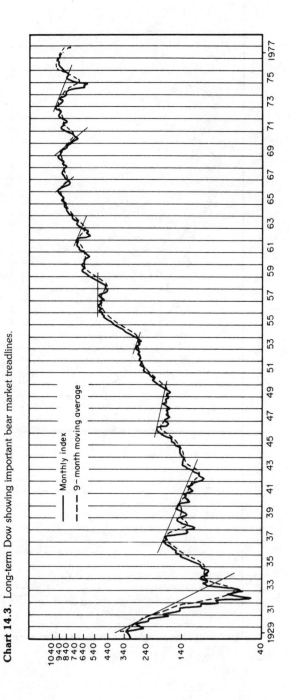

214

was later confirmed by a downward penetration of the line joining the 1932 and 1942 bottoms in 1969. It is also important to note how many of these lines, once violated, became resistance levels to further price advance. This is especially marked for the 1942–1943 and 1962–1966 advances.

Trendlines can also be drawn for bear markets, and these are shown on Chart 14.3. Although this very simple trendline technique provides a reasonable indication of a reversal in trend, some degree of subjectivity and judgment is necessary in the interpretive process. For example, the relatively shallow declining trend in the 1957, 1962, and 1973–1974 bear markets resulted in some unreasonably late signals. *In cases when it is obvious that a trendline is going to be "late," it is better to disregard it and fall back on another technique.* In the three cases outlined above, for instance, the completion of weekly price patterns could have been used to determine a reversal in trend.

The Market Averages and MAs

When experimenting with an MA from the point of view of trend determination, it is necessary first to assess the type of cycle to be considered. The 4-year stock market cycle has corresponded to the U.S. business cycle for many decades. Since the stock market is greatly influenced by business cycle developments, this 4-year (or to place it more exactly, 41-month) cycle is of great significance in trend determination. Consequently, the choice of an MA to detect such swings is limited to anything less than the full period, i.e., 41 months, since an MA covering this whole time span would smooth out the complete cycle and theoretically become a straight line. In practice the MA does fluctuate, since the cycle is rarely limited exactly to its average 41 months and varies in magnitude of price change. Through computer research[1] it has been found that a 12-month MA for the S&P Composite was the most reliable between 1910 and the early 1990s. This was not true for every decade, but for the period as a whole.

In his book *The Stock Market Indicators*, William Gordon calculated that a 40-week crossover gave 29 buy and sell signals for the DJIA between 1897 and 1967.[2] The average gain for all bull signals (i.e., be-

---

[1]Robert W. Colby and Thomas A. Meyers, *The Encyclopedia of Technical Market Indicators*, Dow Jones–Irwin, Homewood, Ill., 1988.

[2]Investors Press, Palisades, N.J., 1968. The actual rule used for buy signals was as follows: "If the 200-day (40-week) average line flattens out following a previous decline, or is advancing and the price of the stock penetrates that average line on the upside, this comprises a major buying signal."

tween the buy and sell signals) was 27 percent, and the average change from sell signals was 4 percent. For investors using the buy signals to purchase stocks, nine of the signals resulted in losses, although none greater than 7 percent, while gains were significantly higher. This approach has worked reasonably well since 1967, though it is important to note that 40-week MA crossovers of the S&P Composite resulted in many whipsaws in the late 1970s. As so often happens after a number of whipsaws, the 1982 buy signal was superb. It captured most of the initial advance of the 1982–1987 bull market, while the second, in late 1984, would have kept investors in the market until the Friday before the 1987 crash.

For intermediate swings, crossovers of 13- and 10-week averages have proved to be useful benchmarks, but naturally an MA covering such a brief time span can result in many misleading whipsaws and is therefore less reliable than the 40-week average. For even shorter swings, a 30-day (6-week) MA works well, although some technicians prefer a 25-day average.

A simpler technique for identifying intermediate trends is to use reversals in the trend of a 13-week ROC of a market average such as the S&P Composite in conjunction with a reversal in the trend in the level of the average itself. The technique used in Chart 14.4 involves the drawing of trendlines for both the weekly closing price of the DJIA and its 13-week momentum. When a break in one index is confirmed by the other, a reversal in the prevailing trend usually takes place. Such signals

Chart 14.4. The DJIA versus 13-week momentum. (*Source: Pring Market Review.*)

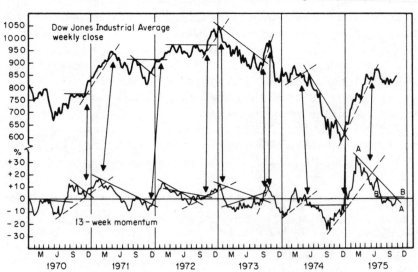

Chart 14.5. The DJIA and a 12-Month ROC. (*Source: Pring Market Review.*)

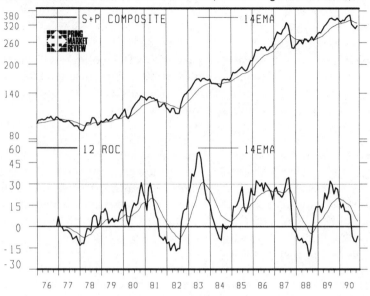

are illustrated in the chart by the arrows. This type of analysis should be supported where appropriate with price pattern analysis for the S&P, and with other techniques utilizing the momentum principles described in Chapter 10. This method does not always give a signal, but whenever there are clearly definable violations of trendlines that have been touched three or more times, the conclusions drawn are usually extremely reliable. A less subjective alternative is to use an MA crossover for the DJIA and either a change in direction of a smoothed rate of change (ROC) for the momentum index, or its penetration of a predetermined level. This combination is shown on Chart 14.5, which uses a 14-month exponential moving average (EMA) for the S&P Composite and a 14-month EMA for a 12-month ROC index. Another useful approach uses the long-term "*k*now *s*ure *t*hing" (KST) indicator or the market cycle model. These are described in Chapter 10.

The Dow Jones Transportation Average

In the last part of the nineteenth century and the early part of the twentieth century, rail was the dominant form of transportation, and therefore an average composed solely of rails represented a good proxy for transportation stocks. In 1970 the Rail Average was expanded to embrace other transportation segments, and the index was renamed the Transportation Average.

The Transportation Average is basically affected by two factors: volume of business and changes in interest rates. First, when a business recovery gets under way, inventories are low and raw materials are needed to initiate production. Transportation volume picks up, and investors anticipating such a trend bid up the price of transportation shares. At business cycle peaks companies typically overbuild their stocks; the result is that when sales start to fall, their requirements for raw materials are reduced. Transportation volume then falls sharply, and the stocks react accordingly. Second, transport companies tend to be more heavily financed with debt than industrials. Because of the leverage of this heavy debt structure, their earnings are also more sensitive to changes in interest rates and business conditions than those of most industrial companies. As a result, the Transportation Average quite often leads the Industrial Average at important juncture points.

The significance of the Dow theory rule requiring confirmation of both the Industrials and Transportations should now be more obvious, since a move by the producer stocks (the Industrials) really has to be associated with an increased volume of transportation, which should be reflected by a similar move in the Transportation stocks. In a similar vein, increased business for the Transportation stocks is likely to be of temporary significance if the industrial companies fail to follow through with a rise in sales and production levels. The longer-term cycles of the Transportation Average and the Industrial Average are more or less the same as a result of their close association with business conditions. The techniques and choice of time spans for MAs, ROCs, etc., are therefore similar to those described above for the Industrials.

One principle which is not normally used for the Industrials but can be applied to the Transportations is that of relative strength (RS). This technique is particularly useful during periods of nonconfirmation between the two averages, when RS can offer a useful clue as to how the discrepancy will be resolved. One such example occurred in early 1974 and is shown in Chart 14.6. The DJIA made an impressive advance in January 1974, reacted in early February, and then rose strongly to a new recovery high in March. The RS for the Transportations, which had been extremely strong up to this point, topped out in early March, and by the time the Industrials made their second peak, the RS of the Transportations had crossed below its 13-week MA. The 13-week momentum index for the RS peaked in January and was also falling sharply during this period. The conclusion drawn from an analysis of

Chart 14.6. Transportations and RS.

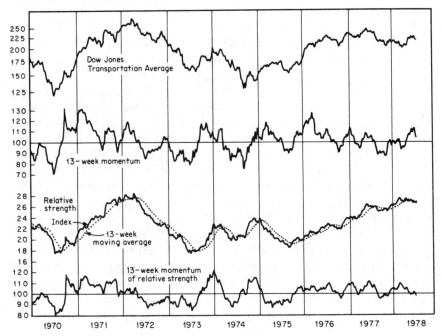

the RS trend at that time would have placed a low probability on the Transportations confirming the March recovery high in the Industrials.

The Utility Average

The Dow Jones Utility Average comprises 15 utility stocks drawn from electric utilities, gas pipelines, telephone companies, etc. This average has historically proved to be one of the most reliable barometers of the Industrials. This is because utility stocks are extremely sensitive to changes in interest rates. Interest rate changes are important to utility stocks for two reasons. First, utility companies require substantial amounts of capital because they are usually highly financed with debt relative to equity. As interest rates rise, the cost of renewing existing debt and raising additional money puts pressure on profits. When interest rates fall, these conditions are reversed and profits rise. Second, utility companies generally pay out their earnings in the form of dividends, so that these equities are normally bought just as much for their yield as for their potential capital gain. When interest rates rise, bonds—which are also bought for their yield—fall in price and thus become relatively more attractive than utilities. As a result, investors are tempted to sell utility stocks and buy bonds. When interest rates fall, the money returns once again to utility stocks, which then rise in price.

Since changes in the trend of interest rates usually occur ahead of reversals in the stock market, the Utility Average more often than not leads the DJIA at both market tops and market bottoms.

Generally speaking, when the Utility Average flattens out after an advance or moves down while the Industrials continue to advance, it is usually a sign of an imminent change in trend for the Industrials. Thus the Utilities led the Industrials at the 1937, 1946, 1953, 1966, 1968, 1973, and 1987 bull market peaks. Conversely, at the 1942, 1949, 1953, 1962, 1966, 1974, and 1982 bottoms the Utilities made their bear market lows ahead of the Industrials. At most major juncture points the Utilities coincided with the Industrials, and occasionally, as at the 1970 bottom and the 1976 top, the Utilities lagged.

The relationship between the Utilities and the Industrials is often overlooked because they usually give their loudest message when other market activity is at its most exciting. At market tops the Utility Average quietly declines while investors, analysts, and the media are excited about huge price advances yet to be seen. Chart 14.7 shows a classic example in 1987. In August the Industrials were at an all-time high, but

Chart 14.7. Dow Jones Industrials versus Dow Jones Utilities. (*Source: Pring Market Review.*)

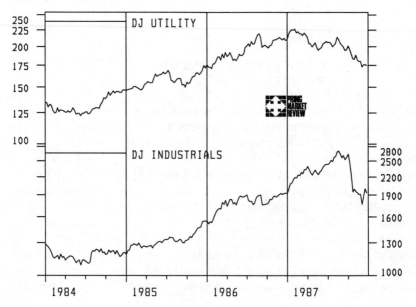

the Utility Average was already in a well-established bear market. At market bottoms fear, depression, and sometimes panic reign, while the Utility Average is very quietly in the process of turning up.

The Unweighted Indexes

An unweighted index is calculated by adding the prices of a universe of stocks and dividing the total by that number. The resulting average is then weighted by price rather than capitalization. The most widely followed is the Value Line Composite.

Unweighted indexes are useful because they closely represent the price of the "average" stock often found in individual portfolios—as opposed to the blue chips, to which institutional investment is more oriented. Unweighted indexes are also helpful in gaining an understanding of the market's technical structure, since they have a tendency to lead the market (i.e., the DJIA) at market tops. When a persistent divergence of this nature between the DJIA and the Value Line develops, it almost always results in the Dow being dragged down as well. Once a divergence starts, a cautious approach should be maintained until both the DJIA and the Value Line break out from price patterns or declining trendlines, etc.

A show of good RS by the unweighted indexes at a time of sustained weakness in the major averages often signifies that a significant rally will follow when the decline is over. This occurred in 1978, when the Value Line Composite Index made its low in late 1977, several months ahead of the DJIA. The Value Line Composite index is shown for a more recent period in Chart 14.8.

General Motors

It has been claimed that "what is good for General Motors (GM) is good for America," and the record for the last 50 years or so certainly bears out this statement as far as the stock market is concerned, for GM is a bellwether stock par excellence.

GM has hundreds and thousands of employees and more than 1 million shareholders, and its business is very sensitive to credit conditions. It is still the largest auto manufacturer in the country, and a significant number of American jobs are either directly or indirectly dependent on the auto industry.

As a result, most of the time GM tends to rise and fall in concert with the trend of the DJIA or the S&P 500. At market tops GM usually leads

Chart 14.8. The Value Line Composite versus the S&P 500. (*Source: Pring Market Review.*)

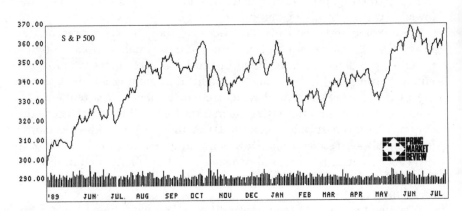

the market, so that a new high in the DJIA which is unconfirmed by GM
is a warning signal of a reversal in trend. On the other hand, GM is not
as helpful at market bottoms because it usually lags. The long-term
chart of GM (Chart 14.9a) shows this quite clearly. It is also worth noting the huge head and shoulders (H&S) formed between 1928 and
1929 as well as the right-angled broadening top between 1964 and
1966. The completion of both these long-term distribution patterns led
to substantial declines in the stock.

Proponents of GM have developed a useful principle. Known as the
4-month rule (although some analysts prefer a 19- to 21-week rule), it
states that if in a bull market GM fails to make a new high within 4 calendar months (for example, February 27 to June 27, or March 31 to
July 31) of its previous peak, the bullish trend of the market has reversed or is just about to do so. Similarly, during a market decline if GM
fails to make a new low within 4 months of its previous trough, a reversal in the downward trend of the market has already taken place or is
just about to occur. The GM rule is not infallible, but its record is extremely good.

Chart 14.9a. Market profile of General Motors, 1924–1935 and 1948–1973. (*Source: M. C. Horsey & Company, Publishers.*)

Chart 14.9b. The DJIA versus General Motors Corporation stock, 1966–1978. (*Source: Securities Research Co., a Division of United Business Service Co., 1978. All rights reserved.*)

15
Price:
Group Rotation

Introduction

Chapter 2 discussed the relationship between the three key financial markets—debt, equity, and gold—and the business cycle. It was established that there are certain periods when these markets move in concert, but more often their trends diverge. The combination depends on the maturity of the business cycle. The most important point to remember is that deflationary forces predominate during the early stages of the cycle, whereas inflationary pressures come to the fore as the recovery matures. No business cycle ever repeats itself exactly, and the leads and lags between the peaks and troughs of the various financial markets differ from cycle to cycle. In spite of this drawback, the concept of the chronological development of the debt, equity, and gold cycles works quite well in practice.

This chapter takes the concept of chronological development of these cycles one step further by categorizing the various industry groups according to their sensitivity to deflationary or inflationary forces, i.e., leading or lagging characteristics. Unfortunately, this categorization is far from an exact process. First, many industries do not conveniently fall into an inflationary or a deflationary category. Second, equities rise and fall in reaction to the outlook for profits and also, what is more important, in response to investor attitudes to those profits. Because interest rates are a significant, but not necessarily dominant, influence on the profits of interest-sensitive stocks, it follows that the price performance of certain interest-sensitive issues may, from time to time, become unlatched from or independent of the price movements in the debt markets. For example, savings and loan stocks declined in 1989 because of a financial crisis in the industry. Normally they would have been expected to rise because interest rates fell during most of that year.

In spite of such drawbacks, the theory of group rotation serves two useful functions. First, it can provide a framework within which to assess the maturity of a primary trend. For example, if there is technical evidence that the stock market is deeply oversold when the primary trend signals a reversal from bearish to bullish, it would be very useful to know that some of the groups which normally lead market turns have failed to confirm new lows made by the market averages. On the other hand, in a situation in which the technical picture is indicating the possibility of a market top, it would be helpful to know that *leading* industry groups had made their highs some weeks or months earlier, and that stronger relative performance was concentrated in industry groups that typically lag the stock market cycle.

Second, the group rotation theory is helpful in determining which groups, and therefore which stocks, should be purchased or pared back. This aspect is discussed in greater detail in Chapter 28.

The comments in this chapter refer to the U.S. stock market, but the concept of group rotation can be extended in principle to other stock markets. Every country experiences business cycles, and there is no reason why Italian or Japanese utilities should not respond to changes in interest rates just as U.S. equities do. Indeed, it is possible to take this concept one step further by saying that markets heavily weighted to the resource area, such as Canada, Australia, and South Africa, ought to perform best at the tail end of the global economic cycle, and in most cases they do.

The Concept of Group Rotation

During a bull market the majority of stocks are rallying most of the time. It follows that most record their bear market lows about the same time as the averages. When utilities are described here as a leading group and steels as a lagging group, the implication is not necessarily that utilities reach their lows ahead of the low in the Dow Jones Industrial Average (DJIA), although they do in most instances. What is more likely to happen is that utilities, being interest-sensitive, will put on their best performance *relative to the market* around the beginning of the cycle. Similarly, steels might advance with the averages during the early stages of the bull market, but their best relative performance *has a ten-*

dency to occur during the later stages of a bull market or the early phases of a bear market.

The sine curve in Figure 15.1 represents growth and contraction of the economy during a typical business cycle. The dashed line reflects intermediate rallies and reactions of the stock market. The idealized peaks and troughs of the other financial markets are also shown. Bond prices typically make their lows (i.e., interest rates reach their cyclical peaks) after the recession has been under way for some months. The stock market, which essentially discounts profits, makes its low about 3 to 6 months before the low in economic activity, whereas the gold market, which discounts inflation, usually comes to life only several months after the recovery has set in. Because the leads and lags vary in each cycle, this approach should be used as a framework, not a mechanical extrapolation.

The overall market consists of many stock groups which are a reflection of the companies making up the various segments of the economy. The economy, as defined by an aggregate measure such as gross national product (GNP), is either rising or falling at any one time. However, there are very few periods in which all segments advance or decline simultaneously. This is because the economy is not one homogeneous unit, but an aggregate of a number of different parts. Some industries respond better to deflationary conditions and the early stages of the productive cycle; others are more prosperous under inflationary conditions which predominate at the tail end of the business cycle.

Economic recoveries are typically led by consumer spending, which is

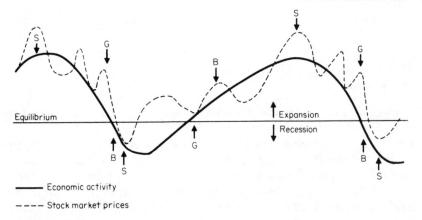

Figure 15.1.

spearheaded by the housing industry. As interest rates fall during a recession, demand for housing gradually picks up. Hence home building and some building and construction stocks can be considered leading groups.

Because they anticipate a consumer spending improvement, retail stores, restaurants, cosmetics, tobacco, and so forth also show leading tendencies, as do certain interest-sensitive areas such as telephone and electric utilities, insurance, savings and loans, and consumer finance companies. As the recovery continues, inventories, which were cut dramatically during the recession, become depleted. Manufacturing industry groups, which might be classified as coincident, then respond by improving in price or relative strength (RS). Finally, as manufacturing productive capacity is used up during the last stages of the recovery, stock groups associated with capital spending, such as steels, some chemicals, and mines, have a tendency to emerge as market leaders.

Confidence is another influence on the group rotation cycle. During the initial stage of a bull market, emphasis is placed on prudence, because investors have lost a considerable amount of money and the news is usually very bad. Stocks with good balance sheets and high yields begin a period of superior RS. As the cycle progresses, stock prices rise, the news gets better, and confidence improves. Eventually the rotation turns to more speculative issues of little intrinsic value. Even though the peak in speculative issues usually leads that of the major averages, their most rapid and volatile period of advance typically occurs in the final or third leg of a bull market.

Some groups are not readily classifiable in terms of the productive process. Air transport, which goes through sharp cyclical swings, is a case in point. This industry average either coincides with or lags slightly at bear market lows but is almost always one of the first groups to turn down before a peak. This could be because these companies are sensitive to interest rates and energy prices, both of which have a tendency to rise at the end of the business cycle. Drug stocks as a group, on the other hand, have a distinct tendency to present their best relative performance at the tail end of the bull market and in this respect should be regarded as a lagging group. They are likely also to lag (in terms of RS) at market bottoms, although this tendency is far less pronounced than their tendency to lag at market tops.

It is also worth noting that the group rotation process has a tendency to work during intermediate-term rallies and reactions as well as cyclical ones.

Splitting the Cycle into Inflationary and Deflationary Parts

Putting the group rotation theory into practice is not an easy matter because the character of each cycle is different. In a rough sense the business cycle can be split into a deflationary part and an inflationary part. A useful starting point is to obtain an inflation/deflation indicator in order to determine that a falling trend in this indicator is deflationary and a rising one inflationary.

The obvious method would be to divide a long-term bond index by a commodity index. After all, bonds usually rise during deflationary periods and fall during inflationary ones. The opposite would be true of commodity prices. Chart 15.1 shows the history of such an indicator between 1969 and 1990. Useful signals of a trend reversal are given by 12-month moving-average (MA) crossovers, though a proper analysis should consider other trend-reversal techniques as well.

The indicator gives us a good sense of whether bonds are outperforming commodities on a price basis, i.e., when the line is falling, but we also need to know whether these movements can be useful from the

Chart 15.1. Commodities versus bonds, 1969–1990. (*Source: Pring Market Review.*)

point of view of giving us a better understanding of the group rotation process.

One way to find out would be to compare the price of a specific deflation-sensitive stock, such as a utility, with an inflation-sensitive one, such as a mining company. The problem with this approach is that one of the stocks may be affected by internal conditions totally unrelated to the business cycle. The same drawback might be true of a comparison of two industry groups, such as utilities versus gold. For instance, the utility group could be suffering from aggressive government regulation whereas the gold group may be unduly stimulated because of a mining strike in South Africa. Neither event would be associated with the business cycle, but both would strongly influence the trend and level of an inflation/deflation ratio.

A better solution is obtained by constructing an inflation indicator from several inflation-sensitive groups and a deflation indicator from deflation-sensitive industry indexes. Thus if one particular industry is influenced by noncyclical forces, it will not unduly distort the total result.

These indicators are shown in Chart 15.2. The Inflation Group Index

Chart 15.2. Inflation-sensitive versus deflation-sensitive groups. (*Source: Pring Market Review.*)

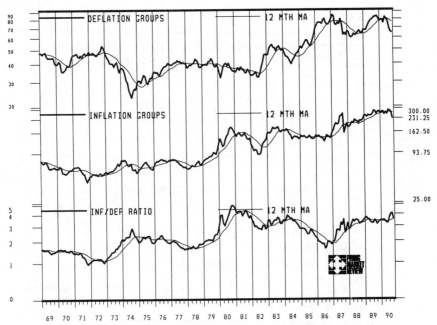

was constructed from a simple average of the Standard & Poor's (S&P) Gold, Domestic Oil, and Aluminum, the Deflation Group Index from Electric Utilities, Savings and Loans, Property and Casualty Companies, and Preferred Stocks.

The ratio of the two is shown underneath. When the ratio is in a rising mode, inflation-sensitive equities outperform their deflation-sensitive counterparts, and vice versa.

In effect, reversals in the trend of this indicator reflect the market's view of whether the cycle is in its inflationary or its deflationary stage. When the line is rising, it indicates that the rotational phase has moved to the inflationary side, and vice versa.

Chart 15.3 features the commodity/bond ratio discussed earlier in this chapter together with the Inflation/Deflation Group Index. By and large, major swings in the two series are very similar, and therefore they reinforce one another.

Most people would find it quite tedious to update the inflation/deflation indicator as described here. A useful shortcut is to calculate a ratio of the Dow Jones Energy Index and the Dow Jones Financial Index, both of which include several inflation- and deflation-sensitive

Chart 15.3. Two inflation/deflation indicators. (*Source: Pring Market Review.*)

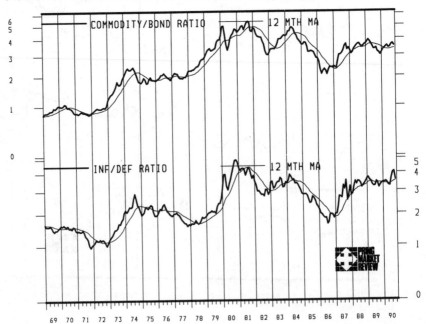

groups respectively. This data is published daily in The Wall Street Journal and weekly in *Barron's,* in conjunction with indexes for a hundred or so other sectors and groups.

Chart 15.4 shows the strength of the S&P Financial Index relative to that of the S&P Composite. Underneath is a momentum indicator of this series and a similar one for the Dow Jones Energy Index. Note that at almost all times these momentum series are moving in *opposite* directions, indicating that they are at opposing ends of the group rotation process. Thus one might consider emphasizing interest-sensitive and other issues with leading tendencies when the Financial Index RS momentum bottoms. A switch to inflation-sensitive areas would be made when the Energy Index bottoms and the Financial Index peaks. It is of course important to make sure that the RS momentum of the groups being purchased or liquidated is consistent with the pattern established by the Energy Index and the Financial Index. For example, it would make no sense to buy gold shares if energy RS was bottoming and gold RS was overbought and peaking. Remember that the momentum series shown in Chart 15.4 are indicators of *relative strength*. Rises and declines in these indicators indicate improving or deteriorating *relative strength.*

Chart 15.4. RS momentum of the Financial Index versus the Energy Index. (*Source: Pring Market Review.*)

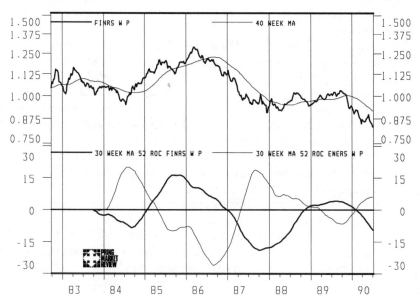

Some Examples

Charts 15.5, 15.6, and 15.7 show three industry groups—utilities, household furnishings, and aluminum—as examples of leading, coincident, and lagging groups, respectively. The upward- and downward-pointing arrows represent bull market peaks and troughs. The charts show that these groups act consistently with what might be expected most of the time, since the actual group, its RS line, or both reflect the leading, lagging, or coincident tendencies. It is also apparent that on several occasions these characteristics do not fit the theory neatly because of investors' attitudes toward the fundamentals. An unusual occurrence of this nature can often be useful in warning of a major turn in the industry's fortunes. For example, in 1953 and 1970 the Utility Index RS line reached its cyclical peak *ahead* of the bear market low. Normally such a development occurs 6 to 18 months after a bull market has begun. In each instance the utility average underperformed in the next bull market. In the 1953–1956 bull trend, the average did in fact rise because this was an extremely powerful advance. However, in the 1970–1974 cycle, the Utility Index exhibited its worst price performance since the 1930s.

In an opposite sense the Utility Index average RS reached its low slightly *ahead* of the 1956 bull market high. Although there were some intermediate periods of weakness, the next 9 years proved to be one of the best periods ever for the average. The action of the RS line is useful in forecasting the group itself, but it also warns that the group, its RS line, or both are likely to offer confusing signals with regard to group rotation analysis.

The coincident nature of the Household Furnishings and Appliances Index can best be seen by comparing the actual peaks and troughs of the index itself to the peaks and troughs in the market. In the two instances, 1973 and 1976, when Household Furnishing and Appliances led the actual market peak by more than 6 months (i.e., deviated from its normal coincident role), the index suffered its two worst bear markets in the post-World War II period.

The S&P Aluminum Index offers some other useful examples. In 1953 the RS index bottomed out ahead of the bear market low and was actually making a 2-year high 1 month later. For a leading group such as the utilities, this would be quite normal, but for a lagging group such as aluminum, it was clearly something out of the ordinary. As Chart 15.7 shows, the next rally was the best one in the post-World War II period. Similarly, at the 1956 and 1959 peaks the uncharacteristic softness of the Aluminum Index, its RS, or both would have provided a

Chart 15.5. The Dow Jones Utilities Index as an example of a leading group. (*Source: Securities Research Co., a Division of United Business Service Co.*)

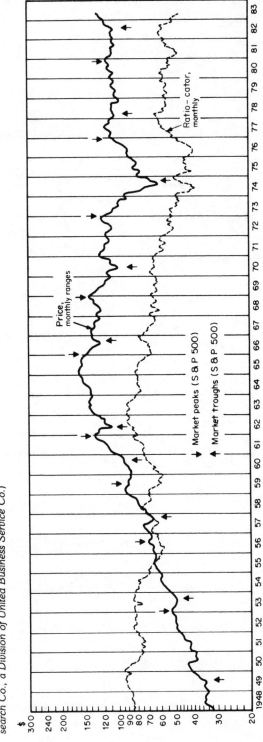

Chart 15.6. S&P's Household Furnishings and Appliances Index as an example of a coincident group. (*Source: Securities Research Co., a Division of United Business Service Co.*)

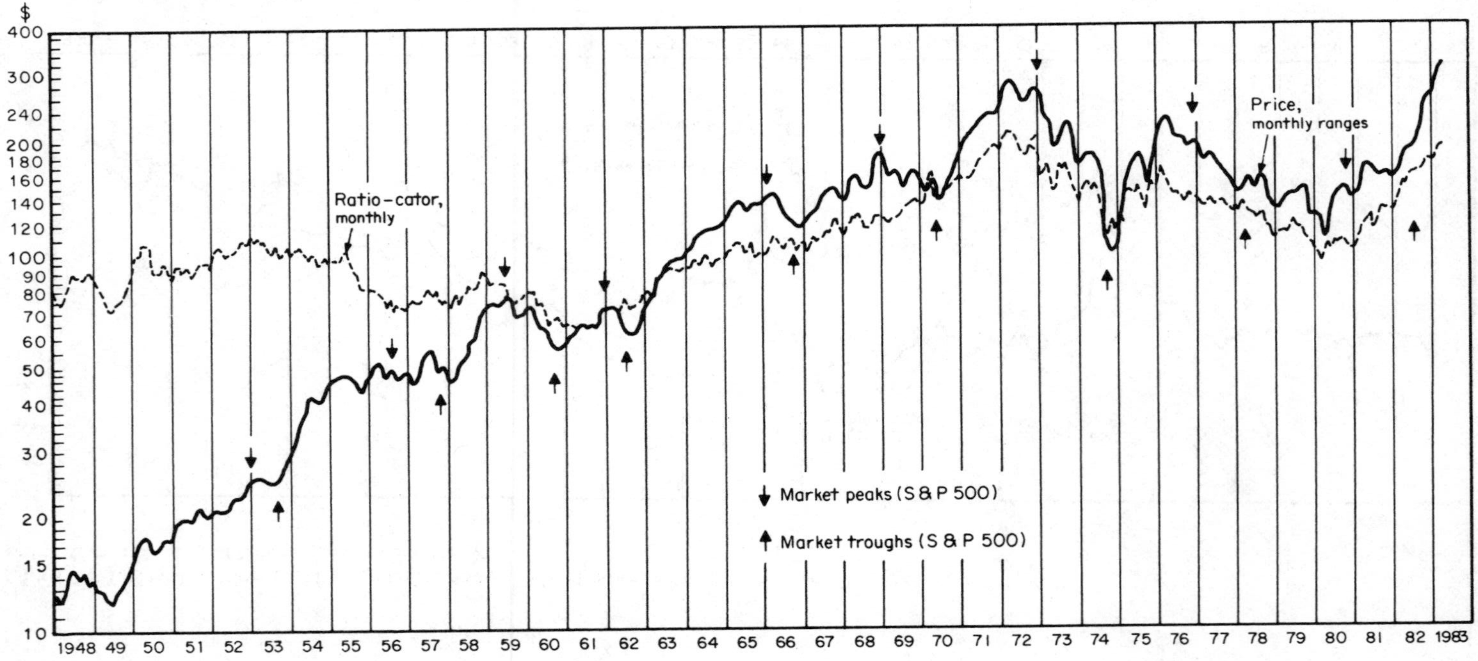

234

Chart 15.7. S&P's Aluminum Index as an example of a lagging group. (*Source: Securities Research Co., a Division of United Business Service Co.*)

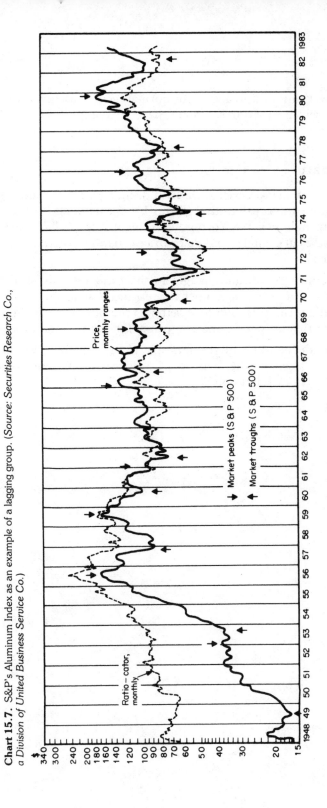

useful warning of a weaker than normal bear market, since this is the point at which superior RS should have been expected.

Summary

1. The stock market cycle includes a distinct pattern of industry group rotation. Interest-sensitive groups have a tendency to lead at peaks and troughs, whereas corporations the profits of which are helped by increases in capital spending or price inflation generally lag the overall market.

2. Sometimes significant changes in the fundamentals of an industry will cause a group to be uncharacteristically strong or weak during a specific cycle. It is therefore better to monitor a spectrum of groups rather than a specific one as a proxy for the rotation process.

3. An understanding of the industry group rotation cycle is helpful both in assessing the maturity of a primary trend and for the purpose of stock selection.

16
Time: Longer-Term Cycles

Time is represented on the horizontal axis of most technical charts. It is normally used in conjunction with price, volume, and breadth—the other three dimensions of psychology that are involved in determining trends in the stock market, which are measured on the vertical axis. Time can also be assessed independently through the analysis of cycles.

Discussions of the importance of time have so far been limited to the idea that the significance of a reversal in trend depends upon the length of time needed for the completion of distribution or accumulation. The longer the period, the greater the magnitude and duration of the next move are likely to be. Removing the speculative excesses of a trend requires a commensurately large corrective movement, just as the discipline of a long period of accumulation provides a sound base from which a substantial and lengthy advance can take place. The very long (8-year) bull market between 1921 and 1929 was interrupted by corrective reactions, but the substantial increase in stock prices during this period resulted in a considerable amount of excess confidence and speculative excesses which were only erased by a sharp and lengthy decline. Similarly, the 1966 stock market peak was preceded by 24 years of basically rising prices and followed by a long period of consolidation involving widely swinging stock prices. When adjusted for inflation, stock prices peaked in 1965 and then went through an extremely severe bear market, which was comparable to the 1929–1932 debacle.

Time is concerned with *adjustment*, because the longer a trend takes to complete, the greater its psychological acceptance and the greater the necessity for prices to move in the opposite direction and adjust accordingly. Investors become accustomed to rising prices in a bull market, each reaction being viewed as temporary. When the trend finally has reversed and the first bear market rally takes place, the majority are still convinced that this too is a temporary reaction and that the bull trend is being renewed. As prices work their way lower in a bear market, the adjustment takes a less optimistic form because the majority of investors forsake their expectations of a rising market and look for prices to move sideways for a time. The psychological pendulum finally swings completely to the other (bearish) side, as investors watch prices slip even further and become overly pessimistic. At this point sufficient time and downside price action have elapsed to complete the adjustment process, and the market in question is then in a position to embark on a new bull cycle.

Time has been viewed here in an emotional context, since time is required for investors to adjust to unrealized expectations. It is important for traders and investors to realize also that time is deeply bound up with the business cycle. This is because a strong and lengthy recovery, like the one between 1921 and 1929, breeds confidence among investors and also among businesspeople, who tend to become inefficient, careless, and overextended as a result of a long period of prosperity. The subsequent contraction in business conditions needed to wipe out these distortions is thus more severe. Equity prices therefore suffer the double influence of (1) losing their intrinsic value due to the decline in business conditions and (2) being revalued downward from the unrealistically high levels that prevailed during the period of prosperity. The reverse set of circumstances apply following a long market decline. This idea of a reaction commensurate with the previous action is known as the *principle of proportionality*.

Measuring time as an independent variable is a complicated process, since prices move in periodic fluctuations known as *cycles*. Cycles can operate for periods ranging from a few days to many decades. At any given moment a number of cycles are operating simultaneously, and since they are exerting different forces at different times, the interaction of their changing relationships often has the effect of distorting the timing of a particular cycle.

The most dominant of the longer ones is the so-called 4-year cycle, in which there is a nominal or average length between troughs of 41 months. Since several other cycles are operating at the same time but with different influences, the length of the 4-year cycle can vary either way by 6 months or so.

Cycles are shown on a chart in the form of a sine wave, as in Figure

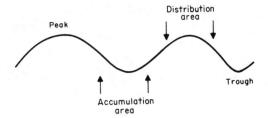

Figure 16.1.

16.1. These curves are usually based on a rate-of-change (ROC), or trend-deviation calculation, which is then smoothed to iron out misleading fluctuations. Since it occurs only rarely that two cycles are of identical length, an average or *nominal* period is calculated. This theoretical time span is used as a basis for forecasting.

In Figure 16.2 this idealized cycle is represented by the dashed line, and the actual cycle by the solid line. The arrows indicate the peaks and troughs of the idealized cycle. In actual fact, price trends rarely reverse exactly at theoretical points, and especially not at peaks, where there is often a long lead time. Nevertheless the theoretical points provide a useful guide.

There are three other important principles concerned with cycle analysis, in addition to those of proportionality and nominality, which were discussed above. The first is the *principle of commonality*, which states that cyclicality of similar duration exists in the price action of all stocks, indexes, and markets. This means that a 4-year cycle exists not only for the U.S. stock, bond, and commodity markets, but also for each individual stock and for international markets as well. The second principle, *variation*, states that while stocks go through similar cycles, the price magnitudes and durations of these nominal cycles will be different because of fundamental and psychological considerations. In other words, all stocks, indexes, and markets go through a similar cycle, but the timing of both their peaks and their troughs differs, and so does the size of their price fluctuations. For example, the interest-sensitive and

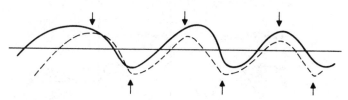

Figure 16.2.

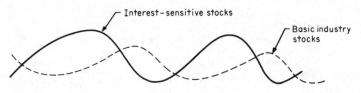

Figure 16.3.

cyclical (basic industry) stocks go through the similar cycle, but because
interest-sensitive stocks (such as utilities) lead the market, cyclicals (such
as steel groups) generally lag behind them. This is shown in Figure 16.3.
Similarly, the interest-sensitive issues may rise by 80 percent from the
trough to the peak of their cycle, while the cyclicals might advance by
only 20 percent, and vice versa.

   Chart 16.1 also illustrates this principle, and shows the interaction of
financial series during a typical business cycle. The rising part of each
cycle usually consists of three stages, which correspond to the three
phases described in the Dow theory. It is normal for prices to reach a
new high as each stage unfolds, but sometimes this does not happen.
This is known as a *magnitude failure,* and is a distinct sign of weakness.
A magnitude failure occurs because of very poor underlying fundamentals. In effect, the cycle misses a beat.

Chart 16.1. Typical cycles with financial series in percentages of their averages: a mechanistic approach to
business cycles. (*Source: L. Ayres, Cleveland Trust
Company, 1939.*)

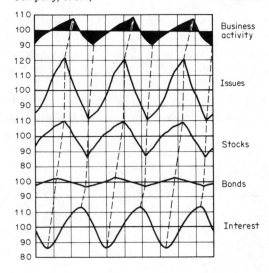

The opposite can also occur: exceptionally strong fundamentals (or the perception of them) can give rise to a fourth stage, in which prices undergo an additional upward leg. For equity markets this final upward surge is often associated with an extended period of declining interest rates. Such strong underlying conditions normally develop when the 4-year cycle occurs in conjunction with the peak of longer-term cycles such as the Kondratieff (50- to 54-year) and Juglar (9.2-year) cycles, which are discussed below.

In cases in which the cyclic turning points of a number of components of a particular market converge, the magnitude of the next move will be much greater. For example, the turning points of individual stock markets around the world can occur at different times. However, in the summer of 1982 most of their cyclical lows coincided. The resulting rally in virtually all markets was explosive.

The third principle is *summation*. Summation is really the combination of a number of cycles into one and is the concept behind the "*k*now *s*ure *t*hing" (KST) market cycle model discussed in Chapter 10. If the result were plotted as one idealized cycle, it would be represented by a curve similar to the one approximated in Figure 16.4.

At any one time there are four influences affecting any time series trend: secular, cyclical, seasonal, and random. The cyclical trend is the starting point for the purpose of analyzing primary bull and bear markets. Specifically, this is the 4-year or *Kitchin cycle*. The secular influence is a very long term one that embraces several 4-year cycles. From the point of view of a stock, bond, or commodity market, the most dominant "secular cycle" is the 50- to 54-year cycle known as the *Kondratieff wave* (after the Russian economist Nicolai Kondratieff). Two other important cycles in excess of 4 years have also been noted, namely the 9.2-year and 18⅓-year cycles.

Chart 16.2*a*, adapted from *Business Cycles*, by Joseph Schumpeter[1] combines the effect of three observable business cycles into one curve. In effect, it shows the summation principle using three longer-term

Figure 16.4.

[1]McGraw-Hill, New York, 1939.

Chart 16.2a. Schumpeter's model of the nineteenth-century business cycle. (*Source: Joseph Schumpeter, Business Cycles, McGraw-Hill, New York, 1939.*)

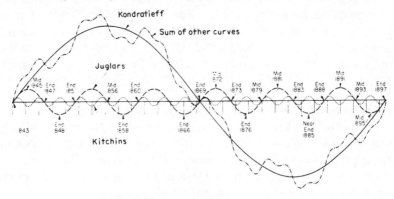

Chart 16.2b. The twentieth-century business cycle and crisis points (calculated path). (*Source: T. J. Zimmerman, Geschichte der theoretischen Volkswirtschafts-lehrs, in an unpublished paper by P. E. Erdman.*)

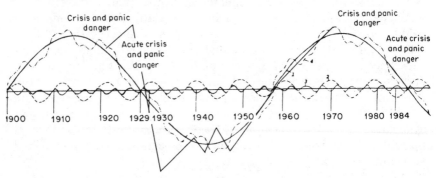

cycles: the 50- to 54-year (Kondratieff), the 9.2-year, and the 41-month (Kitchin) cycles. The model is not intended to be an exact prediction of business conditions and stock prices but rather to indicate the interaction of the shorter cycles with the longer ones. Even so, it is worth noting that the long-term curve crossed below the zero line in 1987, i.e., the year of the stock market crash—and this model was originally constructed in the early part of the 1920s. Comparing this model with Chart 16.3 reveals that the long upmove dating from about 1942 to about 1966 was associated with rising stock prices interrupted by relatively mild cyclical corrections.

Since the underlying force of this model is concerned with the 54-

Chart 16.3. United States stock prices, 1790–1976, showing Kondratieff bull markets (annual mean monthly averages). The Foundation for the Study of Cycles has spliced together the following series: 1790–1831, Bank & Insurance Companies; 1831–1854, Cleveland Trust Rail Stocks; 1854–1871, Clement-Burgess Composite Index; 1871–1897, Cowles Index of Industrial Stocks; 1897–1974, Dow Jones Industrial Averages (DJIA). The shaded areas represent the plateau period in the Kondratieff cycle. (*Source: Pring Market Review.*)

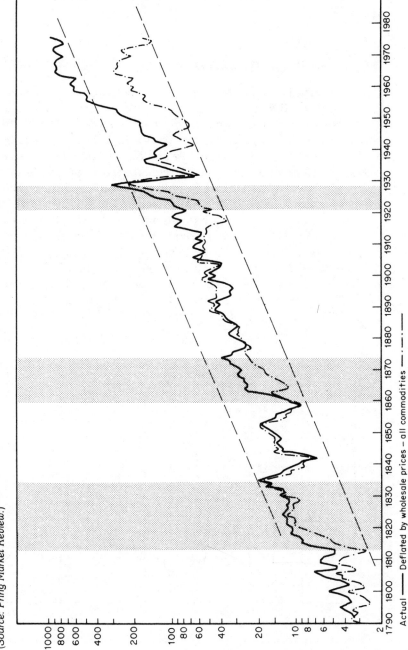

Actual ——— Deflated by wholesale prices – all commodities — · — · —

year Kondratieff wave, that wave will be a good starting point for this discussion.

The Long Wave (Kondratieff)

The 54-year wave is named after a little-known Russian economist who observed in 1926 that the United States had undergone three long economic waves, each lasting between 50 and 54 years.[2] It is worth mentioning that while only three such cycles have been recorded for the United States, E. H. Phelps Brown and Sheila Hopkins of the London School of Economics have noted a regular recurrence of 50- to 52-year cycles of prices in the United Kingdom, between 1271 and 1954. The crest for the most recent cycle was projected for the 1974–1978 period. In terms of global commodity prices and bond yields this was a pretty close call. The same cycle has been observed in interest rates, as shown in Chart 16.4.

Kondratieff used wholesale prices as the focal point of his observations, as shown in Chart 16.5a and b. My own view is that this cycle reflects the balance between long-term inflationary and deflationary forces. For example, there is little doubt that there were serious deflationary pres-

Chart 16.4a. Index numbers of 1780–1925 commodity prices (1901 – 1910 = 100).

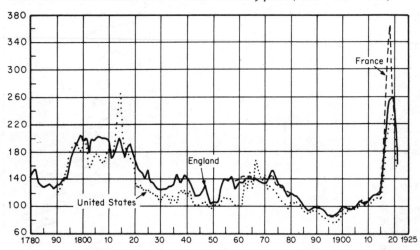

[2]The cycle was also noted by Professor William Stanley Jevons, an English economist, in the second half of the nineteenth century.

Chart 16.4b. Interest rates for the United Kingdom and France, 1815–1925. (*Source: N. D. Kondratieff, The Long Waves of Economic Life.*)

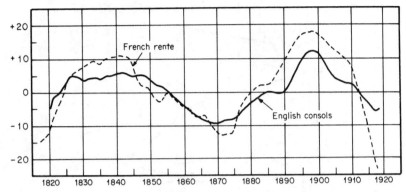

sures in the 1980s, and yet the Consumer Price Index (CPI) rose during this period. This anomaly can be explained by the fact that the antideflationary, or recessionary, activity of governments has been much greater in previous years. This has had the effect of offsetting the deflationary symptoms of lower prices. Kondratieff noted that each wave had three phases: an upwave lasting about 20 years, a transition or plateau period of 7 to 10 years, and a downwave of about 20 years. He observed that each upwave was associated with rising prices, the plateau with stable prices, and the downwave with declining prices. He also noted that a war was associated with both the beginning and the end of each upwave.

At the start of a cycle, business conditions are very depressed. Because of a considerable excess capacity of plant and machinery, there is really no incentive to invest in capital projects. Most people prefer to save money rather than invest it, because of extreme uncertainty. The war at the bottom of the downwave, known as the *trough war* (see Chart 16.5), acts as a catalyst to get the economy moving again. In view of the tremendous economic slack in the system, this war is not associated with inflation. As time progresses, each cyclical upwave becomes stronger and stronger; confidence returns and business once again reaches full productive capacity. Because price inflation is almost absent, interest rates are very low. Credit, a necessary fuel for any recovery, is both abundant and cheap. During this phase, businesses replace old plant and equipment and also invest in new capacity, which improves productivity and creates wealth. This rising phase is usually associated with widespread exploitation of a previously developed technology, such as canals in the 1820s and 1830s, railroads in the mid-nineteenth century,

Chart 16.5. The Kondratieff wave, based on annual averages with a ratio scale of 1967 = 100. (Source: *The Media General Financial Weekly, June 3, 1974.*)

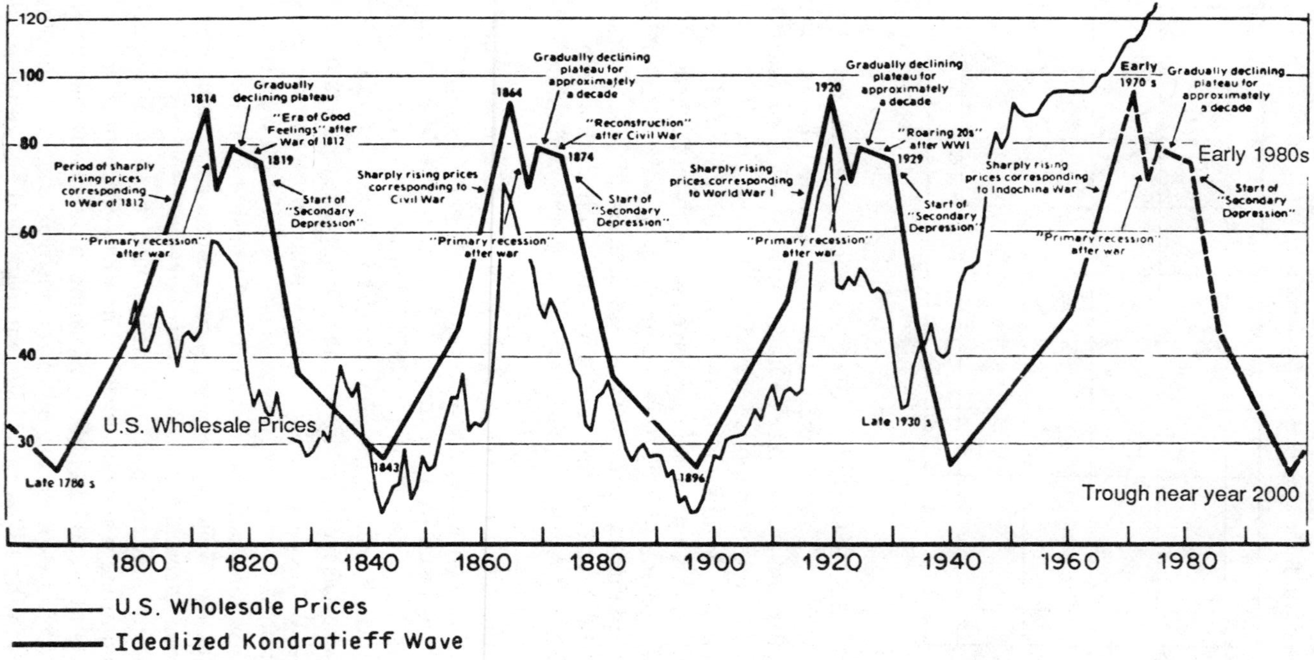

U.S. Wholesale Prices

Idealized Kondratieff Wave

Trough near year 2000

246

automobiles in the 1920s, and electronics in the 1960s. As the rising phase progresses, inflationary distortions caused by overinvestment start to develop. This development has a tendency to cause social tensions and economic instability. A common characteristic around this period is another war, known as the *peak war*. Unlike the trough war, which acts as a catalyst to the economic recovery, the peak war places undue pressure on a system that is already close to full capacity. As a result, commodity prices and bond yields move to very significant 20- to 25-year new highs. This was true of the peaks of 1814, 1864, 1914, and the late 1970s.

This long-term background is important because it influences the cyclical movements of the financial markets (see Chart 16.3). For example, during the up phase and the associated shallow recessions, it would be reasonable to expect mild and brief bear phases for equity markets. The relatively stable plateau period has always been associated with a very powerful bull market (e.g., 1820, 1860, 1920, and 1982). Finally, if a sharp and devastating bear market is to develop, it usually occurs during the down phase.

In a similar vein, commodity bull markets are long and bear trends are short during the up phase. Trends in bond prices are the opposite. The tables are turned during the down phase since commodity bear markets tend to be prolonged but cyclical advances in bonds are quite strong. The interpretation of the technical indicators should be adjusted accordingly. For example, the time span for a cyclical bear market in stocks might be 12 months during the up phase, with the annual rate of monthly price change limited to a −20 percent reading, but the standards would be different during the Kondratieff downwave, when each business cycle becomes weaker and weaker. Under these conditions, bear markets would be expected to last considerably longer and to be far more devastating. The same sort of perspective should be applied to cyclical trends of commodities and bonds, where the Kondratieff cycle is far more reliable.

A study and appreciation of the Kondratieff cycle is a fine example of why any market predictions based on the experience of only the two or three previous cycles are likely to prove unfounded. The Kondratieff wave has occurred only three times in the United States, and on each occasion the conditions have been different. *It should therefore be used as a framework on which to base a better understanding of the very long term trends of inflationary and deflationary forces, rather than as a basis for mechanistic prediction.*

The 18-Year Cycle

Normally the amplitude of a cycle is a function of its duration; i.e., the longer the cycle, the bigger the swing.

The 18-year (or, more accurately, the 18⅓-year) cycle has occurred fairly reliably in stock market prices since the beginning of the nineteenth century. This cycle gains credibility because it operates in other areas, such as real estate activity, loans and discounts, and financial panics.

Chart 16.6 shows a 3-year centered moving average (MA) of common-stock prices from 1840 to 1974. This average helps to smooth the trend and isolate the long-term picture more clearly. The beginning of the 18-year cycle at major market bottoms is self-evident.

While the average cycle lasts 18⅓ years, actual cyclical lows can vary 2 to 3 years either way. These troughs are marked on the chart above the 3-year MA. The increase in government interference in the economy resulting from the Keynesian revolution and the postwar commitment to full employment appears to have had two effects on the cycle that spanned 1952–1970. First, it was stretched out from 18 to 25 years (1949–1974), and second, it prolonged the up phase. This is especially

Chart 16.6. The 18⅓-year cycle of stock prices, 1840–1974 (3-year centered MA). (*Source: Pring Market Review.*)

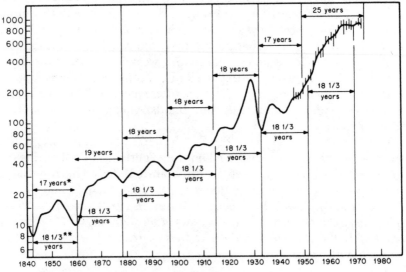

*Actual cycles spanning 17–25 years marked above

**Idealized cycles averaging 18 1/3 years marked below

noticeable for the 1949 low, which on a 3-year MA hardly shows as a trough.

There is a question of whether this cycle is still operating since the conceptual low last bottomed out in 1988, which did not coincide with a bottom associated with a business cycle. However, 18 years from the actual low recorded in 1974–1975 would place the cyclical low in the 1992–1993 period.

The 18-year cycle fits in well with the Kondratieff picture, since three such cycles form one Kondratieff wave. In the last two Kondratieffs, when the upwave part of the 18-year cycle coincided with the plateau period, an explosive bull market and only a mild correction took place. This was also true for the 1980s.

Since 1840, the 18-year cycle has operated fairly consistently. Except for the prolonged nature of the last cycle, there are few grounds for suspecting that this 18-year periodicity no longer exists.

The 9.2-Year Cycle

Chart 16.7 shows the 9.2-year cycle in stock prices from 1830 to 1946. The dashed lines represent the ideal cycle in which stock prices reversed exactly on schedule, and the solid line shows the actual annual average as a percentage of its 9-year MA trend.

The cycle occurred 14 times during the 1930–1946 period, and according to the Bartels test of probability, it could not occur by chance more than once in 5000 times. Further evidence of the significance of this cycle is given by observation of the 9.2-year periodicity in other

Chart 16.7. The 9.2-year cycle in stock prices, 1830–1946. (*Source: Edward R. Dewey, Cycles: The Mysterious Forces That Trigger Events, Hawthorne Books, New York, 1971, p. 119. Reproduced by permission of the Foundation for the Study of Cycles.*)

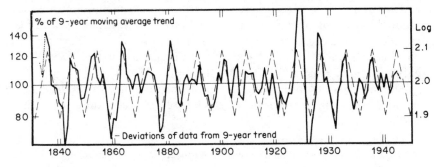

phenomena as unrelated as pig iron prices and the thickness of tree rings.

One problem with using the technique illustrated in the chart is that the annual average is expressed as a percentage of a centered 9-year MA. This means that the trend is not known until 4 years after the fact, so that there is always a 4-year lag in learning whether the 9.2-year cycle is still operating. Nevertheless, if the theoretical crest in 1965.4 is used as a base and the 9.2 years are subtracted back to 1919, the peaks of the 9.2-year cycle correspond fairly closely to major stock market tops. Unfortunately, one of the most recent theoretical peaks occurred in mid-1974, almost at the bottom of the 1973–1974 bear market, and represents the worst "signal" since 1947! However, the 1983 peak was right on target.

One interesting characteristic of the 9-year cycle that is probably of greater forecasting significance is the so-called decennial pattern.

The Decennial Pattern

This pattern was first noted by Edgar Lawrence Smith, who in 1939 published a book called *Tides and the Affairs of Men*.[3] His previous book, *Common Stocks as a Long-Term Investment*, had been a best-seller in the late 1920s.[4] Smith researched equity prices back to 1880 and came to the conclusion that a 10-year pattern, or cycle, of stock price movements had more or less reproduced itself over that 58-year period. He professed no knowledge as to why the 10-year pattern seemed to recur, although he was later able to correlate the decennial stock patterns with rainfall and temperature differentials.

Smith used the final digit of each year's date to identify the year in his calculations. The years 1881, 1891, 1901, etc., are the first years; 1882, 1892, etc., are the second; and so forth. Inspired by the research of Dr. Elsworth Huntington and Stanley Jevons, who both emphasized the 9- to 10-year periods of recurrence in *natural* phenomena, Smith experimented by cutting a stock market chart into 10-year segments and placing them above each other for comparison, as shown in Chart 16.8. He concluded from this data that a typical decade consists of three cycles, each lasting approximately 40 months.

The late Edson Gould, who came into prominence in the mid-1970s because of his uncannily accurate stock forecasts, used the decennial cy-

[3]Macmillan, New York, 1932.
[4]Macmillan, New York, 1939 (available in reprint from Fraser Publishing, Burlington, Vt., 1989).

Chart 16.8. The decennial pattern of industrial stock prices. (*Adapted from Edson Gould's 1974 "Stock Market Forecast." The years 1974–1980 represent our own proximations for major waveforms in the DJIA.*)

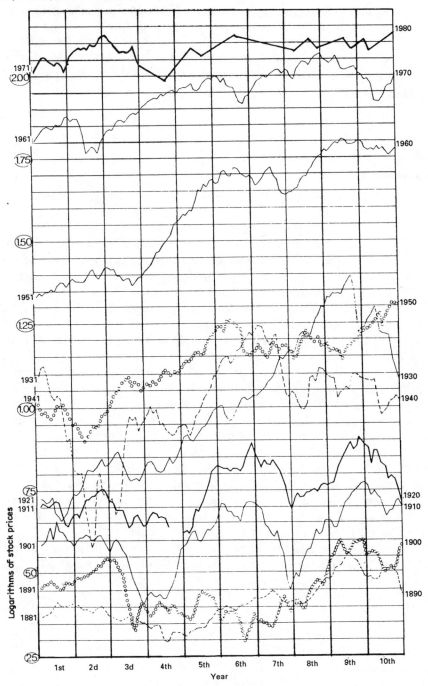

cle as a cornerstone for his research. In his 1974 stock market forecast Gould wrote, "In the 35 years that have passed since Mr. Smith's book was published – 35 years of wars, inflation and vast changes in our economic monetary set up and background – the action of the stock market has, much of the time, fitted unusually well with the 10-year pattern."[5] Smith's discovery has stood the test of time.

The 1980s versus the Average Decennial Cycle

The stock series in Chart 16.9 represents a simple average of the decennial pattern from 1880 to 1989, giving equal weight to the proportional movements of each period. The swings in the 12-month rate-of-change (ROC) indicator show three distinct cycles troughing in the first, fourth, and eighth years. I have calculated this average for other time spans and find that the first cycle low of the decade has more of a tendency to fall between the end of year 1 and the middle of year 2. In a similar vein, the final cycle low for the decade often comes at the tail end of the seventh year rather than in the middle of the eighth. Since this index represents an average, it is highly unlikely that a typical decade will duplicate it exactly.

The decennial pattern can be of greater value if it is used to identify where the strong and weak points usually occur, and then to see whether other technical phenomena are consistent. For example, in the middle of year 9, the 12-month ROC indicator for the average cycle is very overbought, which is consistent with a decline or consolidation starting at the end of that year and following through to the tenth, i.e., the year ending in zero. In 1949, *the 12-month ROC was very oversold and was inconsistent* with its normal position in the decennial pattern. Instead of declining into 1950, the market actually rose. This experience is a good example of why the decennial approach should be used with other technical indicators and not in isolation.

Bearing this in mind, note that Chart 16.10 shows the decade beginning in 1981. The swings in the 6-month MA of the 12-month ROC are very close to the decennial average shown in Chart 16.9, with lows in 1982, 1984, and 1988.

[5]From Smith, *Tides and the Affairs of Men.*

Chart 16.9. U.S. stock prices decennial average, 1881–1989.

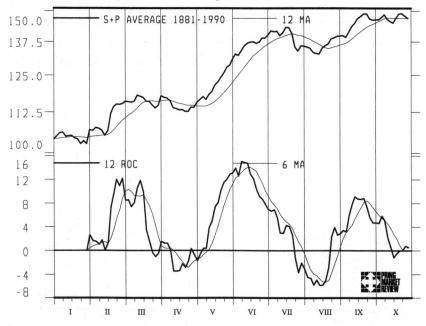

Chart 16.10. S&P Composite, 1981–1990.

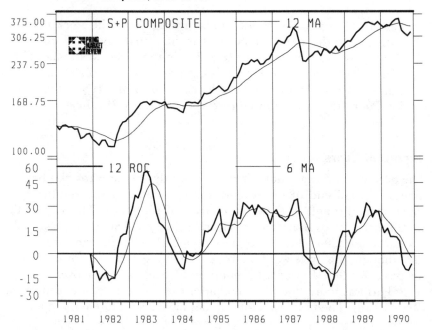

Chart 16.11. The average decennial cycle versus the S&P Composite, 1981–1989.

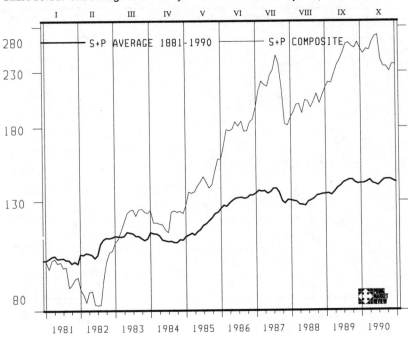

Chart 16.11 compares the decennial average with the stock market performance in the 1980s. It shows that the actual rhythms were very close to the average, and that price action in the 1980s was remarkably strong relative to normal events. Stock prices have typically risen about 1½ times between the first and ninth years, but in the 1980s, the Standard & Poor's (S&P) Composite rose approximately 2½ times.

Important Years

The decennial average shows that there is a distinct upward bias beginning at the tail end of the seventh or the middle of the eighth year, which runs through to the third quarter of the ninth. The 12-month ROC for the 1980s showed quite clearly that the 1988–1989 market followed the normal cyclical rhythm extremely closely. In terms of magnitude though, this cycle was far stronger than the average. For example, the peaks in 1989 showed a 12-month ROC reading at well over 20 percent. This was more than double that of the average decade (shown in Chart 16.10). The best years for equities have been those ending with a

Table 16.1.

Market movements	Years ending in:									
	1	2	3	4	5	6	7	8	9	0
1939–1989, % of months rising	57	62	63	62	75	50	44	61	55	58
1939–1989, % of months falling	43	38	37	38	25	50	56	39	45	42
1881–1989, % of months rising	56	60	55	60	73	53	45	65	60	53
1881–1989, % of months falling	44	40	45	40	27	47	55	35	40	47

5. Table 16.1 shows that between 1881 and 1989, 73 percent of these years were bullish. The other strong years appear to be those ending with 2, 4, and 8.

Weakness is most pronounced in the years ending with 1, 3, 6, 7, and 0. Only the seventh year has declined on more occasions than it has advanced, and it is therefore the weakest. The optimum periods for investment appear to be during the second, fourth, late seventh, and early eighth years. Since these comments relate to "average" years, they only indicate a bias. Investment decisions should take other indicators, such as the position of the 12-month ROC, into consideration. For example, if the market is extremely overbought at the end of the ninth year, the chances are that its "peaking" characteristic will result in weakness. On the other hand, if the market is oversold, as it was in 1949, this is likely to outweigh the normal decennial weakness.

The 41-Month (4-Year) Cycle

One perceptive observation made by Smith was that the decennial pattern appeared to "contain three separate cycles in a decade, each one lasting for approximately forty months,"[6] which is also apparent from the rhythmic action of the 12-month ROC, shown on Chart 16.9. This is most interesting, as it ties in with the so-called 4-year cycle of stock prices. More precisely, the 4-year cycle is a 40.68-month (41-month) cycle. It has been observed to operate in stock prices since 1871. Around 1923 Professor Joseph Kitchin was also able to show a cycle of 41 months in bank clearings, wholesale prices, and interest rates in the

[6]Smith, *Tides and the Affairs of Men*, pp. 55ff.

United States and United Kingdom. This cycle has since carried his
name.

The Kitchin cycle applied to stock prices is illustrated in Chart 16.12*a*
and *b*. Between 1871 and 1946 it has occurred 22 times with almost uncanny consistency. Then in 1946, as Edward Dewey describes it, "Almost as if some giant hand had reached down and pushed it, the cycle
stumbled, and by the time it had regained its equilibrium it was march-

Chart 16.12*a*. The 41-month rhythm in stock prices, 1868–1945. (*Source: Edward R.
Dewey, Cycles: The Mysterious Forces That Trigger Events, Hawthorne Books, New York,
1971. Courtesy of the Foundation for the Study of Cycles.*)

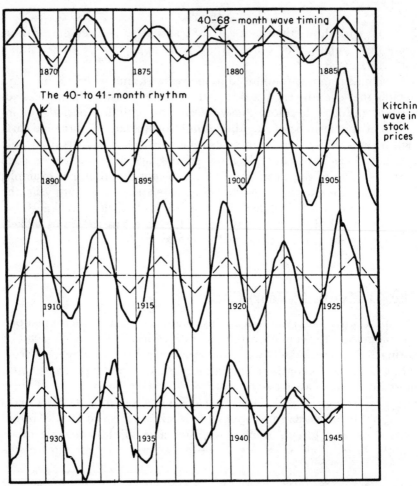

Chart 16.12b. The "reversed" cycle from 1946. (*Source: Courtesy of the Foundation for the Study of Cycles.*)

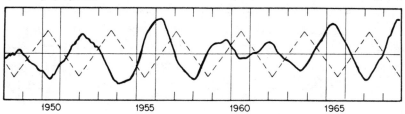

ing completely out of step from the ideal cadence it had maintained for so many years."[7]

Not only did the cycle reverse, it also extended to an average period of about 50 months, as shown in Charts 16.13*a* and *b*. This reversal and extension in the Kitchin wave is a fine example of how a cycle that has appeared for a long time to be working consistently can suddenly, for no apparent reason, become totally distorted. Once again, the fact that a particular indicator or cycle has operated successfully in the past is no guarantee that it will continue to do so.

Chart 16.13a. The 4-year cycle in the post-World War II period for the United States. (*Source: Edward R. Dewey, Cycles: The Mysterious Forces That Trigger Events, Hawthorne Books, New York, 1971.*)

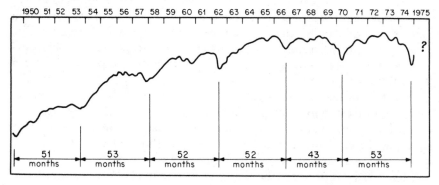

[7]*Cycles: The Mysterious Forces That Trigger Events,* Hawthorne Books, New York, 1971, p. 121.

Chart 16.13b. S&P Composite indicating cycle lows, 1974–1990. (*Source: Pring Market Review.*)

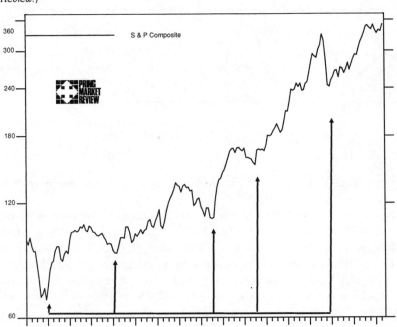

Seasonal Pattern

There is a distinct seasonal pattern of stock prices which tends to repeat year after year. Stocks seem to have a winter decline, a spring rise, a late-second-quarter decline, a summer rally, and a fall decline. The year-end witnesses a rally that usually extends into January. Stocks purchased in October have a high probability of appreciating if held for a 3- or 6-month period.

Apart from seasonal changes in the weather that affect economic activity and investor psychology, there are also some seasonal patterns in financial activities. For example, July and January are heavy months for dividend disbursement, retail trade around the year-end (Christmas) period is the strongest of the year, and so on.

Chart 16.14 represents the seasonal tendency of the stock market to rise in any given month. The probabilities were calculated over the period from 1952 to 1971. As the chart shows, January is normally the strongest month of the year and May the weakest. All movements are

Chart 16.14. Market probability chart. Shown here are the chances of the market's rising on any trading day of the year, based on the number of times the market rose on a particular trading day (the usual number of trading days in each month are included, and Saturdays, Sundays, and holidays excluded) during the period May 1952–April 1971. (*Source: Stock Traders Almanac, Hirsch Organization, Old Tappan, N.J.*)

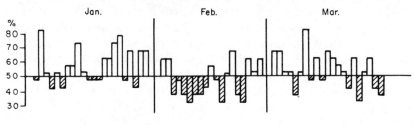

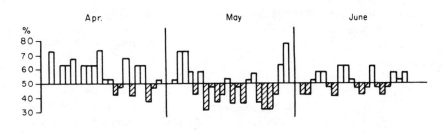

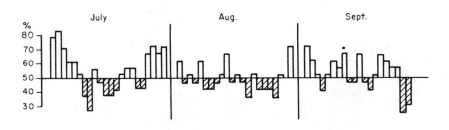

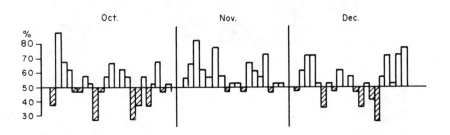

Shows the usual number of trading days in each month (Saturdays, Sundays, and holidays excluded)

relative, since a month with a strong tendency will be accentuated in a bull market, and vice versa.

Generally if the market rises in the first 5 days of January it is likely to maintain the rise during the month. And if the market rises in January, it tends to end the year at a higher level than it started at.

Small-capitalized stocks have a tendency to outperform large-capitalized issues at the turn of the year. For example, in the 11-year period from 1970 to 1981, small stocks average 16.4 percent versus 1.9 percent for large stocks during the 5-day period starting with the last day in December. This year-end effect of superior returns also seems to apply to the month-end. Data covering the 89-year period ending in 1986 show that returns from the last trading day of a month (day − 1 in Figure 16.5) are consistently good. The rationale for this effect may well come from higher month-end cash flows, such as salaries.

Indeed, these four trading days average 0.118 percent versus 0.015 percent for all trading days. Turn-of-the-month returns can be said to account for all the positive capital gain returns generated by the market. In an article entitled "Calendar Anomalies",[8] Bruce Jacobs and Kenneth Levy point out that this effect was less prevalent in the 1980s, which goes to show that it is not a wise policy to follow one indicator exclusively. However, it does make sense to integrate this reliable long-term seasonal effect with short-term oscillators. Clearly, the potential

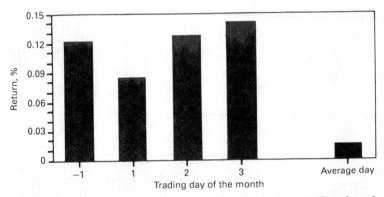

Figure 16.5. The turn-of-the-month effect (average daily returns). (*Data from J. Lakonishok and S. Smidt, "Are Seasonal Anomalies Real? A Ninety-Year Perspective," Johnson working paper 87-07, Cornell University, Ithaca, N.Y., 1987.*)

[8]*MTA Journal,* winter 1989–1990.

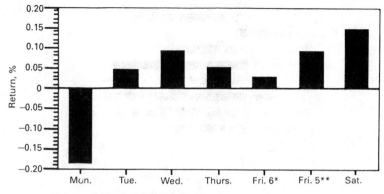

*Fri. 6 = Friday in a 6 day trading week.
**Fri. 5 = Friday in a 5 day trading week.

Figure 16.6. The day-of-the-week effect (average daily returns). (*Data from D. Keim and R. Stambaugh, "A Further Investigation of the Weekend Effect in Stock Returns," Journal of Finance, July 1984, pp. 819–837.*)

for the market to advance at this time will be much greater if it is over-sold going into the last (presumably) bullish day of the month.

Days of the Week

The term "blue Monday" is very much justified. The influence of weak Mondays originated during the 1929–1932 crash. During the Depression, the market advanced, on average, every day of the week except Mondays. It could be said that the entire market decline took place over weekends, during the periods from Saturdays to closings on Mondays.

Figure 16.6 shows the average return for each day from 1928 to 1982. Monday is the only down day. Remembering that this takes account of "black Thursday" in 1929 but does not include the 500-point drop that occurred on "black Monday" in 1987 just goes to emphasize the point.

There does not appear to be any acceptable rationale for this effect, which also occurs in non-U.S. equity markets, debt instruments, and even orange juice.

Preholiday Advances

The day preceding holidays is statistically a bullish period. This is indicated in Figure 16.7, which covers the period between 1963 and 1982.

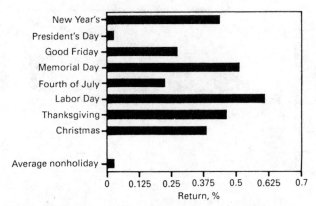

Figure 16.7. The holiday effect (average preholiday returns). *(Data from R. Ariel, "High Stock Returns Before Holidays," Sloan working paper, Massachusetts Institute of Technology, Cambridge, Mass., 1984.)*

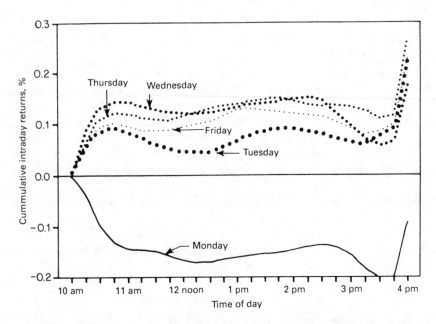

Figure 16.8. The time-of-day effect. *(Data from L. Harris, "A Transaction Data Study of Weekly and Intradaily Patters in Stock Returns," Journal of Financial Economics, vol. 16, 1986, pp. 99–117.)*

With the exception of Presidents' day, all these (average) preholiday trading sessions handsomely beat the average day.

Time of Day

Recent studies[9] have indicated that there is a definite time-of-day effect, as shown in Figure 16.8. There is little difference in the activity from day to day, except for Monday mornings. All days, however, show an upward bias going into the last ½ hour. The study showed that this rallying effect was emphasized even to the closing bell, with the average return of the last trade equal to 0.05 percent or 0.6 cents per share. The nearer the return took place to the closing bell, the higher it was. Trades after 3:55 P.M. averaged 0.12 percent returns or 1.75 cents per share. That upbeat note is a good place to close this chapter.

[9]Jarris, "How to Profit from Intradaily Stock Returns," *Journal of Portfolio Management,* winter 1986.

17
Time:
Practical
Identification
of Cycles

Computers can be very helpful in giving a quick approach to the identification of cycles. Among the software programs and data bases that facilitate this process are MetaStock and Computrac. This chapter discusses some of the basic principles of cyclic analysis, and uses examples to illustrate some simple techniques that help in their identification.

Cycles Defined

A *cycle* is a recognizable price pattern or movement that occurs with some degree of regularity in a specific time period. A market, stock, or indicator that has a relatively consistent price low at 6-week intervals is said to have a 6-week cycle. That successive lows are higher or lower than their predecessor is of no importance in identifying the cycle. What is significant is that there is a clearly definable "low" point every 6 weeks, separated from its predecessor by a high point known as the *cycle high*. Figure 17.1 shows some possible examples.

Figure 17.1 also shows that while cycle lows occur at approximately 6-week intervals, cycle highs can vary. Occasionally they arrive early, as at point *A*; sometimes they occur in the middle of the cycle, as at point *B*; but they may also appear late, as at point *C*. Generally when the cycle high develops shortly after the cycle low, the implications are that the

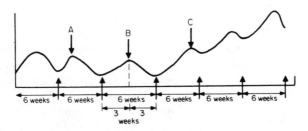

Figure 17.1.

upward part of the cycle is weak and that its overall strength lies on the downside. In this situation each cycle low is normally below that of its predecessor. Similarly, a cycle high that is "late" in arriving, i.e., that arrives well after the halfway period, usually indicates a strong cycle, with the implication that the cycle low will be above the low of the previous cycle. A number of different cycles can be observed for any market or stock, some long and some short in duration. The task of the technician is not to identify as many as possible but to isolate the most dominant and reliable.

There are several principles:

1. The longer the cycle, the greater the amplitude in price is likely to be; e.g., a 10-week cycle will have far greater trading significance than a 10-hour cycle.

2. It follows from item 1 that the larger the cycle, the greater the significance of the low.

3. The larger the number of cycles reaching a low at around the same time, the stronger the ensuing price movement is likely to be.

4. In a rising trend the cycle high has a tendency to "translate to the right," i.e., to occur after the halfway point of the cycle. The same principle holds in reverse for bear markets; i.e., there is a tendency for the cycle high to translate to the left.

5. It is possible to observe cyclic highs that occur at regular time intervals.

6. A projected cyclic high or low may develop in the opposite way to that anticipated. In such cases the cycle is said to be "inverted."

Methods of Detection

Many mathematical techniques have been used to identify cycles. Fourier analysis, for example, isolates the existence of various cycles by length, amplitude, phases, etc. Systematic reconnaissance is a technique that tests for periods requested. The result is a periodogram that shows the most dominant cycles. Although such techniques can be useful, they tend to make technical analysis look as if it is an exact science, which it very definitely is not. These approaches fall outside the scope of this book, but materials listed in the Resources section will give more information. This chapter will be confined to three methods of cycle identification: deviation from trend, momentum, and simple observation.

Deviation from Trend

This method takes a series of data and divides each item by a moving average (MA). The period under observation represents the deviation, and the MA represents the trend.

Chapter 8 explained that since an MA is designed to reflect the underlying price trend, ideally it should be plotted halfway along its span. This is because the "average" price occurs halfway through the time span, e.g., in the seventh week for a 13-week MA. However, changes in direction of the MA usually occur far too late to offer timely signals for the purpose of identifying trend reversals. For this reason technicians normally use an MA crossover for generating signals. Since only historical data are used in cycle identification, this disadvantage is not important. The MA deviation is therefore calculated by dividing the period in question by the midpoint of the MA. The price observation for February 27 is divided by a 13-week MA, as calculated on April 18; i.e., the MA is "moved" back 7 weeks. The result is then plotted as an oscillator which isolates the cyclical high and low points.

It is then a relatively simple task to see whether any consistent time periods separate these points. One method is to note down the time differences between all the cycle lows (and highs) in order to determine which ones come up most frequently. Since MAs smooth out all cycles within their time span, it is important to experiment with several averages in order to identify as many cycles as possible. The more reliable ones should then be used in the analysis.

Momentum

A simpler method is to calculate a momentum oscillator and smooth it by an appropriate MA, as determined by trial and error. This approach will bring out the underlying rhythm in the price movement, just as a deviation-from-trend calculation does. It is doubtful whether the momentum approach alone can be successfully used for cycle identification, but it can prove to be an invaluable confirmation of cyclical reliability when used in conjunction with the technique of simple price observation discussed below.

Chart 18.12 shows the New York Stock Exchange (NYSE) Composite daily close plotted against the 8-day most active indicator. In the 1977–1978 period this indicator appeared to be going through a regular 4- to 5-week cycle, as shown by the upward-sloping arrows on the chart.

The position of a momentum index can also be useful in warning of potential cyclic inversions, i.e., when a projected cyclic low might turn out to be a cyclic high, and vice versa. For example, a cyclic inversion may occur when the observed data project that a cyclic low is likely to develop around a specific date, while the momentum indicator used in conjunction with this study is at, or coming down from, an overbought level.

Simple Observation

The easiest method of identifying cycles is to start by observing, on a price chart, two or three major lows that appear to be relatively equidistant. The next step is to pencil in the projections for that particular cycle. If a substantial proportion of those projections result in either highs or lows, it is a good idea to mark them with a colored pencil. If most projections result in failure, the cycle should be abandoned and a new one sought. A cycle high occurring at any of these points should be treated as a successful projection since the first objective of cycle analysis is to determine potential turning points. Once a reliable cycle has been established, the analyst should look at all the important cycle lows which are "unexplained" by the first cycle and try to "explain" them by discovering another cycle. The chances are that the second cycle not only will fit some of the unexplained lows but also will occur at or near some of the cycle lows previously established. This is very important because a basic principle of cycle analysis is that the greater the number of cycles making a low around a certain time, the stronger the ensuing move is likely to be. Such knowledge *must* be used in conjunction with other technical evidence, but if that too offers a green light, the odds that a significant upwave will occur are increased.

This method for finding cycle bottoms may also be done for cycle highs; an example is given in Chart 17.1.

The next step in the method is discussed in the following section.

Chart 17.1. U.S. Treasury 8⅜ percent bonds, 1995/2000, and a 30-day ROC. (*Source: Pring Market Review.*)

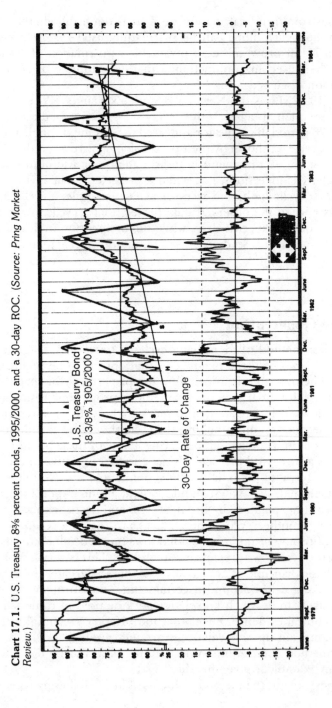

Combining Cycle Highs and Lows

The final part of the exercise is to try to combine certain cyclical high and low points into a projected cycle. Chart 17.1 shows this approach using daily prices for the U.S. Treasury 8⅜ percent bonds of 1995/2000. The arrows above and below the bond price point up a fairly reliable pattern for both cycle highs at approximately 24-week intervals and cycle lows at approximately 18-week intervals. The next step is to join up some of these points in order to construct an overall, idealized cycle wave. Since the cycles of lows and highs are of unequal length, the periods between the cyclic lows and highs (i.e., the upwaves and downwaves) vary in duration. Because of this variance a cycle low can occur before the next cycle high, which happened in December 1980. This low was followed by a very brief but sharp rally. In November 1982 the cyclic low occurred very close to the October high, but the price went sideways rather than rallying. A valuable clue that this was going to take place was given by the 30-day rate-of-change (ROC) index, which was at an extremely overbought condition. Also, that the two cycle points occurred at about the same time suggested that a major turning point was at hand. In effect the November high represented the top of the 1981–1982 bull market.

It should not be assumed that a reliable combination of cycles will always work out as shown in Chart 17.1. For example, the July-August 1980 low was accompanied by a deeply oversold condition, and yet a worthwhile rally failed to materialize.

One of the advantages of combining high and low cycles is that this approach makes it possible to obtain some idea of how long a rally or reaction might last. For example, the proximity of the May 1982 high to the June low suggested a short reaction, whereas the somewhat longer period between the May low and the projected November high indicated a rally of somewhat longer duration than average. Again, it should be emphasized that it is important to combine the interpretation of cyclic analysis with the position of an important ROC index. For example, the high and low cycle points occurred very close together in April 1983, suggesting that a major move was at hand. The ROC indicator did not offer a clear-cut signal about the direction of the impending move. If anything, the moderately overbought level suggested that the move would be down. This in fact proved to be the case, but only after a marginal new high had been set. This cycle is portrayed in Chart 17.1 by a dashed line, because the April peak and the August low seem to better reflect the actual course of prices.

Not all examples work out quite as accurately as that shown in Chart 17.1. Readers are cautioned not to try to make a cycle "work." If it does not fit naturally and easily, the chances are that it either does not exist or is likely to be highly unreliable and therefore should not be used.

Summary

1. Recurring cycles, both of low points and high points, can be observed from charts of financial markets.

2. A cycle turning point is significant both for the time interval between cycles and for the number of cycles that are turning at the same time.

3. Cycle lows and highs that recur at regular intervals may be connected to form an idealized complete cycle.

4. Suspected cycles that do not easily fall into a consistently recurring pattern should not be made to "work" and should be discarded.

18
Volume

Knowing the principle that volume goes with the price trend is a useful confirmation of price action, but studying volume is even more helpful because volume often *leads* price, which offers an advance warning of a potential price trend reversal. Before we take a look at the various methods of volume measurements, the general observations made earlier, in particular, in Chapter 5, will be briefly reviewed.

1. A price rise accompanied by expanding volume is a normal market characteristic and carries no implications of a potential trend reversal.

2. A rally that reaches a new (price) high on expanding volume but has an overall level of activity lower than the previous rally is suspect, and warns of a potential trend reversal (see Figure 18.1, example *a*).

3. A rally that develops on contracting volume is suspect and warns of a potential trend reversal in price (see Figure 18.1, example *b*).

4. Sometimes both price and volume expand slowly, gradually working into an exponential rise with a final blow-off stage. Following this development, both volume and price fall off equally sharply. This represents an exhaustion move and is characteristic of a trend reversal. The significance of the reversal will depend upon the extent of the previous advance and the degree of volume expansion (Figure 18.1, example *c*).

5. When prices advance following a long decline and then react to a level at, slightly above, or marginally below the previous trough, it is a bullish sign if the volume on the second trough is significantly lower than the volume on the first (Figure 18.1, example *d*).

6. A downside breakout from a price pattern, trendline, or moving av-

erage (MA) that occurs on heavy volume is a bearish sign which helps to confirm the reversal in trend (Figure 18.1, example *e*).

7. A selling climax occurs when prices fall for a considerable time at an accelerating pace, accompanied by expanding volume. Following a selling climax, prices may be expected to rise, and the low established at the time of the climax is unlikely to be violated for a considerable time. A price rise from a selling climax is by definition accompanied by declining volume. This is the only time when contracting volume and a rising price may be regarded as normal. Termination of a bear market is often, but not always, accompanied by a selling climax (Figure 18.1, examples *f* and *g*).

8. When the market has been rising for many months, an anemic price rise (Figure 18.1, example *h*) accompanied by high volume indicates churning action and is a bearish factor. Following a decline, heavy volume with little price change is indicative of accumulation and is normally a bullish factor (Figure 18.1, example *i*).

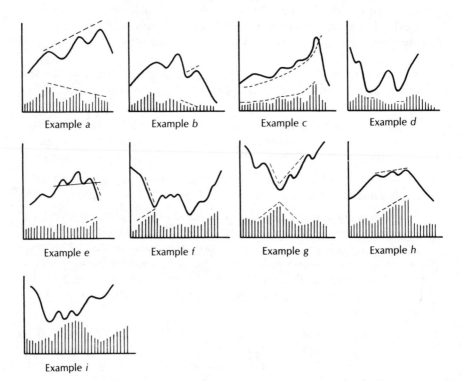

Example *a*   Example *b*   Example *c*   Example *d*

Example *e*   Example *f*   Example *g*   Example *h*

Example *i*

Figure 18.1.

Rate of Change (ROC) of Volume

Primary Trend

In his book *The Stock Market Indicators* William Gordon noted that, between 1877 and 1966, "In 84 percent of the bull markets the volume
high did not occur at the price peak but some months before."[1] Of the
18 bull markets, two uptrends ended with volume and price reaching a
peak simultaneously (January 1906 and March-November 1916), and in
one uptrend (October 1919) volume lagged by a month. The lead time
of volume in the remaining 15 cycles was from 2 months (April 1901
and December 1965) to 24 months (January 1951). The average for all
cycles was 9 months. My own research shows that volume has consistently continued to lead major price peaks since 1966.

In technical analysis the level of volume is usually compared to that of
a recent period in order to determine whether it is high or low.

Chart 18.1 shows the annual rate-of-change (ROC) price for the Standard & Poor's (S&P) Composite and a similar measure for a 3-month
MA of total New York Stock Exchange (NYSE) volume. In most instances the ROC of volume led that of price, especially at market bottoms. This method of showing volume suffers from the fact that the
movements are jagged, and it is therefore difficult to interpret when a
reversal in trend has taken place. Chart 18.2 attempts to surmount this
problem by smoothing the data. The technique used is a 6-month MA
of these two annual ROCs. When used together, the two series can be
extremely instructive.

There are several observations that can be made:

1. The volume curve has an almost consistent tendency to peak out
   ahead of price during both bull and bear phases.

2. In most instances, fairly reliable indications of a *potential* trend reversal can be obtained when the volume momentum crosses price.

3. When the price index is above its zero reference line and is falling,
   but volume is rising (e.g., 1953, early and late 1976, 1981, and late
   1987; the experience in early 1964 appeared to be an exception), the
   expanding activity represents distribution and should be interpreted
   as a very bearish factor once the rally has terminated.

4. A reversal in volume at a market bottom should be confirmed by a
   reversal in price momentum as well.

[1]Investors Press, Palisades Park, N.J., 1968.

Chart 18.1. Price versus volume momentum. (*Source: Pring Market Review.*)

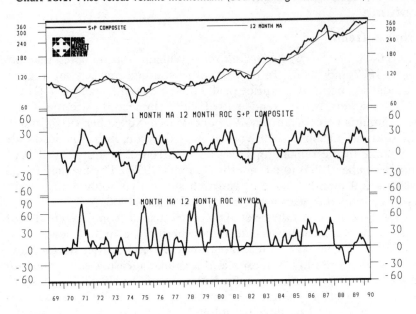

Chart 18.2. Price versus volume momentum smoothed. (*Source: Pring Market Review.*)

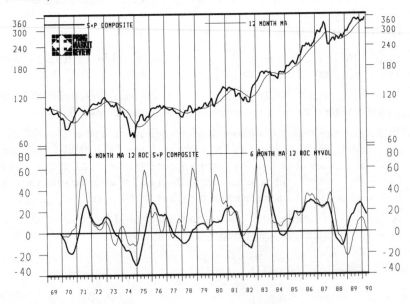

5. Very high readings in the volume indicator are usually followed by strong bull markets.

6. When volume crosses below zero, it is normally, but not always, a negative sign. The most bearish situations seem to arise when the price indicator is well above zero. In 1988, for instance, price momentum was well below zero when volume moved into negative territory, but the market rallied. On the other hand, in 1969, 1973, and 1977 volume crossed below zero just after price momentum had started to roll over from an overbought level, and this was followed by a major decline.

7. During the initial stages of a bull move, volume momentum is always above price. (The 1988–1989 rally represents the *only* exception.)

Chart 18.2 shows that a reversal in one curve unaccompanied by a reversal in the other at market bottoms gave a premature signal. For example, volume turned up ahead of price at the end of 1973 and 1977. Consequently, it is wiser to await a signal from both, even though it may occur at a slightly higher price level.

Intermediate-Term Trend

A useful volume/price crossover model can be constructed by using a 3-week MA of the 26-week ROC of price with a 10-week MA of a 26-week ROC for volume. This is shown in Chart 18.3. The movements and crossovers are to some extent similar to the primary trend model discussed above. The signals come faster and are more sensitive, but the seven principles outlined earlier are still relevant. There is nothing sacred about the time spans and MAs used in this approach. It works reasonably well, but there is no reason for the curious reader not to search for, and find, a better-fitting model.

An alternative method for monitoring intermediate-term trends is to calculate an 8-week MA for an 8-week ROC of volume, as shown in Chart 18.4.

In most instances, when this indicator peaks, it is associated with a consolidation or reversal in the prevailing price trend. Similarly, when the ratio bottoms, it usually provides a good trading opportunity. Since some signals occur while the price is declining and is therefore bearish, it is important to make sure that a positive volume signal is confirmed by a similar one for price.

It should be remembered that a specific time span will be a useful market indicator only as long as the implied cycle reflected by the momentum indicator is still in force. In other words, most of the time the

Chart 18.3. Price versus volume momentum model. (*Source: Pring Market Review.*)

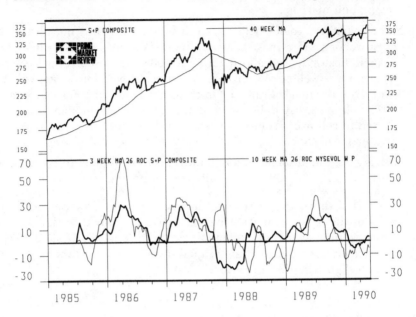

Chart 18.4. Eight-week volume momentum. (*Source: Pring Market Review.*)

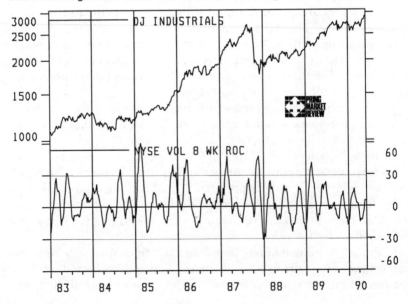

market rises and falls on a fairly consistent basis—for example, 4 years for a cyclical movement, and 13 to 26 weeks on an intermediate basis. The moment price movements diverge significantly from these set movements, indicators based on these cycles will fail to operate successfully. For example, the 1970–1974 cycle was a textbook case of the 4-year cycle in operation. However, the ROC indicators used to successfully signal the peak of this cycle would have been extremely early in forecasting the termination of the 1921–1929, 1942–1946, and 1962–1966 and 1982–1987 bull market peaks.

Short-Term Trend (Volume Oscillator)

Most of the indicators used in technical analysis are derived from price. For example, MAs and oscillators represent manipulation of the same price data, but they look at it from different aspects.

On the other hand, volume is totally different from price, which means that oscillators derived from this data give additional and independent evidence of a potential trend reversal. Volume is most commonly presented on daily charts as a histogram, plotted for a specific period under price.

The histogram approach can be very helpful when there are rapid changes in volume which can be easily identified. Often changes in activity are quite subtle and are not readily apparent from the histogram representation. In this respect, it is often better to express market activity in an oscillator format. Volume changes incorporating an ROC calculation for primary and intermediate trends were introduced above, but an alternative method compares the relationship between two MAs of volume. For short-term price movements, comparing a 10- to a 25-day MA seems to offer good results.

The indicator is constructed by calculating first a 10-day MA and then a 25-day MA of volume. Then the 10-day MA is divided by the 25-day MA and the result is plotted in an oscillator format (see Figure 18.2, steps 1, 2, and 3). The resulting indicator is an oscillator that revolves around a zero reference line. A zero reading in the indicator occurs when both MAs are at identical levels. Positive readings develop when the 10-day MA is above its 25-day counterpart, and vice versa.

Volume oscillators move between bands of extremes just as price momentum does, but with one important difference. When a price index is overextended on the upside, it usually indicates an overbought market with the implication that a reversal to the downside is due. An unusual rise in activity is also associated with an imminent trend reversal, but

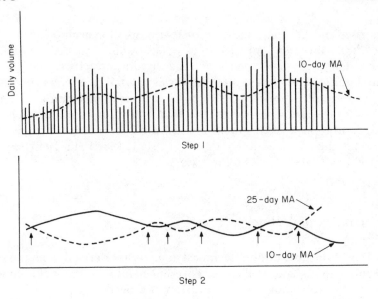

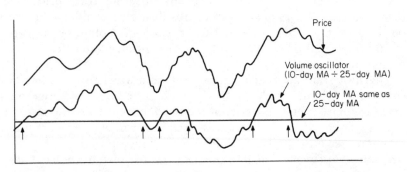

Figure 18.2 . Volume oscillator, steps 2 and 3.

overbought readings in the volume oscillator can occur at market bottoms as well as market tops. For example, during a selling climax, prices move down precipitously as volume expands.[2] Naturally this is reflected in the volume oscillator by a sharp rise. In a similar vein, a rally in price is always accompanied by a rising oscillator, but a weak rally is associated with declining volume; in such a case, the volume oscillator will fall. *It is*

---

[2]Because selling climaxes are short-term affairs, they are reflected in daily volume oscillators. They are also occasionally reflected in weekly data, as in 1987 (Chart 18.3), but not usually in longer-term indicators based on monthly data.

therefore essential to relate the movement of the volume oscillator to the prevailing movement in price.

Apart from this important difference, volume oscillators should be interpreted in the same way as price oscillators. Chart 18.5 shows Banca Commerciale, an Italian stock, and its volume oscillator. The overbought and oversold levels were determined on a trial-and-error basis in which the extreme readings encompassed the majority of the important swings. It is evident that, on most occasions on which the indicator reaches an overbought or oversold zone and then reverses back toward the zero line, an important *short-term* reversal in the price of the stock develops.

The volume oscillator should of course be used in conjunction with price oscillators and an analysis of the price trend of the market or stock in question before a major trading or investment decision is made. This relationship is not always exact. If volume and price changes are not closely related for the stock or market being followed, this approach should not be used.

The second example of a volume oscillator shows ASA, a closed-end gold share fund (see Chart 18.6). The oscillator would have been very

Chart 18.5. Banca Commerciale and a volume oscillator. (*Source: Pring Market Review.*)

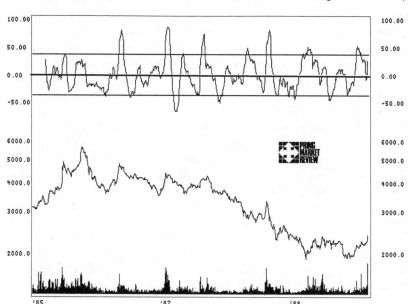

Chart 18.6. ASA and a volume oscillator. (*Source: Pring Market Review.*)

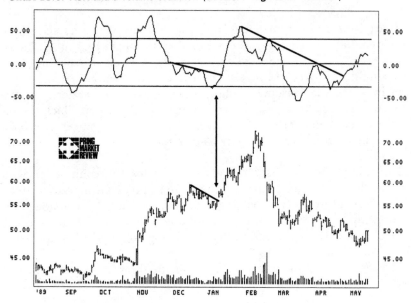

helpful in identifying some short-term peaks in August and October of 1989. It is also worth noting that the volume oscillator also lends itself to trendline construction. For example, in January 1990, a downtrend was broken just at the time the price was also rallying above a small down trendline.

The volume oscillator can also be used for identifying divergences. In the case of ASA, the price traced out a series of three successively higher peaks in January and February, but the volume oscillator peaked in the middle of January and was in a downtrend at a time when ASA was at its final high.

The oscillator later indicated that volume was expanding as the price started to fall. This of course represented a bearish characteristic since volume usually moves in the same direction as price. There was no way of knowing from this particular study that the price would fall from $70 to $50, but the declining series of peaks in the oscillator, later followed by an expansion in volume as the price started to decline, should have warned investors to avoid the stock until the technical position improved.

In late April a trendline joining the January and February peaks was violated, which indicated that volume was expanding. However, this was not a bullish sign because prices started to fall and continued to do so until well after May. Chart 18.7 shows this same oscillator together with

Chart 18.7. The Hang Seng index and an intermediate volume oscillator. (*Source: Pring Market Review.*)

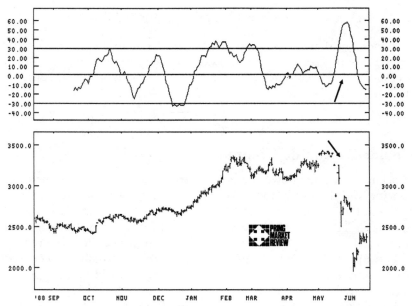

a 3-month perpetual contract for Hang Seng futures. The oscillator was actually falling when the index experienced a breakout in May 1989. This in itself should have warned that all was not well, but the subsequent expansion in volume as the index started to decline was the clincher. The severity of the price retreat was caused by the Tienenman Square massacre, but the technical picture had already deteriorated to the point that the market was clearly vulnerable to bad news.

Summarized below are the main rules for interpreting the volume oscillator.

1. When the oscillator reaches an extreme and starts to reverse, it is indicating the potential for a reversal of the prevailing trend.

2. Volume oscillators occasionally lend themselves to trendline and pattern construction.

3. Expansion in price, associated with a contraction in the volume oscillator, is bearish.

4. An expansion in the oscillator, associated with a contraction in price,

is bearish, except when volume reaches an extreme, in which case a selling climax is usually signaled.

5. The volume oscillator usually leads the price oscillator.

Remember that this is by no means a perfect indicator; therefore you should first make sure that it bears resemblance to the price trend being measured, and then that there is corroborating evidence from other indicators.

Upside/Downside Volume

Measures of upside/downside volume try to separate the volume in advancing and declining stocks. Using this technique makes it possible to determine in a subtle way whether distribution or accumulation is taking place. The concept sounds good, but in practice, volume momentum based on ROC or trend-deviation data appears to be more reliable.

The upside/downside volume data is published daily in *The Wall Street Journal* and weekly in *Barron's*. Upside/downside volume is measured basically in two ways.

The first is an index known as an *upside/downside volume line*. It is constructed by cumulating the difference between the daily plurality of the volume of advancing and declining stocks. Since an indicator of this type is always started from an arbitrary number, it is a good idea to begin with a fairly large one; otherwise there is the possibility that if the market declines sharply for a period, the upside/downside line will move into negative territory, which unduly complicates the calculations. If a starting total of 5000 million shares is assumed, the line will be constructed as shown in Table 18.1.

Table 18.1.

Date	Volume of advancing stocks, in millions	Volume of declining stocks, in millions	Difference	Upside/downside line
Jan. 1	101	51	+50	5050
2	120	60	+60	5110
3	155	155	0	5110
4	150	100	+50	5160
5	111	120	−9	5151

Figure 18.3.

These statistics are not published on a weekly or monthly basis, so longer-term analysis should be undertaken by recording the value of the line at the end of each Friday, or taking an average of Friday readings for a monthly plot. The appropriate MA can then be constructed from these weekly and monthly observations.

It is normal for the upside/downside line to rise during market advances and to fall during declines. When the line fails to confirm a new high (or low) in the price index, it warns of a potential trend reversal. The basic principles of trend determination discussed in Part 1 may be applied to the upside/downside line. (See Figure 18.3.)

When a market is advancing in an irregular fashion, with successively higher rallies interrupted by a series of rising troughs, the upside/downside line should be doing the same. Such action indicates that the volume of advancing issues is expanding on rallies and contracting during declines. When this trend of the normal price/volume relationship is broken, a warning is given that one of two things is happening. Either upside volume is failing to expand sufficiently or volume during the decline has begun to expand excessively on the downside. Both are bearish factors. The upside/downside line is particularly useful when prices may be rising to new highs and overall volume is expanding. In such a case, if the volume of declining stock is rising in relation to that of advancing stocks, it will show up either as a slower rate of advance in the upside/downside line or as an actual decline.

The upside/downside line from 1986 to 1987 is shown in Chart 18.8 together with its 65-day MA. For most of this period the line remained above its MA despite some fairly large short-term corrections in the S&P Composite, but in early October it fell below the MA—just before the crash. An important up trendline was violated simultaneously with the MA, which had the effect of emphasizing the bearish signal.

Also worth noting were the positive divergences that occurred in October 1986, when the S&P made a new short-term low, which was not confirmed by the cumulative upside/downside line.

Chart 18.8. Upside/downside volume, 1986–1987, versus the S&P Composite. (*Source: Pring Market Review.*)

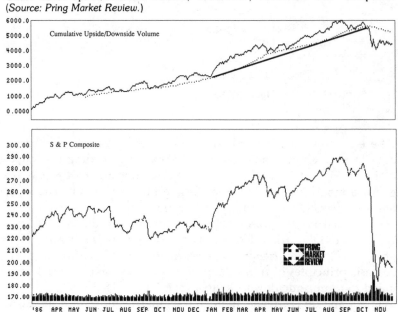

An alternative method of showing upside/downside volume is to construct an oscillator based on the following formula:

$$\text{Oscillator} = (M \times UVOL/M \times DVOL) - 1$$

In this case $UVOL$ = upside volume, $DVOL$ = downside volume, and M is an MA. 1 is subtracted from the formula in order to place the equilibrium line at zero. This additional manipulation does not alter the performance of the indicator. It merely changes the numbers below the equilibrium level to negative numbers.

This formula, based on a 15-day MA, is plotted in Chart 18.9. Most of the time a decline in the oscillator below the +50 level warns of a short-term decline or consolidation. It occasionally lends itself to price patterns (October 1988) and trendline construction (February 1989).

Another method of measuring upside/downside volume is to plot a moving total of both series on the same chart and compare the two (see Chart 18.10). Significant rises in the downside indicator to an overbought level indicate a selling climax, e.g., the one that occurred in late 1988. However, it is usually the upside volume indicator that offers the most reliable pointer of a possible trend reversal.

As long as successive highs in the market are associated with new

Chart 18.9. Intermediate upside/downside volume oscillator. (*Source: Pring Market Review.*)

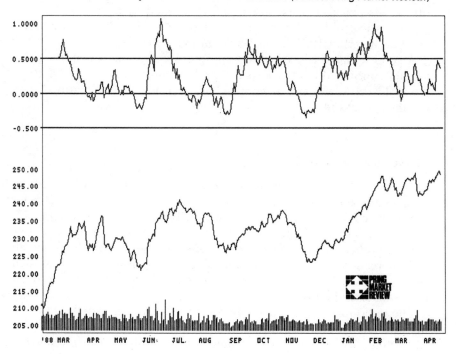

Chart 18.10. Wilshire 5000 and NYSE up volume and NYSE down volume. (*Pring Market Review.*)

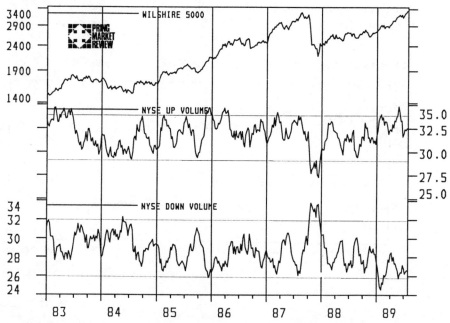

highs in the volume indicator, there is not much chance of a major sell-off because market peaks are usually preceded by at least one diver-gence in the upside volume indicator. Examples of this type of phenom-enon occurred in 1981, 1983, 1987, and late 1989.

A good signal of a market bottom occurs when new lows in the price are not confirmed by new lows in upside volume as in 1978 and 1982. Normally this is also associated with less downside volume (expressed by declining peaks in this indicator).

Most Active Stocks

Statistics on the most active stocks are published in the popular press on both a daily and a weekly basis. Usually the 20 most active NYSE issues are recorded, but results do not seem to differ significantly whether 10, 15, or 20 issues are used. Active stocks are worth monitoring since they not only reflect the actions of institutions but also account for some 20 to 25 percent of total NYSE volume. Since the net price changes of such issues are recorded, it is possible to derive an indicator that can confirm movements in the upside/downside line.

The indicators derived from most active statistics are similar to those derived from upside/downside data. Chart 18.11 shows an oscillator constructed by taking a 30-day moving total of the net difference be-tween the 10 most active advancing and declining stocks. The calcula-tion is made by totaling the number of the 10 most active stocks each day that advance and those that decline. Sometimes the 15 or 20 most actives are used as a basis for the indicator, but results do not differ ap-preciably. In order to obtain the 30-day oscillator, the number of ad-

Chart 18.11. The NYSE Composite versus the 30-day most active indicator.

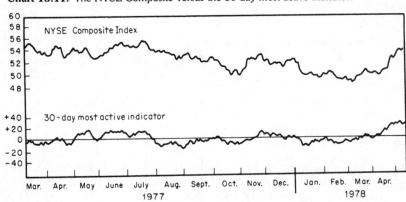

Chart 18.12. The NYSE Composite versus the 8-day most active indicator.

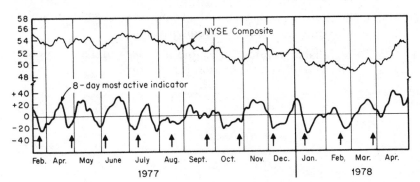

vancing stocks over the 30-day period are then totaled. The same calculation is made for the declining stocks, and one total is taken from the
other. If the number of advancing stocks over the 30-day period is
greater than the number of those declining, the oscillator will have a
reading above zero, and vice versa. As new data are received each day,
they are added to the two totals, and the data for the previous thirty-
first day are deleted. The resulting index appears to be useful for confirming intermediate advances and declines as it crosses above and below its zero reference line. In order to reduce the possibility of
whipsaws, it is a good idea to wait for the index to cross its zero reference line more decisively. An alternative method is to construct an oscillator in a similar manner but using weekly data, i.e., the 10, 15, or 20
most active stocks based on weekly volume.

Shorter-term market movements can be indicated by using a smaller
time span; in Chart 18.12 an 8-day total has been used. The second
method of using the most active stocks is to take a cumulative difference
between the number of advancing and the number of declining stocks
each day. The result is an index which is not dissimilar to the
upside/downside line. Although most of the time these two indicators
move in concert, keeping up both series is well worthwhile, since the
points at which their courses differ are often most informative about a
potential reversal in the overall market trend.

Summary

1. Most indicators are a statistical deviation from price data. Since volume indicators are totally independent of price, they offer a more
   objective view of the quality of the price trend.

2. Volume normally leads price.

3. Volume gives strong indications of a trend reversal when it moves in the opposite direction to the prevailing trend.

4. The more reliable volume indicators are derived from smoothed ROCs or smoothed trend-deviation calculations.

19
Breadth

Breadth indicators measure the degree to which the vast majority of issues are participating in a market move. They therefore monitor the extent of a market trend. Generally speaking, the fewer the number of issues that are moving in the direction of the major averages, the greater the probability of an imminent reversal in trend. Breadth indicators were originally developed to monitor trends in the stock market, but in recent years they have been expanded to embrace any market which can conveniently be subdivided into components. Even though most of the comments in this chapter refer to U.S. equities, it should be remembered that breadth can just as validly be applied to other financial markets.

The concept of breadth can probably be best explained using a military analogy. In Figure 19.1, lines *AA* and *BB* indicate military lines of defense drawn up during a battle. It might be possible for a few units to cross over from *AA* to *BB*, but the chances are that the *BB* line will hold unless an all-out effort is made. In example *a,* the two units represented by the arrows are quickly repulsed. In example *b,* on the other hand, the assault is successful since many units are taking part, and army B is forced to retreat to a new line of defense at *B1*.

A narrowly advancing stock market can be compared to example *a,* where it *looks* initially as though the move through the line of defense

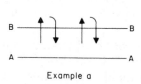

Example a

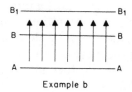

Example b

Figure 19.1.

289

(in stock market terms, *a resistance level*) is going to be successful, but because the move is accompanied by such little support, the overall price trend is soon reversed. In the military analogy, even if the two units had successfully assaulted the *BB* defense, it would not be long before army B would have overpowered them, for the farther they advanced without broad support, the more vulnerable they would have become to a counteroffensive by army B.

The same is true of the stock market, for the longer a price trend is maintained without a follow-up by the broad market, the more vulnerable is the advance.

At market bottoms, breadth is not such a useful concept for determining major reversals, since the majority of stocks usually coincide with or lag behind the major indexes. On the few occasions when breadth reverses its downtrend before the averages, it can be a useful indicator of market bottoms. For the moment, attention will be concentrated on the reason why the broad market *normally* leads the averages at market tops. The word "normally" is used because, in the vast majority of cases, the broad list of stocks does peak out ahead of a market average such as the Dow Jones Industrial Average (DJIA). This rule is not invariable, however, and it should not be assumed that the technical structure is necessarily sound just because market breadth is strong.

Advance/Decline Line

The most widely used indicator of market breadth is an *advance/decline (A/D) line*. It is constructed by taking a cumulative total of the difference (plurality) between the number of New York Stock Exchange (NYSE) issues that are advancing over those that are declining in a particular period (usually a day or a week). Similar indexes may be constructed for the American Exchange (AMEX), or from the U.S. over-the-counter (OTC) issues. A/D lines for other markets are discussed in Part 5. Because the number of issues listed on the NYSE has expanded since breadth records were first kept, an A/D line constructed from a simple plurality of advancing over declining issues gives a greater weighting to more recent years. For the purpose of long-term comparisons it is better to take a ratio of advances versus declines, or a ratio of A/D divided by the number of unchanged issues, rather than limiting the calculation to a simple plurality.

One of the most useful measurements of breadth is a cumulative running total of the formula square root of $A/U - D/U$, where A = the number of stocks advancing, D = the number declining, and U = the number unchanged. Since it is not mathematically possible to calculate a

Table 19.1.

Date	Issues traded (1)	Advances (2)	Declines (3)	Unchanged (4)	Advances ÷ unchanged (5)	Declines ÷ unchanged (6)	Col. 5 – col. 6 (7)	$\sqrt{\text{Col. 7}}$ (8)	Cumulative A/D line (9)
Jan. 7	2129	989	919	221	448	416	32	5.7	2475.6
14	2103	782	1073	248	315	433	-118	- 10.9	2464.7
21	2120	966	901	253	382	356	26	5.1	2469.8
28	2103	835	1036	232	360	447	-87	- 9.3	2460.5
Feb. 4	2089	910	905	274	332	330	2	1.4	2461.9
11	2090	702	1145	243	289	471	-18.2	- 13.5	2448.4
18	2093	938	886	269	349	329	20	4.5	2452.9
25	2080	593	1227	260	228	472	244	-15.6	2437.3

square root of a negative answer (i.e., when the number of declining stocks is greater than the number of those advancing, the calculation cannot be done), the D and A are reversed in such cases, so that the formula becomes the square root of $D/U - A/U$. The resulting answer is then subtracted from the cumulative total, as opposed to the answer in the earlier formula, which is added. Table 19.1 illustrates this calculation using weekly data.

Inclusion of the number of unchanged issues is useful, because at certain points a more reliable advance warning of an imminent trend reversal in the A/D line can be given. This is because the more dynamic the move in either direction, the greater the tendency for the number of unchanged stocks to diminish. Consequently, by giving some weight to the number of unchanged stocks in the formula, it is possible to assess a slowdown in momentum of the A/D line at an earlier date, since an expanding number of unchanged issues will have the tendency to restrain extreme movements.

The A/D line normally rises and falls in sympathy with the major market averages, but it usually peaks well ahead of the top in the major averages. There appear to be three basic reasons why this is so, as follows:

1. The market as a whole discounts the business cycle and normally reaches its bull market peak 6 to 9 months before the economy tops out. Since the peak in business activity is itself preceded by a deterioration of certain leading sectors such as financial, consumer spending, and construction, it is logical to expect that the stocks representing these sectors will also peak out ahead of the general market.

2. Many of the stocks listed on the NYSE, such as preferred stocks and utilities, are sensitive to changes in interest rates. Since interest rates

start to rise before the market peaks, it is natural for the interest-sensitive issues to decline as rates rise.

3. Poorer-quality stocks offer the largest gains, but they are also representative of smaller, less well-financed and less well-managed companies that are more vulnerable to reduced earnings (and even bankruptcy) during a recession. Blue-chip stocks normally have good credit ratings, reasonable yields, and sound underlying assets; thus they are typically the last stocks to be sold by investors during a bull market.

The DJIA and other market averages are almost wholly composed of larger companies which are normally in better financial shape. These popular averages continue to advance well after the broad market has peaked out.

Interpretation

Listed below are some observations that should be borne in mind in interpreting A/D data.

1. Some A/D lines appear to have a permanent downward bias. It is therefore important to observe the relationship between an A/D line and an index over a very long period to see whether this bias exists. Examples include breadth data for the AMEX market, the U.S. OTC market, and the Japanese market.

2. Divergences between a market average and an A/D line at market tops are almost always cleared up by a decline in the average. However, it is mandatory to await some kind of trend-reversal signal before concluding that the average will also decline.

3. It is normal for the A/D line to coincide or lag at market bottoms. Such action is of no forecasting value. When the A/D line refuses to confirm a new low in the index, the signal is unusual and very positive, but only when confirmed by a reversal in the average itself.

4. Breadth data may diverge negatively from the averages, but an important rally is often signaled when a down trendline violation is signaled along with a breakout in the market average itself.

5. In most cases daily A/D lines have more of a downward bias than lines constructed from weekly data.

One of the basic principles of the breadth/price relationship is that the longer and greater the divergence, the deeper and more substantial the implied decline is likely to be. For this reason divergences between the A/D line and the major market averages at primary peaks are more significant than those which occur at intermediate tops. For example, Chart 19.1 shows that the weekly A/D line peaked in March 1971, almost 2 years ahead of the DJIA, a very long period by historical standards. The ensuing bear market was the most severe since the Depression. On the other hand, *the absence of a divergence does not necessarily mean that a steep bear market cannot take place,* as the experience of the December 1968 top indicates. This is also shown in Chart 19.1.

Positive divergences develop at market bottoms where the A/D line refuses to confirm a new low in the Dow. The most significant one occurred in the 1939–1942 period. The DJIA (shown in Chart 19.2) made a series of lower peaks and troughs between 1939 and 1941, while the A/D line refused to confirm. Finally in the middle of 1941 the A/D line made a post-1932 recovery high unaccompanied by the DJIA. The immediate result of this discrepancy was a sharp sell-off into the spring of 1942 by both indicators, but even then the A/D line held well above its 1938 bottom, unlike the DJIA. The final low in April 1942 was followed by the best (in terms of breadth) bull market on record. This positive action by the broad market is unusual. Typically at market bottoms the A/D line either coincides with or lags behind the low in the DJIA and has no forecasting significance until a reversal in its downtrend is signaled by a breakout from a price pattern, a trendline, or a moving average (MA) crossover. Chart 19.3 shows a more up-to-date comparison of the A/D line and the Standard & Poor's (S&P) Composite.

A/D Lines Using Daily Data

Because daily A/D lines have a tendency toward a downward bias, some care should be used in comparing recent highs with those achieved 2 to 3 years ago. Daily A/D lines come into their own when they fail to confirm new highs in the market average that have occurred within an 18-month period. An example is shown in Chart 19.4*a*, where the A/D line peaks in April 1987 but the S&P Composite does not top out until late August. The S&P did not fall right away but eventually followed the leadership of the A/D line. Quite often a number of divergences will be set up. Initially these might be well publicized, but since the widely expected decline fails to materialize, many technicians give up, stating that the divergence "won't work this time." Invariably it does work, though much later than most would anticipate. This was very much the case at the market peak in January 1973, which was followed by a 2-year divergence.

Because bottoms in the daily line usually coincide with or lag behind bottoms in the average, they are not very useful at this point for the purpose of identifying a trend reversal.

A more practical approach is to construct a down trendline for both

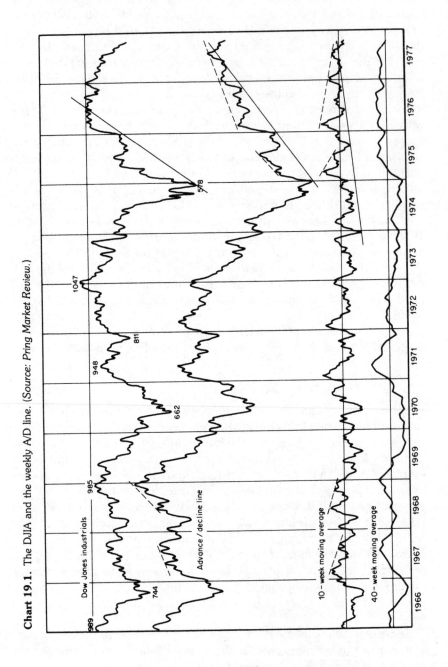

Chart 19.1. The DJIA and the weekly A/D line. (*Source: Pring Market Review.*)

Chart 19.2. The DJIA and the long-term A/D line. (*Source: Pring Market Review.*)

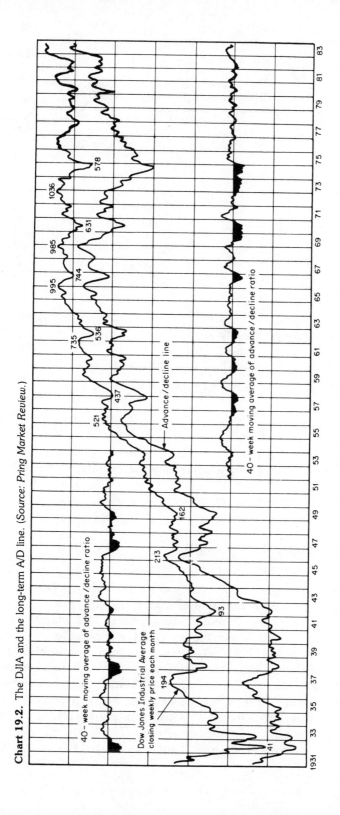

Chart 19.3. The S&P Composite versus the weekly NYSE A/D line.

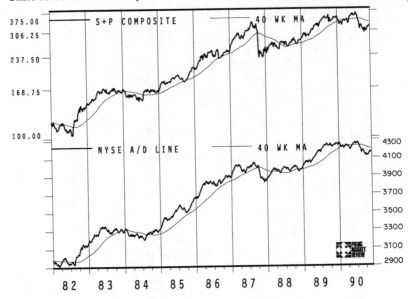

the A/D line and the market average. Violation of both lines usually signals that an important rally is under way. An example is shown in Chart 19.4*b*.

Breadth Oscillators (Internal Strength)

For historical comparative purposes, the rate-of-change (ROC) method of determining momentum is useful in measuring price indexes, because it reflects moves of similar proportion in an identical way. This method, however, is not suitable for gauging the vitality of the indicators that monitor internal market structure, such as those that measure volume or breadth, since the construction of such indexes is often started from a purely arbitrary number. Under certain circumstances this might require an ROC to be calculated between a negative and a positive number, which would obviously give a completely false impression of the prevailing trend of momentum. The following sections provide a brief summary of some oscillators constructed from breadth data.

Chart 19.4a. The S&P Composite versus the daily NYSE A/D line, 1987–1988. (*Source: Pring Market Review.*)

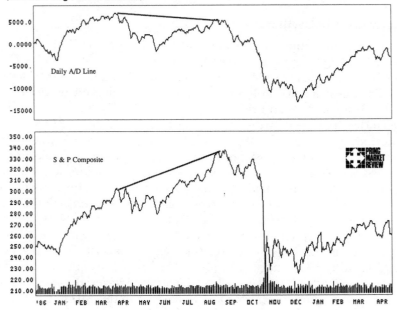

Chart 19.4b. The S&P Composite versus the daily NYSE A/D line, 1988–1989. (*Source: Pring Market Review.*)

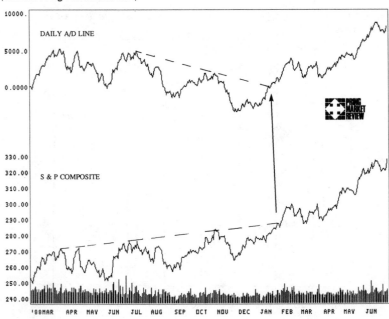

Ten-Week A/D Oscillator

Chart 19.5 shows the A/D line and its 10-week oscillator. The oscillator is constructed by taking a 10-week MA of the square root of $A/U - D/U$ formula discussed above. A comparison of the A/D line and the oscillator illustrates the principle of divergence, as evidenced by declining peaks of momentum and rising peaks in the A/D line itself. These discrepancies are shown by the dashed lines just above the two indexes. It is not possible to know at the time how high the A/D line will extend, only that the technical position (indicated by the declining peaks in the 10-week momentum) is deteriorating. The best method of determining when the A/D line has made its final advance is to wait for a downside trendline penetration or an MA crossover to confirm the action of the momentum index. Normally, as shown on Chart 19.1, the A/D line will sell off quite sharply following a combination of such trend breaks, but sometimes an extended sideways fluctuation results as the A/D line struggles to regain some momentum. The same principle can also be applied during bear markets, when signals are triggered as a series of higher troughs in the oscillator and lower lows in the A/D line are confirmed by a break in the negative trend of the A/D line itself.

Chart 19.5. The NYSE A/D line and a 10-week breadth oscillator. (*Source: Pring Market Review.*)

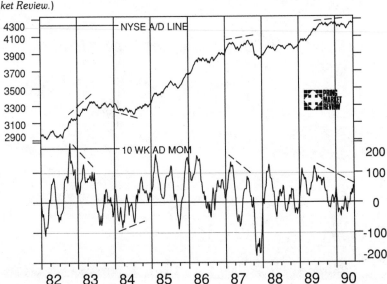

Chart 19.6. The S&P Composite and a 10-day breadth oscillator. (*Source: Pring Market Review.*)

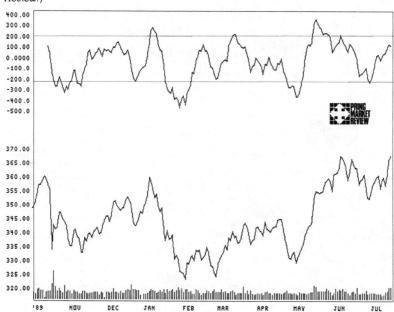

Ten- and Thirty-Day A/D Oscillators

These indicators are calculated by taking a 10- or 30-day MA of the $A \div D$ or the $A - D$ ratio. An alternative calculation can be made by dividing the total of advancing issues by the total of declining issues over a specific time span. Their interpretation is exactly the same as with other momentum indicators, bearing in mind their relatively short time span. An example of a 10-day breadth momentum series is shown in Chart 19.6.

The Arms (Trin) Index

This indicator is named after its innovative inventor, Richard Arms.[1] It represents the relationship between advancing and declining issues, and the volume in advancing and declining stocks.

The Arms Index is calculated by dividing the A/D ratio by the upside/downside volume ratio over a specific period. (Ten days is the normal time span, although tick-by-tick data is published intraday by

[1]Arms-Equivolume Corp., 1650 University Boulevard N.E., Albuquerque, NM 87102.

Chart 19.7. The S&P Composite and a 10-day Arms (Trin) Index. (*Source: Pring Market Review.*)

several of the financial media as well as by the major quotation services.) An example is shown in Chart 19.7.

The Arms Index is used mostly as a short-term trading tool. The idea behind the indicator is to see whether volume is flowing into advancing or declining stocks. It differs from most other momentum indicators in that a falling Trin is bullish (because it shows that more volume is flowing into advancing stocks), and a rising one is negative. Although this inverse relationship should be kept in mind, the Arms Index should be interpreted in exactly the same way as any other breadth oscillator.

The McClellan Oscillator

The McClellan oscillator is a short-term breadth momentum indicator that measures the difference between a 19- and a 39-day exponential moving average (EMA) of advancing minus declining issues. In this respect, it is based on the same principle as the moving-average convergence divergence (MACD) indicator discussed in Chapter 10. The generally accepted rules are that buy signals are triggered when it falls to the oversold area of −70 to −100 and sell signals when it rises to the

+70 to +100 area. My own experience suggests that its interpretation should be based on the same principles as those described in Chapter 9. An example is shown in Chart 19.8.

The McClellan Summation Index is often more reliable. It is calculated as a cumulative total of the daily readings. The result is plotted as a slow-moving curve that changes direction whenever the raw oscillator (described above) crosses above or below its zero line. The slope of the summation curve is determined by the difference between the actual reading and the zero line. In other words, an overbought reading will cause the summation index to rise sharply, and vice versa. Many technicians use these changes in direction as buy and sell signals, but this can result in a lot of whipsaws. My own preference is to use an MA crossover. This is often less timely, but it filters out a significant number of false signals. Trial and error have indicated that over the long haul a McClellan Summation crossover of a 35-day MA works best. An example is shown in Chart 26.1.

Chart 19.8. The McClellan oscillator.

Diffusion Indicators

A diffusion indicator is a form of momentum measure which is constructed from individual series that are used in the calculation of an aggregate index.

It measures the percentage of the universe that is in a positive trend.
When all members are in a bullish mode, the picture is as positive as it
can get. The implication is that the aggregate measure is vulnerable and
therefore likely to peak out. The reverse set of conditions, in which
none of the series is in a positive trend, produces the opposite effect;
i.e., the aggregate index may be reaching its low point and may therefore be a "buy." This simple interpretation of diffusion indexes is a
good starting point, but in practice it does not always work out, as we
will see later.

Since a diffusion measure is a form of momentum indicator, it is subject to the principles outlined in Chapter 9. An example would be the
percentage of the 30 Dow stocks that are in a positive trend.

What Is a Positive Trend?

In technical analysis a market or stock that forms a series of rising peaks
and troughs, or is above a trendline, may be classified as being in a positive trend. However, the only way trends can be monitored through
this interpretation is on the basis of individual judgment, which would
make the construction of a diffusion index covering many series over
many years a very laborious process. For this reason and because of the
need for greater objectivity, a statistical measure that can be easily calculated on a computer is normally used.

The most common measurements calculate the percentage of a series
that are above a specific MA or that have a rising MA. Another popular
alternative is to take the percentage of a universe of series that have a
positive ROC, i.e., a reading above 0 or 100. The choice of MA or ROC
is very important. For example, if we were to take the percentage of
S&P groups above a 3-week MA, the resulting series would be plotted as
an oscillator that would be continuously moving up and down the page
from 0 to 100 and back in an almost meaningless fashion. Plotting the
number of groups above a 52-week (1-year) MA, on the other hand,
would also be relatively unhelpful as the diffusion index would hardly
move at all.

In practice it seems that the MAs and ROCs commonly used in other
areas of technical analysis offer superior results. These are 30-day for
short-term trends; 10-, 30-, and 40-week for intermediate-term trends;
and 12-, 18-, and 24-month for longer-term trends. Even using these

Chart 19.9. The S&P Composite versus the Group Momentum Indicator. (*Source: Pring Market Review.*)

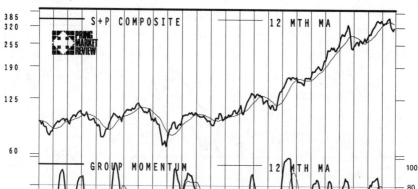

measurements, the resulting data usually needs to be smoothed. For example, the Group Momentum Indicator series shown in Chart 19.9 is calculated from the percentage of 20 industry groups that are above a 12-month MA. This data in turn has been smoothed, and thus the solid line actually represents a 6-month MA of the percentage of groups above their respective 12-month MAs. The smoother line is a 12-month MA of the 6-month MA.

How Many Items Should Be Measured?

A natural tendency is to use as many items as possible to calculate a diffusion indicator, but this involves the maintenance of a very large data base. Chart 19.10 shows a similar measure for three different universes: all stocks on the NYSE, just the 80 or so industry groups, and the 30 specific stocks included in the DJIA. From time to time their movements are different, but the basic swings are very similar. Clearly it is better to be able to compare the movements of all three, but the really significant changes can be observed by making the simpler Dow 30 cal-

Chart 19.10. The percentage of all stocks, Dow stocks, and industry groups in positive trends. (*Source: Courtesy of Dow Theory Letters, Inc., La Jolla, Calif., based on data provided by Chartcraft Ltd.*)

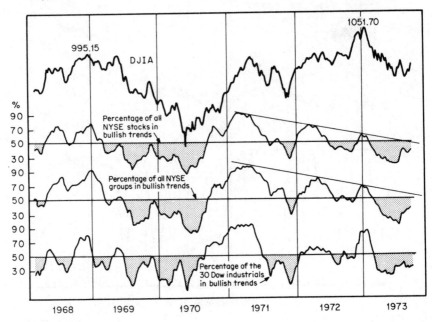

culations. The main thing to bear in mind is that the basket of items used in the calculation reflects the diverse nature of the market's components.

Interpretation

When a diffusion indicator moves to an extreme, it reflects an overbought or oversold condition. However, such readings do not in themselves constitute actual buy or sell signals. Obviously the odds favor a profitable investment made at the time of a zero reading, and vice versa. However, it is usually much safer to wait for a reversal in the trend of the diffusion index, or it is even better to wait for a trend break in the aggregate index being monitored.

Whenever the diffusion index in Chart 19.9 has risen to, or above, the 80 level and then reversed direction, it has almost always been associated with a decline of at least intermediate-term proportions. The same is also true, in an opposite sense, for the trend reversals that have taken place when the index has fallen below 20 percent. This approach works well most of the time, but there are some glaring examples of signals being unduly and misleadingly early, such as that which developed in the beginning of 1974, when it reversed to an upward direction almost a year ahead of the bear market low. The same sort of thing happened in 1986, when a prematurely bearish signal was generated.

The only satisfactory solution seems to be to rely on combining a signal from the diffusion indicator with the aggregate index itself. In such instances an extreme reading in the diffusion index is used as a pointer for a reversal in the intermediate or primary trend, which is confirmed when the index itself crosses a long-term MA, or violates a significant trendline. For instance, the two premature signals discussed above could have been filtered out by waiting for the S&P to cross above its 12-month MA.

Chart 19.11 shows three other popular diffusion indicators: the percentage of NYSE stocks above their 30-week MA, a similar measure for a 10-week time span, and net new highs.

Relative Strength (RS) Diffusion Indexes

It is also possible to develop a diffusion index for a specific stock group, commodity, etc., using an RS approach. The series in Chart 19.12 is calculated from the percentage of a universe of industry groups against which the Oil Composite is rising. In order to construct such a series, it

Chart 19.11. The S&P Composite and three breadth indicators. (*Source: Pring Market Review.*)

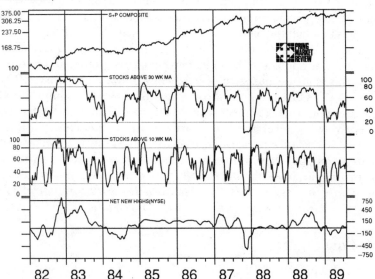

Chart 19.12. The RS of the Oil Composite (versus the S&P Composite) and an oil RS diffusion index. (*Source: Pring Market Review.*)

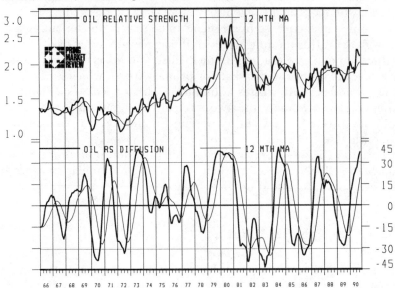

is first necessary to calculate an RS index and its 12-month MA for the Oil Composite against a basket of other industry groups. The percentage of RS lines that show the Oil Composite in a positive trend is then calculated (i.e., when the Oil Composite versus Autos is above its MA, the Oil Composite versus Utilities is above its 12-month MA, etc.). Since the results of these raw calculations are very volatile, the data are then smoothed. In the chart, a reading of 0 means that half the oil RS lines are above their 12-month MAs and half are below. An extreme reading of + 30 to + 45 means that oil is in a strong relative trend as opposed to 80 to 95 percent of the groups, and so on.

Since this is an RS measure, it has been compared in Chart 19.12 to the RS of the Oil Composite group against the S&P Composite. The best investment opportunities occur when the diffusion index has fallen to a relatively low level and then starts to rise. Remember that this is a buy signal for relative performance. Price and RS normally move in the same direction, but there is no guarantee that a rising RS line will result in a profitable investment. *For large portfolio managers who are substanaially invested most of the time, such RS diffusion indicators can be a very helpful guide to optimum portfolio weightings.*

High-Low Figures

The popular press publishes daily and weekly figures for stocks reaching new highs and new lows. These "statistics" relate to the number of *issues making new highs or lows over a 52-week period. There are various methods of measuring the high-low figures, but since the raw data is very jagged, displaying it in an MA format is almost always better.*

Some technicians prefer to plot an MA of the two series individually, others an MA of the net difference between highs and lows. The basic principle is that a rising market over a period of time should be accompanied by a healthy, but not necessarily rising, number of net new highs. When the major averages trace out a series of higher peaks following a long advance but the net number of new highs forms a series of declining peaks, this is a warning of potential trouble. This state of affairs indicates that the technical picture is gradually weakening because successive peaks in the market average are accompanied by fewer and fewer stocks making breakouts (new highs) from price patterns. The net number of new highs also takes into consideration stocks making new lows. In a bear market a new low in the S&P Composite, or other market average, which is not accompanied by a declining number of net new highs is a positive sign.

In this case a declining number of stocks reaching new lows implies fewer downside breakouts, i.e., a shrinkage in the number of stocks resisting the downtrend in the major averages (see Chart 19.13).

An alternative method of calculating high-low data is shown at the bottom of Chart 19.11, where a 6-week MA of net weekly new highs has been plotted against the S&P Composite. This is a particularly good indicator for identifying major turning points. For example, when the S&P Composite was making a new low in early 1978 the high-low indicator refused to confirm. Similarly, in 1982 the S&P Composite made a series of consecutive lows which began in September 1981, whereas the high-low index was making a series of ascending lows. The reverse situation occurs at virtually every market top where a negative divergence appears to develop before the final peak. This was true in 1973, 1976, 1980, 1981, 1983, and 1987.

Seasonal Breadth Momentum

The Seasons Defined

Every cycle effectively goes through four stages before completion, as shown in Figure 19.2. The first occurs after downside momentum has reached its maximum. At this point the series turns up but is still below its equilibrium level. The second is signaled when it crosses above its zero reference line. The third phase starts when it peaks out from above zero. Finally phase 4 is triggered when the indicator crosses below the equilibrium point.

For simplicity's sake we have labeled the respective stages as spring,

Chart 19.13. The daily A/D line versus the 5-day high/low differential. A classic signal of improving technical strength was given in December 1974, when the DJIA fell below its October low. The high/low had fallen to its lowest level in September, thereby pointing up that the majority of stocks were in better technical shape than the DJIA. Between March and July the reverse situation occurred as the DJIA made new highs unaccompanied by an exanding high/low differential. This suggested a weakening technical structure, so that once the A/D line had violated the trendline joining the April-May and June bottoms, an intermediate reaction got under way.

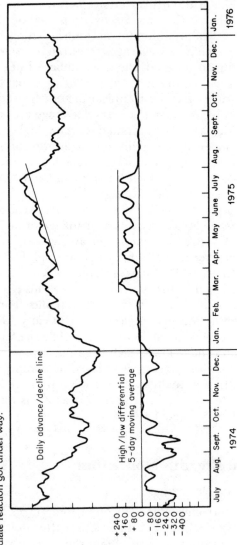

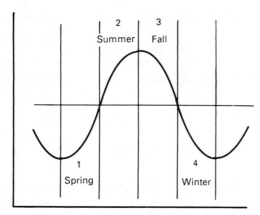

Figure 19.2. (*Source: Pring Market Review.*)

summer, fall, and winter. From both an agricultural and an investment point of view, the best results occur when planting (investing) is done in the spring, and harvesting in late summer or fall.

In effect, spring represents accumulation, summer the markup phase, fall distribution, and winter the markdown phase. This idea was covered in Chapter 9 for an individual series. In situations in which a market can be subdivided into components, it is possible to take this approach one step further by calculating a diffusion index based on the position of the seasonal momentum of its various components, e.g., industry groups for a stock market average, commodity prices for a commodity index, etc.[2] This seasonal momentum approach has two merits. First, it helps to identify the prevailing stage in the cycle, i.e., whether the stock market is in an accumulation, markup, distribution, or markdown phase. Second, it also helps identify major buying and selling opportunities.

Choice of Time Span

The choice of time span is critical for all momentum indicators, including those used in the seasonal momentum studies. For example, a series based on a smoothed 13-week ROC will have far less significance in terms of long-term investment strategy than a series based on a 48-month ROC. This approach can be used for daily, weekly, and monthly data. However, I have found that daily and weekly calculations, even

[2]This approach was first brought to my attention by Ian S. Notley, Notley Group, Yelton Fiscal Inc., Unit 211-Executive Pavilion, 90 Grove Street, Ridgefield, CT 06877.

when greatly smoothed, do not give as reliable a picture as the monthly series. Monthly seasonal momentum also works well for commodities (see Chapter 31) and international markets (see Chapter 27). The indicators represented in the charts included in this chapter have been constructed by adding and weighting the smoothed ROCs of four different monthly time spans, as in the monthly *k*now *s*ure *t*hing (KST) formula described in Chapter 10.

Seasonal (Diffusion) Momentum for the Stock Market

Chart 19.14 shows four seasonal momentum curves based on a basket of S&P Industry groups such as auto, distillers, and computers. Each month the position of the individual groups is calculated and classified. A high reading in the spring series, for example, indicates that the momentum of a significant proportion of the groups is in phase 1, i.e., below zero and rising, and therefore in a position to begin a major advance.

It is important to note that in most cycles there is a chronological sequence as the majority of groups move from spring to summer and

Chart 19.14. The S&P Composite and seasonal momentum, 1966–1990. (*Source: Pring Market Review.*)

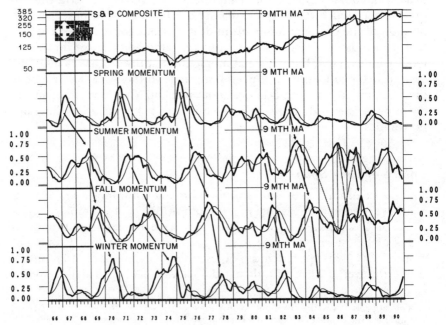

then winter. This is shown by the arrows. Bear market lows typically occur around the time winter momentum peaks out and crosses below its 9-month MA. Confirmation occurs when the S&P Composite penetrates its MA as well.

The peaking out of spring momentum is often associated with the first intermediate-term peak in the bull market, but it is *not* a bearish sign. It simply means that the majority of groups are moving from the spring (accumulation) to the summer (markup) phase. It's bearish only if a significant number of groups are moving from spring back to winter.

Potential market weakness is signaled when the summer momentum, i.e., the third series, starts to turn down. This is not an actual sell signal because the market often moves sideways or even higher after summer momentum peaks. It does, however, indicate that the environment has become much more selective as the smoothed momentum for more and more groups moves to the fall (distribution) phase.

The S&P Composite sometimes declines during the transition from the summer to the fall phase, but it is more normal for downside momentum to pick up as the cycle moves from fall to winter, i.e., at the point at which the momentum indicators for most groups cross below their zero reference lines.

Bear Market Bottoms. *Major buying points occur when winter momentum reaches its peak and starts to turn down.* Generally speaking, the higher the peak, the greater the potential for upside activity. This is because a movement out of winter momentum must flow into spring. A high and falling level in winter momentum therefore indicates that a significant number of groups have the potential to move into the spring position, i.e., to move to the point from which they have the greatest potential to rise. This is shown more clearly in Chart 19.15.

Normally the winter momentum series moves up steadily toward a peak and then reverses direction. Reversals that come from high readings are usually a reliable indication that the downtrend in the overall market has reversed. Occasionally, winter momentum temporarily peaks out but the market itself does not bottom, as in late 1973. This is a very unusual state of affairs, but it does point out that no system is perfect. Intermixing the seasonal momentum analysis with other indicators is very important. In 1973, for example, bond yields were in a persistent rising trend. This is one of the reasons why it is often important to wait for the momentum indicator to cross above or below its MA before concluding that its trend has reversed.

New bull markets are sometimes signaled by a reversal in the downtrend in spring momentum, but since the lead times can also be

Chart 19.15. The S&P Composite and winter momentum, 1966–1990.(*Source.* Pring Market Review.)

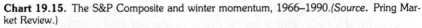

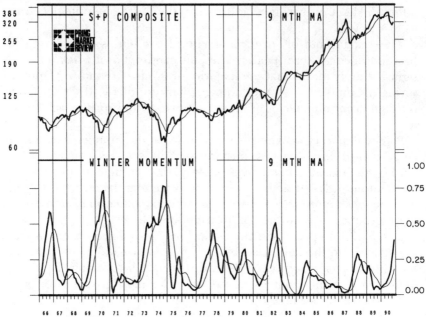

extremely long, upward movement in spring momentum by itself is no guarantee that the market will rally.

A confirming signal of a major bottom is often given by a reversal in trend of summer momentum occurring simultaneously with, or very close to, a peak in winter velocity. *Generally speaking, the lower the level of summer velocity when a reversal occurs, the greater the potential for a market rise.*

Signs of a Market Peak. Market tops are far more elusive than bottoms, but advance warning is usually given by a reversal in the uptrend of spring momentum. Lead times can vary, but it is normally safe to assume that as long as summer and spring momentum are both rising, higher prices are in store. It is also generally true that *the market will rise for at least a month or so following a peak in spring momentum,* usually much longer.

Market tops normally occur at some point between the peak in summer and fall momentum. For example, the stock market peaked in 1983 at the time when summer momentum peaked. Even a topping out in the fall momentum is not always sufficient to trigger a full-fledged bear market. Declining fall momentum is usually associated with a distribution, or topping-out phase, as in 1973 and 1977. Occasionally group momentum swings back to summer, thus averting a major market decline. *It is only when a large and expanding number of groups fall below their zero reference lines, i.e., move into winter, that a bear market picks up downside momentum.*

Indian Summer. During periods such as 1984–1987, which are associated with a strong, persistent linear uptrend, the normal spring-summer-fall-winter sequence does not occur. Instead, a sequence of a different nature, alternating between summer and fall, enables the market to regain its internal strength without suffering a major decline. In a sense, the market undergoes an Indian summer rally.

As a result, *it is not possible to conclude that a peak in summer momentum will always lead to a market decline.* It is more important to watch the beginning of the decline in fall momentum to see whether the flow of groups moves into winter or back into summer.

How to Identify Indian Summers. The best way to determine whether fall momentum will flow back to summer or on to winter is to watch both winter and summer momentum. As long as the winter quadrant continues to rise, this is a bearish sign, and it indicates that an expanding number of groups are declining in price. This will clearly have a negative impact on the S&P Composite.

It is important to note that during the Indian summer phase between 1985 and early 1987 the winter momentum series never succeeded in decisively crossing above its MA.

Conclusion

The construction and calculation of these indicators are available only to technicians who have access to a computer and large data base. However, the concept of progressive seasonal momentum is important to understand even for those who cannot follow this approach on a regular basis since it explains how a market goes through its various stages and the kind of conditions required for major bull and bear moves.

Summary

1. Market breadth measures the degree to which a market index is supported by a wide range of its components.
2. Market breadth is useful from two aspects. First, it informs the tech-

nician about whether the environment for most items (normally eq-uities) is good or bad. Second, market breadth indicators signal ma-jor turning points through the establishment of both negative and positive divergences.

3. Indicators constructed from breadth data include A/D lines, breadth oscillators, diffusion indicators, and net new highs.

4. Breadth divergences are a fine concept, but should be confirmed by a trend reversal in the market averages themselves.

PART 3

Interest Rates and the Stock Market

20
Why Interest Rates Affect the Stock Market

Changes in interest rates affect the stock market for three basic reasons. First, fluctuation in the price charged for credit is a major influence on the level of corporate profits and therefore on the price which investors are willing to pay for equities. Second, movements in interest rates alter the relationships between competing financial assets, of which the bond/equity market relationship is the most important. Third, a substantial number of stocks are purchased on borrowed money (known as *margin debt*). Changes in the cost of carrying that debt (i.e., the interest rate) influence the desire or ability of investors and speculators to maintain these margined positions. Because *changes in interest rates usually lead stock prices*, it is important to be able to identify primary trend reversals in the debt market.

The Effect of Interest-Rate Changes on Corporate Profits

Interest rates affect profits in two ways. First, almost all companies borrow money to finance capital equipment and inventory, so the cost of money, i.e., the interest rate they pay, is of great importance. Second, a substantial number of sales are in turn financed by borrowing. The level of interest rates therefore has a great deal of influence on the ability and willingness of customers to make additional purchases. One of

317

the most outstanding examples is the automobile industry, in which both producers and consumers are very heavily financed. The capital-intensive utility and transportation industries are also large borrowers, as are all the highly leveraged construction and housing industries.

Interest Rates and Competing Financial Assets

Interest-rate changes also have an impact upon the relative appeal of various investment sectors. The most significant relationship is that of stocks to bonds. For example, at any point in time there is a balance between bonds and stocks, in the judgment of investors. However, if interest rates rise faster than dividends can increase, bonds will become more attractive and, at the margin, money will flow out of stocks into bonds. Stocks will then fall in value until the relationship is perceived by investors to be more reflective of the higher level of interest rates.

The effect of interest-rate changes on any particular stock group will depend upon the yield obtained combined with the prospects for profit growth. Most sensitive will be preferred shares, which are primarily held for their dividends and which do not generally permit benefit from profit growth. Utility stocks are also highly sensitive to interest-rate movement since they are held as much for their current dividend yields as for potential growth. Changes in the level of interest rates therefore have a very direct effect on utility stocks. On the other hand, companies in a dynamic stage of growth are usually financed by corporate earnings and for this reason pay smaller dividends. These stocks are less affected by fluctuations in the cost of money, since they are purchased in anticipation of fast profit growth and future yield rather than an immediate dividend return.

Interest Rates and Margin Debt

Margin debt is money loaned by brokers for which securities are pledged as collateral. Normally this money is used for the acquisition of equities, but sometimes margin debt is used for purchases of consumer items, such as automobiles. The effect of rising interest rates on both forms of margin debt is similar in that rising rates increase the cost of carrying the debt. There is therefore a reluctance on the part of investors to take on additional debt as its cost rises. When the service charges become excessive, stocks are liquidated and the debt is paid off. Rising interest rates have the effect of increasing the supply of stock put up for sale with consequent downward pressure on prices.

Bond Yields

The relationship between interest rates and bond prices and the calculation of bond yields will now be examined.

When a bond is brought to market by a borrower, it is issued at a fixed interest rate (coupon) which is paid over a predetermined period. At the end of this maturity period, the issuer agrees to repay the face amount. Since bonds are normally issued in denominations of $1000 (known as *par*), this figure usually represents the amount to be repaid at the end of the (loan) period. Because bond prices are quoted in percentage terms, par ($1000) is expressed as 100. Normally bonds are issued and redeemed at par, but they are occasionally issued at a discount (i.e., at less than 100) or at a premium (i.e., at a price greater than 100).

While it is usual for a bond to be issued and redeemed at 100, over the life of the bond its price can fluctuate quite widely because interest-rate levels are continually changing. Assume that a 20-year bond is issued with an 8 percent interest rate (coupon) at par (i.e., 100); if interest rates rise to 9 percent, the bond paying 8 percent will be difficult to sell, because investors have the opportunity to earn a return of 9 percent. The only way in which the 8 percent bondholder can find a buyer is to reduce the price to a level that would compensate a prospective purchaser for the 1 percent differential in interest rates. The new owner would then earn 8 percent in interest together with some capital appreciation. When spread over the remaining life of the bond, this capital appreciation would be equivalent to the 1 percent loss in interest. This combination of coupon rate and averaged capital appreciation is known as the *yield*. If interest rates decline, the process is reversed, and the 8 percent bond becomes more attractive in relation to prevailing rates, so that its price rises. The longer the maturity of the bond, the greater will be its price fluctuation for any given change in the general level of interest rates.

The Structure of the Debt Markets

The debt markets can be roughly divided into two main areas, known as the *short end* and the *long end*. The short end, more commonly known as the *money market,* relates to interest rates charged for loans up to 1 year in maturity. Normally, movements at the short end lead those at the longer end, since short rates are more sensitive to trends in business conditions and changes in Federal Reserve policy. Money-market instruments are issued by the federal, state, and local governments as well as corporations.

The long end of the market consists of bonds issued for a period of at least 10 years. Debt instruments are also issued for periods of between 1 and 10 years, and are known as *intermediate-term* bonds.

The bond market (i.e., the long end) has three main sectors, which are classified as to issuer. These are the U.S. government, tax-exempt issuers (i.e., state and local governments), and corporate issuers.

The financial status of the tax-exempt and corporate sectors varies from issuer to issuer, and the practice of rating each issuer for quality of credit has therefore become widespread. The best possible credit rating is known as AAA; next in order are AA, A, BAA, BA, BB, etc. The higher the quality, the lower the risk undertaken by investors, and therefore the lower the interest rate required to compensate them. Since the credit of the federal government is higher than that of any other issuer, it can sell bonds at a relatively low interest rate. The tax-exempt sector (i.e., bonds issued by state and local governments) is able to issue bonds with the lowest rates of all, in view of the favored tax treatment assigned to the holders of such issues.

Most of the time, price trends of the various sectors are similar, but at major cyclical turns some will lag behind others because of differing demand and supply conditions in each sector.

Debt and Equity Markets

Debt prices typically top out ahead of the equity market at cyclical peaks. The lead characteristics and degree of deterioration in debt prices required to adversely affect equity differ from cycle to cycle. There are no hard-and-fast rules that relate the size of an equity decline to the time period separating the peaks of bond and equity prices. For example, short- and long-term prices peaked 18 and 17 months, respectively, ahead of the 1959 bull market high in the Dow. This compared with 11 months and 1 month for the 1973 bull market peak. While the deterioration in the bond and money markets was sharper and longer in the 1959 period, the Dow, on a monthly average basis, declined only 13 percent, as compared to 42 percent in the 1973–1974 bear market. The most important point, though, is that every cyclical stock market peak in this century was preceded by, or has coincided with, a peak in both the long and the short ends of the bond market.

A further characteristic of cyclical peaks is that high-quality bonds (such as Treasury or AAA corporate bonds) decline in price ahead of poorer-quality issues (such as BAA-rated bonds). This has been true of nearly every cyclical turning point since 1919. This lead characteristic of high-quality bonds results from two factors. First, in the latter stages of an economic expansion, private-sector demand for financing accelerates. Commercial banks, the largest institutional holders of government securities, are the lenders of last resort to private borrowers. As the demand for financing accelerates against a less accommodative central bank posture, banks step up their sales of these and other high-grade investments and reinvest the money in more profitable bank loans. This sets off a ripple effect, down the yield curve itself and also to lower-quality issues. At the same time these pressures are pushing yields on high-quality bonds upward and are also reflecting buoyant business conditions which encourage investors to become less cautious. Consequently, investors are willing to overlook the relatively conservative yields on high-quality bonds in favor of the more rewarding lower-rated debt instruments; thus, for a temporary period, these bonds are rising while high-quality bonds are falling.

At cyclical bottoms these relationships are similar, in that good-quality bonds lead both debt instruments and poorer-quality equities. The lead characteristics of the debt markets are not quite so pronounced as at cyclical peaks, and occasionally bond and stock prices trough out simultaneously.

The trend of interest rates is therefore a useful benchmark for identifying stock market bottoms.

Chart 20.1 shows primary stock market troughs between 1919 and 1974 which have been associated with tight monetary conditions. The monthly average of stock prices is represented on the top line, with the yields of 4- to 6-month commercial paper and AAA corporate long-term bonds shown underneath. The respective yields have been plotted inversely so that they correspond to the trend in equity and bond prices.

The chart shows that in every case either one or both yield curves bottomed out ahead of stock prices. This relationship between debt and equity markets can be traced back through the early nineteenth century, and shows that virtually every major cyclical stock market bottom was preceded by strength in one or both areas of the debt market. Where this relationship did not hold, the ensuing rise in stock prices proved to be spurious in most cases, and more often than not, prices eventually moved well below the previous low.

Chart 20.1. Interest rates at cyclical stock market troughs. (*Source: Pring Market Review.*)

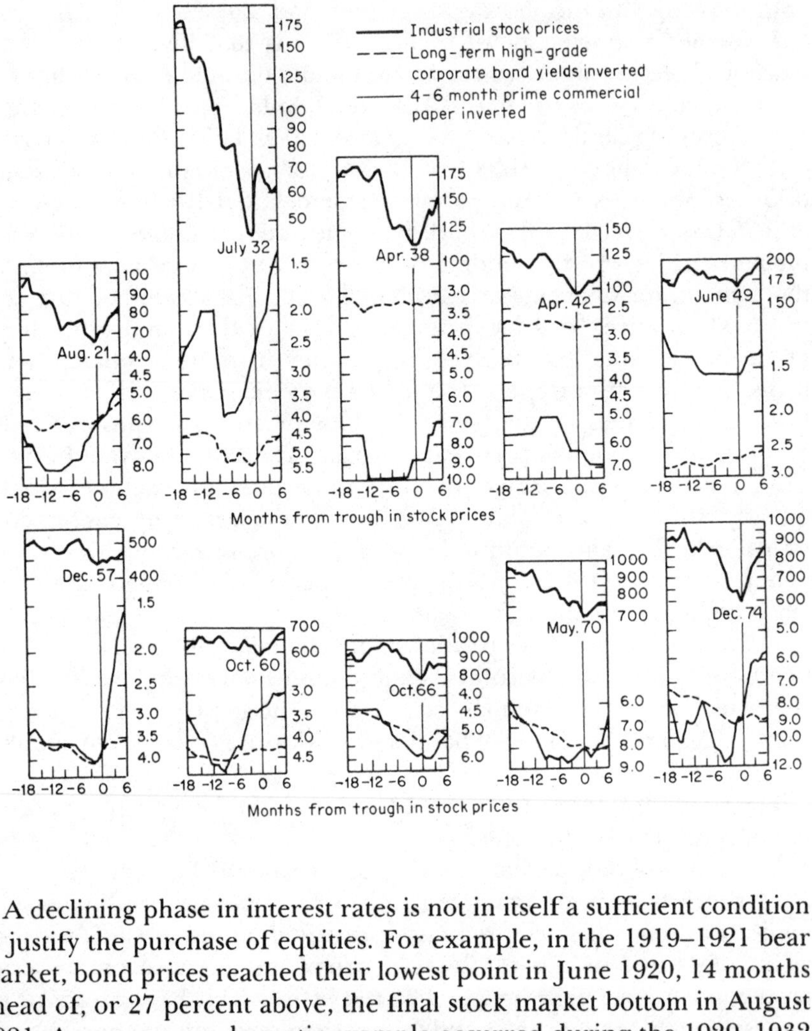

A declining phase in interest rates is not in itself a sufficient condition to justify the purchase of equities. For example, in the 1919–1921 bear market, bond prices reached their lowest point in June 1920, 14 months ahead of, or 27 percent above, the final stock market bottom in August 1921. An even more dramatic example occurred during the 1929–1932 debacle, when money-market yields reached their highs in October 1929. Over the next 3 years the discount rate was cut in half, but stock prices lost 85 percent of their October 1929 value. The reason for such excessively long lead times was that these periods were associated with a great deal of debt liquidation and many bankruptcies. Even the sharp reduction in interest rates was not sufficient to encourage consumers and businesses to spend, which is the normal cyclical experience. Although falling interest rates alone do not constitute a sufficient basis for an expectation that stock prices will reverse their cyclical decline, they are a necessary part of that basis. On the other hand, a continued trend of rising rates has in the past proved to be bearish. Chart 20.2 shows the same three series between 1976 and 1990.

The principles of trend determination apply as well to the bond market as to the stock market. In fact, trends in bond prices are in many ways easier to identify, since the bulk of the transactions in bonds are made on the basis of money flows caused by a need to finance and an ability to purchase. Consequently, while emotions are still important from the point of view of determining the short-term trends of bond prices, money flow is generally responsible for a far smoother cyclical trend than is the case with equities.

Relating Changes in Interest Rates to Equity Market Turning Points

That interest rates lead stock prices at virtually every cyclical turning point has already been established. However, the leads, lags, and level of interest rates required to affect equity prices differ in each cycle. For example, 1962 experienced a sharp market setback with short-term in-

Chart 20.2. Stock prices and inverted interest rates, 1976–1990. (*Source: Pring Market Review.*)

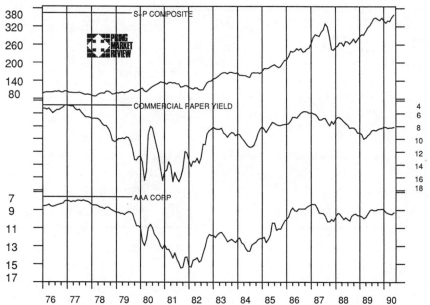

terest rates at 3 percent. On the other hand, stock prices were very strong in the latter part of 1980, yet rates never fell below 9 percent.

The key to the dilemma is that *it's not the level of interest rates that affects equity prices, but their rate of change (ROC)*.

One method for determining when a change in rates is sufficient to influence equities is to overlay a smoothed ROC of short-term interest rates with a similar measure for equity prices. This is shown in Chart 20.3. Buy and sell signals are triggered when the interest-rate momentum crosses above and below that of the Standard & Poor's (S&P) Composite.

We know that the stock market can rally even in the face of rising rates, but this relationship tells us when the rise in rates is greater than that of equities, and vice versa. At times this approach gives some very timely signals, as happened at the 1973 market peak. At other times it is not so helpful. For example, it failed to signal the 1978–1980 rally. Even so, it is interesting to note that the total return on equities and cash during the 2-year period was approximately the same. This approach is far from perfect, as is clearly demonstrated by the confusing signals in the 1988–1990 period. Generally, though, it is better to be cautious when the interest-rate momentum is above that of equities and to take on more risk when the reverse set of conditions holds true.

Chart 20.3. The stock market versus interest-rate momentum. (*Source: Pring Market Review.*)

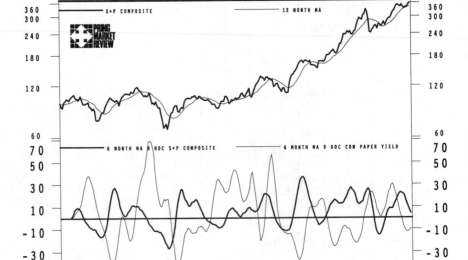

Chart 20.4. The stock market versus the Money Flow Index. (*Source: Pring Market Review.*)

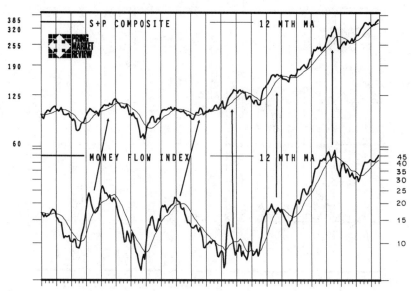

An alternative approach to the interest-rate/equity relationship recognizes that rallies in equity prices are normally much stronger when supported by falling rates, and vice versa. It follows that if a measure of the equity market, such as the S&P Composite, is divided by the yield on a money-market instrument, such as 4-month commercial paper, the series will either lead or fall less rapidly at bear market bottoms and peak out ahead or rise at a slower pace at market tops, if interest rates are experiencing their usual leading characteristics.

An indicator constructed in this way, called the Money Flow Index, is plotted underneath the S&P Composite in Chart 20.4. The arrows point up the lead characteristics.

Chart 20.5 overlays the ROC of the two series. Buy signals are generated when the money-flow momentum crosses above that of the S&P, and vice versa. They are flagged by the upward- and downward-pointing arrows.

Chart 20.6 plots the S&P Composite together with an indicator constructed by subtracting the ROC of the S&P from the ROC of the Money Flow Index (i.e., from Chart 20.5). The zero line represents the crossover points that were flagged by the arrows in Chart 20.5. This final format is a simple way of presenting this interest-rate/stock market relationship. Research back to the 1950s shows that every buy signal

Chart 20.5. The stock market versus money-flow momentum. (*Source: Pring Market Review.*)

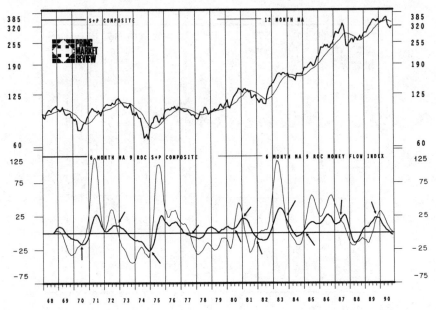

Chart 20.6. The S&P Composite versus the Money Flow Index. (*Source: Pring Market Review.*)

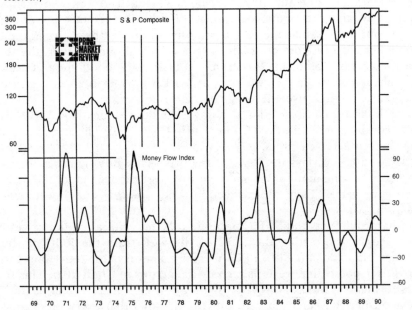

(i.e., zero crossover) has been followed by a *major* stock rally. The only exception occurred in 1989, but in this case the crossover took place when both momentum series (see Chart 20.5) were in an overbought condition. However, when a crossover develops from below the zero reference line, as shown in Chart 20.5, it has normally represented an extremely powerful signal that a new bull market was under way. Sell signals have also been reasonably timely for the most part.

Summary

1. Interest rates influence stock prices because they affect corporate profitability, alter valuation relationships, and influence margin transactions.

2. Interest rates have led stock prices at major turning points in virtually every recorded business cycle.

3. It's the ROC of interest rates, rather than their actual level, that affects equity prices.

21
Short-Term (Money-Market) Interest Rates

Short-term interest rates are more sensitive to business conditions than are long-term rates. This is because decisions to change inventories, for which a substantial amount of short-term money is required, are made much more quickly than decisions to purchase plant and equipment, which form the basis for long-term corporate credit demands. The Federal Reserve, in its management of monetary policy, is also better able to influence short-term rates than those at the longer end.

Federal Funds Rate

The Federal Funds rate is the most closely monitored short-term interest rate because it is directly influenced by the Federal Reserve. Changes in its level often give important clues to changes in monetary policy. Banks are required to hold a certain level of reserves with the Federal Reserve against deposits held by their customers. At the end of the day some banks end up with a surplus of reserves over the required amount, while others have a deficiency. The practice that has evolved is that surplus banks lend to deficient ones, thereby enabling the latter to meet their reserve requirements. The Federal Funds rate is the rate of interest charged for these loans. The Federal Reserve enters into the picture because it is able to control the amount of reserves in the banking system through various techniques, and it is therefore able to influence the level of Federal Funds rate. The trend in the Federal Funds rate is therefore a good indication of the direction of monetary policy and financial pressures in the system as well as a guide to the future course of short-term rates in general.

Chart 21.1 shows one technique that has proved useful in determining the intermediate movements in the Federal Funds Indicator rate. A reversal in the trend of the rate is signaled when the Federal Funds rate crosses over its 10-week moving average (MA) (as shown by the dashed line), and this is confirmed when the momentum index [the 13-week rate of change (ROC)] crosses its zero reference line in the same direction. The trend is assumed to be in existence until both indexes signal a reversal. For instance, at the beginning of 1970 the prevailing trend was down. It appeared to be reversed when the Federal Funds rate crossed above its 10-week average, but this was not confirmed by the momentum index, which remained below its zero reference line. It was not until 1971 that the two indexes confirmed each other and a valid warning of a reversal was given.

Chart 21.2 shows this mechanical technique for the period since 1984. In recent years the Federal Funds rate has been subject to the occasional technical distortion. This does not appear to have unduly affected the results of this type of approach since most of the distortions moved in the direction of the prevailing trend.

Four-Month Commercial Paper

From time to time corporations have a substantial amount of surplus cash which is available for a relatively brief period. Other corporations find themselves in need of money. Normally the two corporations would lend each other money through the intermediacy of a bank. However, the practice has evolved of bypassing the banks and acting through an investment dealer, or money broker, who is paid considerably less than the bank. Consequently, both borrower and lender are able to obtain more favorable terms. This form of debt is known as *commercial paper*. The monitoring of the yield on commercial paper rates is very useful, since these interest rates give a good indication of financial pressures and trends of short-term interest rates in the private sector.

There are, of course, many techniques that can be used to determine the change in trend of the commercial paper rate, but one that has been found most useful from the point of view of confirming reversals in cy-

Chart 21.1. The Federal Funds Indicator rate and 13-week momentum. (*Source: Pring Market Review.*)

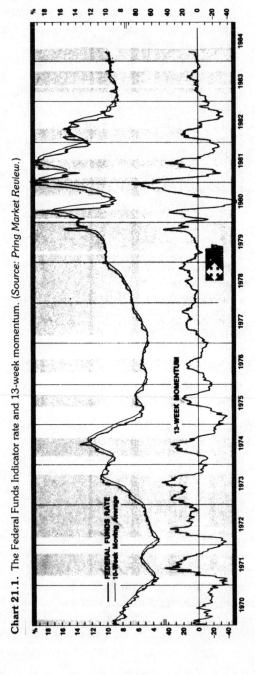

Chart 21.2. The Federal Funds Indicator rate and a 13-week ROC. *(Source: Pring Market Review.)*

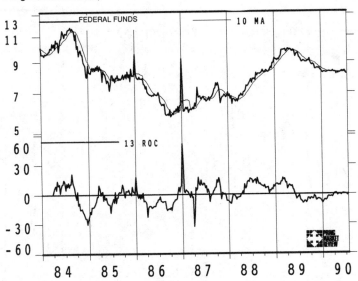

clical movements is determining a reversal in direction of an 18-month exponential moving average (EMA). This is shown in Chart 21.3. An 18-month time span has proved to be useful in determining the cyclical trend of short-term interest rates, since it smooths out whipsaws (such as the 1971 rise) yet retains sufficient sensitivity to respond fairly quickly to changes in longer-term trends. In the 64-year period between 1919 and 1989, a reversal in the downward movement of the EMA, following a cyclical decline in short-term rates, has, with only two exceptions, failed to confirm that a cyclical rise in rates was under way. The two exceptions occurred in 1931 and 1933, when the discount rate was temporarily raised and then lowered in response to specific crises.

Treasury Bills

Treasury bills (T-bills) are short-term debt instruments (i.e., 3-month to 1-year) issued by the U.S. government. The bills are redeemed at face value when they mature, but they pay no interest. The holder obtains a return by purchasing them at a discount (i.e., a price below the face value), which compensates for the loss of interest. Unlike the purchaser of commercial paper, who earns an actual interest rate, a T-bill holder effectively receives a guaranteed capital gain from the investment. The

Chart 21.3. The 3-month commercial paper yield and an 18-month EMA. (*Source: Pring Market Review.*)

rate of return on a T-bill is calculated by relating the capital gain to the time remaining to maturity. Bills are usually quoted on a yield basis, enabling their rate of return to be easily compared with those of other short-term instruments. Most of the time the rate on 90-day T-bills will move in the same direction as the commercial paper rate, since both instruments are influenced by domestic financial conditions. However, the movement of T-bills occasionally diverges for short periods, since they are also bought by foreign investors and foreign central banks. T-bill yields often lead other money-market rates at major turning points. Their trends are analyzed by means of essentially the same techniques as the other money-market rates discussed above.

Three-Month Eurodollar Yields

A *Eurodollar yield* is the interest rate paid on dollar deposits held outside the United States. Trading of 3-month Eurodollars has expanded dramatically since the mid-1970s. Because futures contracts on Eurodollars maturity in 3 months are traded in several countries, including the United States, in many respects it has become a proxy for short-term nongovernment U.S. interest rates. Eurodollar yields move very closely with commercial paper yields or the yields paid on bank certificates of deposit (CDs), since the substitution effect is very close. Chart 21.4 shows the 3-month Eurodollar yield together with three *know sure thing* (KST) indicators. The KST is calculated from the formulas described in Chapter 10.

By and large, reversals in the trend of this yield can be reasonably accurately identified through a combination of 40-week MA crossover, trendline breaks, and KST EMA crossovers.

Many traders and investors monitor the relationship between Eurodollar and 3-month T-bill yields—known as the *Treasury-Eurodollar spread,* or *TED spread).* The idea is that when the differential between the two yields is widening, investors are losing confidence in the financial system and are prepared to take a much larger return in high-quality T-bills. Similarly, if the spread narrows, this means that traders are quite confident and don't need the added implied security of T-bills.

Chart 21.5 shows the TED spread (calculated on a ratio basis) together with an ROC indicator. Trends in this spread should be analyzed in the same way as any price series or relative-strength (RS) relation-

Chart 21.4. Three-month Eurodollar rates and three KST indicators. The KST is a smoothed weighted summed rate of change. The three series in the chart represent a proxy for short, intermediate, and primary trends. Important buy signals occur when all three series are above their EMAs and vice versa. (*Source: Pring Market Review.*)

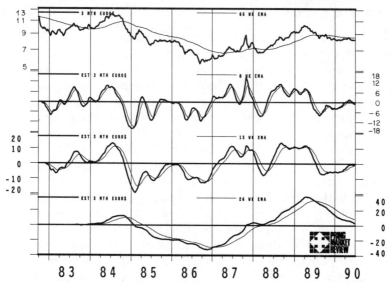

Chart 21.5. Three-month Eurodollar yields versus three-month T-bill yields (the TED spread). (*Source: Pring Market Review.*)

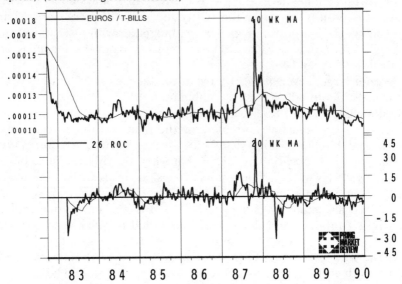

ship. The only problem is that it is a very volatile series and does not really lend itself to trend-reversal techniques.

The Yield Curve

The yield curve in its simplest form measures the relationship between short- and long-term rates. The most common approach is to divide the yield on corporate AAA obligations by that of 3-month commercial paper, as shown in Chart 21.6. The curve is said to be normal when long rates are above short rates, because lenders require a higher yield for a longer time period than for a shorter one, owing to the greater degree of risk and uncertainty.

When short rates rise above long rates, creating a condition that is known as an *inverted yield curve,* the indication is that a tight money policy is in effect.

Trends in the yield curve are very similar to general trends in interest rates. Consequently, if short-term rates and the yield curve both cross their 12-month MA, they have the effect of reinforcing each other.

From time to time, divergences occur between the yield curve and the commercial paper yield. For example, 1982 and the late 1984 highs in the commercial paper yield were not confirmed by the yield curve. Sim-

Chart 21.6. The yield curve versus the 3-month commercial paper yield. *(Source: Pring Market Review.)*

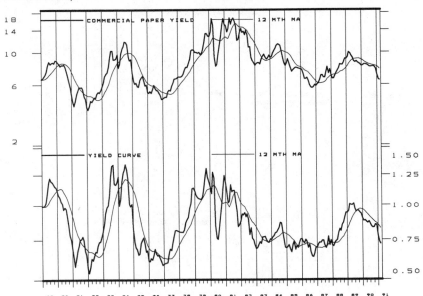

ilarly, the yield curve made only a very marginal new low in late 1986, but the commercial paper yield made a significant new trough. After this, both series rallied quite sharply. In effect the yield curve often acts as a *leading* indicator of short-term rates. Since the yield curve is a reflection of prevailing monetary policy, inverted curves tend to be an early sign of a stock market peak. Consequently, an inverted curve is a distinct sign of caution for equity investors. On the other hand, a reading below the 0.75 level is usually bullish for equities.

Short-Term Interest Rates and Intermediate Trends in Equities

In Chart 21.7 the Value Line Composite and its 13-week ROC index are compared to a 13-week ROC index of the yield on 4- to 6-month commercial paper. The momentum of short-term interest rates has been plotted *inversely* to correspond with stock prices. The downward arrows relate to periods when the commercial paper yield has risen by 20 percent over a 13-week period, i.e., when the inversely plotted index has

Chart 21.7. The Value Line Composite Index and two measures of momentum. (*Source: Pring Market Review.*)

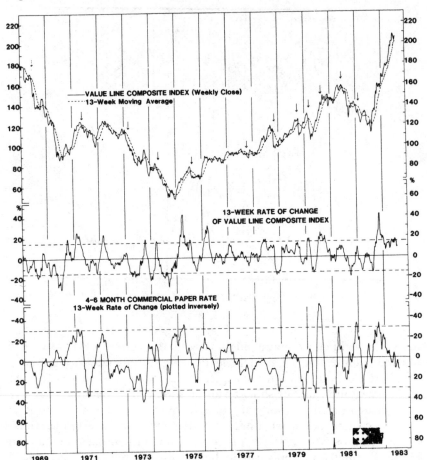

fallen to the 120 percent level. The degree of decline has varied, but for the 10 signals shown on the chart, the average was 20 percent. Rising rates usually result in greater damage during a bear market. The decline is normally well under way by the time the index has fallen to the 120 percent level. However, it is worth noting that a 20 percent rise in yields over a 13-week period was sufficient to kill even the most powerful rallies during the 1969–1983 period.

Chart 21.8 shows a similar approach expressed in a slightly different way. In this instance the ROC of equity prices is overlaid onto the ROC for the commercial paper yield. Buy signals are generated when the stock series crosses above the yield momentum, and vice versa. This is

Chart 21.8. The S&P Composite versus stock market and yield momentum. (*Source: Pring Market Review.*)

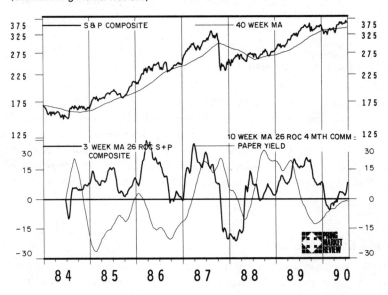

by no means a perfect approach, but it does give another dimension to the technical arsenal. The quality of a signal is also important. For instance, a buy signal was indicated in the late spring of 1989, but it occurred at a time when the stock momentum series was at a very high, and therefore suspicious, level. The market did not fall immediately, but the signal eventually proved to be sub-par.

The Importance of Changes in the Discount Rate

Changes in the discount rate reflect changes in monetary policy, and thus they are more important than changes in any other short-term interest rate. The discount rate is therefore a good indication of the future direction of market-oriented rates and has a strong psychological influence on both debt and equity markets. In addition, since the Federal Reserve does not reverse policy decisions on a week-to-week basis, a change in the discount rate implies that the trend in market interest rates is unlikely to be reversed for at least a few months. A corporation does not like to cut dividends shortly after they have been raised. In a similar vein, the central bank wishes to create a feeling of continuity and consistency. A change in the discount rate is therefore helpful in confirming trends in other rates which, when taken by themselves, can sometimes give misleading signals because of temporary technical or psychological factors.

For Trends in Short-Term Interest Rates

Market rates usually lead the discount rate at cyclical turning points. Even so, a discount rate cut after a series of hikes acts as a confirmation that a new trend of lower rates has begun. The same is true at cyclical bottoms. It's often a good idea to monitor the relationship between the discount rate and its 12-month MA (see Chart 21.9), because crossovers almost always signal a reversal in the prevailing trend at a relatively early stage.

For the Stock Market

Since the incorporation of the Federal Reserve System, every single bull market peak in equities has been preceded by a rise in the discount rate,

Chart 21.9. The discount rate and a 12-month MA versus the 3-month commercial paper yield. (*Source: Pring Market Review.*)

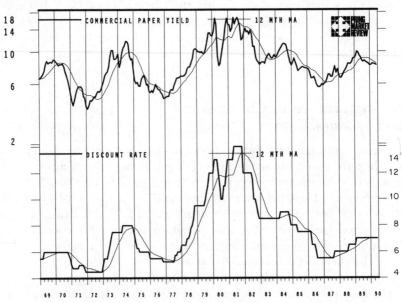

with the exception of the Depression and the war years of 1937 and 1939 and, more recently, 1976. The leads have varied. In 1973 the discount rate was raised on January 12, 3 days before the bull market high, whereas the 1956 peak was preceded by no fewer than five consecutive hikes.

There is a well-known rule on Wall Street: *Three steps and stumble!* The rule implies that after three consecutive rises in the discount rate, the equity market is likely to stumble, i.e., to enter a bear market. In effect, this reflects the fact that interest rates bottom out ahead of the peak in equities. The "three-steps" rule is therefore a recognition that a significant rise in interest rates and tightening in monetary policy have already taken place. Table 21.1 shows the dates when the discount rate was raised for the third time, together with the duration and magnitude of the subsequent decline in equities from the data of the third hike.

Discount-rate cuts are equally as important. Generally speaking, as long as the trend of discount-rate cuts continues, the primary bull market in stocks should be considered intact. Even after the final cut, the market usually continues to go up for a considerable period.

Most of the time the cyclical course of discount-rate cuts resembles a series of declining steps, but occasionally this is interrupted by a temporary hike before the downward trend is resumed. The *discount-rate low* is defined as a low that occurs after a series of declining steps has taken place, and that either remains unchanged at this low level for at least 15 months or is followed by two or more hikes in 2 different months. In other words, if the series of cuts is interrupted by one hike, the trend is

Table 21.1.

Date of discount rate 3d hike		Months between 3d hike and market low	Magnitude of loss, %
November	1919	21	29.86
May	1928	49	77.45
August	1949	0	0
September	1955	27	9.04
March	1959	19	4.31
December	1965	10	15.92
April	1968	27	20.99
May	1973	16	36.47
January	1978	2	1.58
December	1980	19	18.06
February	1989	20	Gain of 4.7

still classified as being a declining one unless the rise occurs after a period of 15 months has elapsed; only when two hikes in the rate have taken place is a low considered to have been established.

Since the data is available for most of this century, it covers both deflationary and inflationary periods and should therefore reflect a number of different economic environments.

Table 21.2 shows that *there have been 13 discount rate lows since 1924. On each occasion the market moved significantly higher from the time the rate was cut.*

The average increase from the date of the cut was 56.7 percent, while the average period between the final cut and the ultimate peak was 31 months.

A discount-rate cut is just one indicator, and while it is invariably bullish, the overall technical position is also important. For example, the low in the discount rate usually occurs just after the market has started a bull phase. If the market is overbought, the odds that the ensuing rally will obtain the magnitude and duration of the average are slim. It should also be noted that even though each discount-rate low has ultimately been followed by a new bull market high, this by no means ex-

Table 21.2.

Discount rate low		S&P Composite high		S&P Composite at time of cut	S&P Composite price peak	Time between last cut and market high (months)	Magnitude of % gain	Average % gain per month
August	1924	September	1929	10.4	31.3	61	200.1	3.3
June	1932	July	1933	4.7	10.9	13	132.0	3.3
January	1934	February	1937	10.3	18.1	125	75.7	10.1
August	1937	June	1946	16.7	18.6	94	11.3	0.1
April	1954	April	1959	27.6	48.1	25	74.3	3.0
April	1958	December	1959	42.3	59.1	20	39.7	2.0
August	1960	February	1966	56.5	92.7	65	64.1	1.0
April	1967*	December	1968	91.0	106.5	20	17.0	0.9
December	1971	January	1973	99.2	118.4	13	19.4	1.5
November	1976	February	1980	101.2	115.3	27	13.9	0.5
July	1980	November	1980	119.8	135.7	4	13.3	3.3
February	1982	July	1983	146.8	167.0	5	13.8	2.8
Average						31	56.7	2.7

*The April 1967 cut did not occur after a series of declines but was associated with the 1966 business slowdown. The exclusion of this cut would improve the average results.

SOURCE: *Pring Market Review*, April 1986.

Chart 21.10. The discount rate and the stock market. (*Source: The Bank Credit Analyst.*)

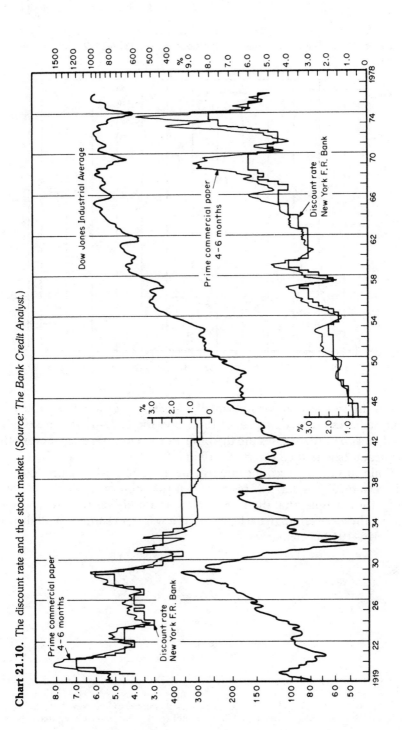

Chart 21.11. The discount rate and the stock market, 1977–1990. (*Source: Pring Market Review.*)

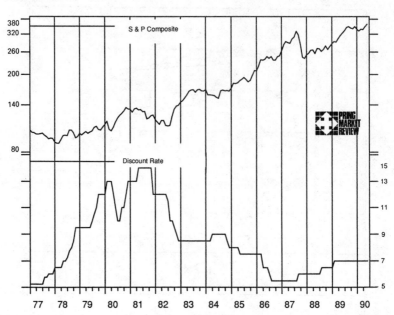

cludes the risk of a major intermediate-term correction along the way. Such setbacks occurred in 1934, 1962, and the 1977–1978 period.[1] Indeed, in two of these cases the discount-rate cut occurred just before the correction began. (See Charts 21.10 and 21.11.)

While cuts in the discount rate usually precede stock market bottoms, this relationship is far less precise than that observed at market tops. Note, for example, that the rate was lowered no fewer than seven times during the 1929–1932 debacle, whereas it was not changed at all during the 1946–1949 bear market.

[1] In the 1977–1978 period the broad market, as measured by the New York Stock Exchange (NYSE) advance/decline (A/D) line, did not correct but moved irregularly higher.

22

Long-Term Interest Rates

The long-term bond market comprises federal government obligations, corporates, and the tax-exempt sector, as illustrated in Chart 22.1. The overall trend of each series is very similar, but at specific points, the demand-supply relationship, peculiar to one or another of the sectors,

Chart 22.1. Representative series from the three bond market sectors. (*Source: Pring Market Review.*)

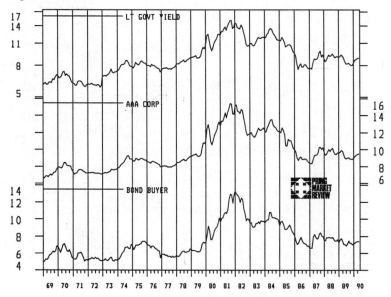

sets it apart from the rest. For example, the long-term corporate market reached its cyclical high in October 1974 (along with most bonds of shorter maturity), but the municipal and government indexes did not peak until October 1975. The government yield index troughed in January 1977, but its municipal counterpart reached its low many months later.

Chart 22.2 shows the Composite Bond Index, which was constructed from the average of all three sectors. This index is useful because it places movements of all three areas in perspective and serves as a base for relative-strength (RS) analysis. This index has been plotted inversely in order to make it correspond to bond prices.

Technical analysis of bonds is very similar to that of stocks, in that trend reversals in yield indexes or price indexes of bonds can be identified by price pattern formations, trendlines, momentum, moving averages (MAs), etc. In a sense, it is possible to extend a crude form of divergence analysis because an advance or decline by one sector, if unconfirmed by the other two, often proves spurious. One major difference between bonds and stocks is that *high-quality bonds generally lead the debt market in both directions,* whereas it is normally the poorer-quality stocks that lead the equity market down; both classes appear to bottom out simultaneously.

Chart 22.2. The Composite Bond Index versus the Composite Debt Index. (*Source: Pring Market Review.*)

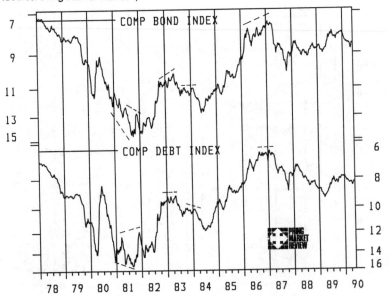

An example of a divergence in the bond market is shown in Chart 22.2, which features the Composite Bond Index and with the Composite Debt Index.[1] The latter is constructed from a simple average of short- and long-term yields from all sectors. Since short-term rates *generally* lead those at the long end, and the Composite Debt Index is heavily weighted in favor of the short end, this indicator often leads the Composite Bond Index. Positive and negative divergences have been highlighted. Whenever these types of disagreements occur, a reversal in the prevailing trend should be anticipated.

Trend Determination of Long-Term Bonds

Analysis of the trend in bond prices (or yields) is approached in the same way as analysis of the various equity market indicators. Because the movement of bonds *tends* to be much smoother than those of stocks, whipsaws resulting from the use of MAs are usually far less troublesome. A useful technique for identifying reversals in primary trends is to calculate a 14-month exponential moving average (EMA) for the yield and a 14-month EMA of the 12-month rate of change (ROC) (see Chart 22.3). Usually a relatively early signal or a reversal in the primary trend is given when both EMAs reverse direction.

Another possibility, shown in Chart 22.4, is to relate 12-month MA crossovers to signals in the long-term *k*now *s*ure *t*hing (KST). This works quite well for most primary trend reversals, but the KST type of approach fails during a period such as the 1960s, when bond prices were in a strong secular decline. Rallies were so brief that the momentum curve had hardly given a buy signal before the price began a new cyclical decline.

Since bond yields are clearly influenced by commodity prices, it is often a good idea to compare the two. Chart 22.3 also includes the CRB Spot Raw Material Commodity Index. The chart shows that on virtually all occasions in the 24-year history covered by the chart, bond yields do not reverse their primary trend until commodity prices do.

---

[1]The Composite Bond Index is a simple average of 20-year U.S. government bonds, Moody's AAA corporate yields, and the Bond Buyer yield. The Composite Debt Index includes the Federal Funds rate, 3-month Eurodollars, CDs, Treasury bills (T-bills), commercial paper, and 1- and 5-year government bonds.

Chart 22.3. Bond prices versus commodity prices. (*Source: Pring Market Review.*)

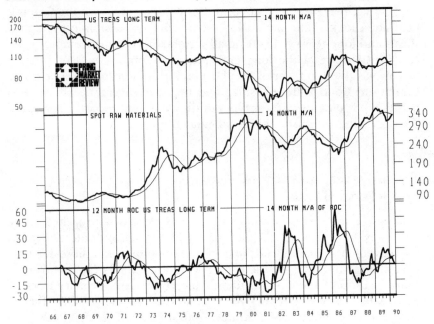

Chart 22.4. Government bond yield and a long-term KST indicator. The KST is a smoothed weighted rate of change. (*Source: Pring Market Review.*)

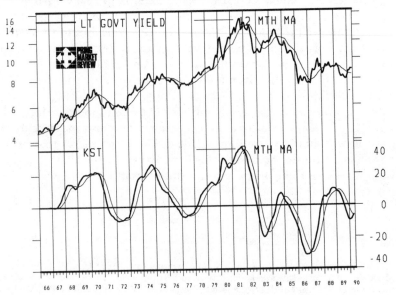

Intermediate- and Short-Term Movements in Bond Prices

As bonds move closer to their maturity date, they cease to behave like long-term instruments. For this reason, it is a good idea to maintain data on a continuous series. Chart 22.5 shows the Lehman Bond Index that is published weekly in Barron's. It is a price index and should not be confused with the Lehman Bond Index that is also reported in *The Wall Street Journal,* which is a total return index (i.e., it includes reinvested interest payments).

The Lehman Bond Index is shown in Chart 22.5 with a 39- and a 13-week ROC indicator. It is interesting to note that the 1986–1987 and 1989 tops were both associated with trend breaks in the 39-week indicator. Remember, the more the indicators agree, the stronger and more reliable the next signal is likely to be.

A good method for determining short-term (2- to 4-week) movements in bonds is to compare the price to a 30-day ROC indicator, as shown in Chart 22.6. In this case the price represents a 3-month perpetual futures contract.[2] A perpetual contract is one that simulates a fu-

Chart 22.5. The Lehman Bond Index and two ROCs. (*Source: Pring Market Review.*)

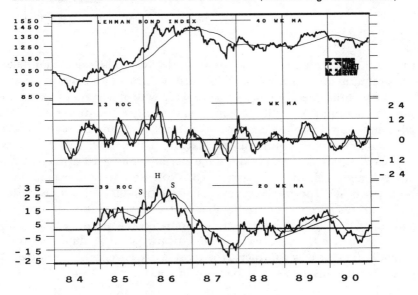

[2]CSI Data, 200 West Palmetto Park Road, Boca Raton, Fl 33432-3788.

Chart 22.6. The 3-Month Perpetual Bond Price versus a 30-day ROC. (*Source: Pring Market Review.*)

tures contract with a perpetual 3-month delivery. The calculation takes the premium and discount of the futures contract into consideration.

Note that the late 1989 top was associated with almost nonexistent upside momentum. Also, the momentum and price trendlines were violated simultaneously. Whenever a joint trendline penetration accompanies momentum weakness of this nature, a major sell-off should be expected. Chart 22.7 shows the same period using a 10-day and a 25-day volume oscillator (see Chapter 18). Note how volume expanded as both price and the oscillator experienced trendline violations at the 1989 top. It's important to remember that volume includes all contracts traded. It is of little value to use the volume of a specific contract because, as the contract moves closer to a nearby status, volume naturally expands. The nearby contract is the most active except for the last week or so. In such instances an expansion in volume is misleading.

Chart 22.7. The 3-Month Perpetual Bond Price versus a volume oscillator. (*Source: Pring Market Review.*)

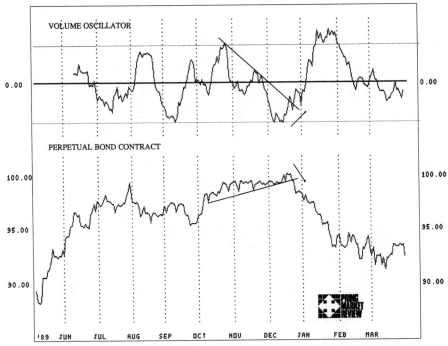

PART 4

Other Aspects of Market Behavior

23

Sentiment Indicators

*I find more and more that it is well to be on
the right side of the minority since it is always
the more intelligent.*   GOETHE

During primary bull and bear markets the psychology of all investors
moves from pessimism and fear to hope, overconfidence, and greed.
For the majority the feeling of confidence is built up over a period of
rising prices, so that optimism reaches its peak around the same point
that the market is also reaching its high. Conversely, the majority is
most pessimistic at market bottoms, at precisely the point when it should
be buying. These observations are as valid for intermediate-term peaks
and troughs as they are for primary ones. The difference is normally of
degree. At an intermediate-term low, for example, significant problems
are perceived, but at a primary market low, they often seem insurmountable. In some respects the worse the problems, the more significant the bottom.

The better-informed market participants, such as insiders and stock
exchange members, tend to act in a manner contrary to that of the majority by selling at market tops and buying at market bottoms. Both
groups go through a complete cycle of emotions, but in completely opposite phases. This is not to suggest that members of the public are always wrong at major market turns and that professionals are always correct; rather, the implication is that, in aggregate, the opinions of these
groups are usually in direct conflict.

Historical data are available on many market participants, making it
possible to derive parameters that indicate when a particular group has

moved to an extreme historically associated with a major market turning point.

Unfortunately, there is a possibility that many of the indexes that worked well prior to the 1980s have been partially distorted because of the advent of listed options trading in 1973 and the introduction of stock index futures in 1982. This is because the purchase and sale of options and index futures substitute for short selling and other speculative activity, which had been used as a basis for the construction of sentiment indicators.

Generally speaking, the data relating to market participants that have not been unduly affected by options trading before the early 1970s are unavailable. Some degree of caution should be exercised in the interpretation of these data in view of their relatively short history. However, since a description of technical analysis would not be complete without some reference to investor sentiment, some of the more reliable indicators are considered below. Use of three or four indexes that measure sentiment is useful from the point of view of assessing the majority view, from which a contrary opinion can be taken.

Specialists Public Ratio

Chart 23.1 shows a 4-week moving average (MA) of what might be regarded as the weekly ratio that pits the smart money against one of the least informed categories of market participant. It measures the round-lot short selling by the public against the New York Stock Exchange (NYSE) specialists on the floor of the Exchange. It has been plotted inversely to correspond with peaks and troughs in the market. The ratio can be interpreted in a number of ways. Generally speaking, it seems to work better in signaling an advance. One might think that an extreme reading below 38 percent was bullish, but this is not usually the case. In some instances, such as late 1983, this type of signal was totally misleading because it occurred just as the market began a major decline. The best signals seem to come when the ratio reverses trend from an extreme level and then either violates a down trendline or crosses above the 38 percent zone, i.e., as shown by the lower dashed line in Chart 23.1.

Sell signals are not so reliable. Indeed, the ratio reached an extreme bearish level right after the 1987 crash, when logic would have indicated that it should have been at a bullish record extreme.

Short Interest Ratio

The short interest is a figure published around the end of the month which reports the number of shares that have been sold short on the

Chart 23.1. Specialists Public Ratio (4-week MA). (*Courtesy Ned Davis Research.*)

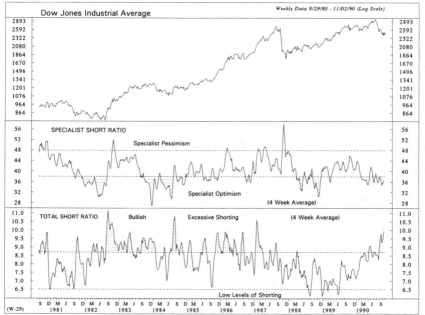

NYSE. Similar data are also published by the other exchanges. The short interest is a flow-of-funds statistic, since every share sold short has to be repurchased (covered), but it is also a measure of sentiment. This is because a large number of shares sold short indicates a predominantly bearish attitude, and vice versa. Over the years, technicians have discovered that the ratio of the short interest to the average daily volume of the preceding month offers more reliable signals than the short interest taken by itself. The ratio is most bullish when it is at a reading of 1.8 or higher. Typically, readings in excess of 2.0 are even more bullish. A short interest ratio of less than 1 has normally reflected a very bullish consensus. Unfortunately, this indicator has shown a tremendous bullish bias since 1982, with consistent readings in excess of 2.0. As a result it failed to signal either the 1983–1984 bear market or the 1987 crash. This distortion has probably developed because of the widespread use of options and futures, and the indicator is therefore unlikely to revert to its previously useful role. Chart 23.2 shows the ratio calculated with an average 12-month daily volume instead of with an average of monthly volume. Recent distortions are self-evident.

Chart 23.2. Short interest ratio versus 12-month daily volume. (*Courtesy Ned Davis Research.*)

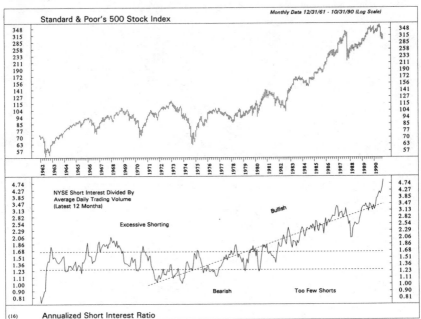

Insider Trading

Stockholders who hold in excess of 5 percent of the total voting stock of a company and corporate officers or other employees who have access to important corporate information are required to file with the Securities and Exchange Commission (SEC) any purchases or sales within 10 days. As a group, these "insiders" are generally correct in their decisions, having a tendency to sell proportionately more stock as the market rises, and vice versa. An 8-week moving average (MA) of the weekly insider sell/buy ratio is shown at the bottom of Chart 23.3. The chart shows that as prices work their way higher, insiders accelerate their sales as a percentage of purchases. Market peaks are signaled when the ratio rises for a period of a few months or more and then reverses trend. In this respect a rise above the 70 percent level and a subsequent reversal in the direction of the index is sufficient under normal circumstances to induce a decline.

At market lows the 60 percent level appears to offer the best warning of an impending advance. If the index either falls below the 60 percent

Chart 23.3. Insider sell/buy ratio. (*Source: Vickers Stock Research Corp.*)

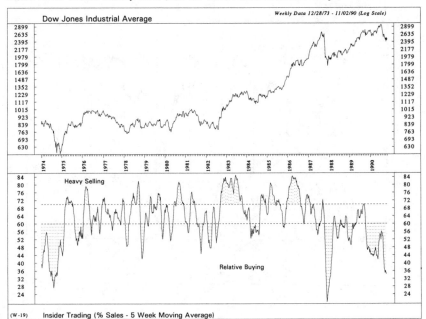

level and then rises above it, or even just declines to briefly touch it, as in early 1978 or March 1980, a rally usually results.

Advisory Services

Since 1963, Investors' Intelligence[1] has been compiling data on the opinions of publishers of market letters. It might be expected that this group would be well-informed and would offer advice of a contrary nature by recommending acquisition of equities at market bottoms and offering selling advice at market tops. The evidence suggests that the advisory services in aggregate act in a manner completely opposite to that of the majority and therefore represent a good proxy for an "anti-majority" opinion.

Chart 23.4*a* shows the percentage of bullish market letter writers in relation to the total of all those expressing an opinion. The data have been smoothed by a 10-week MA to iron out misleading fluctuations. The re-

[1]New Rochelle, N.Y.

Chart 23.4a. Advisory Services Sentiment Indicator. (*Source: Investors' Intelligence, Inc., Larchmont, N.Y.*)

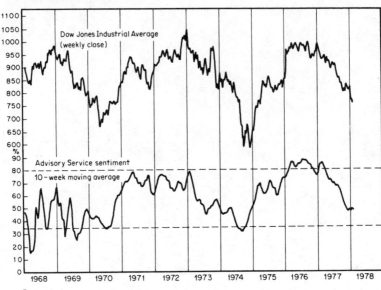

* Bulls as a percentage of bulls and bears

sulting index shows that the advisory services follow the trend of equity prices by becoming most bullish near market tops and predominantly pessimistic around market bottoms. Investors would clearly find it more profitable, then, to take a position contrary to that of the advisory service industry.

This index also gives a good indication of how market psychology can swing from outright pessimism to extreme overconfidence. In early 1968, for example, virtually all services were putting out bearish forecasts right at a major low. Then, as prices began to rise, their prognostications became more optimistic and turned to outright bullishness at the peak. This indicator would have proved very useful during the 1973–1974 bear market. The averages experienced two substantial declines in 1973, but at no time did the index reach an extreme level that would have been consistent with a market bottom.

Whenever the Advisory Services Sentiment Indicator has moved below the 35 percent level and then risen above it, important buy signals have usually resulted. The two weakest signals occurred during the 1969–1970 bear market in 1969, and each was followed by a bear market rally. At market tops a decline from the eighties or high seventies to below the 75 level appears to offer a fairly consistent warning of impending trouble.

The principles of divergence can also be applied to the interpretation of this index. For example, market peaks in 1973, 1983, and 1987 were not confirmed by new highs in the Advisory Services Sentiment Indicator, which indicated a subtle but significant shift in opinion. During the 1969–1970 bear market, prices worked their way lower, but confidence was markedly higher in May 1970 than in July 1969, thereby setting up a positive divergence.

Quite often the *trend* of sentiment can be as important as the *level* in identifying important market reversals. For example, the beginnings of both the 1970 and the 1975 advances were associated with positive trendline breaks in the Advisory Services Sentiment Indicator (Chart 23.4*a*. In a similar vein, the 1973–1974 and 1977–1978 bear markets were preceded by the completion of a major sentiment top. Chart 23.4*b* shows a 4-week MA of the same indicator between 1965 and 1990. The buy and sell signals indicated by the arrows result from crosses of the two dashed lines.

Chart 23.4*b*. Advisory Services Sentiment Indicator. (*Source: Investors' Intelligence, Inc., Larchmont, N.Y.; courtesy Ned Davis Research.*)

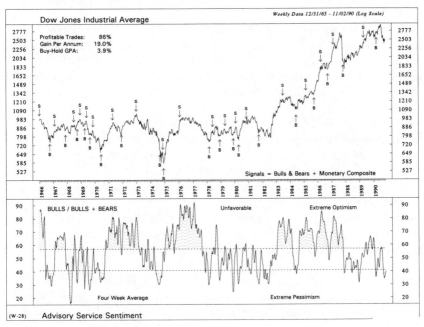

Chart 23.5. The Lehman Bond Index and the Bullish Consensus. (*Source: Pring Market Review; source for bullish consensus: Market Vane's poll of futures-trading advisers.*)

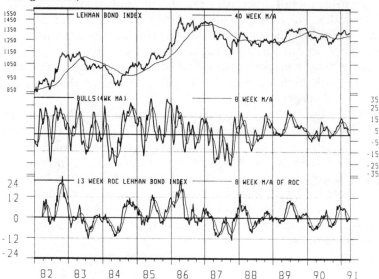

Market Vane and Bond Market Sentiment

Sentiment indicators are also published for the futures market. The most widely followed are data issued by *Market Vane.*[2] Each week *Market Vane* polls a sample of market participants. The results are published as the percentage of participants that are bullish. The theory is that when a significant number of participants are bullish on a particular market, they are already positioned on the long side and there is very little potential buying power left. The implication is that the price has only one way to go, and that is down. In a similar manner, if most participants are bearish, selling pressure has reached an extreme, and therefore prices will reverse to the upside.

One problem with these statistics is that they are based on the opinion of short-term traders, which makes them somewhat erratic and which therefore has implications only for near-term price movements. One way of surmounting this drawback is to calculate an MA of the raw data, so as to smooth out the week-to-week fluctuations.

A 4-week MA of the *Market Vane* data and a long-term Treasury-bond (T-bond) index are plotted in Chart 23.5. Because a reading below 50 percent in the published numbers indicates that the majority of participants are bearish, the data has been reduced by 50, which means

---

[2]Haddaday Publications Inc., Pasadena, CA 91101.

that the zero level in the chart corresponds to a 50 percent reading by the published Bullish Consensus figures. Actual numbers below 50 percent are therefore represented by a negative reading in the chart. The two dashed lines at plus and minus 15 percent represent readings in the published figures of 70 percent and 20 percent, respectively.

Important sell signals often occur when the indicator crosses above the 20 percent level and then recrosses below it on its way toward zero. Readings that have fallen below 15 percent and then risen above it (i.e., the lower dashed line) have often generated timely buy signals. The main drawback in interpreting this data is that premature buy and sell signals often result when a persistent trend is under way. For example, in January 1986 a sell signal was triggered as the index fell below the 20 percent level, but bond prices themselves rallied sharply higher in what turned out to be the most explosive advance of the whole 1984–1986 period. Moreover, a buy signal was given in the spring of 1987. The bond price did experience a small rally, but this was soon followed by a very sharp decline. Other premature sell and buy signals were also given in late 1982 and early 1984.

These flaws demonstrate the necessity of using this indicator in conjunction with a number of others in order to obtain a more balanced picture.

The Bullish Consensus numbers appear to offer very timely signals when the indicator moves to an extreme during a contratrend move. For example, when it reached a bullish extreme during a bear market in early 1984, the rally attracted a large number of bulls, pushing the index above the 20 percent level, but prices collapsed when it recrossed below this area. By the same token, when it moves to a bearish extreme in a bull market, a major buying opportunity is usually signaled. A classic example occurred in the spring of 1985, when the Bullish Consensus moved to an extreme below the 20 percent level and then rallied above it. Some understanding of the prevailing nature of the main trend is therefore an important prerequisite for identifying such turning points.

Combining Sentiment and Momentum

One useful approach for identifying early reversals in trend is to combine sentiment and momentum into one series. Chart 23.6 shows an indicator which combines the smoothed Bullish Consensus numbers, described above, with an 8-week MA of a 13-week rate of change (ROC) of the Lehman Bond Index.

Buy and sell alerts occur when the Bullish/Momentum Index crosses

Chart 23.6. The Lehman Bond Index and a sentiment momentum indicator. (*Source: Pring Market Review and Market Vane.*)

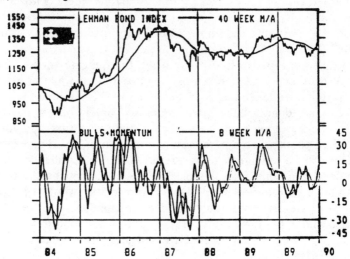

through the oversold and overbought zones and then recrosses on its way back to zero. With the exception of early 1986, every sell signal has been followed by a fairly lengthy correction which has taken the form of either a major sell-off or a long period of consolidation.

Sometimes important clues of a potential trend reversal occur if the Bullish Consensus numbers move to an extreme but are not confirmed by a similar move in momentum. Such action represents an exception to the rule that bulls are attracted only by sharply rising prices and bears only by sharply falling prices.

For example, Chart 23.5 shows that in mid-1982 the sentiment indicator moved to a bearish extreme, but momentum hardly declined at all. In 1986 the reverse set of conditions occurred: the sentiment indicator moved to a bullish extreme with virtually no upside price momentum. Such contradictions do not occur very often, but when they do, there is a high degree of probability that an important trend reversal is in the wind.

The rationale probably lies in the fact that rising prices (momentum) attract bulls, whereas falling prices (momentum) attract bears. However, when sentiment moves to an extreme and prices do not, the degree of optimism or pessimism is misplaced, and the price must adjust accordingly.

Unfortunately, I have been unable to correlate the Bullish Consensus data for most of the other futures markets with their respective price trends; consequently I have found it more difficult to extend this bond analysis to other futures markets with a similar degree of confidence.

Mutual Funds

Data on mutual funds are published monthly by the Investment Company Institute. The statistics are useful because they monitor the actions of both the public and the institutions. In recent years money-market and tax-exempt mutual funds have become widespread; therefore, the data used here have been modified to include only equity funds. Technical analysts usually calculate mutual fund cash as a percentage of assets. In a sense this data should be treated as a flow-of-funds indicator, but it is discussed here as a measure of sentiment.

Mutual Fund Cash/Assets Ratio

Mutual funds consistently hold a certain amount of their portfolios in the form of liquid assets in order to accommodate investors wishing to cash in or redeem their investments. A useful indicator is derived when this cash position is expressed as a percentage of the total value of mutual funds' portfolios (a figure known as *total asset value*) (see Chart 23.7). The index moves in the direction opposite to the stock market, because the proportion of cash held by mutual funds rises as prices fall, and vice versa. There are three reasons for this characteristic. First, as the value of a fund's portfolio falls in a declining market, the proportion of cash held will automatically rise even though no new cash is raised. Second, as prices decline, the funds become more cautious in their buying policy, since they see fewer opportunities for capital gains. Third, the decision is made to hold more cash reserves as insurance against a rush of redemptions by the public. In a rising market the opposite effect is felt, as advancing prices automatically reduce the proportion of cash, sales increase, and fund managers are under tremendous pressure to capitalize on the bull market by being fully invested.

One of the drawbacks of this approach is that mutual fund cash data has, by and large, remained above the 8.5 percent level since 1978. It is true that the market has been in a rising trend since then, but one of the functions of an indicator of this nature is to warn of setbacks such as the 1980 and 1981–1982 bear markets, not to mention the 1987 crash.

One way around this problem, originally devised by Norman Fosback

Chart 23.7. Mutual funds cash/assets ratio. (*Source: Investment Company Institute; courtesy Ned Davis Research.*)

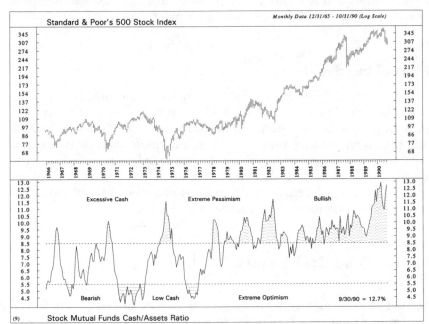

of Market Logic, is to subtract the prevailing level of short-term interest rates from the cash percentage levels themselves. In this way the incentive for portfolio managers to hold cash due to high interest rates is neutralized. This adjustment to the cash/assets ratio is shown in Chart 23.8. It is a definite improvement on the raw data, but unfortunately it does not explain the 1987 crash.

A final alternative, devised by Ned Davis Research, compares switch fund cash and mutual fund managers cash to total mutual fund assets. This series is also adjusted for interest rates and appears to offer the best results of all. The labeled buy (*B*) and sell (*S*) signals in Chart 23.9 are generated when this series crosses below the lower dashed line; they remain in force until it crosses above the upper dashed (selling) line.

Margin Debt

Trends in margin debt are probably better classified as flow-of-funds indicators, but since the trend and level of margin debt are also good indications of investor confidence (or lack of confidence), they are discussed in this section.

Chart 23.8. Mutual funds cash/assets ratio adjusted for interest rates. (*Source: Investment Company Institute; courtesy Ned Davis Research.*)

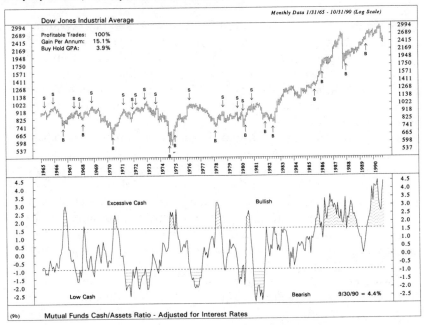

(9b) Mutual Funds Cash/Assets Ratio - Adjusted for Interest Rates

Chart 23.9. Switch fund cash/assets ratio. (*Source: Investment Company Institute; courtesy Ned Davis Research.*)

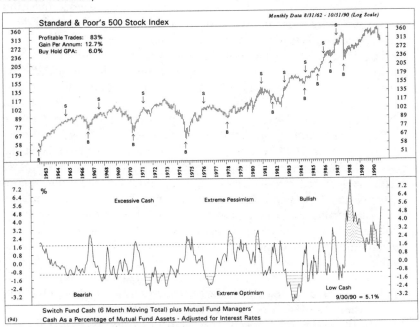

(9d) Switch Fund Cash (6 Month Moving Total) plus Mutual Fund Managers' Cash As a Percentage of Mutual Fund Assets - Adjusted for Interest Rates

Margin debt is money borrowed from brokers and bankers using securities as collateral. The credit is normally used for the purchase of equities. At the beginning of a typical stock market cycle, margin debt is relatively low; it begins to rise very shortly after the final bottom in equity prices. As prices rise, margin traders as a group become more confident, taking on additional debt in order to leverage larger stock positions.

During a primary uptrend, margin debt is a valuable source of new funds for the stock market. The importance of this factor can be appreciated when it is noted that margin debt increased almost tenfold between 1974 and 1987. The difference between stock purchased for cash and stock bought on margin is that margined stock must at some point be sold in order to pay off the debt. On the other hand, stock purchased outright can theoretically be held indefinitely. During stock market declines, margin debt reverses its positive role and becomes an important source of stock supply.

This occurs for four reasons. First, the sophistication of margin-oriented investors is relatively superior to that of other market participants. When this group realizes that the potential for capital gains has greatly diminished, a trend of margin liquidation begins. Margin debt has flattened or declined within 3 months of all but one of the 14 stock market peaks since 1932.

Second, primary stock market peaks are invariably preceded by rising interest rates, which in turn increase the carrying cost of margin debt, therefore making it less attractive to maintain.

Third, since 1934 the Federal Reserve Board (the "Fed") has been empowered to set and vary margin requirements, which specify the amount that can be lent by a broker or bank to customers for the purpose of holding securities. This measure was considered necessary in view of the substantial expansion of margin debt that occurred in the late 1920s. The liquidation of this debt pyramid contributed to the severity of the 1929–1932 bear market. When stock prices have been rising strongly for a period of time, speculation develops, often resulting in a sharp rise in margin debt. Sensing that things could get out of control at this stage, the Fed raises the margin requirement, which has the effect of reducing the buying power of the general public from what it might otherwise have been. Normally, it takes several margin-requirement changes to significantly reduce the buying power of these speculators. This is because the substantial advance in the price of stocks—which was responsible for the requirements' being raised in the first place—normally creates additional collateral at a rate which is initially sufficient to offset the rise in reserve requirements.

Fourth, the collateral value of the securities used as a basis for the margin debt falls as stock prices decline. The margin speculator is faced

Chart 23.10. Margin debt and a 12-month MA. (*Courtesy Ned Davis Research.*)

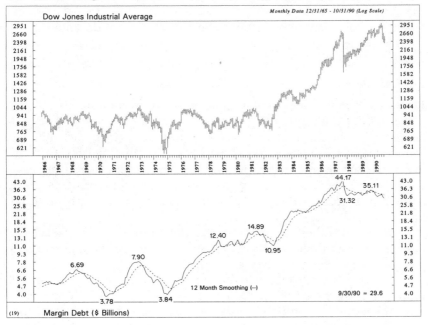

(19)   Margin Debt ($ Billions)

with the option of putting up more money or selling stock in order to pay off the debt. At first, the margin call process is reasonably orderly, as most traders have a sufficient cushion of collateral to protect them from the initial drop in prices. Alternatively, those who are undermargined often choose to put up additional collateral or cash. Toward the end of a bear market, prices fall more rapidly, and this unnerving process, combined with the unwillingness or inability of margin customers to come up with additional collateral, triggers a rush of margin calls. This adds substantially to the supply of stock that must be sold regardless of price. The self-feeding downward spiral of forced liquidation continues until margin debt has contracted to a more manageable level.

Margin debt is a useful indicator when expressed in relation to its 12-month MA, as shown in Chart 23.10. Crossovers offer confirmation of major trend reversals.

Put/Call Data

Sentiment indicators based on short selling data appear to have been distorted in recent years, in part because of the introduction of listed options. The other side of the coin is that options can themselves be used as a basis for the construction of sentiment indicators. Their performance is far from perfect but definitely worth consideration.

Put/Call Ratio

Perhaps the most widely followed option-derived indicator is the one that measures the ratio of the volume of puts to the volume of calls. A *put* gives an investor or trader the option to *sell* a specific stock index or commodity at a predetermined price over a specified period. In effect the purchaser of a put is betting that the price of the underlying asset will go down. This is a form of short sale in which the trader's risk is limited to the cost of the put. (The risk on a short sale is theoretically unlimited.)

A *call*, on the other hand, is a bet that the underlying asset will rise in price. It gives a purchaser the option to *buy* a stock index or commodity at a predetermined price over a specified period.

It is normal for call volume to outstrip that of puts, and so the put/call ratio invariably trades below the 1.0 or (100) level. This indicator measures the swings in sentiment between the bulls and the bears. In theory, the lower the ratio, the more bullish the crowd and the more likely the market is to decline, and vice versa. A low ratio means that very few people are buying puts relative to calls, whereas a high ratio indicates that a larger number of traders than normal are betting that the market will go down.

The put/call ratio is shown in Chart 23.11 as a 4-week MA of puts divided by a 4-week MA of calls. This series has been "normalized" to take account of the predominance of call volume. This has the effect of changing the scale but not the swings in sentiment.

The 4-week MA of the ratio often signals a rally when it moves through and then crosses back below the upper dashed line. Its timing of tops (based on a recrossing above the lower dashed line) generally offers reliable signals, but it experienced some notable failures during 1986.

The series at the bottom of Chart 23.11 measures the relative premium of puts to calls. The concept is that when investors are bullish, they bid up the premium of calls against their intrinsic value. Intrinsic value is based on the current price in relation to the strike price, taking into consideration the time premium and the volatility of the underlying stock. On the other hand, when investors are bearish, they are willing to place a higher relative premium on puts. The chart shows that this is a contrary indicator, since a high reading indicates pessimism. It

Chart 23.11. Put/call ratio (4-week MA). (*Courtesy Ned Davis Research.*)

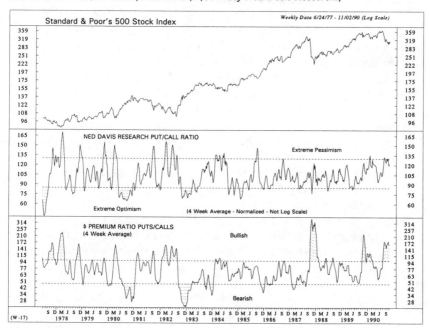

is useful to compare the levels of the put/call volume and the put/call premium series. In a very general sense, larger moves seem to develop when the two are in agreement.

Put/Call Open Interest

Bob Prechter and Dave Allman[3] introduced another put/call indicator in an article in the *Market Technician's Journal.*[4] Their approach compares the open interest on puts and calls on the Standard & Poor's (S&P) 100 (OEX). *Open interest* is the total number of outstanding options at the end of the day.

Prechter and Allman use a 10-day MA of the ratio, which has the advantage of being far less erratic. The theory behind this indicator is basically the same as that for other put/call ratios. However, because the open interest figure is far less erratic than daily volume, there are fewer signals. As a result, the signals are quite useful for identifying intermediate-term as opposed to short-term reversals.

[3]New Classics Library, Gainesville, GA.
[4]Issue 34, winter 1989–1990.

The major drawback is that data has been available only since 1983, which is a relatively short time compared to other sentiment indicators. The actual indicator is constructed from a 10-day MA of daily ratios. A reading of 2.0 in either direction is unusual and typically signals an important turning point in the market.

Market bottoms appear to be associated with declines below 0.50. Three buy signals triggered in this way are shown in Chart 23.12. Following the first signal, in February 1984, the market essentially moved sideways before moving down. This was not a particularly good signal. The second, in December 1984, occurred just before the market began a significant new bull market upleg. A further buy signal occurred in November 1987, when it briefly broke to the 0.31 level before crossing back above 0.50, giving an important buy signal which was followed by an over 50 percent market advance.

Market peaks appear to be signaled when the ratio moves above the 1.9 percent level and then falls back below it. This is shown in Chart 23.13. Two signals were given in 1983. The first was followed by a small intermediate decline, the second by a 16 percent market drop. Three signals were given in 1987. The first failed, the second signaled a small intermediate decline, and the third occurred at the time of the then all-time peak.

It is apparent that not every signal results in a significant reversal in the market. In effect, a signal should be used as an alert that an important move may be in the offing and that a closer than normal examination of the overall technical position is warranted. After all, every major market turn between 1983 and 1990 was signaled by this useful indicator.

Contrary Opinion as a Sentiment Indicator

The crowd is typically wrong at major market turning points, and the news media normally reflect majority opinion. Therefore a sentiment indicator based solely on reports, cover stories, network news items, and other public sources would probably be extremely useful. Unfortunately, in practice it is not possible to construct a precise indicator. However, a careful study of popular magazine publications (such as *Time, Newsweek, U.S. News & World Report, Fortune,* and *Business Week*), the network evening news, financial books on the best-seller list, and other such sources can offer a very useful supplement to the indicator approach.

Typically, at the top or bottom of an established move, the story of a market crashing, the gold price soaring, or some other extreme event is in itself newsworthy, and the story will appear as either a prominent article or a cover story. I do not mean to imply that the media are incom

Chart 23.12. The Dow Jones Industrial Average (DJIA) versus the OEX 10-day MA open interest put/call ratio (extremely low readings). (*Source: New Classics Library, Gainesville, Georgia.*)

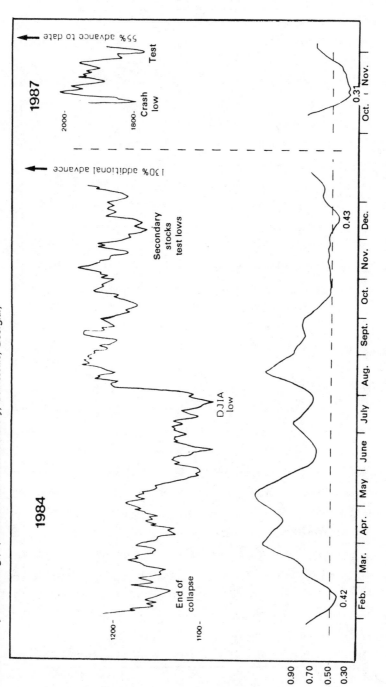

Chart 23.13. The DJIA versus the OEX 10-day MA open interest put/call ratio (extremely high readings). (*Source: New Classics Library, Gainesville, Georgia.*)

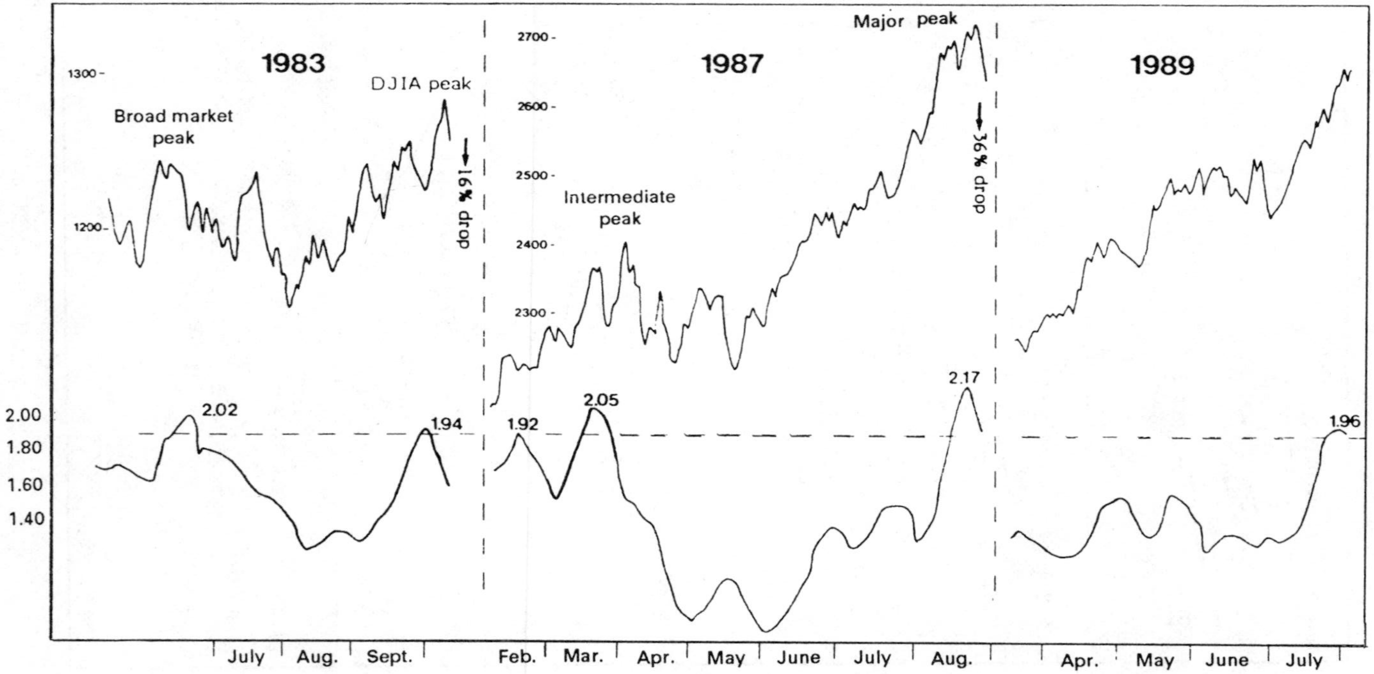

petent because they emphasize financial stories at the wrong time—quite the reverse, in fact, because their function is to publish newsworthy stories. From a market aspect, of course, nothing is more newsworthy than a panic-stricken or euphoric market. Unfortunately, by the time the facts have been widely disseminated, they have usually been well discounted by the markets; it is thus much more likely that the media are publicizing the end rather than the beginning of a move. Occasionally a cover story or article will prove timely for investment purposes, as happened with the famous "Birth of the Bull" *Time* cover at the beginning of the 1982–1983 advance. In this case some interpretation would have been necessary since the stock market had grabbed the news on record volume and a very sharp price rise off a deeply oversold condition, each of which is characteristic of the beginning of a major move. It is very important, therefore, to make sure that such stories are consistent with the other technical indicators.

Typically, the news story will not be an isolated example but will appear in many publications in one form or another, making it easier to identify a basic theme. After a sustained run-up in stock prices, for example, one article may be quoting experts who are forecasting significantly higher prices, and another may feature analysts touting their favorite stocks or the tremendous incomes being earned by America's leading stockbrokers. Such a trend will almost invariably indicate that the pendulum has swung too far in the bullish direction. At major market lows the opposite type of story will emerge, highlighting a panic decline, some financial problem seemingly impossible to resolve, or a major bankruptcy. The videotaping of a major feature right from the floor of the NYSE during the early evening network news usually proves to be a classic tip-off that a decline is either finished or in its very late stages.

At other times an isolated article or story on an obscure topic will offer a vital clue that a trend has gone too far. For example, in late 1981, just before a major debt market sell-off, an article pointing out the profit potential for Treasury-bill/Treasury-bond (T-bill/T-bond) spreads was printed in one of the major magazines. In the summer of 1983, just before a major sell-off, another magazine ran a long article on stock index futures. Although experienced investors are familiar with such concepts and trading vehicles, this type of article is very unusual for a magazine with a wide circulation among the general public. Another classic was a CBS evening news feature on the price of sugar in 1980, which was broadcast within 1 or 2 days of the bull market peak. It is doubtful whether the sugar price has been discussed on that program either before or since.

The art of forming a correct contrary opinion based on an observation of the media is not easy, since such articles and features are usually published or aired at a time when no one in his or her right mind would expect a market reversal. In other words, the reports appear to be perfectly logical. Putting this approach into practice is therefore not a simple matter, and this discussion is intended only to illustrate the possibilities which exist for augmenting a more orthodox technical approach.

Markets' Reactions to News

Another extremely important, though imprecise, approach to appraisal of market sentiment is to observe the reaction of any market to news events, especially unexpected ones. This is a helpful exercise, since markets look ahead and factor all foreseeable events into the price structure. If a news event that would normally be expected to move the price does not affect it, the likelihood is that all the news – good or bad – is already reflected in the price.

A classic example occurred at the end of 1986, when the famous insider stock scandals began to appear, starting with the indictment of David Levine and Ivan Boesky. Under normal circumstances the market would be expected to decline, but in this instance, equity prices stalled for a while and then embarked on a significant rally.

The discount rate was raised in the spring of 1978. This should have been followed by a weak market, but instead, equities rallied on heavy volume. This situation also fitted well into the technical position, which on a long-term basis was very oversold. Also, just after the bottom, the Net New High list expanded rapidly.

Examples could be cited for many other markets, but the basic principle that holds true is that if a market does not respond to a news event in the manner one might normally expect, it is probably in the process of turning. Evaluation of this factor is most definitely a judgment call but can act as a very useful adjunct to an appraisal of technical indicators.

Summary

1. Sentiment indicators are useful supplements to the trend-determining techniques discussed in other chapters. They should be used for the purpose of assessing the consensus view from which a contrary position can be taken.

2. Since sentiment indicators are susceptible to institutional changes, it is mandatory to consider them as a group rather than on an individual basis.

24
Speculative Activity in the Stock Market

Speculation has been defined as the undertaking of substantial risk in the hope of gain. Some degree of speculation is always present in market activity, in the sense that there are always individuals willing to bear a risk. However, since virtually all bull markets in their late stages have clearly defined characteristics of speculation, an examination of some indicators that measure this phenomenon of excessive confidence is well worthwhile.

Over the course of the stock market cycle, investors move from outright pessimism and sometimes panic at market bottoms to an outlook of overconfidence and avarice at market tops. On the assumption that, once set in motion, a trend in market psychology perpetuates itself, it is important to determine the level of emotion at any point compared with previous periods, and also to detect any reversal in its trend at a relatively early stage.

Measuring Speculation

As discussed in Chapters 14 to 19, there are four main aspects or dimensions of psychology in the stock market: price, volume, time, and breadth. Price reflects the level of enthusiasm; volume, its intensity; breadth, the extent of participation; and time, the extent of the period.

The farther these four factors work in any one direction, the greater the significance of the counteraction.

For example, by late 1929, stock prices had been rising almost uninterruptedly for 8 years. Prices had increased fivefold, and volume at the time of the peak was exceptionally heavy. The counteraction was naturally extreme, with an almost total collapse in equity prices. Since speculation is one of the most emotional aspects of the stock market, examination from all four dimensions—price, volume, breadth, and time—is relevant.

Price

One method of evaluating speculation is to compare the prices of low- and high-quality issues. The rationale is that low-quality stocks are more volatile and, in a bull market, will rise proportionately faster than better-quality stocks. The high potential for profit in these equities makes them very popular with speculators. In addition, members of the public who like to buy in 100-share "round" lots but do not have the capital to purchase higher-priced stocks in these quantities find low-priced equities a natural vehicle.

The upper portion of Chart 24.1a shows the Standard & Poor's (S&P) Low-Priced Stock Index and the S&P High-Grade Stock Index. The relatively high volatility of the low-priced stocks is self-evident and is a good reflection of the exaggerated emotions of investors during a market cycle. At market bottoms the Low-Priced Stock Index either lags or coincides with the Dow Jones Industrial Average (DJIA) and is therefore a confirming indicator. At market peaks the index usually leads by anywhere from 0 to 15 months. Considered in isolation, the index itself is not too helpful in determining levels of speculation, though obviously a sustained but controlled uptrend points to a good underlying improvement in confidence, while a more exponential trend after a slow but lengthy rise is a good tip-off to a speculative peak.

The lower portion of Chart 24.1a shows what amounts to a relative-strength (RS) line comparing the S&P Low-Priced Stock Index to the S&P High-Grade Stock Index. It is calculated by dividing the low-priced index by the high-grade index. Whenever the resulting ratio is below 100, the value of the high-grade index is greater than that of the low-priced. Such a condition reflects a relatively defensive posture by speculators and is normally associated with major bottom areas. With the exception of 1961, the ratio has always been above 100 at major tops.

There is no absolute level that indicates a peak in speculation. However, the high readings in the late 1920s and in 1937, 1946, 1968, and 1983 (all of which followed lengthy periods of rising stock prices) were clearly pointing out that activity was reaching an extreme from which a

Chart 24.1a. Low-priced versus high-priced stocks. (*Source: Pring Market Review.*)

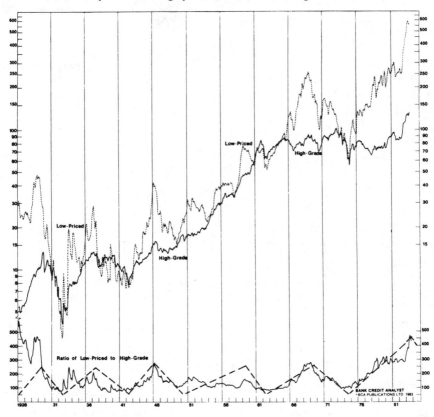

major counteraction could be expected. It is important to distinguish between the high levels that occur in this index after a long and substantial rise in equities and, for example, those that occurred in 1933–1934 and 1951, which were strong upward reactions in low-priced stocks following a long and sharp decline. In retrospect it can be seen that the 1971–1972 rally was really a temporary interruption of what proved to be a long corrective period.

Chart 24.1*b* shows the ratio together with a long-term *k*now *s*ure *t*hing (KST) indicator. In some respects peaks and troughs in the KST indicate extremes in speculative activity.

Volume

Chart 24.2 shows the average monthly volume of the American Stock Exchange (AMEX) expressed as a percentage of that on the New York

Chart 24.1b. Low-priced versus high-priced stocks, 1972–1990. (*Source: Pring Market Review.*)

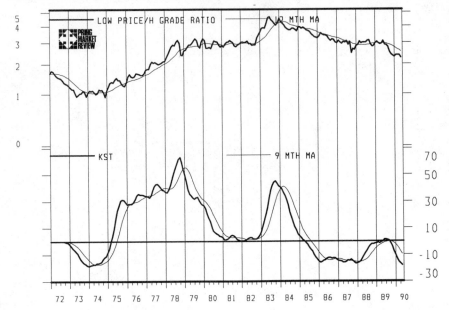

Stock Exchange (NYSE). The rationale for using this index is basically the same as that for using the high-grade/low-priced comparison. Generally speaking, because of less stringent listing requirements, stocks trading on the AMEX are of lower quality than those on the NYSE. Since speculators normally deal in low-quality issues, rises and falls in the index therefore reflect volume trends toward more or less speculation. Historically, levels in excess of 50 percent have been associated with major tops. Normally these high readings lead peaks in the major averages by several months or more. Conversely, levels of 20 percent or less (when speculation in terms of volume is low) have often been good buying points. However, purchases would have been more profitably made if this somewhat erratic indicator had been used in conjunction with the others.

Since the 1970s, the AMEX has lost considerable market share to the NYSE and more particularly to the over-the-counter (OTC) market. For this reason and because of the advent of options and futures it is unlikely that the AMEX/NYSE volume ratio will again be useful as a reliable speculative index. Chart 24.3 shows the ratio of OTC volume in the NYSE.

Chart 24.2. AMEX volume as a percentage of NYSE volume (monthly). (*Source: Pring Market Review.*)

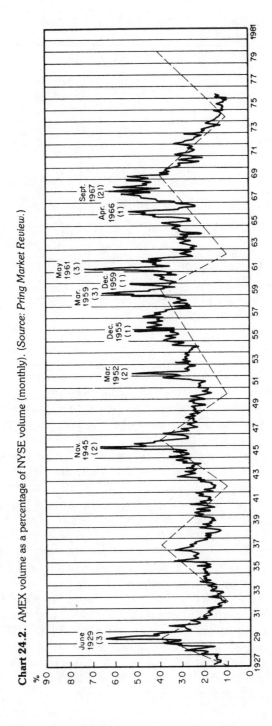

Chart 24.3. OTC volume compared to NYSE volume.

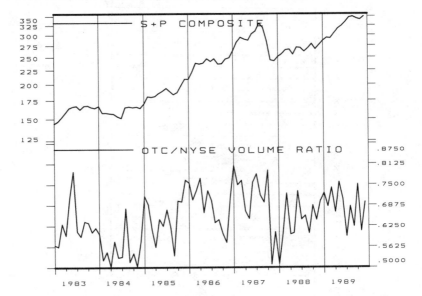

Breadth

One prerequisite for a strong surge in speculation is that equities should have been rising on a broad front for a relatively long period of time. For the general level of confidence to mature into a speculative orgy, it is first necessary for a broad spectrum of stocks to advance rather than for the price rise to be confined to a relatively select group.

If only a few investors are making money, overconfidence is unlikely to develop, but if virtually everyone is profiting, the ingredients are in place for a self-feeding spiral resulting in an excess of optimism.

Breadth is portrayed in Chart 19.2 by an advance/decline (A/D) line constructed on the basis of the square root of the $A/U - D/U$ formula discussed in Chapter 19. Until 1969 every cyclical peak in the Dow since 1931 had been confirmed by the A/D line. At the speculative peak in 1968 the line made a new cyclical high unaccompanied by the DJIA. On the other hand, the then all-time high in 1973 for the Dow was not confirmed by the A/D line, which had at that time been unable to surpass its 1968 high. These examples illustrate the necessity for strong breadth rather than a strong average to presage a speculative flurry. The 1968–1969 rise in the A/D line was a cumulation of the rise in speculation begun in 1962, but it was not reflected in the Dow. On the other hand, a notable high for the DJIA was achieved in January 1973 against an overall declining trend in breadth.

The 1983 speculative peak was preceded by a rise in the A/D line, but this was less obvious than other tops in speculation. Even so, it is well worth noting that the DJIA moved sideways between 1976 and 1982, reaching an all-time high only at the end of 1982. On the other hand, the NYSE weekly A/D line, shown in Chart 19.3, was in a persistent, confidence-building uptrend through the 1976–1982 period.

The other speculative peaks were preceded not only by strong rises in breadth but also by a rise that had extended for a number of years. Only after a long advance was confidence able to develop into excessive optimism.

Time

For a strong speculative wave to get under way, it is necessary not only to correct the excesses of the previous speculative peak but also to establish a fairly lengthy period of rising stock prices, so that a feeling of gradually improving confidence can erase the fears and caution involved in the corrective process. Since many investors suffer staggering loses during the declining period, time is also needed either to restore their financial viability or to develop a new generation of participants who have not undergone the sobering experience of a speculative cleansing. Once confidence resumes, a self-feeding spiral can occur, when investors begin to undertake risks as a group which they would never contemplate as independent and clear-thinking individuals.

In observing the patterns of the speculative indicators discussed above, it becomes clear that this repetitive emotional transition from greed to fear and back to greed forms an approximate cycle. Since the 1920s, for example, four outstanding speculative peaks (1928–1929, 1946, 1967–1968, and 1983) have occurred, about 20 years apart. These major peaks were separated by three other peaks at roughly 10-year intervals—in 1937, 1959, and 1978—so that there were really seven peaks of speculation in all, each falling in the latter part of their respective decade. Between these periods of excesses, troughs also occurred at 10-year intervals when risk-bearing was at a minimum. These points happened in 1932, 1942, 1950, 1962, and 1974, and to some extent in 1982. Following these low points, there was a period either of bounceback or of speculative recovery, such as 1934 or 1951–1952, or the beginning of a slow, but sustained, rise in speculation, as in 1942–1946 or 1962–1968. This idealized cycle has been superimposed on the AMEX/NYSE volume and high-grade/low-priced price indicators discussed above. There are some obvious flaws in this concept, since turning points in volume, price, and breadth do not always coincide. For ex-

Chart 24.4a. Dividend yields (Barron's 50-Stock Average) and the 10-year cycle in speculation. (*Source: Pring Market Review.*)

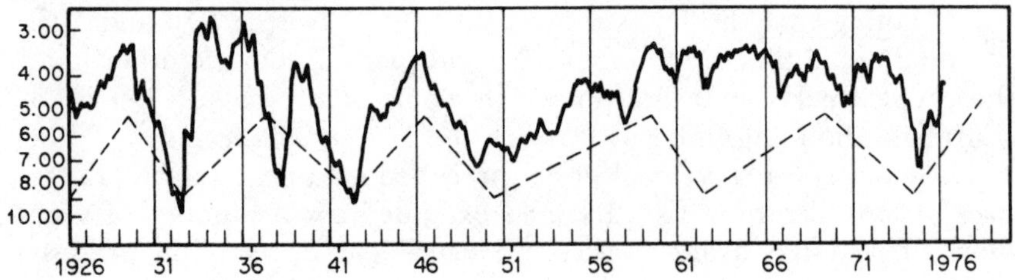

ample, in 1936–1937 the high-grade/low-priced ratio was quite high, and breadth had risen sharply for a fairly lengthy 5 years. On the other hand, AMEX/NYSE volume was high (34 percent) compared with 1932 (10 percent), but it was still well below other speculative peaks. Conversely, the AMEX/NYSE volume reached its highest recorded level in 1961, at around 74 percent, against a relatively short 6-month advance in breadth and a price ratio that showed low-priced stocks only marginally above high-grade issues.

Yield

Another approach to the 10-year-cycle concept of speculation is to examine stock yields since they reflect an important form of equity valuation. If stocks are overvalued (i.e., if they possess low yields), some degree of speculation is implied, and vice versa. Chart 24.4a shows the idealized 10-year cycle superimposed over the dividend yield plotted inversely, and Chart 24.4b shows the same relationship for the yield on the S&P Composite. There are two obvious periods in which the relationship does not fit. The first occurred in 1936–1937, when yields rose as speculation and stock prices advanced. The second occurred in 1983, when blue chips were bargains on a yield basis and OTC stocks were reaching a secular peak in RS terms.

Even so, the blue chips, as measured by the DJIA, soon caught up and experienced a record high in dividend valuation in 1987.

The Influence of Options and Stock Index Futures

The traditional methods of speculation have become distorted to some extent by the advent of listed options and trading in stock index futures.

Chart 24.4b. S&P yield, 1969–1990. (*Source: Pring Market Review.*)

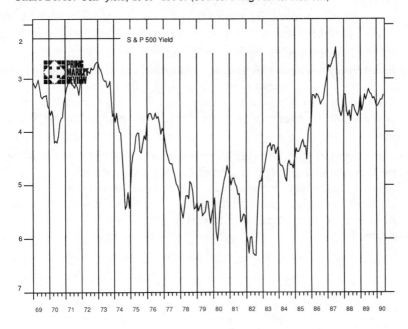

Unfortunately, data on these new vehicles do not go back far enough to be of any predictive value; indeed, it is not clear what proportion of such trading is due to arbitrage and hedging and what to speculation. Although their introduction may dilute some of the activity associated with lower-quality issues, the concept of a wasting asset or an ultra-high gearing is not palatable to all speculators. Consequently, it should be fair to assume that though some of the indicators discussed above may not reach the fervent levels witnessed on previous occasions, they will continue to give some indication of the general trend and level of speculative activity.

Summary

1. From the point of view of the long-term investor, the establishment of a major cyclical peak in speculation is an important factor, because it often represents the last but most dynamic stage of any bull market.

2. Since the 1920s, there have been six such peaks (1928–1929, 1936–1937, 1946, 1959, 1967–1969, and 1983), separated by about

10 years. With the exception of 1983, a major decline followed these excesses of optimism from which the market, as measured by the A/D line, did not recover to a new high for at least 4 years. In most cases the retracement of these losses took much longer.

3. In addition to these speculative peaks, there is also an approximate 10-year cycle of troughs characterized by a dearth of speculative activity and a general disgust with equities. There is normally an initial rebound or recovery in speculation following these major cyclical lows.

4. The speculative indicators discussed in this chapter are not precise tools; rather, they offer a longer-term perspective on how far the trend of optimism or pessimism has matured and should be treated as background indicators that can lead to a more enlightened interpretation of other trend-identification techniques.

25
Automated Trading Systems

In recent years there has been a substantial increase in the use of personal computers (PCs) for the purposes of technical analysis. Not surprisingly, this has encouraged many traders and investors to try to devise their own mechanical, or automated, trading systems. These systems can be very helpful as long as they are not used as a substitute for judgment and thinking. Throughout this book I have emphasized that technical analysis is an *art* — the art of interpreting a number of different and reliable, scientifically derived indicators.

This chapter will not reveal a perfect mechanical trading system, i.e., the holy grail. I believe that mechanical trading systems should be used in either of two ways. The preferred method is to incorporate a well-thought-out mechanical trading system *to alert* the trader or investor that a trend reversal has probably taken place. In this method the mechanical trading system is an important filter but represents just one more indicator in the overall decision-making process.

The other way in which a mechanical trading system can be used is to take action on *every* signal. If the system is well-thought-out, it should generate profits over the long term. However, if you pick and choose which signal to follow without other independently based technical criteria, you run the risk of making emotional decisions, losing the principal benefit of the mechanical approach.

Unfortunately, most mechanical trading systems are based on historical data and are constructed from a more or less perfect fit with the past, in the expectation that history will be repeated in the future. Again unfortunately, this expectation will not necessarily be fulfilled, because market conditions change. A well-thought-out and well-designed mechanical system, however, should do the job reasonably well. In this respect it is better to design a system that gives a less-than-perfect fit but more accurately reflects normal market conditions. Remember that you are interested in future profits, not perfect historical simulations. If special rules have to be invented to improve results, the chances are that the system will not operate successfully when extrapolated to future market conditions.

Advantages of Mechanical Systems

The advantages listed below assume that the investor or trader will follow the buy and sell signals consistently.

One of the great difficulties of putting theory into practice is that a new factor — emotion — enters the scene as soon as money is committed to the market.

1. A major advantage of a mechanical system is that it automatically decides when to take action; this has the effect of removing emotion and prejudice. The news may be atrocious, but when the system moves into a positive mode, a purchase is automatically made. In a similar vein, when it appears that nothing can stop the market from going through the roof, the system will override all possible emotions and biases and quietly take you out.

2. Most traders and investors lose in the marketplace because they lack discipline. Mechanical trading requires only one aspect of discipline, the commitment to follow the system.

3. A well-defined mechanical system will give *greater consistency of profits* than will a system in which buying and selling decisions are left to the individual.

4. A mechanical system will let profits run in the event that there is a strong uptrend but will automatically limit losses if a whipsaw signal occurs.

5. A well-designed model will allow the trader or investor to participate in the direction of every important trend.

Disadvantages of Mechanical Systems

1. No system will work all the time, and there may well be long periods when it will fail to work.

2. Using past data to predict the future isn't necessarily a valid approach because the character of the market often changes.

3. Most people try to get the best or optimum fit when devising a system, but experience and research tell us that a historical "best fit" doesn't usually translate into the future.

4. Random events can easily jeopardize a badly conceived system. A classic example occurred in Hong Kong during the 1987 crash, when the market was closed for 7 days. There would have been no opportunity to get out even if a sell signal had been triggered. True, this was an unusual event — but it's surprising how often special situations upset the best rules.

5. Most successful mechanical systems are trend-following in nature. However, there are often extended periods during which markets are in a nontrending mode, which renders the system unprofitable.

6. "Back-testing" won't necessarily simulate what actually would have happened. It is not always possible to get an execution at the price indicated by the system, because of illiquidity, failure of your broker to execute orders on time, and so forth.

Design of a Successful System

A well-designed system should try to capitalize on the advantages of the mechanical approach but should also be designed to overcome some of the pitfalls and disadvantages discussed above. In this respect there are eight important rules that should be followed:

1. Back-test over a sufficiently long period with several markets or stocks. The more data that can be tested, the more reliable the future results are likely to be.

2. Evaluate performance by extrapolating the results over an earlier period. In this case the first step would involve the design of a system based on data for a specific time span, for example, 1977 to 1985 for the bond market. The next step would be to test the results from 1985 to 1990 to see whether or not your approach would have worked in the subsequent period. In this way, rather than "flying blindly" into the future, the system is given a simulated but thorough testing using actual market data.

3. Define the system precisely. This is important for two reasons. First, if the rules occasionally leave you in doubt about their correct interpretation, some degree of subjectivity will permeate the approach. Second, for every buy signal there should be a sell signal, and vice versa. If a system has been devised using an overbought crossover as a sell and an oversold crossover as buy, it might work quite well for a time. An example is shown in Figure 25.1, example *a*. On the other

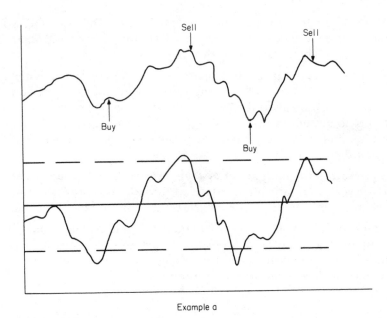

Example a

Figure 25.1

hand, there could be long periods during which a countervening signal is not generated simply because the indicator does not move to these extremes. Failure to define the system precisely can therefore result in significant losses, as shown in Figure 25.1, example *b*.

4. Make sure that you have enough capital to survive the worst losing streak. When you are devising a system, it is always a good idea to assume the worst possible scenario and to make sure that you start off with enough capital to survive such a period. In this respect, it is worth noting that the most profitable moves usually occur *after* a prolonged period of whipsawing.

5. Follow every signal without question. If you have confidence in your system, do not second-guess it. Otherwise, unnecessary emotion and undisciplined action will creep back into the decision-making process.

6. Use a diversified portfolio. Risks are limited if you place your bets over a number of different markets. If a specific market performs far worse than it ever has in the past, the overall results will not be catastrophic.

7. Trade only markets that show good trending characteristics. Chart 25.1 shows the lumber market between 1985 and 1989. During this

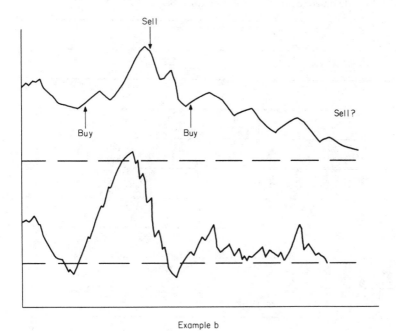

Example b

Figure 25.1 (Continued)

period the price fluctuated in a volatile, almost haphazard fashion and clearly would not have lent itself to a mechanical trend-following system. On the other hand, the Commodity Research Bureau (CRB) Spot Raw Industrial Index (shown in Chart 25.2), although it is subject to the odd confusing trading range, has by and large moved in consistent trends.

8. Keep it simple. It is always possible to invent special rules to make back-testing more profitable. Overcome this temptation. Keep the rules simple, few in number, and logical. The results are more likely to be profitable in the future, when profitability counts.

Trading-Range and Trending Markets

There are basically two types of market conditions: trending and trading-range. A trending market, as shown in Figure 25.2, is clearly suitable for moving average (MA) crossovers and other types of trend-following systems. In this kind of situation it is very important to define

Chart 25.1. Lumber. (*Source: CRB Weekly Chart Service.*)

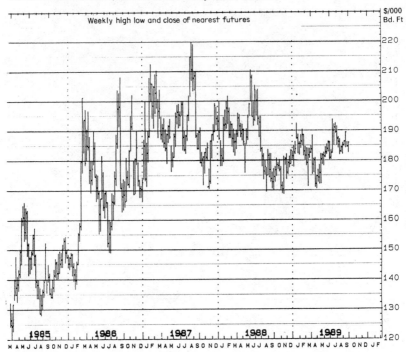

Chart 25.2. CRB Spot Raw Industrial Index (1967 = 100). (*Source: CRB Weekly Chart Service.*)

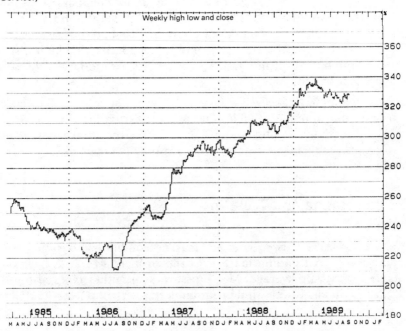

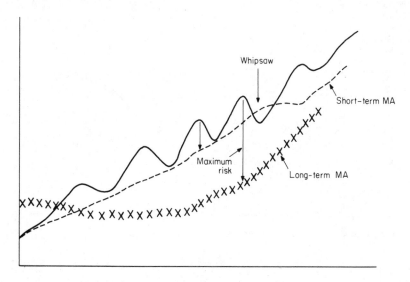

Figure 25.2. Trade-off between timeliness and sensitivity.

the risk since an MA is a trade-off between volatility and sensitivity. In the example in Figure 25.2, the maximum distance between the short-term MA, shown as the dashed line, and the series, shown as the solid line, is the maximum risk. Unfortunately, the short-term MA whips around and gives several false signals. Although the risk of the individual trade defined by the crossover of this MA is small, the chances of unprofitable signals are much greater.

On the other hand, a longer-term MA, shown by the X's, offers a larger maximum risk but fewer whipsaws.

MAs, as shown in Figure 25.3, are virtually useless in a trading-range market since they move right through the middle of the price fluctuations and almost always result in unprofitable signals. Oscillators, on the other hand, come into their own in a trading-range market. They are continually moving from overbought to oversold extremes, which trigger timely buy and sell signals. During a persistent uptrend or downtrend, the oscillator is of relatively little use because it gives premature buy and sell signals, often taking the trader out at the beginning of a major move. The ideal automated system therefore should include a combination of an oscillator and a trend-following indicator.

The risk and reward for oscillator-type signals generated from overbought and oversold extremes are shown in diagrammatic form in Figure 25.4. The number of potential trading opportunities is represented on the horizontal axis, and the risk on the vertical axis. There are very few times when an oscillator is extremely overbought or extremely oversold,

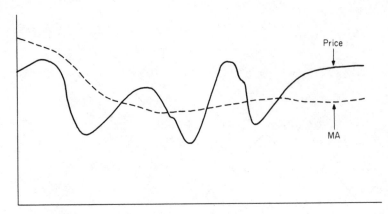

Figure 25.3. MA crossovers in trendless markets equal whipsaws.

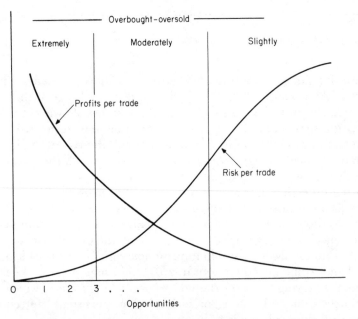

Figure 25.4. Relationship between profits and risk per trade, based on opportunities. (*Source: Perry Kaufman, New Commodity Trading Systems, John Wiley & Sons, Inc., New York, 1987.*)

but these are the occasions when the profit per trade is at its greatest and the risk the smallest. Moderately overbought conditions are much more plentiful, but the profits are lower and the risk higher. Taken to the final extreme, slightly overbought or oversold conditions are extremely plentiful, but the risk per trade is much higher and profits are significantly lower. Ideally, a mechanical trading system should be designed to take advantage of a situation in which profits per trade are high and risk is low. Execution of a good system therefore requires some degree of patience because these types of opportunities are limited.

Turning points in price trends are often preceded by a divergence in the oscillator, so it is a good idea to combine signals from extreme oscillator readings with some kind of MA crossover. This won't result in a perfect indicator, but it might help to filter out some of the whipsaws.

Guidelines for Appraising Results

When one is reviewing the simulated results of a mechanical system, there is a natural tendency to look at the bottom line to see which system would have generated the most profits. However, top results do not always indicate the best system. There are several reasons for this, as follows:

1. It is possible that most, or all, of the profit was generated by one signal. If so, this would place lower odds on the system's generating good profits in the future since the system would lack consistency. An example of an inconsistent system is shown in Table 25.1, which represents signals generated by a 10-day MA crossover of an oscillator that was constructed by dividing a 30-day MA by a 40-day MA (a form of moving average convergence divergence, or MACD). The market being monitored was Hong Kong during the 1987–1988 period. Over the whole period, the system would have *gained* nearly 1200 points, compared to a buy-hold approach, which would have *lost* 800 points. However, this excellent gain would have actually resulted in a loss had it not been for the fact that a prescient short-sale signal occurred just before the 1987 crash.

2. Another consideration involves the identification of the worst string of losses (the longest drawdown). After all, it is no good having a system that generates a large profit over the long term if you do not have sufficient capital to ride out the worst period. There are two things to look for in this respect: the string of losing signals, and the maximum amount lost during these adverse periods.

3. A system that generates huge profits but requires a significant number of trades is less likely to be successful in the real world than is a system based on a moderate number of trades. This is true because the more trades that are executed, the greater the potential for slippage through illiquidity, etc. More transactions also require more time and involve greater commission costs and so forth.

Table 25.1. Hong Kong H39/89 30–40 Oscillator
10-unit MA of Indicator (07/29/87 to 08/08/88)

Date	Trade	Price	Profit or loss					
			Current trade		Cumulative			
			Points	Percent	Points	Percent	Dollars
08/19/87	Sell	@ 3559.900	0.000	0.000	0.000	0.000	0.00
09/03/87	Buy	@ 3843.900	−284.000	−7.978	−284.000	−7.978	−79.78
09/09/87	Sell	@ 3696.900	−147.000	−3.824	−431.000	−11.802	−114.97
09/25/87	Buy	@ 3918.900	−222.000	−6.005	−653.000	−17.807	−168.12
10/14/87	Sell	@ 3999.000	80.100	2.044	−572.900	−15.763	−151.11
12/15/87	Buy	@ 2099.900	1899.100	47.489	1326.200	31.726	252.02
02/04/88	Sell	@ 2269.900	170.000	8.096	1496.200	39.822	353.38
02/22/88	Buy	@ 2374.900	−105.000	−4.626	1391.200	35.196	290.77
03/28/88	Sell	@ 2459.900	85.000	3.579	1476.200	38.775	336.97
04/08/88	Buy	@ 2639.900	−180.000	−7.317	1296.200	31.458	239.14
04/19/88	Sell	@ 2584.900	−55.000	−2.083	1241.200	29.374	213.32
06/06/88	Buy	@ 2612.900	−28.000	−1.083	1213.200	28.291	200.18
07/05/88	Sell	@ 2702.900	90.000	3.444	1303.200	31.736	241.52
07/06/88	Buy	@ 2774.900	−72.000	−2.664	1231.200	29.072	208.45
07/18/88	Sell	@ 2722.900	−52.000	−1.874	1179.200	27.198	185.80

Total long trades	7		Total short trades	7
Profitable longs	4 (57.1%)		Profitable shorts	1 (14.3%)
Total buy stops	0		Total sell stops	0
Biggest gain	1899.100		Biggest loss	−284.000
Successive gains	3		Successive losses	3
Total gain or loss	$1179.200		Average gain or loss	84.229
			Total gain or loss	18.58%

SOURCE: *Pring Market Review*/MetaStock.

A Simple Technique

A technique that allows investors to take advantage of both trending and trading-range markets is to combine an MA and an oscillator in such a way that buy signals are triggered when the oscillator has fallen to a predetermined oversold level and the price itself subsequently crosses above an MA. The position is liquidated if the price crosses below the MA. On the other hand, if the oscillator crosses to an overbought level prior to an MA crossover, part of the position will be sold in recognition of the possibility that the market might be experiencing a trading range. The other part of the position will continue to ride until an MA sell signal is triggered.

This approach will make it possible to capitalize on the potential of a trending market, but some profits will be taken in case subsequent market action turns out to be part of a volatile trading range.

Recognizing that oscillators often diverge at important market turning points, an alternative might be to wait for the oscillator to move to an extreme for a second time before buying on an MA crossover. The same rules as previously described would be used for selling.

The Best Signals Go with the Trend

In virtually every situation the *best signals invariably occur in the direction of the main trend.* It is easy to pick out the direction of the primary trend in hindsight, of course, but in the real world we have to use some kind of objective approach to determine the direction of the main trend.

One idea might be to calculate a 12-month MA and to use the position of the price relative to the average as a basis for determining the primary trend. The trading system would be based on daily and weekly data and would be acted upon on the long side only when the index was above the average; short signals would be instigated when it was below.

There are two drawbacks to this approach. First, the market itself may be in a long-term trading range in which MA crossovers do not correctly identify the main trend. Second, the first bear market rally quite often occurs while the price is above its 12-month MA. In effect, the buy signal associated with that rally would be operating against the main trend.

By and large, though, most markets trend, and this approach will filter out a lot of the countercyclical moves.

An alternative is to use a long-term momentum series, such as the monthly *know sure thing* (KST), calculated along the lines discussed in Chapter 10. When the KST is rising and the price is above its 12-month MA, a bull market environment is indicated, and all trades would be made from the long side. When the KST is falling and the price is above its 12-month MA, the chances are that the primary trend is in the process of peaking; no positions would be instigated. If you already had some exposure, the topping-out action of the KST would indicate that some profits should be taken, but total liquidation of the position would probably be better achieved at the time of a negative MA crossover. A trade would be activated only when the KST and the price, vis-à-vis its MA, were in a consistent mode. For example, when the KST peaks out and the market itself falls below its 12-month MA, a bear market environment is indicated and only trades on the short side should be initiated.

Some Very Simple Mechanical Approaches

The McClellan Summation Index and a 35-Day Moving Average Crossover

The McClellan Summation Index was discussed in Chapter 19. It is one indicator that has proved to be consistently profitable in the stock market over a long period. Table 25.2 summarizes the results between 1979 and 1981 using a simple 35-day MA crossover to generate buy and sell signals. Chart 25.3 shows the results graphically. There have been a few periods of losing streaks, but the indicator has by and large consistently earned money from the long side.

Table 25.2. Technician Profitability Test: MA Indicator Penetration (Both Long and Short Positions)

S&P 500 McClellan Summation, 35-Unit MA of Indicator (02/27/79 to 05/18/81)

| | | | Profit or loss | | | | |
| | | | Current trade | | Cumulative | | |
Date	Trade	Price	Points	Percent	Points	Percent	Dollars
03/20/79	Buy	@ 100.500	0.000	0.000	0.000	0.000	0.00
04/23/79	Sell	@ 101.560	1.060	1.055	1.060	1.055	10.55
06/08/79	Buy	@ 101.480	0.080	0.079	1.140	1.133	11.34
07/23/79	Sell	@ 101.580	0.100	0.099	1.240	1.232	12.34
08/02/79	Buy	@ 104.090	-2.510	-2.471	-1.270	-1.239	-12.67
09/10/79	Sell	@ 108.160	4.070	3.910	2.800	2.671	25.93
11/20/79	Buy	@ 103.680	4.480	4.142	7.280	6.813	68.42
02/07/80	Sell	@ 116.270	12.590	12.143	19.870	18.956	198.16
04/15/80	Buy	@ 102.620	13.650	11.740	33.520	30.696	338.83
07/30/80	Sell	@ 122.220	19.600	19.100	53.120	49.796	594.54
01/05/81	Buy	@ 137.960	-15.740	-12.878	37.380	36.917	389.19
02/17/81	Sell	@ 127.800	-10.160	-7.364	27.220	29.553	286.88
03/03/81	Buy	@ 130.550	-2.750	-2.152	24.470	27.401	259.19
04/28/81	Sell	@ 134.320	3.770	2.888	28.240	30.289	295.55

Total long trades	7		Total short trades	6
Profitable longs	6 (85.7%)		Profitable shorts	3 (50.0%)
Total buy stops	0		Total sell stops	0
Biggest gain	19.600		Biggest loss	-15.740
Successive gains	5		Successive losses	3
Total gain or loss	28.240		Average gain or loss	2.172
Total gain or loss	$295.55		Total gain or loss	29.56%

SOURCE: *Pring Market Review/Technician.*

Chart 25.3. The McClellan Summation Index versus a 35-day MA, 1979–1981. (*Source: Pring Market Review/Technician.*)

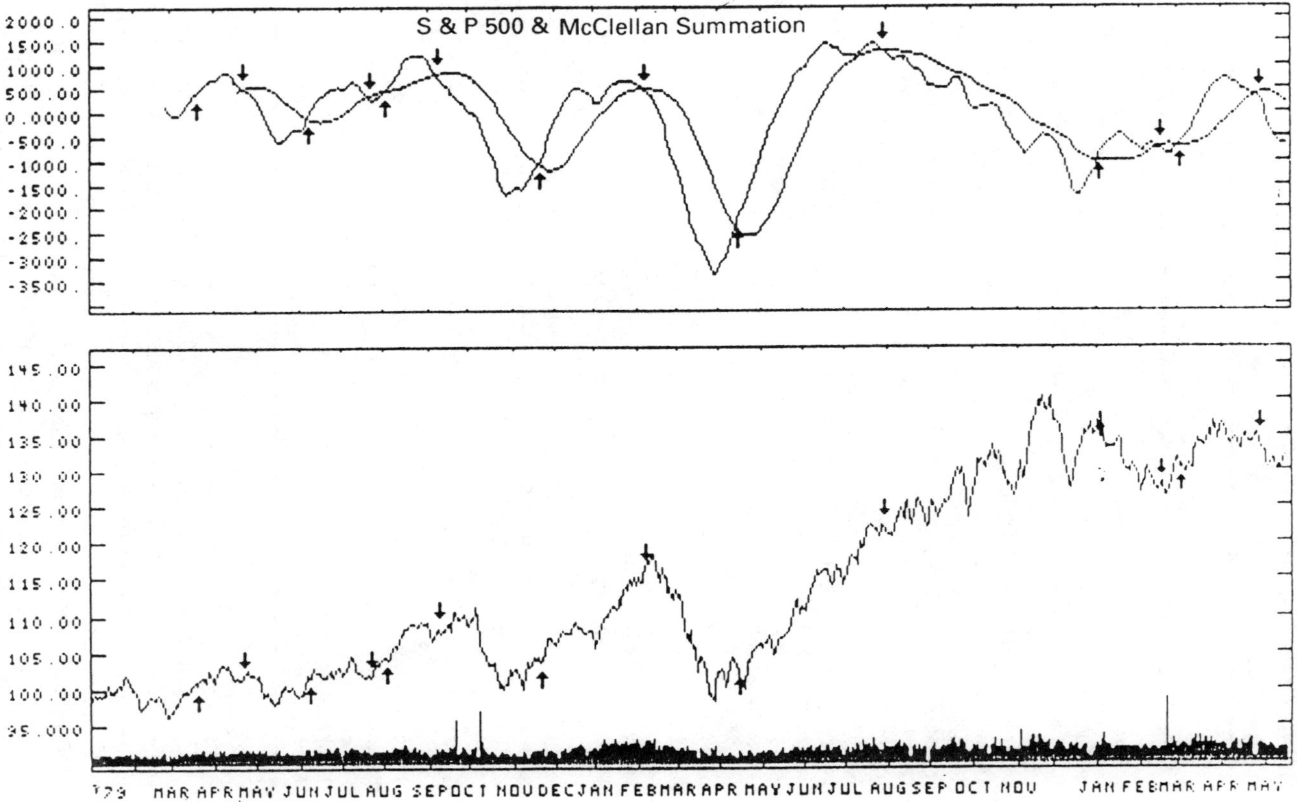

S & P 500 & McClellan Summation

Table 25.3. S&P 500, McClellan Summation
35-Unit MA of Indicator (05/01/81 to 02/21/84)

| | | | Profit or loss | | | | |
| | | | Current trade | | Cumulative | | |
Date	Trade	Price	Points	Percent	Points	Percent	Dollars
06/10/81	Buy	@ 132.310	0.000	0.000	0.000	0.000	0.00
07/01/81	Sell	@ 129.760	−2.550	−1.927	−2.550	−1.927	−19.27
08/14/81	Buy	@ 132.480	−2.720	−2.096	−5.270	−4.023	−39.83
08/21/81	Sell	@ 129.220	−3.260	−2.461	−8.530	−6.484	−63.46
10/08/81	Buy	@ 122.300	6.920	5.355	−1.610	−1.129	−13.30
12/18/81	Sell	@ 124.000	1.700	1.390	0.090	0.261	0.41
02/25/82	Buy	@ 113.200	10.800	8.710	10.890	8.971	87.54
05/21/82	Sell	@ 114.880	1.680	1.484	12.570	10.455	103.68
07/16/82	Buy	@ 111.060	3.820	3.325	16.390	13.780	140.38
08/10/82	Sell	@ 102.830	−8.230	−7.410	8.160	6.370	55.88
08/18/82	Buy	@ 108.520	−5.690	−5.533	2.470	0.836	−2.55
11/22/82	Sell	@ 134.210	25.690	23.673	28.160	24.509	233.58
01/14/83	Buy	@ 146.650	−12.440	−9.269	15.720	15.240	119.24
01/25/83	Sell	@ 141.750	−4.900	−3.341	10.820	11.899	81.84
02/07/83	Buy	@ 146.930	−5.180	−3.654	5.640	8.245	42.31
03/23/83	Sell	@ 152.810	5.880	4.002	11.520	12.246	84.02
04/22/83	Buy	@ 160.420	−7.610	−4.980	3.910	7.266	30.03
06/01/83	Sell	@ 162.550	2.130	1.328	6.040	8.594	43.71
09/06/83	Buy	@ 167.890	−5.340	−3.285	0.700	5.309	9.42
10/20/83	Sell	@ 166.980	−0.910	−0.542	−0.210	4.767	3.95
11/25/83	Buy	@ 167.180	−0.200	−0.120	−0.410	4.647	2.75
12/19/83	Sell	@ 162.320	−4.860	−2.907	−5.270	1.740	−26.40
01/06/84	Buy	@ 169.280	−6.960	−4.288	−12.230	−2.548	−68.15
01/31/84	Sell	@ 163.410	−5.870	−3.468	−18.100	−6.015	−100.46

Total long trades	12		Total short trades	11
Profitable longs	5 (41.7%)		Profitable shorts	3 (27.3%)
Total buy stops	0		Total sell stops	0
Biggest gain	25.690		Biggest loss	−12.440
Successive gains	5		Successive losses	6
Total gain or loss	−18.100		Average gain or loss	−0.787
Total gain or loss	$−100.46		Total gain or loss	−10.05%

To balance out the picture, Table 25.3 and Chart 25.4 show the worst period, i.e., 1981–1984, in which a loss of 10 percent would have been generated. Although this system tacked on a gain of 43 percent between 1985 and 1988, its overall results are far from perfect. After all, McClellan is measuring breadth, but the trading vehicle is the Standard & Poor's (S&P) Composite. Like all indicators described in this book, it is suggested as a starting point from which to develop other systems and strategies.

Chart 25.4. The McClellan Summation Index versus a 35-day MA, 1981–1984. (*Source: Pring Market Review.*)

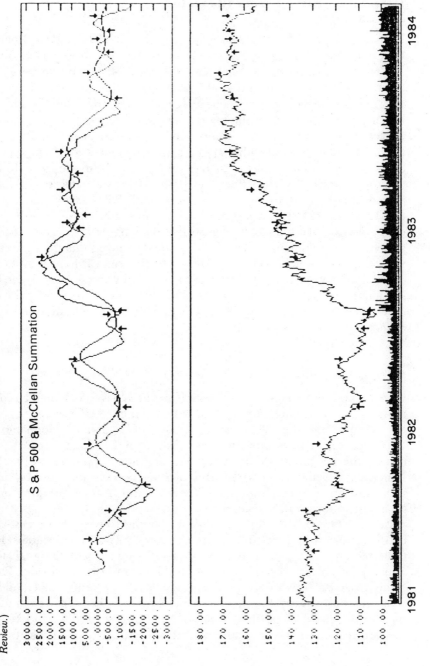

The S&P Composite and a 12-Month MA Crossover

In their book *The Encyclopedia of Technical Market Indicators*, Robert W. Colby and Thomas A. Meyers[1] indicate that, over the period from 1910 to 1986, 12-month MA crossovers of the S&P Composite were the most profitable monthly and weekly averages. Table 25.4 shows the results between 1941 and 1988. There were 27 trades on the long side, of which 17 were profitable; the biggest loss was 7 percent.

I have tested this approach using many monthly series and find that by and large it is successful, although it may fail in an occasional market because of extraordinary volatility. An example occurred in the Hong Kong market between July 1987 and July 1988, when two panic sell-offs occurred before an MA crossover was generated. Back-testing has shown that 12-month MA crossovers of the S&P Composite are far more effective than more complicated approaches such as the long-term KST crossing its 9-month MA. In defense of the KST, it should be noted that this indicator was designed as much to gauge the maturity of a trend as to be used as an actual trading vehicle. I noted earlier that actual buy and sell signals can be legitimately triggered only by a reversal in the trend of the actual price or index itself. Remember that the KST is a momentum indicator, and you cannot buy and sell momentum!

A Triple Indicator System

One method that has proved extremely profitable is to combine an MA crossover with a signal from two rate-of-exchange (ROC) indicators. In the example here, we will be using the pound/U.S. dollar relationship. I introduce this approach with some degree of hesitancy because, of course, there is no guarantee that it will continue to operate profitably. Usually it is better to choose different time periods for the MA and ROC indicators so that the signals have a better chance of taking into account two different market cycles.

Let's start by looking at the results of a simple 10-week MA crossover between 1974 and 1976. The pound and the buy and sell signals are indicated on Chart 25.5. Table 25.5 shows that there were 22 signals for a total profit of 62.5 cents from both the long and the short side. This compares to the buy-hold approach, with a loss of 58 cents. Taken on its own, this was a fairly commendable performance, but let's remember that for a significant portion of the time, i.e., most of 1975 and 1976, the British pound was in a sustained downtrend. It is true that there

---

[1]Dow Jones–Irwin, Homewood, Ill., 1988.

Table 25.4. MetaStock Profitability Test: MA Price Penetration (Both Long and Short Positions)

S&P Composite, Monthly Average (12-Unit MA of Security)

			Profit or loss				
			Current trade		Cumulative		
Date	Trade	Price	Points	Percent	Points	Percent	Dollars
02/00/41	Sell @	9.890	0.000	0.000	0.000	0.000	0.00
07/00/41	Buy @	10.260	-0.370	-3.741	-0.370	-3.741	-37.41
08/00/41	Sell @	10.210	-0.050	-0.487	-0.420	-4.228	-42.10
09/00/41	Buy @	10.240	-0.030	-0.294	-0.450	-4.522	-44.92
10/00/41	Sell @	9.830	-0.410	-4.004	-0.860	-8.526	-83.16
09/00/42	Buy @	8.680	1.150	11.699	0.290	3.173	24.10
11/00/43	Sell @	11.330	2.650	30.530	2.940	33.703	336.76
01/00/44	Buy @	11.850	-0.520	-4.590	2.420	29.113	275.41
09/00/46	Sell @	15.090	3.240	27.342	5.660	56.455	624.13
07/00/47	Buy @	15.770	-0.680	-4.506	4.980	51.949	550.94
09/00/47	Sell @	15.060	-0.710	-4.502	4.270	47.446	481.11
10/00/47	Buy @	15.450	-0.390	-2.590	3.880	44.857	442.76
12/00/47	Sell @	15.030	-0.420	-2.718	3.460	42.138	403.54
04/00/48	Buy @	15.400	-0.370	-2.462	3.090	39.676	368.99
11/00/48	Sell @	15.290	-0.110	-0.714	2.980	38.962	359.21
08/00/49	Buy @	15.290	0.000	0.000	2.980	38.962	359.21
04/00/53	Sell @	24.710	9.420	61.609	12.400	100.571	1196.60
12/00/53	Buy @	24.830	-0.120	-0.486	12.280	100.085	1185.93
10/00/56	Sell @	46.240	21.410	86.226	33.690	186.312	3070.78
05/00/57	Buy @	46.780	-0.540	-1.168	33.150	185.144	3023.24
08/00/57	Sell @	45.840	-0.940	-2.009	32.210	183.135	2942.40
05/00/58	Buy @	43.700	2.140	4.668	34.350	187.803	3126.45
02/00/60	Sell @	55.780	12.080	27.643	46.430	215.446	4267.12
06/00/60	Buy @	57.260	-1.480	-2.653	44.950	212.793	4127.37
07/00/60	Sell @	55.840	-1.420	-2.480	43.530	210.313	4000.22
12/00/60	Buy @	56.800	-0.960	-1.719	42.570	208.594	3914.25
04/00/62	Sell @	68.050	11.250	19.806	53.820	228.400	4887.58
12/00/62	Buy @	62.640	5.410	7.950	59.230	236.350	5355.65
06/00/65	Sell @	85.040	22.400	35.760	81.630	272.110	7628.42
08/00/65	Buy @	86.490	-1.450	-1.705	80.180	270.405	7481.30
03/00/66	Sell @	88.880	2.390	2.763	82.570	273.168	7715.67
04/00/66	Buy @	91.600	-2.720	-3.060	79.850	270.108	7448.94
05/00/66	Sell @	86.780	-4.820	-5.262	75.030	264.846	7004.36
02/00/67	Buy @	87.360	-0.580	-0.668	74.450	264.177	6950.86
02/00/68	Sell @	90.750	3.390	3.881	77.840	268.058	7259.39
04/00/68	Buy @	95.670	-4.920	-5.421	72.920	262.636	6811.61
03/00/69	Sell @	99.300	3.630	3.794	76.550	266.431	7108.01
05/00/69	Buy @	104.620	-5.320	-5.358	71.230	261.073	6673.62
06/00/69	Sell @	99.140	-5.480	-5.238	65.750	255.835	6271.67
10/00/70	Buy @	84.370	14.770	14.898	80.520	270.733	7355.02

Table 25.4. MetaStock Profitability Test: MA Price Penetration (Both Long and Short Positions) (*Continued*)

			Profit or loss				
			Current trade		Cumulative		
Date	Trade	Price	Points	Percent	Points	Percent	Dollars
11/00/71	Sell	@ 92.780	8.410	9.968	88.930	280.701	8187.85
12/00/71	Buy	@ 99.170	−6.390	−6.887	82.540	273.814	7555.06
04/00/73	Sell	@ 110.270	11.100	11.193	93.640	285.007	8512.61
02/00/75	Buy	@ 80.100	30.170	27.360	123.810	312.367	11115.28
02/00/77	Sell	@ 100.960	20.860	26.042	144.670	338.410	14270.39
05/31/78	Buy	@ 97.410	3.550	3.516	148.220	341.926	14807.33
11/30/78	Sell	@ 94.710	−2.700	−2.772	145.520	339.154	14369.19
12/29/78	Buy	@ 96.110	−1.400	− 1.478	144.120	337.676	14142.00
03/31/80	Sell	@ 104.690	8.580	8.927	152.700	346.603	15493.77
05/30/80	Buy	@ 107.690	−3.000	− 2.866	149.700	343.737	15021.13
07/31/81	Sell	@ 129.130	21.400	19.909	171.140	363.646	18210.77
09/30/82	Buy	@ 122.430	6.700	5.189	177.840	368.835	19207.54
02/29/84	Sell	@ 157.670	35.240	28.784	213.080	397.619	25024.04
08/31/84	Buy	@ 165.020	−7.350	− 4.662	205.730	392.957	23810.89
10/30/87	Sell	@ 284.320	119.300	72.294	325.030	465.251	41747.75
09/30/88	Buy	@ 269.200	15.120	5.318	340.150	470.569	44021.06

Total long trades	27		Total short trades	28
Profitable longs	17 (63.0%)		Profitable shorts	8 (28.6%)
Total short stops	0		Total long stops	0
Biggest gain	119.300		Biggest loss	−7.350
Successive gains	4		Successive losses	6
Total gain or loss	340.150		Average gain or loss	6.185
Total gain or loss	$44021.06*		Total gain or loss	4402.11%

*Assumes $ per point expressed as cumulative gain.

were a number of whipsaws in late 1975 and early 1976, but they were of minor consequence.

The next step is to introduce a 13-week ROC. Buy and sell signals are triggered when the 13-week ROC crosses above and below its zero reference line. The results are shown in Table 25.6 and graphically portrayed in Chart 25.6.

This approach nets a gain of 58 cents, which is similar to the results with the MA crossover. However, it is important to note that only 10 momentum signals were generated, as compared to 22 signals for the MA crossover. The profits were slightly less, but the number of signals and therefore the possibility of whipsaws were dramatically reduced by using the ROC indicator. Even so, there were a couple of nasty whipsaws in 1976.

The next step is to introduce a second ROC indicator in order to try to

Chart 25.5. The British pound and a 10-week MA, 1974–1976. (*Source: Pring Market Review.*)

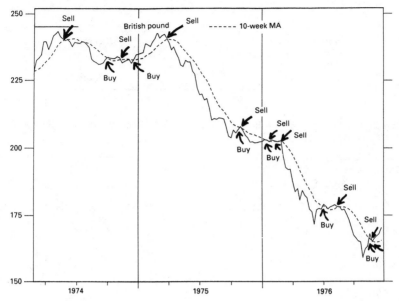

Table 25.5. 1974–1976

Method		Long and short signals	Net profit (loss)
Buy	*Hold*	–	(58.1 cents)
03/74	$2.283		
12/76	$1.702		
10-week MA		22	62.5 cents

filter out some of the whipsaws. A 6-week ROC was chosen mainly because it spans approximately half the time of its 13-week counterpart. Buy signals are generated only when all three cycles, as measured by the 10-week MA, the 13-week ROC, and the 6-week ROC, are in agreement.

The rule is that buy signals are triggered only when *all three* indicators go positive, and sell signals only when *all three* go negative. The results are shown in Table 25.7 and plotted in Chart 25.7. Profits were improved marginally, but what is most important is that the number of signals is reduced dramatically. Since only four buy signals were given, this obviously reduces commission costs and the emotional factor of having to monitor the market closely to see when the next buy and sell signals will be generated.

Table 25.6. 1974–1976

Method		Long and short signals	Net profit (loss)
Buy	*Hold*	–	(58.1 cents)
03/74	$2.283		
12/76	$1.702		
13-week ROC		10	58.0 cents

Chart 25.6. The British pound in U.S. dollars and a 13-week momentum. (*Source: Pring Market Review.*)

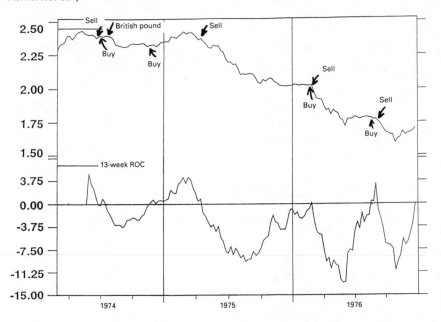

I originally introduced this concept in *International Investing Made Easy.*[2] At that time, the results tested back to 1971 would have turned $10,000 into more than $1 million. This calculation was based on reinvestment of all profits from a 10 percent margin position. It assumed that the movement in the nearby contract months did not differ appreciably from the cash rate. Commission costs, positive and negative carrying costs, and taxes were ignored.

The figures were updated for the second edition of this book, showing that the $10,000 had grown to over $4 million by 1983. The system has continued to operate profitably into the 1990s.

[2]McGraw-Hill, New York, 1978.

Table 25.7. 1974–1976

Method		Long and short signals	Net profit (loss)
Buy	*Hold*	–	(58.1 cents)
03/74	$2.283		
12/76	$1.702		
10-week MA		22	62.5 cents
13-week ROC		10	58.0 cents
6-week ROC, 13-week ROC, and 10-week MA combined		4	65.6 cents

Chart 25.7. The British pound trading system. (*Source: Pring Market Review.*)

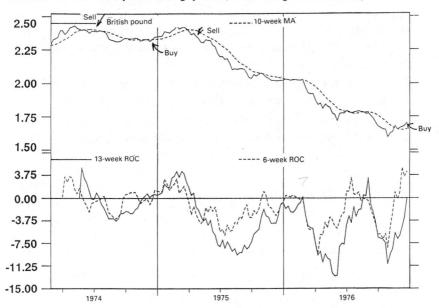

It is very important to understand that this approach will not necessarily offer such large rewards in the future. Indeed, experimentation
with other currencies has also proved profitable, but the results have always been inferior to the hypothetical example discussed above.

The example of the British pound must be treated as the exception
rather than the rule, but it is introduced to give you an incentive to experiment along these lines.

Summary

1. The use of automated systems has the prime advantage of reducing emotion and encouraging greater discipline in the investment process.

2. No system will work all the time. It is important to understand the disadvantages of a mechanical trading system so that some of the pitfalls can be programmed out.

3. Mechanical trading systems may be used as a filter to identify important buy and sell junctures. In this approach, actual market decisions are based on appraisal of *other* indicators. Alternatively, every signal of a mechanical trading system may be followed consistently, to allow the system to stand on its own.

4. Any system should be designed to take into consideration the fact that markets not only trend but also undergo periods of volatile trading activity. In appraising results of the system, it is important to look for consistency and maximum drawdown (losses).

5. Because no system works perfectly, any approach should involve exhaustive testing over long periods and with many markets.

6. The use of any system should involve diversification to filter out periods when the system does not operate for a specific market.

26

Putting the Indicators Together

It is now appropriate to examine an actual market cycle by putting the indicators together and observing how they work in practice. The 1970–1974 period has been chosen because that particular cycle offers a substantial variety of technical conditions that are worth studying.

Using the Dow Jones Industrial Average (DJIA), Chart 26.1 illustrates the market action of this period in a simplified waveform, showing the three upward phases of the 1970–1973 bull market and the three downward phases of the 1973–1974 bear market. The description here will focus upon these two primary moves and the intervening secondary corrections.

Chart 26.1. The DJIA and major movements, 1970–1974.

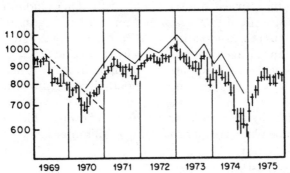

The cycle begins in the dark days of late May 1970. The market had declined dramatically for 6 weeks on gradually expanding volume, the trend of virtually all the technical indicators was down, and no obvious end to falling prices seemed to be in sight. Nevertheless, there were some tentative indications that prices would soon bottom out, since short-term interest rates and long-term government bonds[1] had already reversed their cyclical trends in late 1969.

By the end of May it was obvious that a selling climax had taken place. While this did not necessarily mean that the ultimate low had been reached, it did imply that the May bottom would hold at least temporarily and that prices were likely to decline for a while. At the same time, many of the oscillators were recording extreme "oversold" conditions. The annual rate of change (ROC) of the Dow had reached a postwar low, while the 10-week moving average (MA) of the advance/decline (A/D) ratio (Chart 19.1) was at a very negative level. In addition, many sentiment indicators were pointing up an extreme degree of pessimism. This can be observed from Charts 23.4a and 23.8, which show the Advisory Services Index and the mutual funds cash/assets ratio, respectively.

At this juncture many indicators were pointing out that a new bull market was in the process of being born, but as yet no long-term trends had been broken, no long-term MAs had been crossed, no bases had been built, and certainly no positive divergences had occurred among the major averages. It was not until the summer months of 1970 that more tangible signs of cyclical reversal appeared. First, a base was formed by most averages as the early June rally petered out and a successful test of the May lows was achieved. As prices rose in July and August, a clearly defined bear market trendline was penetrated on the upside (see Chart 26.1). During this period, the 18-month exponential moving average (EMA) of the 3-month commercial paper rate turned down (see Chart 21.3), confirming that a cyclical reversal in short-term rates had taken place. Finally, longer-term indicators of price and volume momentum turned up (see Chart 18.2). These indicators offered fairly conclusive proof that a new bull market had begun in May, especially as they were accompanied by a Dow theory buy signal in December. Finally, encouragement was given by the World Stock Index, which had crossed above its 14-month exponential average (Chart 27.1), accompanied by a rising trend in the smoothed momentum index (Chart 27.1).

Prices generally rose until March 1971, following which an 8-month correction took place. Advance warning of this intermediate decline was

[1]See Charts 20.1 and 22.1.

given by interest-sensitive indexes. The Federal Funds Indicator rate, for example, had already given a sell signal in February as it moved above its 10-week MA, and its momentum index had crossed above its zero reference line (see Chart 21.1). This signal validated the action of the Utility Index, which had topped out in January and refused to confirm the March high in the DJIA. The A/D line had also peaked ahead of the industrial average. Many of the oscillators had also reached extremely overbought conditions earlier in the year, but this was quite a normal and healthy phenomenon for the early stages of a bull market. Only a decline in momentum accompanied by a break in the trend of the index being monitored really flashes a red light.

The position at the March peak in the Dow was therefore one in which the interest-sensitive and breadth indexes had begun to diverge, and the oscillators were declining from an overbought condition. In addition, many of the sentiment indicators were also at bearish extremes. Certainly no distribution had formed, the strong uptrend dating from May 1970 was still intact, and the longer-term momentum indicators were still positive. The primary trend of the commercial paper rate was also positive, as evidenced by the strongly rising 18-month EMA. The situation appeared to be one of cyclical strength but potential intermediate weakness.

Not surprisingly, prices broke and continued falling until August. During this period, the strong July 1970–April 1971 uptrends of many averages were decisively violated on the downside, but since these trends were unsustainably steep, this development merely indicated that the market was adjusting to a more subdued rate of advance. By August the technical picture suggested that the market was oversold and a rally was called for. The 13-week ROC of the DJIA, for example (see Chart 14.4), reached a low reading of −10 percent, and the percentage of 30 DJIA stocks in bullish trends was moderately oversold (see Chart 19.10). The rally did take place, and at the same time, debt markets began to recover from their decline, which had started earlier than the stock market decline.

This was a very difficult period, since most long-term factors pointed to a continuation of the bull cycle, and the intermediate trends of interest-sensitive securities (normally a good lead indicator for the stock market) had also turned positive. Given the oversold nature of the market in August and the fact that the April-August downtrend had been violated on the upside, it would have been easy to come to the conclusion that the reaction was over, especially as volume expanded very sharply during late August. But this proved to be one of those times when patience would have paid off, since not all the indicators were in a positive position.

In addition, while some of the major averages (such as the DJIA) were able to better their July highs, others (such as the A/D line) failed to surpass theirs. Finally, despite the positive trend in the bond and money markets, the Utility Index continued to remain in its intermediate downtrend, while the Morgan Stanley Capital International World Stock Index showed absolutely no indication of a reversal in its intermediate downtrend.

It was not until early December, when the market was much lower, that there were many more signs that the bull market was about to resume. First, the debt markets had failed to make new lows in November and had therefore set up some positive divergences from the stock market. Second, the 10-week oscillator of the weekly A/D line had failed to significantly penetrate its August low, which created another positive divergence between it and the A/D line itself. Third, the indicators of long-term momentum measuring price and volume (Chart 18.2), while falling slightly, had not confirmed a bear market by falling below their zero reference lines. Finally, the Dow Jones Transportation Index refused to confirm the November low in the Dow, thereby indicating that the Dow theory bull market was still intact.

The rally continued until April 1972, when the DJIA returned to the 950 resistance level, which again served to halt the advance as it had done 1 year earlier. The Dow did not sell off as it had in 1971, but began a period of consolidation in the 900–950 area that was to last for most of the balance of the year. The action over the ensuing months provided the first indication that the bull market was reaching maturity. First, the up phase of the 4-year cycle was rapidly running out of time, since it was 2 years off by May 1972. This did not necessarily mean that the rise could not continue longer (as shown by the 1962–1966 experience); but in view of renewed weakness of (1) the debt markets during this period, (2) the Utility Average, (3) the A/D line, and (4) the Most Active Indicator, some ominous rumblings were developing. Indeed, not only was the A/D line falling while the DJIA was marking time, but it had also failed to surpass its old 1971 high (see Chart 19.1). Moreover, even though long-term interest rates held steady until January 1973, the Federal Funds Indicator (Chart 21.1) went negative in the late spring of 1972, suggesting that the intermediate trend of short-term interest rates was up. Later on, the 18-month EMA of 3-month commercial paper (Chart 21.3) started to rise, thereby confirming that the cyclical trend in short-term rates had also been reversed. To make matters worse, the Transportation Average, which had previously outperformed the DJIA during the 1971 decline, began to fall off rather badly. Finally, all the sentiment indexes were painting a picture of widespread confidence and optimism, which, from a contrary-opinion stand-point, suggested that a top was being made.

By October 1972 many of the oscillators measuring intermediate movements began to reach oversold conditions or, in the case of the 10-week A/D ratio, to create a positive divergence. The indications therefore were that a short-term rally would then take place, but the overbought nature of the long-term *know sure thing* (KST) (Chart 10.16) indicated that it would be a high-risk one. The DJIA experienced an intermediate rise as it rallied 15 percent from 900 to 1065, a new all-time high. Because of the rally, even greater divergences were set up, as this strong performance was not confirmed by many of the other indicators. As if things were not bad enough, short-term interest rates during this period began to rise even more sharply, accompanied by a hike in the discount rate and a rise in margin requirements in December. By late January, the long end of the bond market (Chart 22.1) also began to fall sharply. The situation in January 1973 was that the DJIA had broken out of what appeared to be a 9-year consolidation pattern but the accompanying technical structure was so weak that the move proved to be spurious. The bear market, which had begun for most issues in mid-1972, had finally reached the blue-chip sector. During the early months of 1973 it also became apparent that the World Stock Index had turned down, although it was not until late winter that the Index fell below its 14-month EMA (Chart 27.1). The first downleg of the new bear market was temporarily halted in July. The DJIA, the A/D line, and several other indicators made a new low in August, after a brief rally. But this secondary bottom was unconfirmed by the NYSE Composite (Chart 14.1a). Moreover, two important oscillators—the 10-week A/D line ratio (see Chart 19.1) and the 13-week ROC (Chart 14.4)—were both well up from their July bottoms at the time of the new Dow low in August. These many divergences and oversold readings suggested that the market was in a position to mount a substantial rally, for the first time since the fall of 1972. However, some of the longer-term indicators were still in the early stages of deterioration, which suggested that this rally was likely to be a bear market correction rather than the first leg of a new bull market. For example, both the 18-month EMA of the commercial paper rate and the Federal Funds Indicator were suggesting that the trend of short-term interest rates was still adverse for stock prices. In addition, the sentiment indicators were reflecting a fair degree of pessimism, but not enough to be commensurate with a bear market low. This can be observed from the Advisory Services Sentiment Indicator (Chart 23.4a).

In 7 weeks the Dow rose 12 percent, from 880 right back to the 1000 level on rapidly expanding volume. The speed and strength of the rally confused many, including myself, into believing that the bear market was over. This deceptive characteristic is most common during the first rally of a bear market, since business conditions are usually still good and negative arguments seem less persuasive against a background of rising stock prices.

However, most of the indicators measuring long-term movements remained in a bearish trend throughout this period. For example, despite the softening in short-term interest rates, the 18-month EMA of the commercial paper rate was still negative, while most of the long-term momentum indicators were below their zero reference lines and falling. Still, some of these more sensitive longer-term indicators began to turn up, and for the first time in many years they gave a misleading signal; generally speaking, however, the proof of a new bull market was far from conclusive. In addition to the negative tone of many of the longer-term indicators, *the rally had taken place during a period of rising interest rates, whereas falling interest rates normally lead or coincide with bear market bottoms.* Also the commodity market was still in a rising trend. Bear market lows are associated with falling commodity prices. In any event, by October the market became overbought and was losing momentum in the face of a very major level of resistance around the Dow 1000 level. When the market runs into significant resistance under such conditions, it is always wiser to await the reaction which invariably takes place, and then to reassess the state of the indicators.

In this case the correction extended for 200 Dow points and left no doubt that the bear market was still very much alive.

The second bear market rally was not difficult to predict. The DJIA had fallen to an extremely significant support area at 800, while the various oscillators had again reached oversold territory. In the case of the 10-week A/D ratio, this was to be its lowest reading of the bear market. Although no major positive divergences were apparent, the Federal Funds Indicator, which had turned positive in November, was still signaling that lower interest rates lay ahead.

The ensuing rally was almost as deceptive as the previous one, but for different reasons. To start with, the oversold condition in December 1973 was much greater than that of the previous July or August, leading many observers to believe that the December selling climax marked the end of the bear market. Moreover, the A/D line and many of the lower-priced stocks were initially acting much stronger than the Dow itself, as can be seen by comparing the two indexes in Chart 19.1.

This strength was short-lived, since the A/D line fell away very sharply following the late March peak in the Dow. Moreover, the 18-

month weighted MA of the commercial paper rate had remained in a negative trend throughout this period and was now joined by the Federal Funds Indicator, which also deteriorated in late March. While the Federal Reserve was obviously easing monetary policy during the December-March period, it did not at any time lower the discount rate. As the rally progressed, the Advisory Services Sentiment Indicator turned over and began to deteriorate.

The subsequent reaction proved to be the third and final leg of the worst bear market since the 1930s. The 1974 bottom was initially signaled by a positive reading in the Federal Funds Indicator in October as well as by a major set of divergences between the DJIA, the S&P 500, and the Transportation and Utility averages during October and December, when most indexes formed classic double bottoms. Several positive divergences were also observed in many of the oscillators. For example, the December reaction in the percentage of stocks above their 200-day MA was far above the October low, thereby indicating a position of growing technical strength. By October most of the sentiment indexes had reached extreme levels of pessimism, adding further confirmation that a major bottom was being formed. By the end of January, all the indicators had formed and broken out of large bases, Dow theory was signaling a new bull market, and most of the long-term momentum indexes had turned up accompanied by an expanding level of volume. The number of groups experiencing winter momentum had also peaked from a very high reading (Chart 19.15). These positive technical developments were also confirmed by the debt markets, most of which had made their cyclical bottoms in the fall, and commodities and the money-flow (Chart 20.5) and long-term KST indicators (Chart 10.14) also gave a buy signal. Finally, the World Stock Index, confirmed by virtually all the foreign stock indexes, made a sharp reversal, and in January 1975 it rose explosively..Prices were in a declining phase typical of equity bear market bottoms. There was little doubt that the 1974–1975 bull market had begun!

PART 5

Specific Financial Markets

27

Technical Analysis of International Stock Markets

Since equities are bought and sold throughout the world for essentially the same reasons, the principles of technical analysis can be applied to any stock market. Unfortunately, the degree of sophistication in statistical reporting of many countries does not permit the kind of detailed analysis that is available in the United States. Nevertheless, it is possible to obtain data on price, breadth, and volume for nearly all countries. Information on industry groups and interest rates is also widely available.

Identifying Primary Global Trends

Chart 27.1 shows the Morgan Stanley Capital International World Stock Index, which is constructed from a selection of blue-chip stocks from many different countries weighted by capitalization. This series has been adjusted to U.S. dollars and is widely published in the financial press. The World Stock Index is a good starting point from which to analyze the cyclical trends of the various stock markets, just as a composite index or the Dow Jones Industrial Average (DJIA) would be used as a focal point in assessing the U.S. market. This is because the stock

Chart 27.1. The World Stock Index. (*Source: Pring Market Review.*)

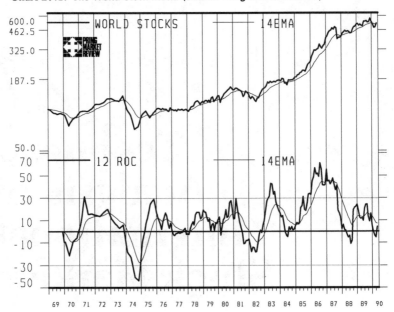

markets of the individual countries tend to move in the same direction, just as the majority of U.S. stocks reflect the primary trend of the DJIA most of the time. The individual stock markets do not all reach their peaks or troughs concurrently. The United Kingdom, for example, has a *tendency* to lead, while the Japanese and Canadian markets are usually late in turning down.

Chart 27.2 shows the existence of the international 4-year cycle, as indicated by the arrows. This average is different from the World Stock Index, since it weights each stock market by an approximate share of world GNP. It can be seen that the peaks in 1961, 1965, 1969, 1973, 1977, and 1981 are separated by approximately 4 years, and that the troughs in 1962, 1966, 1970, 1974, 1978, and 1982 are separated by the same period.

Chart 27.1 shows that the cycle underwent a distortion in the mid- to late 1980s, since the idealized peak in 1985 materialized 2 years late, in 1987, and the 1986 idealized low appeared in 1988.

Shown beneath the World Stock Index in both Chart 27.1 and Chart 27.2 is a 12-month rate-of-change (ROC) index and a 14-month exponential moving average (EMA). When used in combination with the moving average (MA) of the World Stock Index itself, crossover of this

Chart 27.2. The World Stock Index versus 12-month momentum. (*Source: Pring Market Review.*)

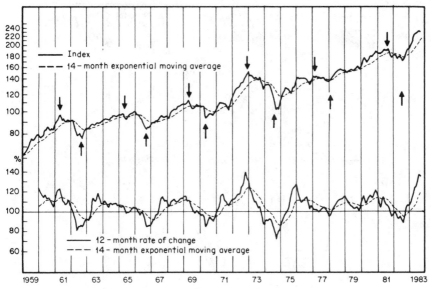

(SOURCE: Pring Market Review.)

momentum MA has offered a useful confirmation of primary trend reversals in world equities. If the world is treated as one unit comprising many parts (i.e., the various stock markets), it is possible to construct several diffusion indicators measuring the global internal technical structure.

Another way of analyzing the global technical position is to calculate a diffusion index based on the percentage of individual-country indexes that are registering a positive ROC. The first step requires an adjustment of the various indexes to U.S. dollars so that a comparison with the U.S. Dollar World Capital International Index can be made.

Because the raw data from the calculation results in a very jagged indicator, the series in Chart 27.3 has been smoothed with a 6-month MA.

Useful buy and sell signals are triggered when the diffusion indicator crosses above and below its 6-month MA from an extreme level. These signals are flagged by the arrows. In most cases they are fairly timely. One notable exception occurred in 1982, when the diffusion index gave a premature buy signal.

Finally, Chart 27.4 shows the seasonal momentum model described in Chapter 10 on a global basis, but this time using dollar-adjusted stock market indexes rather than industry groups. The history is not as long as that of the U.S. market, but the same principles appear to work very

Chart 27.3. The World Stock Index and a diffusion indicator (U.S. dollar-adjusted). (*Source: Pring Market Review.*)

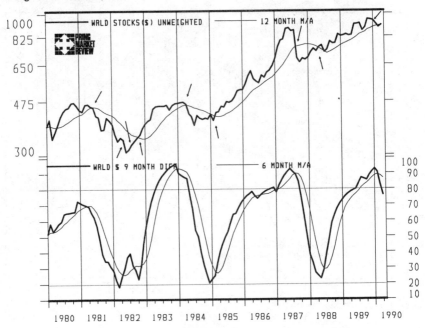

well. Note the major buying junctures that were signaled by peaks in the winter quadrant in 1980, 1982, and 1988.

Intermediate-Term Turning Points in Global Equities

One useful method for identifying important juncture points is to calculate the number of (U.S. dollar-adjusted) markets making new 39-week highs. A 20-week MA of a series based on this calculation is shown in Chart 27.5. The principles of net new high divergence discussed in Chapter 19 apply equally as well to the global picture. Note the negative divergence that took place in 1988 and 1989, and the trendline break in late 1989 that signaled the 1990 decline.

Not all countries will rise or decline with the World Stock Index, because the principle of variation (see Chapter 16) applies just as much to

Chart 27.4. The World Stock Index and seasonal momentum. (*Source: Pring Market Review.*)

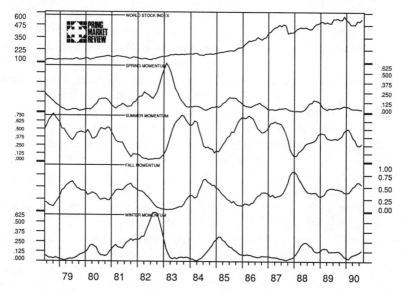

Chart 27.5. Net new global highs (U.S. dollar-adjusted). (*Source: Pring Market Review.*)

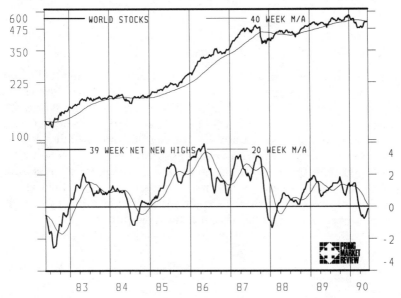

countries as to individual stocks or groups. In addition, the long-term economic, financial, and political situations of countries will vary, so that a good world bull market in equities may be brief or almost nonexistent for a country undergoing severe financial distortions, such as Hong Kong between 1986 and 1990. Generally speaking, improvements in technology and communications have broken down geographical and trading patterns, and countries have become more interdependent, with the result that their stock market and business cycles are now much more closely related than they used to be. A giant leap in this direction appeared to take place after the 1987, crash in which all markets participated on a synchronized basis. The introduction of international mutual funds of both the closed- and the open-ended varieties in the late 1980s in the United States is a striking example of this growing sense of international awareness.

The three stages of the 1974–1977 bull market shown in Charts 27.6 through 27.8 point up that this principle of commonality (see Chapter 16) was already in existence. The arrows above and below the various stock indexes correspond to intermediate buy and sell signals on the DJIA, as derived from a momentum indicator.[1] The charts show that the termination of each upleg was followed sooner or later by a fall in each individual stock index. As the global cycle developed into the third phase, several stock markets (such as the French and Italian) failed to make a new bull market high, resulting in a third upleg magnitude failure.

Individual Country Selection

A further aid in assessing the technical position of an individual country can be obtained through the construction of a relative-strength (RS) index using a country index such as the Nikkei Dow and the World Stock Index itself. The trend of the RS line does not indicate whether a market is rising or falling in an absolute sense, but only whether it is outperforming or underperforming the rest of the world. Once it has been established that the World Stock Index is in a rising trend, it is important to compare it with a stock market experiencing a favorable RS trend. In this respect all these calculations should be adjusted to a common currency in order to distinguish the true picture.

---

[1]This momentum indicator was developed by I. S. Notley of the Notley Group, Yelton Fiscal Inc., Unit 211, Executive Pavilion, 90 Grove Street, Ridgefield, CT 06877.

Chart 27.6. Commonality applied to world stock indexes, phase 1.

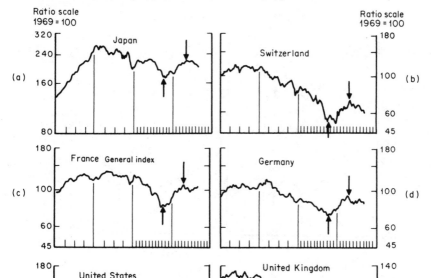

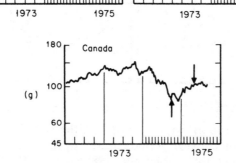

Chart 27.9, for instance, shows the Toronto Stock Exchange (TSE) Composite Index (adjusted for U.S. dollars) together with its RS (against the World Stock Index).

Most of the time these indicators conflict, but in late 1978 they were in total agreement; the price, RS, and momentum indicators all violated important down trendlines. These conjunctions are very unusual, but when they occur, they are usually followed by strong price moves. Another joint signal by price and RS was triggered in late 1971. It is im-

Chart 27.7. Commonality applied to world stock indexes, phase 2.

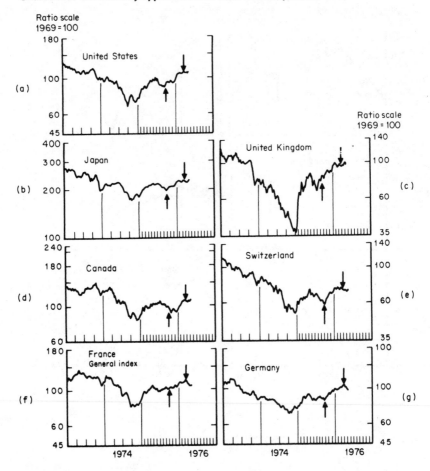

portant to note that both were followed by the strongest *relative* bull markets in the whole 20-year period covered by the chart. Even though the Toronto market rallied between 1982 and 1989, the persistent weakness in the relative-strength indicator (RSI) shows that an investor would have underperformed the global market.

See Chart 27.10, for example, which shows the German stock market in yen, expressed as RS against the World Stock Index, also adjusted to yen. In effect, this chart shows how the German equity market looked to a yen-based investor.

A major buying opportunity was clearly signaled in early 1985 because the German stock index and its RS line both violated significant down trendlines and their respective 12-month MAs. The 12-month

Chart 27.8. Commonality applied to world stock indexes, phase 3.

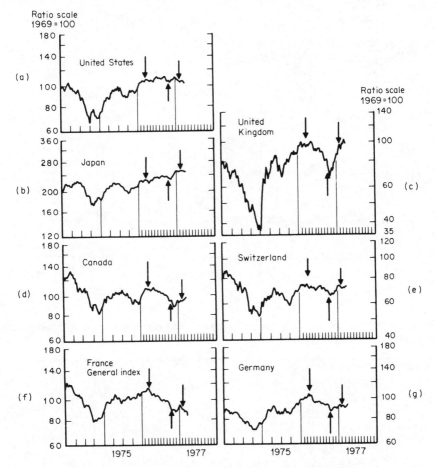

ROC indicator also emphasized the strong underlying technical structure by bottoming out and rallying above a 2-year trendline.

These kinds of what we might call AAA buying opportunities do not occur very often on an individual market, as the Canadian and German examples demonstrate. However, given the myriad of possible markets and cross-currency relationships, it should not be difficult to pick out one or two major opportunities each year.

Chart 27.9. The TSE Composite Index versus the World Stock Index (both U.S. dollar-adjusted). (*Source: Pring Market Review.*)

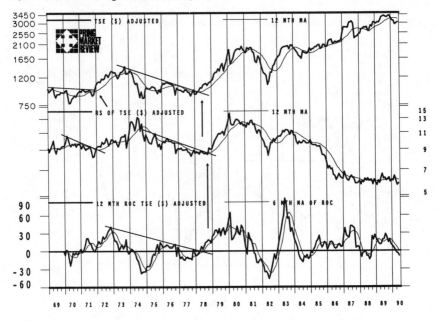

Chart 27.10. The German Stock Market versus the World Stock Index (both in yen). (*Source: Pring Market Review.*)

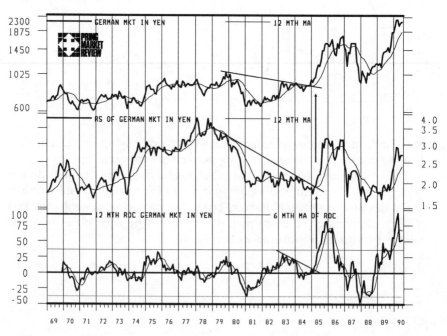

28
Technical Analysis of Individual Stocks

A useful systematic method for stock selection is what is known as the *top-down approach*. In this case the "top" is an analysis of whether the equity market is in a primary bull or a primary bear phase. Since most equities rise during a bull market and decline during a bear trend, this first step establishes whether the overall environment is likely to be positive or negative.

The next step involves an appraisal of the technical position of the various industry groups, since equities in the same industry generally move together. Once an attractive group has been isolated, the final stage involves the selection of individual stocks. This approach is discussed below. First, here are some general observations.

All investors would like their investments to appreciate rapidly in price, but stocks that may satisfy this wish tend to be accompanied by a substantially greater amount of risk than many investors are willing to accept. Stocks that move up rapidly in price usually have a high beta (i.e., they are very sensitive to market movements), a very small float (i.e., they are illiquid and very price-sensitive to a small increase in volume), or a very strong earnings momentum resulting in constant upward revisions in the price/earnings multiple. Others may be experiencing a turnaround situation in which the price has fallen to unrealistically low levels, so that even the slightest good news has an explosive effect on the price.

These are all fundamental factors and really fall outside the scope of this book. However, it is important to understand that investors can be very fashion-conscious when it comes to stock ownership. When prices have been bid up to unrealistically high levels and the media are covering positive developments in cover stories, major articles, etc., the chances are that the bullish arguments are understood by virtually all market participants. At this point virtually everyone who wants to buy has already done so, and the stock is said to be *overowned*. This happened to the pollution-control group in the late 1960s, the so-called glamour growth stocks in 1973, the oils in 1980, and certain "hi-tech" stocks in the early 1980s. When the news is so bad that it appears that profits will never recover or that the company might even go into bankruptcy, the opposite condition sets in and the stock is said to be *underowned*. Real Estate Investment Trusts in 1974 and tire stocks in 1980 are examples of underownership. Not all companies go through such extreme cycles, but it is still important to recognize that the psychological process exists.

A position of overownership usually develops over several cyclical advances, creating what is called a *secular rise*. Similarly, a position of underownership, in which a stock becomes totally out of fashion, usually takes many years to develop.

Stock Selection from a Secular Point of View

General

The selection process should begin by trying to identify whether a stock is in a secular advance or decline in order to try to establish its position within its ownership cycle. Chart 28.1a shows Allis Chalmers Corp. (ALL), a company which went through several such cycles between 1948 and 1983. Stocks in basic industries, such as ALL, are called *cyclical stocks* since they offer great profit opportunities over one or even two business cycles but are rarely profitable using the buy-hold approach.

Because of the long-term growth characteristics of the global economy, most stocks exhibit characteristics of a long-term secular advance interrupted by mild secular corrections. Chart 28.1b shows such a trend for Bristol Myers (BMY). Between 1948 and 1953, and later between 1967 and 1974, the stock was in a small secular decline, since successive bear market lows were lower than their predecessors. For the rest of the time Bristol Myers was in a secular uptrend. The dominant period of rapid price advance occurred between 1953 and 1967. By 1968 the violation of the 10-year uptrend line in the stock and the 12-year uptrend in relative strength (RS), labeled "ratio-cator" in the chart, suggested that the stock was in an overowned state and might need a lengthy corrective period.

By 1974 BMY had experienced a "double" bear market in which it lost almost two-thirds of its value. Having corrected the excesses of the previous secular advance, BMY was then in a strong technical position to begin a new advance.

Republic Steel Corp., shown in Chart 28.1c, provides an opposite example; this stock spent most of its time between 1959 and 1982 in a secular bear market. From the point of view of investing and using a 5- to 7-year time horizon, it would have been relatively difficult to make money in Republic compared to BMY.

These three examples point up the differing life cycles and characteristics of individual stocks. Investors who are able to identify secular trends in price and RS are in a position to profit from extremes in the ownership cycle. Consequently, a very long term price chart of stocks can provide a useful starting point for stock selection.

Major Price Patterns (Long Bases)

The discussion of price patterns in Chapter 5 pointed out the relationship between the size of a formation and the ensuing price move in terms of both magnitude and time. One of the best approaches to stock selection is to search through the chart books for issues that are emerging from or pulling back to long-term bases, since there are almost always some stocks in this position. It should be noted that whenever the chart books are full of emerging long-term bases, as occurred in the early 1940s and the late 1970s, the odds of a long-term, broad-based general market advance are greatly enhanced.

Some examples of these large formations in action are shown in Charts 28.1 and 28.2. BMY (Chart 28.1b) broke out of a 14-year inverse head-and-shoulders (H&S) consolidation pattern in 1980; this break was accompanied by a similar move in the company's RS line.

Smithkline Beecham Corp. (SKB), shown in Chart 28.2a, traced out a broadening formation with a flat top during the 1967–1975 period, ending the long interval of consolidation which began in 1959. Since the RS line had broken above its 13-year downtrend in 1974 almost a year before, the two trends had the effect of strongly reinforcing one another. A second opportunity to purchase SKB occurred in mid-1977 as the price pulled back to the upper portion of the base. The dramatic rise above the flat top, once this correction was completed, is typical of the type of move to be expected from these formations. In this case, it was not a classically symmetrical formation, since the flat top declined slightly; even though there were some false breakouts along the way, the general "feel" of this trading action was one of a broadening type.

Chart 28.1a. Allis Chalmers. (*Source: Securities Research Co., a Division of United Business Service Co.*)

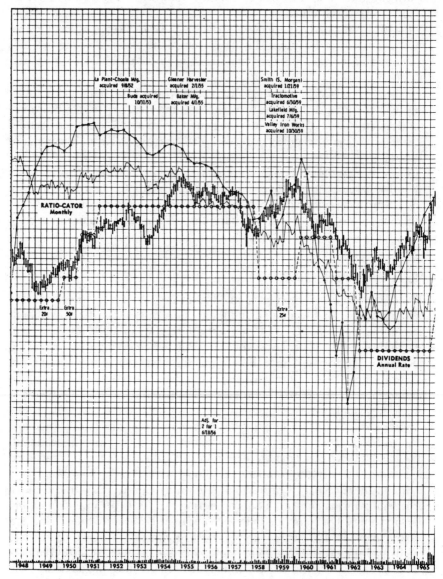

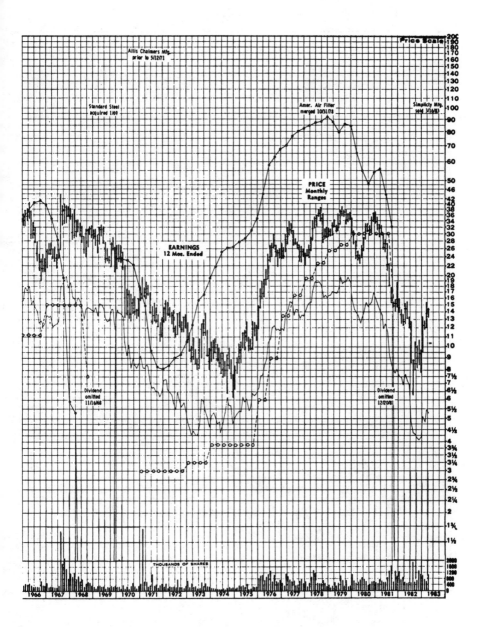

Chart 28.1b. Bristol Myers. (*Source: Securities Research Co.*)

Chart 28.1c. Republic Steel Corp. (*Source: Securities Research Co.*)

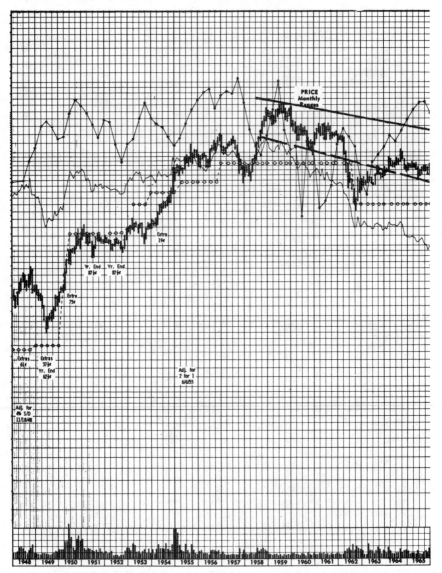

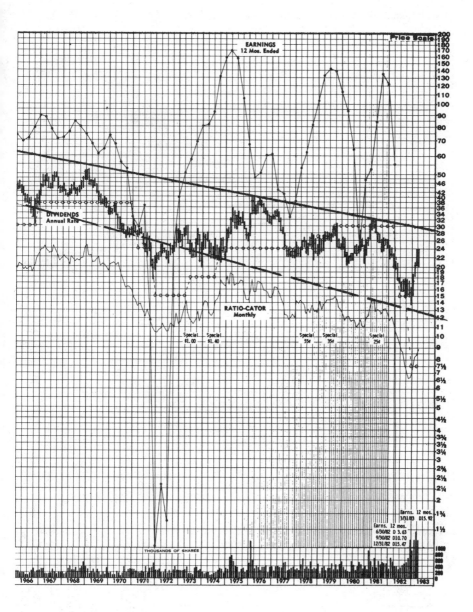

Chart 28.2a. Smithkline Beecham. (*Source: Securities Research Co.*)

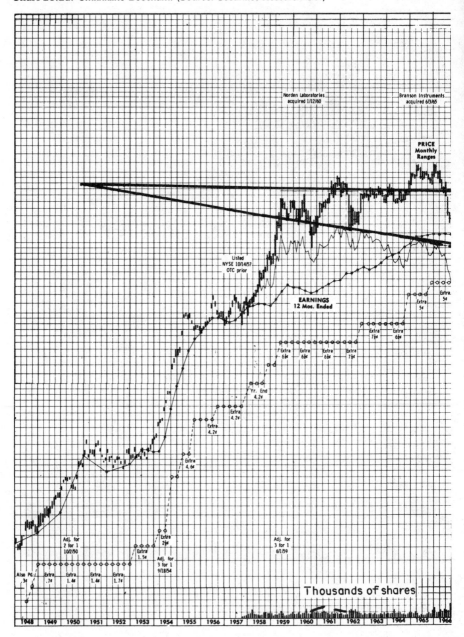

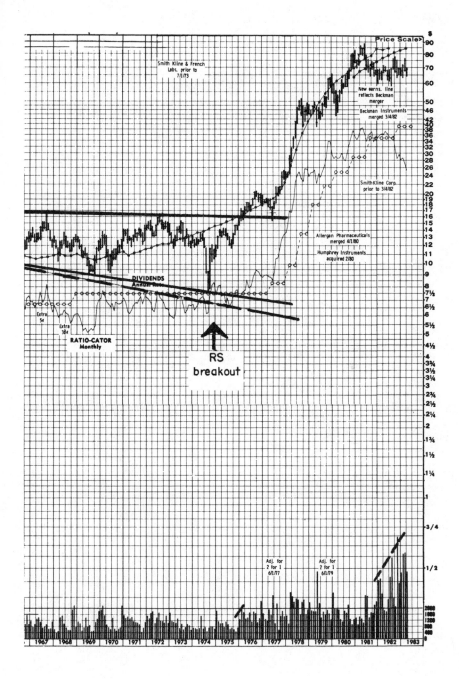

Price Scale

Smith Kline & French
Labs. prior to
7/1/73

New earns. line
reflects Beckman
merger

Beckman Instruments
merged 3/4/82

SmithKline Corp.
prior to 3/4/82

Allergan Pharmaceuticals
merged 4/1/80

Humphrey Instruments
acquired 2/80

DIVIDENDS
Annual Rate

Extra
5¢

Extra
38¢

RATIO-CATOR
Monthly

RS
breakout

Adj. for
2 for 1
6/1/77

Adj. for
2 for 1
6/1/79

Chart 28.2b. Whirlpool Corp. (*Source: Securities Research Co.*)

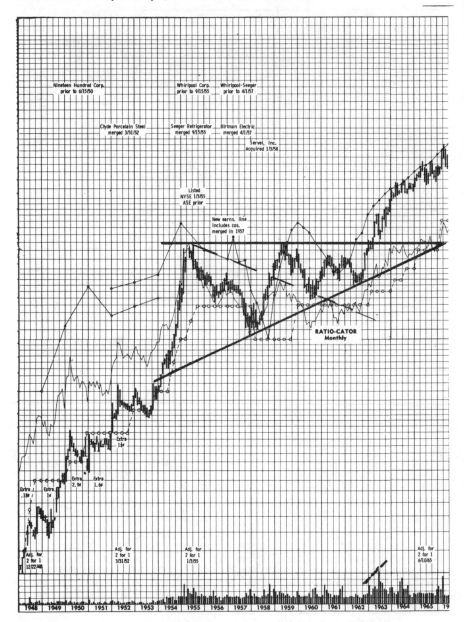

Chart 28.2c. Fedders Corporation. (*Source: Securities Research Co.*)

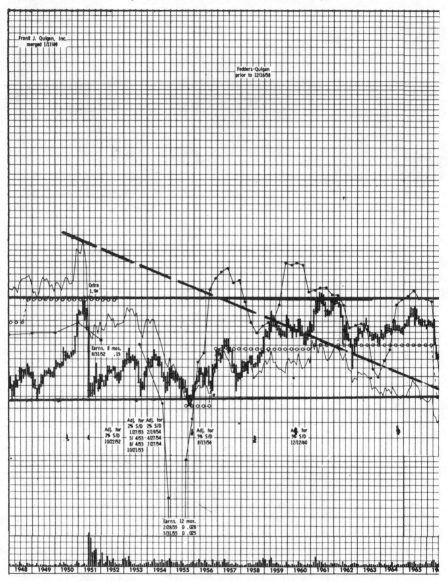

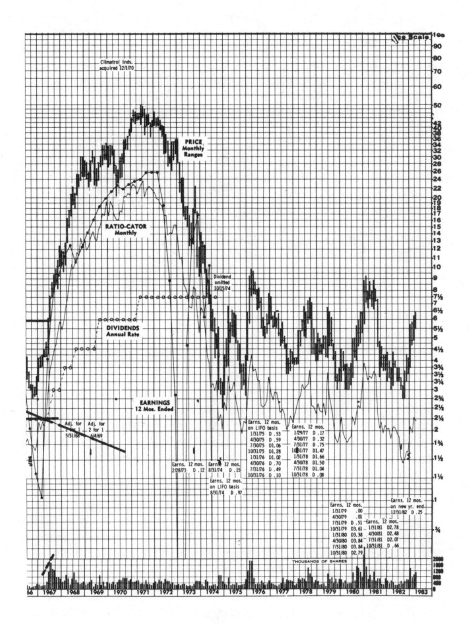

Climatrol Inds.
acquired 12/1/70

PRICE
Monthly
Ranges

RATIO-CATOR
Monthly

Dividend
omitted
10/15/74

DIVIDENDS
Annual Rate

EARNINGS
12 Mos. Ended

Adj. for   Adj. for
1   2 for 1
5/31/68   6/4/69

Earns. 12 mos.   Earns. 12 mos.
2/28/73   D .12   8/31/74   D .15

Earns. 12 mos.
on LIFO basis
8/31/74   D .97

Earns. 12 mos. on LIFO basis	
1/31/75	D .53
4/30/75	D .59
7/30/75	D1.06
10/31/75	D1.28
1/31/76	D1.02
4/30/76	D .70
7/31/76	D .49
10/31/76	D .10

Earns. 12 mos.	
1/29/77	D .17
4/30/77	D .32
7/31/77	D .75
10/31/77	D1.47
1/31/78	D1.66
4/30/78	D1.50
7/31/78	D1.04
10/31/78	D .08

Earns. 12 mos.	
1/31/79	.00
4/30/79	.01
7/31/79	D .51
10/31/79	D3.61
1/31/80	D3.38
4/30/80	D3.84
7/31/80	D3.84
10/31/80	D2.79

Earns. 12 mos.	
1/31/81	D2.78
4/30/81	D2.48
7/31/81	D2.07
10/31/81	D .66

Earns. 12 mos. on new yr. end	
12/31/82	D .25

THOUSANDS OF SHARES

66 | 1967 | 1968 | 1969 | 1970 | 1971 | 1972 | 1973 | 1974 | 1975 | 1976 | 1977 | 1978 | 1979 | 1980 | 1981 | 1982 | 1983

Whirlpool Corp. (Chart 28.2*b*) offers a fine example of an ascending triangle that took 8 years to complete. The breakout was accompanied by good volume and preceded by a long-term reversal in RS. The stock consolidated its gains in the form of what might be loosely described as a 10-year inverse H&S pattern in the mid-1970s. Whether the 1977 sell-off qualifies as a left shoulder is open to debate. The important point is that the 1982 breakout above the heavy resistance at the neckline was accompanied by improving RS and expanding volume.

Finally, Fedders Corporation (Chart 28.2*c*) formed a huge rectangle base between 1948 and 1957. This example has been chosen for two reasons: First, it illustrates that when a valid breakout occurs, the surprises are usually on the upside. Second, even though a large base normally implies a long and steady rise following the breakout, once a dynamic rise of the type experienced by Fedders has occurred, investors should be on the lookout for some price vulnerability and should not greedily assume that the move can extend indefinitely.

Some Basic Principles of Stock Selection during a Primary Bull Market

General

A bull market has been defined as a period in which most stocks are moving up most of the time. A bear market, in contrast, is a period in which most stocks are declining the vast majority of the time. When one is investing or speculating in the market, it is clearly important to be committing money during the bull phase; although some stocks can rise during a bear market, the law of probability indicates that it is much more difficult to make profitable investments.

The performance of specific issues can differ widely, not only over the course of the total bull move, but also during its various stages. This phenomenon was discussed in Chapter 15, which described the group rotation process. Once it has been established that the overall environment for equities is positive on a primary or intermediate-trend basis, or both, two questions need to be answered:

1. Which industry groups look technically sound not only in their own right but also *relative* to the market?

2. Which stock or stocks within the group look strong technically in their own right, in relation to the market as a whole, and in relation to the group or industry index?

In this respect the obvious starting point would be an analysis of the relative positions of the various industry groups in terms of the group rotation process described in Chapter 15. Not all groups fit into the cycle, but an analysis of the relative positions of the energy and financial sectors (see Chapter 15) would be a good starting point from which to determine whether the cycle was in its inflationary or deflationary part. The next step would be to analyze the groups that were akin to the sector that looked more promising.

Chapter 24, in discussing speculation, pointed out that there have been distinct cycles in the relationship between low-priced and high-grade stocks since the 1920s. This should also have a bearing on the decision-making process. Chart 28.3, for example, shows the NASDAQ (Over-the-Counter) Composite, a proxy for low-capitalized stocks. Shown at the bottom is its relative performance against the Standard and Poor's (S&P) Composite. This RS line broadly follows the cycles in the relationship of low-priced/high-grade issues. An understanding of the prevailing trend of this relationship therefore offers a good perspective on which type of investment is likely to offer superior results. For example, between 1975 and 1983 low-capitalized stocks were outperforming blue chips. Other things being equal, an investor would have been better off exposed to this sector. Between 1983 and 1990 it was the turn of the blue chips. Remember, this is a *relative* choice, for in

Chart 28.3. The NASDAQ (Over-the-Counter) Composite versus the S&P Composite. (*Source: Pring Market Review.*)

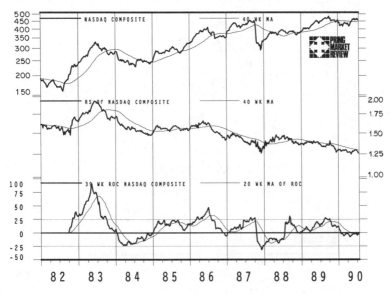

the 1983–1990 period, both low-capitalized stocks and blue chips rallied in price. It was just that the heavier-capitalized issues went up faster.

This high-capitalization/low-capitalization analysis does not preclude the necessity for group rotation analysis. Indeed, low-capitalization issues go through the same process. What such an analysis does do is to give the investor an additional dimension, which enables him or her to determine which *type* of issues are likely to perform well.

Stock Selection at a Major Market Bottom

An Example Using Retail Stocks.   Chart 28.4 shows the S&P General Merchandise Store Index between 1971 and 1983. Since retail stores are considered a leading group, it would be reasonable to expect this index to show an improving trend in RS at the beginning of the cycle. However, this was certainly not the case at the 1974 bear market low. The index itself was able to rally along with the market in late 1974–early 1975, but the RS line continued on its downward path. If a group with leading tendencies cannot put on an impressive performance at the beginning of the cycle, when it should be at its strongest,

Chart 28.4. S&P General Merchandise Store Index, 1971–1983. (*Source: Pring Market Review.*)

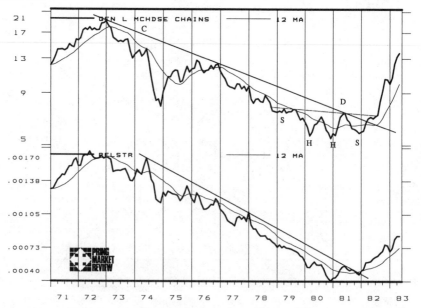

this is normally a sign of underlying technical weakness. In the case of the group in the General Merchandise Store Index, the implication was that even if the index itself could put on a rally and result in a profitable trade, there were likely to be far better opportunities in other stock groups in which RS was actually improving. The chart shows that the index did manage to rally into January 1976 but subsequently declined in price for another 4 years. It was apparent that this group had begun a period of underperformance at the 1982 bottom.

By the time the market bottomed in 1982, the General Merchandise Store Index was about the same, but the technical action had improved dramatically. The secular low was touched in December 1980. However, an improvement in RS did not become apparent until late 1981, when the down trendline, which had begun in 1974, 7 years before, was broken on the upside. By the summer of 1982 it became apparent that this group had begun an important bull market, for not only did the index fail to confirm the 1981 low in the Dow Jones Industrial Average (DJIA), but it had already broken above the downtrend (line *CD*) in March 1982, 5 months before the bull market began. Since this declining trendline could be drawn back to 1973 and was therefore 9 years in length, it was quite clear that a major change in the long-term technical picture had taken place.

By late August 1982, 3 weeks after the start of the bull market, the index broke out from a massive, 4-year, complex, inverse H&S accumulation pattern, thereby leaving little technical doubt that this group had embarked on a major bull move.

Once this fact was established, the question that would then arise was which general merchandise stock or stocks would constitute the most profitable investment. Possible candidates were K-Mart Corp.; J. C. Penney Co., Inc.; Sears, Roebuck & Co.; Wal-Mart Stores, Inc.; and F. W. Woolworth Co. These five stocks are shown in Charts 28.5*a* to *e*. Clearly, the outstanding stock throughout the 8-year period between 1975 and 1983 was Wal-Mart, which rose from just over $1 to over $40.

By August 1982, at the beginning of the bull market, Wal-Mart and its RS line had been in an uptrend for 7 years. Since there was no sign of a reversal in either of these trends, there was no technical justification for selling the stock. On the other hand, since Wal-Mart had been rising sharply for a very extended period, it could quite easily have become vulnerable to profit taking if some bad news had come out. Should it therefore have been bought? Because buying the leading stock or group at the beginning of a bull market normally pays off, it would have made sense to allocate some funds to Wal-Mart even though the stock looked overextended. As it happened, the stock doubled during

Chart 28.5a. K-Mart Corp. (*Source: Securities Research Co.*)

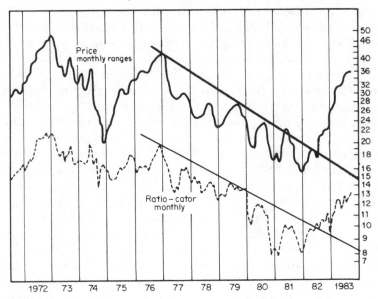

Chart 28.5b. J. C. Penney Co., Inc. (*Source: Securities Research Co.*)

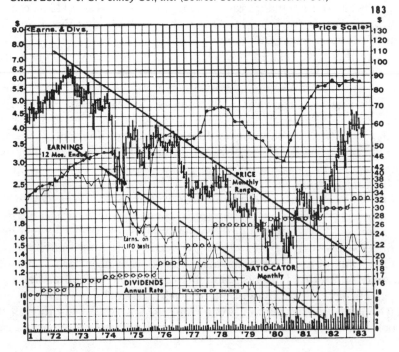

Chart 28.5c. Sears, Roebuck & Co. (*Source: Securities Research Co.*)

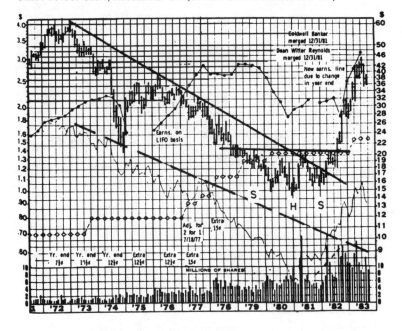

the next year. However, from an investment management point of view, it would nevertheless have made sense to spread the risk.

In this respect one stock, Sears, stands out—for whereas other stocks had violated major downtrends on the upside, Sears had actually completed and broken out from a major inverse H&S pattern. In the ensuing 12 months the performance of Sears closely matched that of Wal-Mart, proving that the diversification strategy would have worked quite well. The performance of the remaining stocks in the group, though less exciting than that of Wal-Mart and Sears, still out-ranked the market as measured by the DJIA.

Trend Changes in RS within a Primary Trend

The example used above concerned a group of stocks the RS trend of which had been improving over a long period of time, i.e., between two stock market cycles. Since moves of an intermediate nature often prove to be highly profitable, it makes sense to consider changes in an RS trend within a primary move, for there is a *tendency* for different

Chart 28.5*d*. Wal-Mart Stores, Inc. (*Source: Securities Research Co.*)

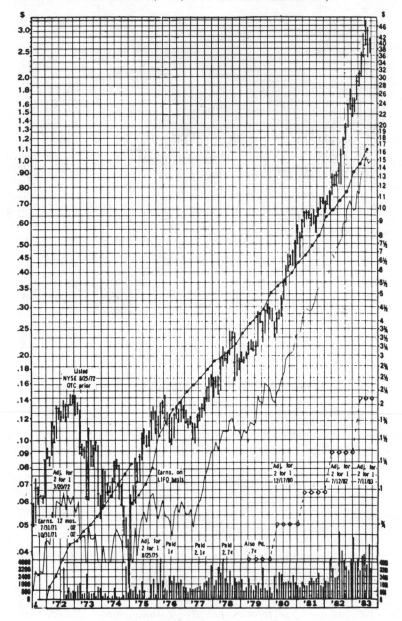

Chart 28.5e. F. W. Woolworth Co. (*Source: Securities Research Co.*)

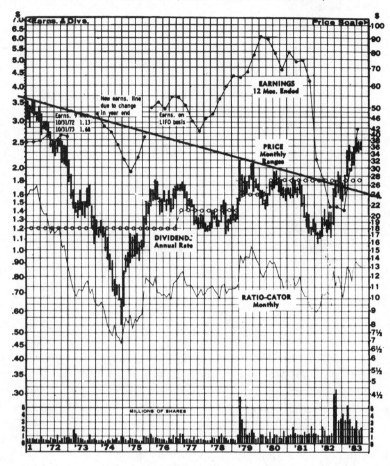

groups to outperform the averages at various stages of a bull or bear market.

Such changes in RS can often first be noticed around important intermediate turning points of the market itself. This can be seen from Chart 28.6, which illustrates the performance of the S&P Electronics–Semiconductor/Components Index. In 1976 this group made a new bull market high, but this was not confirmed by the RS line, which had peaked earlier, in 1975. When the bull market trendline of the index itself was violated on the downside (*AB*), the negative action of the RS line was confirmed. Even more bearish was the fact that the index had just completed a 9-month H&S distribution pattern (which

Chart 28.6. S&P Electronics–Semiconductor/Components Index, 1972–1983. (*Source: Pring Market Review.*)

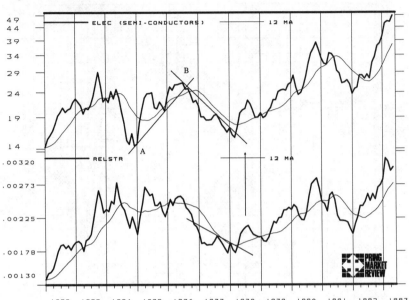

was apparent only on a monthly high, low, close chart). By early 1978[1] the technical position of this group had completely reversed itself. The index itself reached a 2-year low in March 1978, but the RS line bottomed out early in 1977 after having been in an uptrend for almost a year. By April 1978 both the index itself and the RS line had broken above their down trendlines, thereby offering a strong buy signal for semiconductor stocks in general. Again the question of which stocks to buy would arise. What is interesting is that all the stocks used in the construction of the index outperformed the market during the following months. The choices, which are shown in Charts 28.7a to e, were AMP, Inc.; Intel Corp.; Motorola, Inc.; National Semiconductor Corp.; and Texas Instruments, Inc. (TI).

National Semiconductor had an improving RS line and had broken out from a double bottom formation by April 1978, but there had been no discernible reversal in trend in terms of either the price itself or its RS line. Moreover, by that time the stock, at about $16, was 60 percent

---

[1] It is debatable whether 1978 marked a bear market or an intermediate low. In a strict Dow theory sense, it represented a bear market low. For broader-based indexes such as the Value Line Composite for March 1978, however, it was an intermediate low; it has therefore been treated as such in this example.

Chart 28.7a. AMP, Inc. (*Source: Securities Research Co.*)

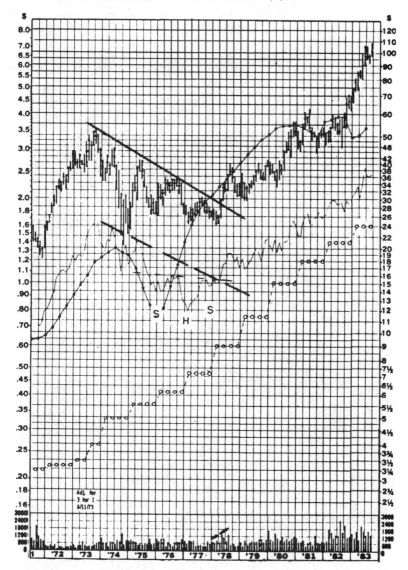

Chart 28.7b. Intel Corp. (*Source: Securities Research Co.*)

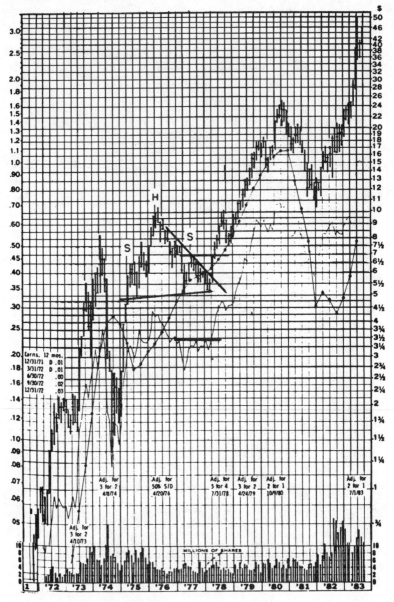

Chart 28.7c. Motorola, Inc. (*Source: Securities Research Co.*)

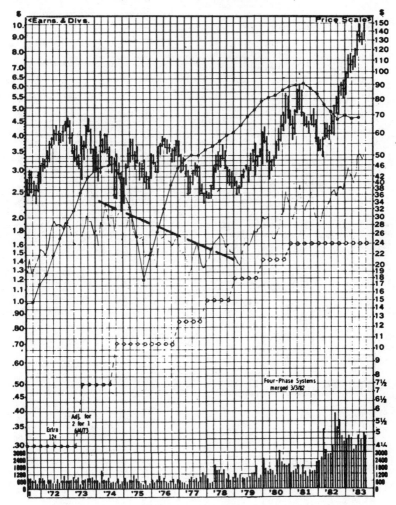

above its low. Motorola was also relatively unattractive since the choppy nature of the stock suggested that technical signals could not be wholeheartedly relied upon. This is a point very well worth noting since certain stocks possess characteristics that result in constant whipsaws, yet other stocks almost consistently give reliable technical signals. Given the choice, reliability is to be preferred, even though the volatile alternative may offer greater profit potential if it is not giving a whipsaw signal. Even though an important break of a 5-year downtrend in Motorola's

Chart 28.7d. National Semiconductor Corp. (*Source: Securities Research Co.*)

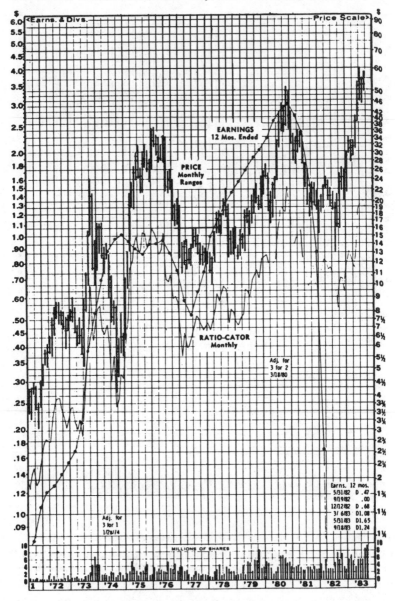

Chart **28.7**e. TI. (*Source: Securities Research Co.*)

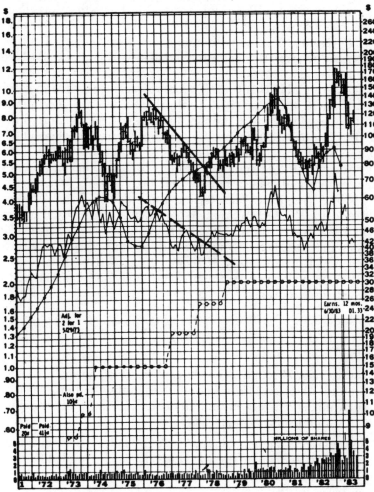

RS had taken place, the general technical unreliability of the stock suggested that there might be better possibilities elsewhere.

TI, on the other hand, looked to be a better prospect; both the stock and its RS line had pushed above very important trendlines accompanied by a modest expansion in volume. Here at last was a possible candidate.

AMP also looked promising. This stock had just broken above a downtrend which had been in force for nearly 5 years. On the whole it had been a more reliable stock than Motorola, and its recent action had been superior to that of TI. This could be seen because AMP had made a marginal new low in 1978 compared to TI's low, which was almost 20 percent lower than that set in 1977. Finally, the RS line of AMP not only broke above a 4½-year down trendline but also completed and broke out from an inverse H&S pattern. On balance, therefore, AMP looked to be a better bet than TI.

The final candidate was Intel. This issue was the only one that did not make a post-1976 low in 1978. It also broke above a very important down trendline in April. Although this line was not as long as that of AMP or TI, it had been touched many times during its descent and its violation therefore represented an important signal. The line was relatively shorter than the comparable ones for the other candidates because the stock had made a new all-time high in 1976, which was actually a point in its favor. The RS line also failed to form a discernible downtrend for the same reason. What made Intel such an intriguing prospect was that the April 1978 breakout above the $7 area strongly suggested that the H&S distribution pattern that seemed to be forming between mid-1975 and early 1978 was going to fail. This conclusion would have been correct, as the breakout above $7 was followed by a very worthwhile move.

Summary

1. Most stocks go through ownership cycles, which normally take a long period to complete. It is important to identify whether a stock is in a secular uptrend or downtrend, in order to better understand its position within its ownership cycle.

2. Substantial profit potential is available to the long-term investor who can identify stocks that are breaking out from extended bases when they are accompanied by expanding volume and an improving long-term trend in RS.

3. Though a bull market generally carries most stocks with it, the performance of individual issues can vary considerably, both over the course of the primary upmove and within it.

4. Once a favorable market environment has been established, the process of selecting stocks should begin with analysis of an appropriate industry group and should lead to final isolation of the stocks that are outperforming the others within the group. Purchases should be made only when price trends and volume support the improving RS.

29
Technical Analysis of Gold

Introduction

Prices in financial markets are determined by psychology—by the attitude of investors and speculators toward the fundamentals. Gold perhaps arouses greater emotion than any other commodity or market. Some investors call gold the "barbaric metal," but others believe that it is the only true store of value and that only a return to the gold standard will restore the world's financial structure to stability.

Emotion moves in trends, and so do gold prices. Price trends in the gold market are no more difficult to detect than those in other financial markets. In fact, the price of gold is relatively easier to analyze from a technical viewpoint than the price of virtually any other commodity because of the depth of the analytical tools available. These tools include trend analysis of the gold price itself, of the relationship between gold and gold shares and between gold and other precious metals, and of the relationship between gold and its advance/decline (A/D) line.

At any given time there are three forces that influence the price of gold: (1) gold as money, i.e., as a currency and store of value; (2) gold as an industrial metal; and (3) gold as an emotional thermometer. The supply of any currency, unlike the supply of gold, can be expanded at will. Therefore the major influence on the gold price is investors' hopes or fears about the future course of inflation. Gold is also purchased as an alternative reserve asset when the U.S. dollar, the world's principal reserve currency, is weak.

Primary bull and bear markets are greatly influenced by the business cycle. Not only does the inflation-hedge demand for gold move up and down with business activity, but so does the demand for gold as an industrial metal. The emotional demand for gold is a result of investors' perceptions of political events. It is not related to the business cycle but has the effect of exacerbating rallies in a bull market and cushioning declines during bear markets. For example, the invasion of Afghanistan took place during a bull market and had a very powerful effect on the gold price, whereas the upward effect of the Sadat assassination and the Iran-Iraq war, which occurred during a bear market, was small and temporary.

Analysis of the Gold Price Itself

The gold price, which is expressed here in U.S. dollars, responds reasonably well to trend-determining techniques such as price pattern behavior, moving averages (MAs), and rates of change (ROCs). For longer-term movements, decisive crossovers of the 12-month MA have been reliable (see Chart 29.1). Buy and sell signals using a monthly *know sure thing* (KST) indicator (see Chapter 10) have also been reasonably accurate.

Chart 29.1. Gold bullion, monthly. (*Source: Pring Market Review.*)

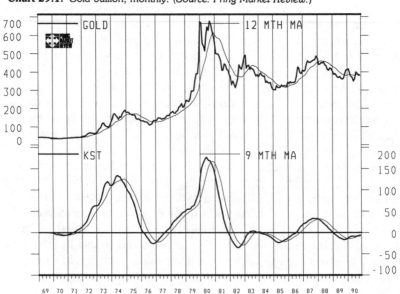

Gold and Gold Shares

General Principles

In most cases gold shares lead the price of bullion. Occasionally the prices of individual gold-mining companies can be distorted by specific company developments that are totally unrelated to the gold price. For this reason it is preferable to relate a gold share index, such as the Toronto Stock Exchange (TSE) Gold and Silver Share Index or the Philadelphia Gold and Silver Index (XAU), to the gold price.

This relationship between the prices of gold and gold shares works so well for several reasons.

First, investors in gold shares are concerned about the flow of profits from those shares, which is predominantly determined by the average price of gold bullion over a particular period. If investors in the shares feel that the average price is likely to fall, they discount this fact by selling in advance, and vice versa.

Second, gold shares are more leveraged than bullion. Not only do gold mines borrow money to go into production, but also, as the gold price rises or falls, marginal ore deposits become commercially profitable or unprofitable, which adds to or subtracts proportionately more from the value of the mine than the change in the actual price of the metal.

Third, the profits of gold mines are a function of the gold price as well as the cost of production. These costs are basically subject to the same influences as other corporations, with the result that trends in profits are also influenced by the business cycle. Since profits are a leading indicator and inflation (which is discounted in the trend of bullion prices) is a lagging indicator, the net effect (other things being equal) is for gold shares to lead the price of bullion.

The general rule is that the prevailing trend is assumed to be intact unless a new high or low in either the stocks or bullion is not jointly confirmed. This represents a disagreement and warns that the prevailing trend is likely to reverse. Usually bullion lags behind the shares, but occasionally it is the shares that are slow to turn. In either case a trend reversal should be expected.

Some Examples

The top of Chart 29.2 shows the price of the London P.M. fix from 1971 to 1983. Underneath is the TSE Gold Share Index (converted to U.S. dollars). The chart shows that the Gold Share Index reached a cyclical high in March 1974, whereas the bullion price topped out 9 months later.

Up to March 1974 the two indexes had been moving together, as each

Chart 29.2. The gold price versus gold shares (in U.S. dollars), monthly. (*Source: Pring Market Review.*)

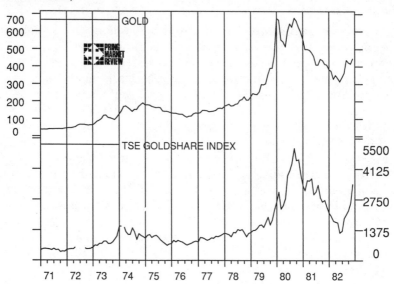

new high was confirmed by the other. It is also worth noting that the Gold Share Index was actually forming a top throughout 1974 from which it eventually broke down. At the beginning of 1975 it was fairly clear that the technical structure of the gold asset markets was very weak; the shares failed by a wide margin to confirm the bullion, and also gave an important indication that they were going to lead the bullion price lower.

At the bottom of the bear market in mid-1976 this technical position had partly reversed itself. Whereas the bullion price made its low in August 1976, the TSE Gold Share Index refused to make a new low, which set up a divergence. Although this was clearly a positive sign, a really bullish signal did not come until later that year, when the bear market trendlines of both the bullion price and the Gold Share Index were penetrated on the upside.

The cyclical peak in gold bullion in January 1980 was one of the few occasions when the shares *lagged* behind the bullion price. During the December 1979–February 1980 period, the gold bullion price formed a small head and shoulders (H&S) pattern in the face of rising share prices, as shown in Chart 29.2. Given the leading characteristic of the gold shares, it might have been expected that the distribution pattern being traced out by the bullion would fail. Since the pattern did not fail, it would have been wise to conclude that the gold price would head lower when the trend in the bullion price broke in early March.

Although the shares tend to lead the bullion price, there are times when they lag. A price move in bullion which remains unconfirmed by the shares, and vice versa, indicates that the gold asset markets are out of gear, and is almost always a sign that the prevailing trend is likely to reverse. Such a development is signaling that the gold asset markets are out of gear.

Another point worth noting is that the asset which takes the lead, whether bullion or gold shares, generally has the largest ensuing price swing. For example, gold bullion peaked at $850 in January 1980, ahead of the shares. Bullion lost almost half its value in the next few months, whereas the losses in the Gold Share Index were limited to about 30 to 40 percent.

By May 1980 the decline had run its course. That the TSE Gold Share Index had formed and completed an important bottom ahead of bullion was highly significant. First, it provided some advance warning that an imminent upside breakout in the metal was likely to take place, and second, it added tremendous validity to the breakout in the metal price when it did in fact occur. This is another example of an important trend reversal, signaled by a disagreement between the shares and the metal.

The September 1980 peak in the gold price was also instructive, since it found the gold asset markets once again in a major disagreement. Gold shares reached a new cyclical peak, but bullion was well below its January high. The ensuing decline was lengthy and painful for both shares and bullion.

Chart 29.3 shows that the December 1987 bullion high was also asso-

Chart 29.3. The gold price in U.S. dollars versus the Toronto Stock Exchange gold and silver share index. (*Source: Pring Market Review.*)

ciated with a disagreement since it was not confirmed by the shares that had already experienced a very sharp decline in October. In a similar vein, the shares started to bottom in early 1988, well over a year ahead of bullion.

Gold and the Gold A/D Line

A weekly A/D line for the NYSE is constructed by taking a cumulative plurality of the number of issues advancing over those declining. The gold A/D line, which is shown in Charts 29.4 and 29.5, is calculated by taking a cumulative weekly plurality of the price of gold expressed in different currencies. Each week the gold price is expressed in 12 differ-ent currencies (the number that happens to be in the basket of cross-currency relationships, as explained in Chapter 30), e.g., U.S. dollar/gold, and yen/gold. The net number of advances or declines is then added to or subtracted from the running total. If the A/D line was at 155 in the previous week and gold rallied in terms of three currencies and declined against the other nine in the basket, the running total (A/D line) would fall to 149. There is no reason why the gold A/D line should not be constructed from any number of currencies, although the larger the universe, the greater the task of data collection and manipulation.

Chart 29.4. Gold versus the gold A/D line, 1974–1983. (*Source: Pring Market Review.*)

Chart 29.5. Gold versus the gold A/D line, 1982–1990. (*Source: Pring Market Review.*)

The concept behind the A/D line construction is to try to estimate whether the price rise (or decline) of gold bullion is a broad one, or whether it is moving up or down merely in response to fluctuations in the U.S. dollar.

The gold A/D line is interpreted in the same way as the gold/gold share relationship. Generally the A/D line leads the price of gold bullion or the gold A/D line remains unconfirmed. The continuation of the prevailing trend is doubtful because of the disagreement. Chart 29.4 shows that the A/D line did not confirm the December 1974 high, the August 1976 low, or the June 1982 low; important trend reversals followed. There was another major disagreement in September 1980 when the A/D line made a new secular high but the gold price did not.

Negative divergences occurred at the 1987 and early 1990 peaks (Chart 29.5). It is important to remember that these disagreements are only characteristics and not outright signals. It is mandatory to await a trend-reversal signal for the yield price itself. For example, the A/D line set up a positive divergence with the gold price in 1984. However, since the price did not reverse its downtrend throughout this period, a purchase based only on a positive divergence would have been very unprofitable.

Gold and Other Precious Metals

Over the course of the business cycle, the fortunes of the four precious metals traded on futures markets—gold, silver, platinum, and palladium—are very similar. Indeed, at almost every trading session they move in tandem; only the magnitude of each move varies.

The three critical markets to monitor are gold, silver, and platinum. If all three confirm new highs or lows in a prevailing trend, they are in gear. These relationships are therefore of no predictive value in terms of potential trend reversals. When one or two of the metals begin to falter, a warning, but not an actual signal, of a trend reversal is given. A more important area to monitor is the relative-strength (RS) action between the various metals. This is because a change in an RS relationship often signals a reversal in the trend of the price of gold. For example, Charts 29.6 and 29.7 show the price of gold with the silver/gold ratio. A rising line means that silver is outperforming gold, and vice versa. These charts indicate reversals associated with a reversal in the silver/gold ratio in late 1974, mid-1976, early 1980, 1982, 1986, late 1987, and early 1990.

Chart 29.6. Gold versus silver, 1974–1982. (*Source: Pring Market Review.*)

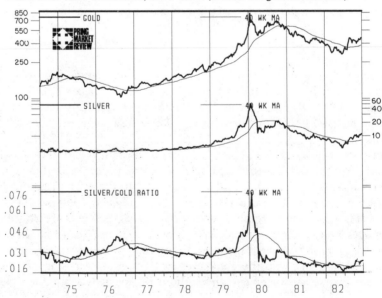

Chart 29.7. Gold versus silver, 1982–1990. (*Source: Pring Market Review.*)

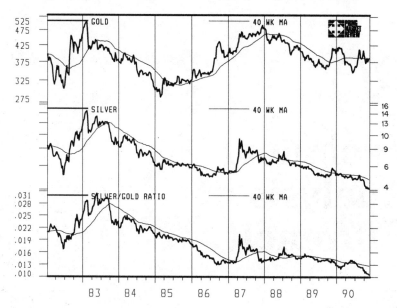

Summary

1. Changes in the trend of the gold price can be determined with the help of price patterns, MAs, volume characteristics, ROCs, etc.

2. Gold shares and the gold A/D line usually lead the price of gold. If their lead remains unconfirmed by the gold price, or vice versa, it represents a disagreement which almost always results in a reversal in the prevailing trend.

3. Changes in the trend of the gold price are usually accompanied by a change in the trend of the gold/silver ratio, the gold/platinum ratio, or both. It is of little concern whether or not gold is outperforming the other two metals; what is important is that the trend in the relationship has changed.

30
Technical Analysis of Currencies

Introduction

The principles that underlie analysis of currencies from a technical aspect are basically the same as those used in any other financial market or for individual stocks. The major difference is that the price, or level, of a currency is always relative to the prices of all other currencies. Hence a rising trend in the U.S. dollar-adjusted Swiss franc will be bullish for Americans and bearish for the Swiss, but when gold or equities are declining sharply, they are bearish for everyone.

There are two questions which must be asked by anyone who invests or speculates in currencies: First, which currency should be bought (or sold)? Second, which cross-currency rate should be bought (or sold)? In other words, the first step is to establish whether a currency is generally strong against most other currencies, and then to try to identify which cross rate or relationship it will be strongest against. Investors with a longer-term horizon also need to take interest-rate differentials into consideration. This factor is discussed later.

From a speculative point of view, there are really only six currencies that are actively traded outside the bank market: the Canadian and Australian dollars, British pound, Swiss franc, German mark, and Japanese yen. All six are listed on the International Monetary Market (IMM) in Chicago, and the last four are also listed on the London International Financial Futures Exchange (LIFFE) in the United Kingdom.

These and other currencies can also be bought or sold in the forward market through the currency trading departments of major international banks.

Isolating a Strong or Weak Currency

The starting point involves the technical appraisal of an overall measure which acts as a proxy for the general fortunes of a specific currency in a similar way that a stock market average, such as the Standard & Poor's (S&P), is used as a proxy measure for the market as a whole. The most convenient form is a trade-weighted (TW) index. TW indexes are constructed from a basket of cross-currency relationships, weighted according to the volume of trade transacted with the country issuing the base currency. For example, Canada is the largest trading partner of the United States; the TW (U.S. dollar) index is therefore heavily weighted in favor of the Canadian dollar. On the other hand, since relatively little trade is transacted between the United States and Switzerland, the changes in the Swiss franc would have only a marginal effect on a TW index. TW indexes are constructed by several institutions, including the Morgan Guarantee Bank, the Bank of England, and the Federal Reserve.

Chart 30.1 shows a Federal Reserve TW index of the U.S. dollar with

Chart 30.1. The TW dollar and a 12-month ROC. (*Source: Pring Market Review.*)

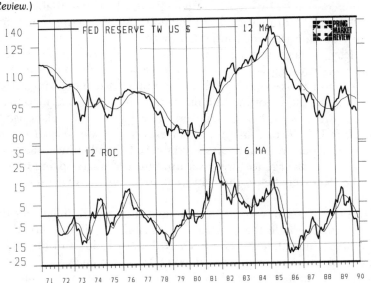

a 12-month rate of change (ROC), a 12-month moving average (MA) of the index, and a 6-month MA of the ROC indicator. When the 6-month MA crosses zero, most of the time it is associated with a major move in the dollar index but only if confirmed by an MA crossover by the index itself. Sometimes these signals are rather late, as for example, the one that was triggered at the end of 1985.

Another technique which has proved useful in analyzing the overall technical structure of a currency is to compare its TW index with an advance/decline (A/D) line, as shown in Charts 30.2*a* and *b*. The A/D line for the U.S. dollar, shown as the middle series of both charts, is constructed by taking a simple cumulative weekly plurality of the U.S. dollar in relation to a basket of currencies using a Friday close as a basis. If the dollar rises against eight currencies and falls against four, the plurality (+4) is added to the cumulated total of the previous week. In this example, 12 currencies and gold have been used in the construction, but there is no reason not to use a larger basket of currencies in the analysis. The comparison between the TW index and the A/D line is useful because the two series do not always move together. When they are moving in concert, the prevailing trend is reaffirmed, but when they move in opposite directions or one does not confirm the other, a warning of a probable reversal in trend is given.

Some examples are shown in Charts 30.2*a* and *b*. For example, the two higher peaks in the TW index in 1979 were not confirmed by a similar action in the A/D line. Although the TW index did not sell off, a new high was seen only after about 10 months. In turn, this new high was not confirmed by the A/D line in 1980, which was unable to surpass its 1979 high. A dramatic sell-off followed. Similarly, the September low in the A/D line was not confirmed by the TW index, and this was followed by a major trend reversal, this time to the upside. One other point worth noting is that between 1978 and early 1980 the A/D line formed and broke out from a broadening formation with a flat top. Throughout the following bull market, each index confirmed the other as new highs were being achieved. The use of this relationship was therefore limited to confirming that everything was in gear technically during this period. This analysis did prove helpful at the 1985 peak. It's true that no divergences were set up, but in the late spring both series crossed decisively below their 40-week MAs for the first time in several years.

The discussion has so far been limited to the U.S. dollar, but there is nothing to preclude the construction of similar indicators for the other currencies. Indeed, it is useful to chart the TW indexes of the major currencies as an important starting point for their analysis. For example, Chart 30.1 shows that the U.S. TW index was forming a top in 1976,

Chart 30.2a. The U.S. dollar and the A/D line. (*Source: Pring Market Review.*)

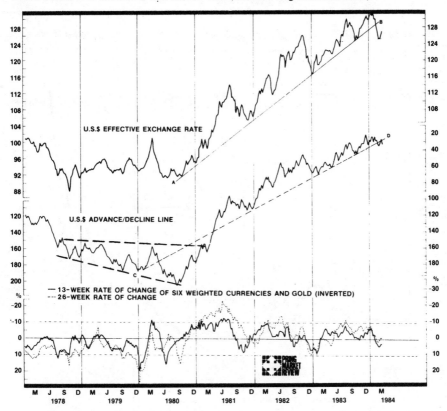

Chart 30.2b. The TW dollar and the dollar A/D line, 1982–1990. (*Source: Pring Market Review.*)

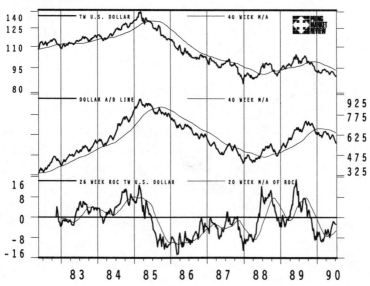

Chart 30.3. The TW Japanese yen and a 12-month ROC. (*Source: Pring Market Review.*)

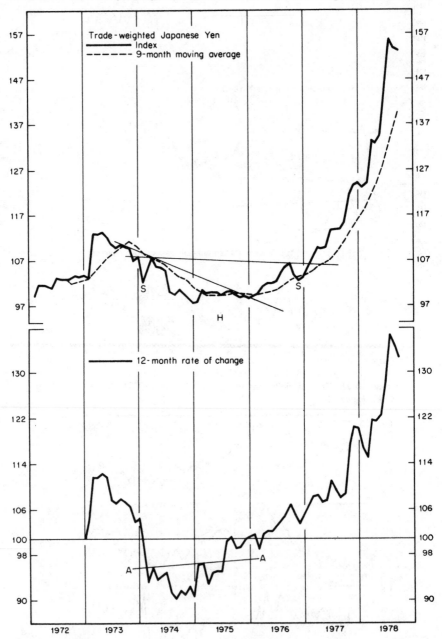

whereas the TW index for the Japanese yen shown on Chart 30.3 reveals the formation of a very large inverse head-and-shoulders (H&S) pattern between 1974 and 1976. It can be seen from this simple comparison that the U.S. dollar was likely to decline and that the yen was probably embarking on a major bull market. It was relatively simple at the time, therefore, to conclude that the yen should be bought against the U.S. dollar.

Analysis of Individual Currency Relationships

Charts 30.4 through 30.8 represent the major currencies against the U.S. dollar from 1978 to 1990. The format for the pound and Canadian dollar includes the currency, an MA, and two ROCs. Since an ROC index measures momentum over a given cycle, using two indexes helps to show whether the two cycles are in gear. For instance, it is normal for them both to move in the same general direction; their *relationship* is not offering any forecasting value. On the other hand, if they have been moving in opposite directions for some time or if they are wide apart, a warning is given that the cycles are not in gear and that *perhaps* an important change in the prevailing trend is going to take place. A classic example of this phenomenon in winter 1980 can be seen

Chart 30.4. The British pound. (*Source: Pring Market Review.*)

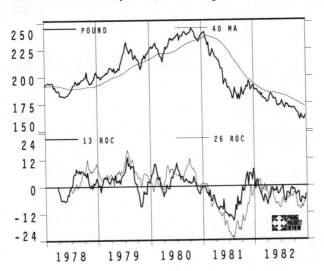

Chart 30.5. The Canadian dollar. (*Source: Pring Market Review.*)

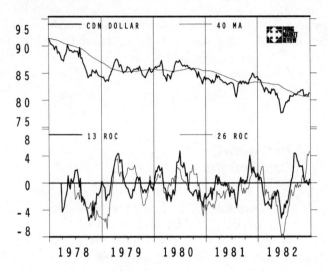

Chart 30.6. The Deutsch mark. The KST is a smoothed weighted summed rate of change. The three series in the chart represent a proxy for short, intermediate, and primary trends. Important buy signals occur when all three series are above their EMAs and vice versa. (*Source: Pring Market Review.*)

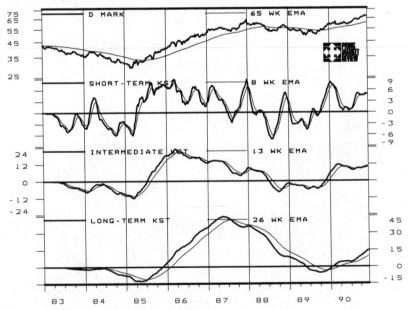

Chart 30.7. The Swiss franc. The KST is a smoothed weighted summed rate of change. (*Source: Pring Market Review.*)

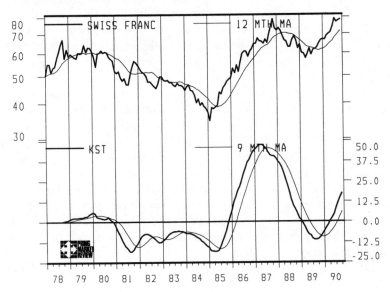

Chart 30.8. The Japanese yen. (*Source: Pring Market Review.*)

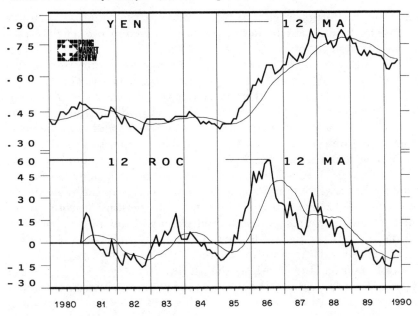

in Chart 30.4, which shows the British pound. At the time of the bull market peak, the 26-week ROC reached a 16-month high, yet the 13-week ROC had been trending in the opposite direction since the summer of that year and was able to rally only anemically at that time. A similar type of divergence from several other currencies could also be observed during that same period; it further emphasized dollar strength.

In Chart 30.5 the Canadian dollar shows many of these divergences. At the beginning of 1979, for example, a bullish divergence developed, since the 26-week ROC index was in a sideways-to-declining trend during late 1978 and early 1979, while its 13-week counterpart was basically in a rising phase. The result of this divergence, which was completely opposite in nature to that of the British pound discussed above, was to signal a reversal of the previous downward trend. Chart 30.5 also reveals that while it is normal for such divergences to result in a sharp sell-off (for a negative divergence) or rally (for a positive divergence), these do not always occur; instead, a fairly lengthy period of consolidation can develop (e.g., mid-1979).

Charts 30.5, 30.6, and 30.7 demonstrate alternative approaches to currency analysis.

Technical Analysis of Interest-Adjusted Currencies

The level of short-term interest rates changes from country to country because of the differing monetary policies pursued by the central banks of the different countries.

Cross-currency rates for future delivery take these interest-rate differentials into consideration and are priced accordingly. For instance, U.K. short-term money-market instruments were yielding 15 percent in the early part of the 1990s, but U.S. rates started the decade at 8.5 percent. This meant that investors who bought pounds and held them for 12 months would be ahead by 6.5 percent in comparison to what they would have had if they had held U.S. dollars (i.e., they would have been ahead by the difference between 15 percent and 8.5 percent). If you believed that there was not going to be any change in the value of the dollar/pound relationship over the coming 12 months, it would make sense to convert your U.S. cash to pounds, invest the money, and then sell the pounds for future delivery. In this way you would obtain the interest differential without the currency risk by being long pounds in the cash market and short in the futures (i.e., you would have a hedge). However, because the sterling money-market instrument would be paying 15 percent and the U.S. only 8.5 percent, you would earn an additional 6.5 percent on your money. There is a catch, however: other people have thought of the same idea, and the sterling you sell for 1-year future delivery actually is priced 6½ percent below sterling for spot or cash delivery. In other words, a discount is built into the price of the currency to compensate for the interest-rate differential.

This market pricing mechanism can be turned to the advantage of the technician, for if a normal spot cross-currency relationship is looking strong technically and the interest-rate differential is also positive, the possibilities of a profitable trade or investment are substantially increased. The top series in Chart 30.9 shows the Australian dollar versus the yen on a normal basis. The second series shows the same relationship, but adjusted for the interest-rate differential (based on 3-month Eurodollar deposits). The significant difference between the two series in the chart is the 12 percent interest-rate differential, which means that a trader on the long side of the yen has to make 12 percent in (yen) appreciation just to break even.

The importance of this market pricing mechanism from a technical aspect is that if you can isolate a trend reversal in an unadjusted currency cross rate and there is a significant interest-rate differential, you can achieve a form of built-in insurance against whipsaws.

The major problem occurs if you are leveraged and the interest-rate

Chart 30.9. The Australian dollar versus the Japanese yen, allowing for interest-rate differentials. (*Source: Pring Market Review.*)

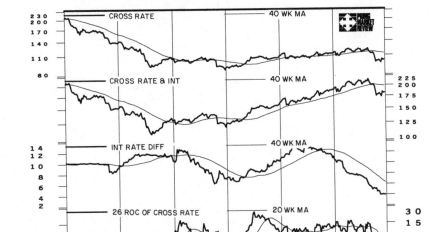

differential gets substantially wider as the position goes against you. In that situation the currency itself declines, and because the differential widens, the discount for delivery also widens.

By and large, though, if the technical position of the currency is positive, the odds of achieving a superior rate of return are far higher when a favorable interest-rate differential is present. It should be noted that the Australian dollar/yen example described above reflects an unusually wide interest-rate differential.

Summary

1. Technical analysis of individual currencies should begin from an analysis of an overall measurement known as a *trade-weighted (TW) index*.

2. Once a strong currency has been isolated, it is important to find a weak currency to sell against it.

3. A/D lines, MAs, and oscillators are also useful in analysis of currencies.

4. Superior results are achieved when a cross relationship shows a positive technical position and a wide and favorable interest-rate differential.

31
Technical Analysis of Commodity Markets

Introduction

Since commodity markets are so highly leveraged and volatile, it is probably true to say that technical analysis is used more widely in this area than any other. Most commodity transactions are consummated within a very short time, quite often within the course of a single day. For this reason, commodity traders have tended to concentrate on charts and systems geared to the very short term. The basic principles outlined in Chapters 5 to 12 can be applied to individual commodities. This chapter will describe how to identify important trend reversals in the overall commodity price structure, and how to capitalize on these situations with the help of relative-strength (RS) analysis. It is oriented toward commodity traders who wish to obtain a longer-term and macro background for these challenging markets. A brief discussion of seasonal aspects is also included.

Establishing a Reference Point

Technical analysis of commodity markets should begin with a commodity index rather than a particular commodity. There is no widely followed index such as the Dow Jones Industrial Average (DJIA), which is constantly quoted in the global press. This is probably because no convenient method of weighting commodities has been found to be widely acceptable.

It is also of note that individual commodities move counter to the general commodity trend more than individual stocks do, often because of specific fundamental factors totally unrelated to the business cycle.

The most widely followed (futures) composite index in the United States is the Commodity Research Bureau (CRB) Composite Index, which is constructed from 21 different industrial and agricultural commodities but is quite heavily influenced by changes in the prices of grains. The same organization also publishes several subindexes based on futures contracts such as grains and livestock. In addition, it calculates and publishes two spot commodity indexes. The CRB Spot Commodity Index is constructed from the cash price of 22 commodities covering the agricultural and industrial sectors. The CRB Spot Raw Materials Index, which used to be published by the Bureau of Labor Statistics, consists purely of industrial raw material prices. Another widely used index is the *Journal of Commerce* Industrial Raw Materials Index. Both industrial indexes are influenced by economic developments rather than weather, which has a tendency to drive agricultural prices.

The Economist, an internationally known publication which is based in London, publishes a composite index in which each commodity is weighted by its share of world trade. (The same data is shown in terms of pound sterling.) *The Economist* also publishes several subindexes such as the Metals Index and the Fibers Index. *The Economist* Dollar Index is shown in Chart 31.1.

The relative performances of the various composite indexes can and do vary considerably. Chart 31.1, for example, compares the performance of the CRB Composite Index with that of *The Economist* and the *Journal of Commerce* Industrial Raw Materials Index. The chart shows that while the indexes move in concert a substantial portion of the time, there are some glaring instances in which they do not.

For example, the performance of the *Journal of Commerce* Index differed greatly from that of the CRB Composite and *The Economist* Index during the 1988–1990 period. These different performances reflect alternative weightings by various commodities, emphasizing that there really is no "perfect" indicator for overall commodity price movements.

Since it is important to be able to use an indicator for monitoring rel-

Chart 31.1. *The Economist* versus the CRB and the *Journal of Commerce*. (*Source: Pring Market Review.*)

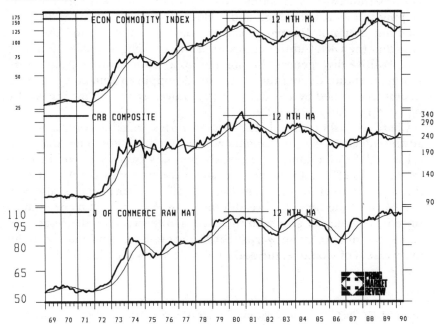

ative strength (RS), a selection must be made. The CRB Index has been selected for the following reasons: First, the formula for spot commodity prices developed by the CRB has been adopted by the U.S. government for reporting purposes. (The spot and futures index formulas are relatively similar.) Second, this organization also publishes subindexes which, along with the spot index, can be used for comparative analytical purposes. Third, the CRB Index and its subindexes can be easily obtained in either data or chart form from the CRB. Fourth, the data are also relatively easy to obtain from the financial press or popular databases.

Analyzing Major and Intermediate Trends

The techniques for determining the trends of commodity indexes are basically the same as those used with other markets. Price patterns, trendlines, moving averages (MAs), and rate-of-change (ROC) indica-

tors are all valid techniques. Chart 31.2, for example, shows the CRB
Futures Index with a 12-month ROC. This indicator was very useful in
helping to identify the 1982 and 1986 bottoms. In both cases, the momentum indicator formed a base and broke out at around the same
time that the CRB Futures Index itself was crossing above its 12-month
MA. Positive divergences also pointed up a distinct shrinkage in downside momentum during these periods. A topping formation in the oscillator, confirmed by a negative MA crossover and trendline break, also
signaled the early 1989 sell-off.

Chart 31.3 shows the CRB Futures Index together with a weekly
advance/decline (A/D) line and a net new high indicator. The A/D line is
calculated from a cumulative weekly plurality of a basket of 16 commodities. In effect, it is identical to the construction of the A/D line for
the equity market (discussed in Chapter 19). Interpretation is also similar. Most of the time this breadth indicator does not tell us very much
since it is moving in gear with the CRB. However, when their paths diverge, the disagreement warns that the prevailing trend may be about
to reverse. For example, the A/D line made a new high in mid-1984, but

Chart 31.2. The CRB and a 12-month ROC. (*Source: Pring Market Review.*)

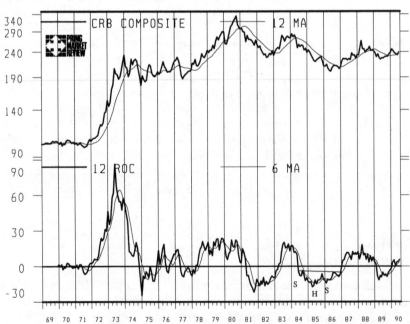

Chart 31.3. The CRB and two measures of breadth. (*Source: Pring Market Review.*)

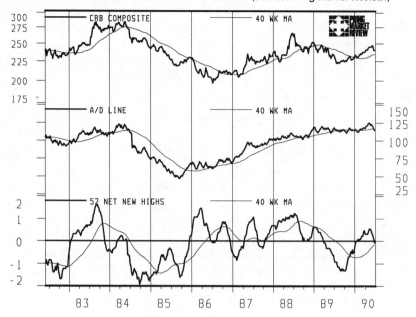

the CRB Futures Index failed to confirm it. In 1986 the A/D line refused to confirm the bear market CRB low. Both divergences, or disagreements, were followed by a reversal in trend. Joint trendline violations can also provide timely and reliable signals of trend reversals, for example, the one that occurred in early 1987.

The Net New High Index is a plot of a 6-week MA of the percentage of a basket of 16 commodities that record net new highs over a 52-week period. It too offers a further clue about the quality of the prevailing trend. For example, the 1984 high in the CRB Futures Index was accompanied by a very low level of net new highs, which pointed up weakness in the underlying upside momentum. More often than not, a sell signal is generated when the Net New High indicator, having crossed through its overbought zone, recrosses back on its way toward zero.

There are many other ways to identify major trend reversals in commodity indexes. Examples include seasonal momentum (see Chart 31.4) and a market cycle model using the *know sure thing* (KST) approach, as shown in Chart 31.5.

Chart 31.4. The *Journal of Commerce* Spot Raw Materials Index and seasonal momentum. (*Source: Pring Market Review.*)

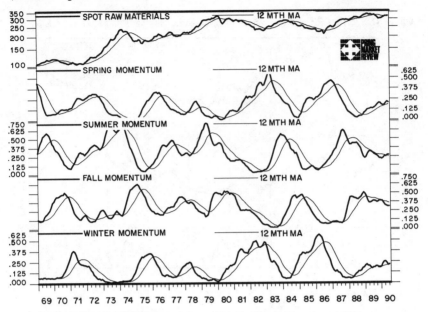

Chart 31.5. The CRB Composite and three KST measures. The KST is a smoothed weighted summed rate of change. The three series in the chart represent a proxy for short, intermediate, and primary trends. Important buy signals occur when all three series are above their EMAs and vice versa. (*Source: Pring Market Review.*)

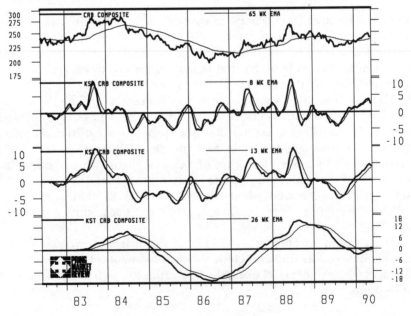

Relative Strength Analysis
Using Commodity Subindexes

General

Analyzing the various subindexes is worthwhile because the trend of individual commodity markets can be very diverse. Commodities in general are lagging indicators, unlike stocks, which usually show some recognizable form of group rotation. Consequently, there is no conceptual rotation pattern which can be used as a framework for further analysis. Each group has to be assessed on its own technical merits. The analysis of subindexes is useful, first, to identify prospective areas in which to trade, and second, as a basis for RS analysis. The approach used is very similar to that described in Chapter 28 for individual stocks. Whereas the stock market can be conveniently subdivided into 70 or 80 groups, commodity subgroupings are effectively limited to grains, soft commodities, livestock, metals, energy, textiles, and fats and oils.

Isolating a Strong Subgroup

Once it is established that commodities in general are in a primary bull market, the next step is to examine the RS position of the various groups.

Chart 31.6 shows the CRB Composite Index with the metals subcomponent. The CRB Composite made an important low in August 1977 but was unconfirmed by the Metals Index, which had bottomed out earlier, in January 1976. The positive action by the metals indicated that this group was likely to outperform the CRB Composite Index in the coming period. Additional evidence emerged when both the Metals Index and its RS line (against the CRB Composite) broke above the intermediate down trendline AB. The chart shows that while the CRB Composite rallied over the following year, the performance of the Metals Index was far superior. A similar situation arose in mid-1982, when both the RS line and the Metals Index successfully broke above major down trendlines.

Chart 31.7 shows the 1982 period in greater detail. After an initial bounce, the Metals Index fell back and successfully tested its low. As the previous high was bettered in September, both the Metals Index and its RS line moved back above their down trendline (CD). The CRB Composite Index itself crossed above its 30-week MA, shown in Chart 31.7, setting the scene for a dynamic rally. The Composite Index rallied between September 1982 and February 1983, but the Metals Index performed even better.

Chart 31.6. The CRB Composite Index versus the CRB Metals Index, 1976–1983. (*Source: Dominion Securities Pitfield Graphics.*)

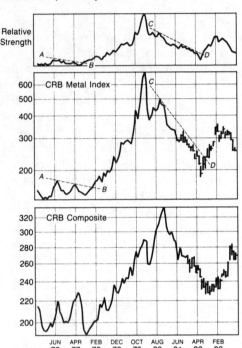

Selecting a Specific Commodity

While metals prices in general did well during this period, it should not be blindly assumed that a long position in all metals would have been profitable. This is illustrated in Chart 31.8, which shows the performance of London spot lead and New York spot silver, both expressed in RS terms against the CRB Metals Index. In the late summer of 1982, silver broke above its steep bear market downtrend (only the last few weeks of which are shown on the chart). As the silver RS indicator rallied above its trendline in July, lead's RS began to break down. Chart 31.8 shows that a long position in silver would have produced substantial profits, as compared to a long position in lead, which declined in price for the rest of 1982.

Identifying Changes in RS

RS analysis helps to determine deteriorating as well as improving technical situations. For example, Chart 31.7 shows that the relationship be-

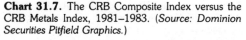

Chart 31.7. The CRB Composite Index versus the CRB Metals Index, 1981–1983. (*Source: Dominion Securities Pitfield Graphics.*)

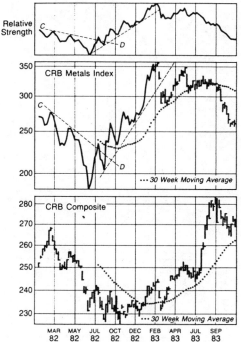

tween the Metals Index and the CRB Composite was changing dramatically in the early part of 1983, since the sharp February commodity price decline broke both the uptrend of the Metals Index and the uptrend of its RS line. Even though the Composite Index picked up steam and rallied sharply into the summer, the deteriorating technical structure of the metals markets would have made it difficult for participants on the long side to make any money.

When the metals began to break down, investors or speculators who were bullish on the overall trend of commodity prices would have found an analysis of RS relationships very helpful at this time. Chart 31.9 shows the CRB Grain Index with its RS against the Metals Index. In the late spring of 1983 several observations could be made. First, the Grain Index itself had been making a series of bullish ascending peaks and troughs. When it crossed its 30-week MA in June, it also broke

Chart 31.8. New York spot silver versus London spot lead. (*Source: Dominion Securities Pitfield Graphics.*)

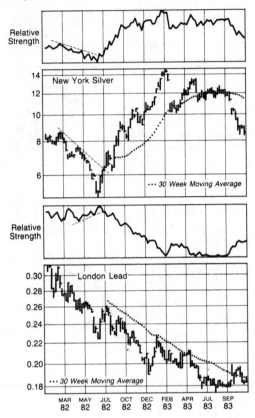

above a small intermediate down trendline, indicating that the test of the February low had been successful. Since the CRB Composite Index had previously broken out of a major inverse head-and-shoulders (H&S) pattern and found support around the neckline, the odds were pretty high that the overall commodity bull market was still intact. An examination of the RS line of the grains against the metals in the upper panel showed that grains were the better candidate. This was because the RS index had not only broken above an important down trendline *EF,* but had also completed a downward-sloping inverse H&S pattern. This view was later validated by the price action.

Seasonal Aspects

Seasonality in commodity prices is influenced by temporary changes in the supply-demand relationship, caused by factors which occur about

Chart 31.9. The CRB Grain Index with its RS against the CRB Metals Index, 1981–1983. (*Source: Dominion Securities Pitfield Graphics.*)

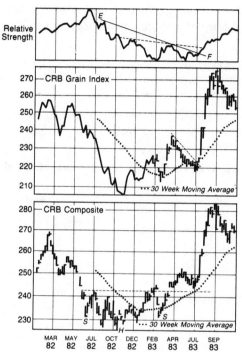

the same time each year. Agricultural commodities appear to have the strongest seasonal tendencies. On the supply side, such factors as harvest, planting, weather patterns, and navigation on the Great Lakes are very important. Demand is affected by seasonal consumption, feed demand, export patterns, soybean crushings, etc. Seasonal tendencies do not always work, since longer-term fundamental factors often outweigh them. Readers who wish to study this subject in greater detail are referred to *Seasonality in Agricultural Futures Markets.*[1]

Metals prices also appear to be affected by seasonality. Typically the best seasonal buying opportunity occurs sometime between late October and early January. Important peaks in prices develop in the February–May period and again following a summer rally, and seasonal highs develop in the late summer and early fall.

[1]Written and published by ContiCommodity Services, Inc.

Summary

1. The overall trends of commodity prices are subject to primary bull and bear markets, but individual commodity prices are generally more independent of the general price trend than are individual stocks.

2. A commodity price index should be used to monitor general commodity price movements. The CRB Composite Index, although far from perfect, is recommended for this purpose.

3. Major buying and selling points for both the indexes and the individual commodities can be identified from price trend, momentum, and breadth analyses.

4. Commodity selection can be profitably made through RS analysis.

Epilog

The suggestion was made at the outset that the keys to success in the stock market were knowledge and action. The "knowledge" part of the equation has been discussed as comprehensively as possible, but the final word has been reserved for investor "action," since the way in which knowledge is used is just as important as understanding the process itself.

Indicated below are some common errors which all of us commit more often than we would like to. The most obvious of these can be avoided by applying the accompanying principles.

1. *Perspective.* The interpretation of any indicator should not be based on short-term trading patterns; the longer-term implications should always be considered.

2. *Objectivity.* A conclusion should not be drawn on the basis of one or two "reliable" or "favorite" indicators. The possibility that these indicators could give misleading signals demonstrates the need to form a a balanced view derived from *all* available information.

3. *Humility.* One of the hardest lessons in life is learning to admit a mistake. The knowledge of all market participants in the aggregate is, and always will be, greater than that of any one individual or group of individuals. This knowledge is expressed in the action of the market itself, as reflected by the various indicators. Anyone who "fights the tape" or the verdict of the market will swiftly suffer the consequences. Under such circumstances, it is as well to become humble and let the market give its own verdict; a review of the indicators will frequently suggest the future direction of the markets. Occasionally the analysis proves to be wrong, and the market fails to act as anticipated. If this unexpected action changes the basis on which the

original conclusion was drawn, it is wise to admit the mistake and alter the conclusion.

4. *Tenacity.*   If the circumstances outlined above develop but it is considered that the technical position has *not* changed, the original opinion should not be changed either.

5. *Independent thought.*   If a review of the indicators suggests a position that is not attuned to the majority view, that conclusion is probably well founded. On the other hand, a conclusion should never be drawn simply because it is opposed to the majority view. In other words, contrariness for its own sake is not valid. Since the majority conclusion is usually based on false assumptions, it is prudent to examine such assumptions to determine their accuracy.

6. *Simplicity.*   Most things done well are also done simply. Because the market operates on common sense, the best approaches to it are basically very simple. If an analyst must resort to complex computer programming and model building, the chances are that he or she has not mastered the basic techniques and therefore requires an analytical crutch.

7. *Discretion.*   There is a persistent temptation to call every possible market turn, along with the duration of every move the stock market is likely to make. This deluded belief in one's power to pull off the impossible inevitably results in failure, a loss of confidence, and damage to one's reputation. For this reason, analysis should concentrate on identifying major turning points rather than predicting the duration of a move—because there is no known formula on which consistent and accurate forecasts of this type can be based.

Appendix **A**

Candle Charts[1]

Candle charts originated in Japan several centuries ago but have recently gained a following in other countries. This system of plotting price data is an alternative to the familiar bar chart. Candle charts can be used to identify price patterns, and they also lend themselves to trendline construction. They are constructed from opening, high, low, and closing data for a specific period such as an hour, day, or week.

Bar charts are expressed as vertical lines, with the left and right handles representing the opening and closing levels. Candle charts, on the other hand, are plotted as vertical rectangular boxes that connect the opening and closing prices, and with vertical lines that extend from the rectangles to encompass the extreme high and low. Bar charts treat all data more or less equally, but candle charts place great emphasis on the trading range between the opening and closing prices, and also differentiate between which is higher. It is important to note that candle charts can be plotted only for markets in which opening prices as well as closes, highs, and lows are known. Proponents of this system believe that it provides all the information contained in bar charts as well as additional ideas contained only in candle charts. Candle charts are not a Holy Grail, but they are certainly a useful adjunct to the technical arsenal. In this description we will refer to days, since they are the most common time frame, but bear in mind that candle charts can be constructed for any time period.

A typical candle really consists of two parts: the "real body," i.e., the rectangular part, and the "shadow" or "wick," i.e., the two vertical extensions. The top and bottom of the rectangle are determined by the opening and closing prices for the day. If the closing price ends up

---

[1]Source for candle chart information: Steve Nison, *Japanese Candlestick Charting Techniques*, New York Institute of Finance, New York, 1991.

491

above the opening (the real body), it is plotted in white. When the price closes *below* the opening, it is plotted in black (Figure A.1). In a black real body, the top of the rectangle represents the opening price and the bottom the close. This is reversed in the case of a white rectangle, where the close is plotted at the top and the open at the bottom.

The thin vertical shadow lines that protrude from the real body reflect the high and low for the day. Since closing and opening prices can be the same as each other, or identical with the high or low, there are a number of possible combinations that need to be represented. Some of them are shown in Figure A.1. Candlesticks provide essentially the same information as bar charts, but their more pronounced visual representation of the material enables technicians to identify characteristics that are less obvious on bar charts. Certain phenomena illustrated in bar charts have been given their own names, such as "key reversal days" or "island reversal days." Likewise, with candle charts, because of the large number of potential variations for both individual days and price formations encompassing several days, it has been common practice to give exotic names to the various possibilities. The characteristics of some of the more common candles are shown in Figure A.1.

Figure A.1*a* shows the "long white line," a wide trading range where the opening is close to the low and the high is near the close—bullish. Figure A.1*b* is the "long black line," a wide trading range where the opening is close to the high and the close near the day's low—bearish. Figure A.1*c*, A.1*d,* and A.1*e* shows "doji lines," where opening and closing prices are identical. Interpretation depends upon the context in which they appear. Figure A.1*f* and A.1*g* illustrates "umbrella lines," where the real body is narrow and develops at the high end of the day's trading range. Umbrella lines are bullish at bottoms and bearish at tops. Figure A.1*h* and A.1*i* shows "spinning tops," representing days when the trading range is very small. They do not have any significance in trading ranges but are important in some of the price formations discussed later.

Candle charts offer indications of both reversal and continuation

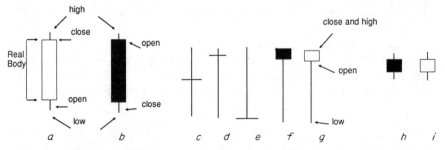

Figure A.1. Examples of daily lines.

phenomena, just as bar charts do. Some examples in this chapter demonstrate these phenomena in candlestick formations (see Charts A.1 to A.4). Candlesticks really come into their own in the identification of shorter-term reversals and continuation situations.

Reversal Phenomena

Hammers and Hanging Men (Takuri and Kubitsuri)

These formations (Figure A.1*f* and A.1*g*) have probably gained more notoriety than all the others because of their imposing titles. A "hanging man" is an umbrella line that develops after a rally. It looks rather like the body of a man with dangling legs and, as its name implies, is a bearish pattern. If a hanging man appears after a prolonged upmove, it should be treated with respect, especially if it occurs after a gap. A hanging man can be identified by the fact that the shadow, or wick, is at least twice the height of the real body. The color of the body is not important.

A "hammer" is identical to a hanging man but occurs after a market decline, when it is a bullish sign. It gets its name from the idea that the price is "hammering out" a bottom. In effect, it represents the kind of trading day when the price temporarily slips quite sharply, for there is a "run" on the selling stops. Nevertheless, the technical position is sufficiently constructive to cause buyers to come into the market and push the price back up toward or above the opening level.

Dark Cloud Cover (Kabuse)

In real life dark clouds (Figure A.2) hint at the possibility of rain, so a "dark cloud" candlestick formation implies lower prices. Its bearish connotations are most pronounced during an uptrend or in the upper part of a congestion zone. It is a form of key reversal, since the price closes down on the day after a gap higher opening. It consists of 2 days. The

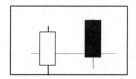

Figure A.2. Dark cloud cover (kabuse).

first is a strong white real body, and the second is a black body in which the close occurs in the lower half of the previous white real body.

Piercing Line (Kirikomi)

This pattern (Figure A.3) would be more aptly named "sunny sky" because it is the exact opposite of the dark cloud and is therefore bullish. It is important to note whether the second day's white body closes more than halfway above the previous body. If it does not, conventional wisdom indicates that additional weakness is likely.

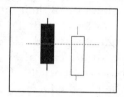

Figure A.3. Piercing line (kirikomi)

Engulfing Pattern (Tsutsumi)

This formation (Figure A.4) develops significance after a prolonged price move. It is characterized by two consecutive shadowless real bodies, in which the second day "engulfs" the first. It is bullish in a downtrend, when the second day is a white body, and bearish in an uptrend, when it appears as a black one.

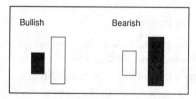

Figure A.4. Engulfing pattern (tsutsumi).

Stars (Hoshi)

Stars (Figure A.5) are common phenomena in candle charts and come in four different reversal varieties. Stars are combinations of wide real bodies and spinning tops. The *morning star* heralds a new day (upmove) and is bullish. It consists of two long real bodies separated by a spinning top. The star is represented by the spinning top, which is made on a gap. The third body should be white and should result in a closing price more than halfway up the body of the first.

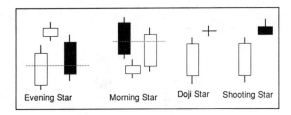

Figure A.5. Stars (hoshi).

The *evening star* is a precursor of night. It has the opposite characteristics and implications of a morning star.

A *doji star* is a bearish sign and occurs after a lengthy rally. It consists of a gap and a doji line.

A *shooting star* is like a short-term top where the daily price action experiences a small gap where the black real body appears at the end of a long wick or upper shadow.

Upside Gap Two Crows (Narabi Kuro)

This bearish formation (Figure A.6) consists of a long white line followed by two black lines. The first black line gaps to the upside. The third day often closes the gap, but because it is a black line where the close is below the open, its implication is bearish.

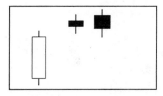

Figure A.6. Upside gap two crows (narabi kuro).

Continuation Formations

Upside Gap (Tasuki)

A tasuki gap (Figure A.7) occurs after an advance. The requirement is an upside white line gap followed by a black line *that does not close the gap.* This type of pattern is usually followed by higher prices. However, if the gap is filled, the formation deteriorates into an upside gap with one crow and therefore loses its bullish portent.

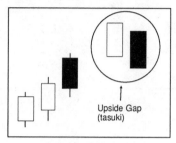

Figure A.7. Upside gap (tasuki).

Rising and Falling Three Methods

These formations (Figure A.8) are very similar in concept to a flag in bar charting, except that they take only a few days, not weeks, to develop. The rising method is a bullish pattern and consists of a powerful white line followed by a series of three or four declining small black lines. These lines should be accompanied by a noticeable contraction in volume which indicates that a very fine balance is developing between buyers and sellers. The final part of the pattern is a very strong white line that takes the price to a new closing high. If volume data are available, this final day should record a significant increase in activity. The bearish falling three methods is exactly the opposite except that volume characteristics are of no significance on the last day.

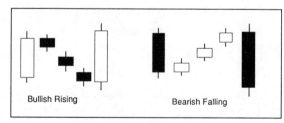

Figure A.8. Rising and falling three methods.

Windows (Ku)

Japanese chartists refer to gaps as "windows" (Figure A.9). Whereas gaps are said to be "filled" in traditional bar charts, windows are "closed" in candle charts. Windows therefore have the same technical implications as gaps.

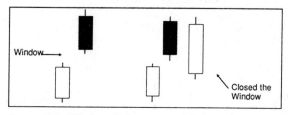

Figure A.9. Windows (ku).

Harami Lines

Chapter 7 mentioned that trendline violations are followed by either a reversal or a temporary consolidation. The meeting line formation (Figure A.10) is similar to the consolidation trendline break in that it indicates a loss of momentum. The main difference is that harami lines are of much shorter duration and consist of 2 days' price action. The second one, i.e., the harami, forms a real body that is sufficiently small to be engulfed by the prior day's *long* real body. If the harami is also a doji, as in Figure A.10, it is called a "harami cross." These patterns often warn of an impending trend change, especially if they follow a series of strong white line up days.

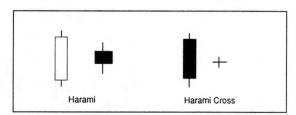

Figure A.10. Meeting lines (harami).

Summary

Candle charts can be constructed only from data that include opening prices, and therefore the technique is not one that can be applied to all markets. Candle charts provide a unique visual effect that emphasizes certain market characteristics not easily identifiable from bar or closing charts. Candlesticks can be plotted automatically through popular software packages such as MetaStock and Computrac, which are listed in the Resource section.

Examples of candle charts are shown in Charts A.1 through A.4.

Chart A.1. *Financial Times* stock exchange 100 cash.

Chart A.2. New York light crude 3-month perpetual (October 1989–March 1990).

Chart A.3. New York light crude perpetual (August–December 1990).

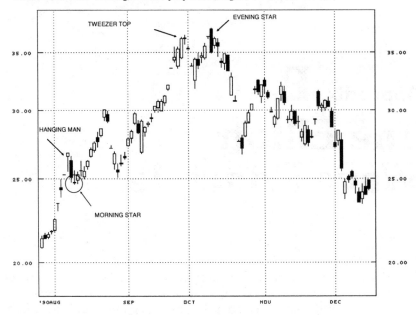

Chart A.4. Treasury bonds.

Appendix B
The Elliott Wave Principle

The Elliott Wave Principle was established by R. N. Elliott and first published in a series of articles in *Financial World* in 1939. The basis of Elliott Wave theory developed from the observation that rhythmic regularity has been the law of creation since the beginning of time. Elliott noted that all cycles in nature, whether of the tide, the heavenly bodies, the planets, day and night, or even life and death, had the capability for repeating themselves indefinitely. Those cyclical movements were characterized by two forces—one building up, the other tearing down.

This concept of natural law also embraces an extraordinary numerical series discovered by a thirteenth-century mathematician named Fibonacci. The series which carries his name is derived by taking the number 2 and adding to it the previous number in the series. Thus $2 + 1 = 3$, then $3 + 2 = 5$, $5 + 3 = 8, 8 + 5 = 13, 13 + 8 = 21, 21 + 13 = 34$, etc. The series becomes 1, 2, 3, 5, 8, 13, 21, 34, 55, 89, 144, 233, etc. It has a number of fascinating properties, among which are:

1. The sum of any two consecutive numbers forms the number following them. Thus $3 + 5 = 8$ and $5 + 8 = 13$, etc.

2. The ratio of any number to its next higher is 61.8 to 100, and the ratio of any number to its next lower is 161.8 to 100.

3. The ratio 1.68 multiplied by the ratio 0.618 equals 1.

The connection between Elliott's observation of repeating cycles of nature and the Fibonacci summation series is that the Fibonacci numbers and proportions are found in many manifestations of nature. For example, a sunflower has 89 curves, of which 55 wind in one direction and 34 in the opposite direction. In music, an octave comprises 13 keys on a piano, with 5 black notes and 8 white. Trees always branch from the base in Fibonacci series, and so on.

Combining his observation of natural cycles with his knowledge of the Fibonacci series, Elliott noted in an 80-year period that the market moved forward in a series of five waves, and then declined in a series of three waves. He concluded that a single cycle comprised eight waves, as shown in Figure B.1 (3, 5, and 8 are of course Fibonacci numbers).

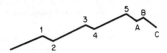

Figure B.1.

The longest cycle in the Elliott concept is called the Grand Super-cycle. In turn each Grand Supercycle can be subdivided into eight supercycle waves, each of which is then divided into eight cycle waves. The process continues to embrace Primary, Intermediate, Minute, Minuette, and Sub-Minuette waves. The various details are highly intri-cate, but the general picture is represented in Figures B.1 and B.2.

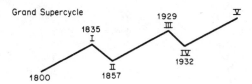

Figure B.2.

Figures B.2 and B.3 show Elliott in historical perspective. Figure B.2 illustrates the first five waves of the Grand Supercycle, which Elliott deemed to have begun in 1800. As the wave principle is one of form, there is no way to determine when the three corrective waves are likely to appear. However, the frequent recurrence of Fibonacci numbers representing time spans between peaks and troughs are probably be-yond coincidence. These time spans are shown in Table B.1.

More recently, 8 years occurred between the 1966 and 1974 bottoms and the 1968 and 1976 tops, and 5 years between the 1968 and 1973 tops, for example.

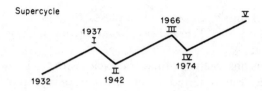

Figure B.3.

Table B.1. Time Spans between Stock Market Peaks and Troughs

Year started	Position	Year ended	Position	Length of cycle (years)
1916	Top	1921	Bottom	5
1919	Top	1924	Bottom	5
1924	Bottom	1929	Top	5
1932	Bottom	1937	Top	5
1937	Top	1942	Bottom	5
1956	Top	1961	Top	5
1961	Top	1966	Top	5
1916	Top	1924	Bottom	8
1921	Bottom	1929	Top	8
1924	Bottom	1932	Bottom	8
1929	Top	1937	Top	8
1938	Bottom	1946	Top	8
1949	Bottom	1957	Bottom	8
1960	Bottom	1968	Top	8
1962	Bottom	1970	Bottom	8
1916	Top	1929	Top	13
1919	Top	1932	Bottom	13
1924	Bottom	1937	Top	13
1929	Top	1942	Bottom	13
1949	Bottom	1962	Bottom	13
1953	Bottom	1966	Bottom	13
1957	Bottom	1970	Bottom	13
1916	Top	1937	Top	21
1921	Bottom	1942	Bottom	21
1932	Bottom	1953	Bottom	21
1949	Bottom	1970	Bottom	21
1953	Bottom	1974	Bottom	21
1919	Top	1953	Bottom	34
1932	Bottom	1966	Top	34
1942	Bottom	1976	Top	34
1919	Top	1974	Bottom	55
1921	Bottom	1976	Top	55

It can readily be seen that the real problem with Elliott is interpretation. Indeed, every wave theorist (including Elliott himself) has at some time or another become entangled with the question of where one wave finished and another started. As far as the Fibonacci time spans are concerned, although these periods recur frequently, it is extremely difficult to use this principle as a basis for forecasting; there are no indications whether time spans based on these numbers will produce tops to tops, or bottoms to tops, or something else, and the permutations are infinite.

The Elliott Wave is clearly a very subjective tool. Its subjectivity in itself can be dangerous because the market is very subject to emotional influences. For this reason, the weight given to Elliott interpretations should probably be downplayed. The old maxim "A little knowledge is a dangerous thing" applies probably more to Elliott than to any other market theory. The sources listed in the Resources section will give a fuller understanding of the principles involved, since the theory has been described here only in its barest outline.

Glossary

Advance/Decline (A/D) Line: An A/D line is constructed from a cumulative plurality of a set of data over a specified period (usually daily or weekly). The result is plotted as a continuous line. The A/D line and market averages usually move in the same direction. Failure of the A/D line to confirm a new high in the market average is a sign of weakness, whereas failure of the A/D line to confirm a new low by the market averages is a sign of technical strength.

Advisory Services: Privately circulated publications which comment upon the future course of financial markets, and for which a subscription is usually required.

Bear Trap: A signal which suggests that the rising trend of an index or stock has reversed but which proves to be false.

(Market) Breadth: Breadth relates to the number of issues participating in a move. A rally is considered suspect if the number of advancing issues is diminishing as the rally develops. Conversely, a decline which is associated with fewer and fewer stocks falling is considered to be a bullish sign.

Bull Trap: A signal which suggests that the declining trend of an index or stock has reversed but which proves to be false.

Customer Free Balances: The total amount of unused money on deposit in brokerage accounts. These are "free" funds representing cash which may be employed in the purchase of securities.

Cyclical Investing: The process of buying and selling stocks based on a longer-term or primary market move. The cycle approximates to the 4-year business cycle, to which such primary movements in stock prices are normally related.

Divergence: A nonconfirmation that is not cleared up. Negative divergences occur at market peaks, while positive divergences develop at market bottoms. The significance of a divergence is a direct function of its size; i.e., over time, the question is whether there is a series of divergences between the indicators and the number of indicators that are diverging.

Insider: Any person who directly or indirectly owns more than 10 percent of any class of stock listed on a national exchange, or who is an officer or director of the company in question.

Margin: Occurs when an investor pays part of the purchase price of a security and borrows the balance, usually from a broker; the "margin" is the difference between the market value of the stock and the loan which is made against it.

Margin Call: The demand upon a customer to put up money or securities with a broker. The call is made if a customer's equity in a margin account declines below a minimum standard set by the exchange or brokerage firm. This happens when there is a drop in price of the securities being held as collateral.

Members: Members of a stock exchange who are empowered to buy and sell securities on the floor of the exchange either for a client or for their own account.

Momentum: The underlying power or thrust behind an upward or downward price movement. Momentum is represented on a graph as a line that is continually fluctuating above and below a horizontal equilibrium level which represents the halfway point between extreme readings. Momentum is a generic term embracing many different indicators, such as rate of change (ROC), relative strength indicators (RSIs), and stochastics.

Moving Average (MA): A simple MA is constructed by taking a mean average of a time series over a given period. When the price crosses above or below the MA, a "buy" or "sell" signal is given. MAs often serve as support or resistance points.

Moving Average Convergence Divergence (MACD): An oscillator that measures the distance between two simple or exponential moving averages (MAs).

Nonconfirmation: A market is said to be "in gear" when most averages and indicators that form a part of it confirm successive highs or lows. For example, when the Dow Jones Industrial Average (DJIA) makes new highs, but the advance/decline (A/D) line does not, a nonconfirmation is said to occur. If other indicators or averages also fail to confirm, conditions are regarded as bearish until the nonconfirmations are cleared up, and vice versa.

Odd Lots: Units of stock of less than 100 shares; these do not customarily appear on the tape.

Odd-Lot Shorts: Odd lots that are sold short. Since odd lots are usually the vehicle of uninformed traders, a high level of odd-lot shorts in relation to total odd-lot sales often characterizes a major market bottom. A low level of odd-lot shorts compared with total odd-lot sales is a sign of a market top.

Option: The right to buy or sell specific securities at a specified price within a specified time. A "put" gives the holder the right to sell the stock, a "call" the right to buy the stock. In recent years options on specific stocks have been listed on several exchanges, so that it is now possible to trade these instruments in the same way that the underlying stocks can be bought and sold.

Overbought: An opinion about the level of prices. It may refer to a specific indicator or to the market as a whole after a period of vigorous buying, following which it may be argued that prices are overextended for the time being and are in need of a period of downward or horizontal adjustment.

Oversold: An opinion about the level of prices. It is the opposite of overbought, i.e., a price move that has overextended itself on the downside.

Over-the-Counter (OTC) Market: An informal collection of brokers and dealers. Securities traded include almost all federal, state, municipal, and corporate bonds and all widely owned equity issues not listed on the stock exchanges.

Price/Earnings Ratio: The ratio of the price of a stock to the earnings per share, i.e., the total annual profit of a company divided by the number of shares outstanding.

Price Patterns: When a trend reverses direction, the price action typically traces out a formation known as a *reversal pattern*. The larger and deeper the pattern, the greater is its significance. Patterns that are formed at market tops are called *distribution formations;* i.e., the stock or market is assumed to be undergoing distribution from strong, informed hands to weak, uninformed buyers. Price patterns at market bottoms are known as *accumulation formations*. Price formations may also represent temporary interruptions of the prevailing trend, in which case they are called *continuation patterns*.

Rally: A brisk rise following a decline or consolidation of the general price level of the market.

Reaction: A temporary price weakness following an upswing.

Relative Strength (RS): An RS line or index is calculated by dividing one price by another. Usually the divisor is a measure of "the market," such as the Dow Jones Industrial Average (DJIA) or the Commodity Research Bureau (CRB) Commodity Index. A rising line indicates that the index or stock is performing better than "the market," and vice versa.

Trends in RS can be monitored by moving average (MA) crossovers, trendline breaks, etc., in the same way as any other indicator.

Relative Strength Indicator (RSI): An oscillator measuring the internal momentum of a price series. The RSI is designed to oscillate between 0 and 100. It can be calculated for any time span, but 14 days is the most commonly used period. It should not be confused with relative strength

(RS), which measures relative performance bewtween two different time spans.

Secondary Distribution or Offering: The redistribution of a block of stock some time after it has been sold by the issuing company. The sale is handled off the exchanges by a securities firm or group of firms, and the shares are usually offered at a fixed price which is related to the current market price of the stock.

Short Covering: The process of buying back stock that has already been sold short.

Short-Interest Ratio: The ratio of the short position to the average daily trading volume of the month in question. A high short-interest ratio (above 1.8) is considered bullish, and a low one (below 1.15) is considered bearish.

Short Position (Interest): The total amount of short sales outstanding on a specific exchange at a particular time. The short position is published monthly.

Short Selling: Short selling is normally a speculative operation undertaken in the belief that the price of the shares will fall. It is accomplished by borrowing stock from a broker in order to sell shares one does not own. Most stock exchanges prohibit the short sale of a security below the price at which the last board lot was traded.

Specialist: A member of a stock exchange who acts as a specialist in a listed issue and who is registered with the exchange for that purpose. The member agrees to efficiently execute all orders and, insofar as is reasonably practical, to maintain a fair and orderly market in the issue or issues for which he or she is a specialist.

Trendlines: Trendlines are constructed by joining a series of descending peaks or ascending troughs. Greater significance is attached to a break in the trendline the more times it has been touched, the longer the line remains viable, and the less steep its angle. A trendline break does not necessarily signal a trend reversal.

Yield Curve: The structure of the level of interest rates through various maturities. Usually the shorter the maturity, the lower the interest rate. Thus, 3-month Treasury bills usually yield less than 20-year government bonds. The slope of the yield curve relates to the speed with which rates rise as the maturity increases. In periods of tight money, short-term rates usually yield more than longer-term rates, and the curve is then called an *inverse yield curve*.

Resources

Books

Appel, G.: *Winning Stock Market Systems*, Signalert Corp., Great Neck, N.Y., 1974.

Ayres, L. P.: *Turning Points in Business Cycles*, August M. Kelly, New York, 1967.

Benner, S.: *Benner's Prophecies of Future Ups and Downs in Prices*, Chase and Hall, Cincinnati, 1875. Reprinted in *Journal of Cycle Research*, vol. 8, no. 1, January 1959.

Bernstein, J.: *The Handbook of Commodity Cycles: A Window on Time*, John Wiley and Sons, Inc., New York, 1982.

Bressert, Walter: *The Power of Oscillator/Cycle Combinations*, Bressert and Associates, Tucson, 1991.

Bretz, W. G.: *Juncture Recognition in the Stock Market*, Vantage Press, New York, 1972.

Colby, Robert W., and Thomas A. Meyers: *The Encyclopedia of Technical Market Indicators*, Dow Jones–Irwin, Homewood, Ill., 1988.

Coppock, E. S. C.: *Practical Relative Strength Charting*, Trendex Corp., San Antonio, Tex., 1960.

Dewey, E. R.: *Cycles: The Mysterious Forces That Trigger Events*, Hawthorne Books, New York, 1971.

——— and E. F. Dakin: *Cycles: The Science of Prediction*, Henry Holt, New York, 1947.

Drew, G.: *New Methods for Profit in the Stock Market*, Metcalfe Press, Boston, 1968.

Edwards, Robert D., and John Magee: *Technical Analysis of Stock Trends*, John Magee, Springfield, Mass., 1957.

Eiteman, W. J., C. A. Dice, and D. K. Eiteman: *The Stock Market*, McGraw-Hill, Inc., New York, 1966.

Fosback, N. G.: *Stock Market Logic: A Sophisticated Approach to Profits on Wall Street*, The Institute for Econometric Research, Fort Lauderdale, Fla., 1976.

Frost, A. J., and Robert R. Prechter: *The Elliott Wave Principle — Key to Stock Market Profits*, New Classics Library, Chappaqua, N.Y., 1978.

Gann, W. D.: *Truth of the Stock Tape*, Financial Guardian, New York, 1932.

Gartley, H. M.: *Profits in the Stock Market*, Lambert Gann Publishing, Pomeroy, Wash., 1981.

Gordon, William: *The Stock Market Indicators,* Investors Press, Palisades Park, N.J., 1968.

Granville, J.: *Strategy of Daily Stock Market Timing,* Prentice-Hall, Englewood Cliffs, N.J., 1960.

Greiner, P., and H. C. Whitcomb: *Dow Theory,* Investors' Intelligence, New York, 1969.

Hamilton, W. D.: *The Stock Market Barometer,* Harper & Bros., New York, 1922.

Hurst, J. M.: *The Profit Magic of Stock Transaction Timing,* Prentice-Hall, Englewood Cliffs, N.J., 1970.

Jiler, W.: *How Charts Can Help You in the Stock Market,* Commodity Research Publishing Corp., N.Y., 1961.

Kaufmann, Perry: *New Commodity Trading Systems,* John Wiley and Sons, Inc., New York, 1987.

Krow, H.: *Stock Market Behavior,* Random House, New York, 1969.

Merrill, A. A.: *Filtered Waves: Basic Theory,* Analysis Press, Chappaqua, N.Y., 1977.

Murphy John J.: *Intermarket Technical Analysis,* Wiley New York, 1991.

———: *Technical Analysis of the Futures Market,* New York Institute of Finance, New York, 1986.

Nelson, S.: *ABC of Stock Market Speculation,* Taylor. New York, 1934.

Nison, Steve: *Japanese Candlestick Charting Techniques,* New York Institute of Finance, New York 1991.

Pring, Martin J.: *How to Forecast Interest Rates,* McGraw-Hill, Inc., New York, 1981.

———: *International Investing Made Easy,* McGraw-Hill, Inc., New York, 1981.

Rhea, Robert: *Dow Theory,* Barrons, New York, 1932.

Shuman, J. B., and D. Rosenau: *The Kondratieff Wave,* World Publishing, New York, 1972.

Smith, E. L.: *Common Stocks and Business Cycles,* William Frederick Press, New York, 1959.

———: *Common Stocks as a Long-Term Investment,* Macmillan, New York, 1939 (now available in reprint from Fraser, Burlington, Vt., 1989).

———: *Tides and the Affairs of Men,* Macmillan, New York, 1932.

Dealers for Out-of-Print Books

James Fraser
Fraser Publishing Co.
P.O. Box 494
Burlington, VT 05402
(802) 658-0322

Rod Klein
Wall Street Books
P.O. Box 24 A 06
Los Angeles, CA 90024
(213) 476-6732

Ron Bever Books
Route 3, Box 243-B
Edmond, OK 73013
(405) 478-0125

Computer Programs

Computrac
1017 Pleasant St.
New Orleans, LA 70115
1-800-535-7990
(504) 895-1474

Downloader (data collection program)
MetaStock Professional (technical analysis software)
The Technician (stock market analysis software)

The above three programs are available from:

Equis International
P.O. Box 26743
Salt Lake City, UT 84126
1-800-882-3040
(801) 974-5115

or

International Institute for Economic Research (agent)
P.O. Box 329
Washington Depot, CT 06794
1-800-221-7514
(203) 868-7772

TechniFilter Plus
RTR Software, Inc.
19 W. Hargett St., Suite 204
Raleigh, NC 27601
(919) 829-0786

Video Courses

Financial Trading Seminars
P.O. Box 20555
Columbus Circle Station
New York, NY 10023
1-800-458-0939
(212) 432-7630

Featuring Alexander Elder:

1. MACD and MACD-Histogram
2. Relative Strength Index
3. Stochastics
4. Triple-Screen Trading System

Featuring Gerald Appel: Day-Trading

International Institute for Economic Research, Inc.
P.O. Box 329
Washington Depot, CT 06794
1-800-221-7514
(203) 868-7772

Featuring Martin J. Pring:

1. Video Course on Technical Analysis (5-tape course)
     Lesson I   The Basic Principles of Technical Analysis
     Lesson II   Price Patterns
     Lesson III Support, Resistance, Trendlines, and Moving Averages
     Lesson IV   Momentum, Relative Strength, and Volume
     Lesson V   Mechanical Trading Systems and Correct Investment Attitudes

2. How to Forecast Interest Rates

3. Asset Allocation and the Business Cycle

New Classics Library
P.O. Box 1618
Gainesville, GA 30503
1-800-336-1618
(404) 536-0309

Featuring Robert R. Prechter, David A. Allman, and Daniel L. Ascani:

1. Introduction to the Elliott Wave Principle
2. Counting Waves Correctly
3. Characteristics of Impulse Waves
4. Characteristics of Corrective Waves
5. Rules, Guidelines, and Wave Personalities
6. Understanding the Fibonacci Ratio in Financial Markets
7. Calculating Fibonacci Relationships with Precision Ratio Compass
8. Real-Time Trading Using the Elliott Wave Principle
9. Trading Options Successfully Using the Elliott Wave Principle
10. Questions and Answers with Prechter, Allman, and Ascani

Data Vendors

Commodity Systems, Inc.
200 West Palmetto Park Road
Boca Raton, FL 33432-3788
(407) 392-8663

Dow Jones News/Retrieval
P.O. Box 300
Princeton, NJ 08543-0300
(609) 452-1511

Reuters Information Services, Inc.
61 Broadway, 31st floor
New York, NY 10006
(212) 493-7100

Warner Computer Systems, Inc.
1701 Pollitt Drive
Fair Lawn, NJ 07410
(201) 797-4633

Index

About the Author

Martin J. Pring is one of the most respected names in the
field of forecasting financial markets. He is editor of *Pring
Market Review*, a technically oriented publication covering
the U.S. stock and bond markets, commodities, and
currencies. He is also president of the International Institute
for Economic Research.

In addition to being a contributor to many financial
publications, including *Barron's*, *Futures*, *Investment Vision*,
and *FNN*, he is the author of McGraw-Hill's highly
acclaimed *How to Forecast Interest Rates*, *The McGraw-Hill
Handbook of Commodities and Futures*, and *International
Investing Made Easy*. He has lectured widely in Europe,
North America, and the Far East on global financial
markets, and has also published a five-tape video course on
technical analysis.

The *Pring Market Review* is designed and written for the resourceful and sophisticated investor who is willing to learn the art of cyclical investing through a study of technical analysis.

Each month the *Pring Market Review* analyzes the trends of the major global financial markets - debt, equity and commodity. By building them together in a framework, it explains how they interrelate, and recommends financial assets suitable for the prevailing stage of the business cycle.

- *Over 75 indicators of the U.S. debt and equity markets alone.*

- *A complete chart service containing a unique and comprehensive set of over 50 charts covering all of the significant world financial markets.*

- *Unique proprietary indicators - such as Advance/Decline lines for commodities, gold and major currencies, and special volume and momentum indicators for the U.S. stock market.*

- *The Pring Barometers - stock, bond, inflation , money market and gold - researched back to the 1950s and identifying major trend reversals.*

International Institute for Economic Research, Inc.

P.O. Box 329
Washington Depot, CT 06794
203/868-7772 Fax 203/868-2683

Return to:

International Institute for Economic Research
P.O. Box 329
Washington Depot, CT 06794
203/868-7772 Fax 203/868-2683

- *Special Introductory Offer:*
  A three-month subscription for $45.00 of the Pring Market Review for readers of this book (coupon must be enclosed).

Name_____

Company Name_____

Address_____

City_____State and Zip_____

Country_____

Telephone_____

☐ MC ☐ Visa ☐ Amex ☐ Check Enclosed

Card No._____

Expiration Date_____

In U.S. Funds Only!

Comments or Specific Interest:

_____

_____

_____

_____